U.S. Defense Policy
in an Era
of Constrained Resources

U.S. Defense Policy in an Era of Constrained Resources

Edited by

Robert L. Pfaltzgraff, Jr.
Richard H. Shultz, Jr.
The Fletcher School of Law and Diplomacy,
Tufts University

Lexington Books
D.C. Heath and Company/Lexington, Massachusetts/Toronto

Library of Congress Cataloging-in-Publication Data

U.S. defense policy in an era of constrained resources / edited by
  Robert L. Pfaltzgraff, Jr., Richard H. Shultz, Jr.
     p.   cm.
    ISBN 0-669-21358-6 (alk. paper).
    1. United States—Military policy.   2. United States—Armed
Forces—Appropriations and expenditures.   I. Pfaltzgraff, Robert L.
II. Shultz, Richard H., 1947–   . III. Title: US defense policy in
an era of constrained resources.   IV. Title: United States defense
policy in an era of constrained resources.
UA23.U185   1989
355.033573—dc0.   89-36935
                                                                       CIP

Published simultaneously in Canada
Printed in the United States of America
Casebound International Standard Book Number: 0-669-21358-6
Library of Congress Catalog Card Number: 89-36935

The paper used in this publication meets the minimum requirements of
American National Standard for Information Sciences—Permanence of
Paper for Printed Library Materials, ANSI Z39.48-1984. ∞ ™

Year and number of this printing:

89 90 91 92 10 9 8 7 6 5 4 3 2 1

Contents

Preface

On November 16–18, 1988, the International Security Studies Program (ISSP) of The Fletcher School of Law and Diplomacy assembled a diverse group of specialists from academia, the military, government, and the private sector to address the topic, "U.S. National Defense Policy: Priorities and Options for the 1990s." These experts were commissioned to present research papers on the challenges the United States is likely to face in meeting existing and new national security commitments in light of changing U.S.-Soviet relations, new technologies, budget restrictions, low-intensity conflict, personnel constraints, and strategy-formulation concerns. The conference was the seventeenth such meeting sponsored by the ISSP since its inception in 1971. Recent conferences have included: "Protracted Warfare—The Third World Arena: A Dimension of U.S.-Soviet Conflict"; "Emerging Doctrines and Technologies: Implications for Global and Regional Political-Military Balances"; "East-West Trade and Technology Transfer: New Challenges for the United States"; and "Terrorism and Other 'Low-Intensity' Operations: International Linkages."

The 1988 conference was co-sponsored with the National Defense University. We are most grateful to Lt. Gen. Bradley Hosmer, USAF, then President of the National Defense University, for his support, encouragement, and participation in the program. We would also like to extend our gratitude to Dr. John Endicott, then Director of the Institute for National Security Studies, National Defense University, for his assistance in planning and coordination.

As with any such effort, success is dependent on the work of the staff. The ISSP has the good fortune of having an outstanding and talented support group. Freda Kilgallen, Administrative Assistant to the ISSP, did an outstanding job handling all conference arrangements and making sure the meeting ran on time and with no bottlenecks. Roberta Breen, Staff Assistant, likewise made an important contribution to the overall success of the program. Steve Adragna, Research Staff Director, played an instrumental role in the editing and preparation of the manuscript for publication. He also contributed an outstanding concluding chapter. Each year the ISSP has the good fortune of having the assistance of a U.S. Air Force Research Associate. This year's officer, Lt. Col. Joseph Moynihan, like those who preceeded him, actively contributed to the success of the conference and other ISSP programmatic activities. We wish to thank both Lt. Col. Moynihan for his outstanding efforts and the U.S. Air Force for having made his participation possible.

Finally, we wish to express our thanks to Mr. Paul O'Connell of Lexington Books for all his assistance. Without his professionalism, organizational skills, and patience, this book would not have been possible. As with previous ISSP publications, this book represents a true team effort, and is but the most recent installment in our ongoing publication series.

Robert L. Pfaltzgraff, Jr.
Richard H. Shultz, Jr.

Introduction

I n an era of constrained defense budgets and uncertain national security priorities, the United States faces difficult choices in the development and maintenance of an adequate military posture. Because the national security policy and military capabilities we choose today will be in operation into the next century, it is essential that such decisions be based on an accurate assessment of the emerging security environment and the threats and challenges we will face. Such factors, considered at a time when the new Bush administration is engaged in a series of major policy reviews, make both timely and necessary an assessment of the national security policy options that will be available to the United States for the years ahead.

This book endeavors to provide just such an assessment. It is intended for a broad spectrum of foreign and defense policy professionals, including civilian government officials, military officers in command and staff positions, members of Congress and their staff assistants, public policy analysts and researchers at major 'think tanks," academics engaged in the study and teaching of international security, the media, and the reader with a particular interest in national security issues. Like other publications of the International Security Studies Program (ISSP) of The Fletcher School of Law and Diplomacy, Tufts University, this book is the product of a collegial effort. In November 1988, ISSP, together with the National Defense University, cosponsored a major conference, "U.S. National Security Policy: Priorities and Options for the 1990s." At this conference, research papers were presented by leading security specialists and strategic thinkers—both civilian and military—drawn from various government agencies, military commands, public policy research institutions, academia, and the private sector. Conference participants were likewise drawn from a broad cross-section of the community of national security specialists, and much of the discussion and deliberation that took place was reflected in the final version of the conference papers. Following the conference, most of those papers were revised and edited to make up this book.

As a point of departure for its analysis, the study proceeds from the question: "What are the requisite elements and what ought to be the policy goals of an integrated long-term ‚strategy for the United States?" Certainly, this question has been addressed before, perhaps most notably by the President's Commission on Integrated Long-Term Strategy. While the recommendations of the commission contributed significantly to the debate over national security policy (indeed, several of the reports by the commission's working groups are excellent), the issue of how best to formulate a sound long-term security strategy requires a more holistic examination. The United States faces and will face multiple challenges, risks, and threats (of a widely varying nature) to its national security both now and throughout the 1990s. In confronting this broad range of troublesome issues, the United States must wisely determine which priorities and options are most crucial for national defense into the next decade and beyond.

Toward that end, this book examines the broad spectrum of issues and choices inherent in shaping national security policy. Although it is not specifically so subdivided, the book focuses on eight separate "segments" of the spectrum of issues pertaining to national security policy. Chapters 1 through 5 establish a foundation for more finely tuned analyses by surveying the horizon in order to anticipate, to the extent possible, various changes and continuities in the emerging global security environment, particularly from the U.S. vantage point. Subsequent chapters proceed to address various other defense-related issues. Chapters 6 through 9, for example, address the land, sea, and aerospace "battlefields" of the future, as well as the impact of developments in high technology on those future warfare environments. Critical issues associated with assessing and interpreting the strategic nuclear balance are examined in chapters 10 through 12. Next, chapters 13 through 15 analyze some of the issues that will affect the ability of the United States and its allies to maintain an effective policy of forward defense and sound alliance relationships. The increasingly complex challenge posed by low-intensity conflict is explored in chapters 16 through 18, along with the evolving requirements for the United States to be able to deal with LIC and to project power effectively in the security environment of the 1990s. The thorny and politically divisive issues associated with fulfilling military personnel needs in light of adverse demographic trends are the subject of chapters 19 through 21. Departing from this pattern, chapters 22, 23, and 24 each address a specific topic central to national security policy formulation, namely: the role and utility of arms control; organization of the national security bureaucracy; and policies and processes for intelligent and efficient defense procurement. Finally, chapters 25, 26, and 27 attempt to come to grips with the nettlesome issue of formulating an integrated long-term strategy for the United States. These chapters essentially address the questions of what national strategy is, and what the elements of an American strategy ought to be.

As the several analyses contained here convincingly attest, U.S. national security planners, defense decisionmakers, and elected officials have their work cut out for them, and the challenges they currently face are likely to become all the more complex in the years ahead. Despite certain enduring hallmarks and characteristics, U.S. defense policy must recognize and prepare for real changes in the emerging security environment. The nature of future conflict will be influenced by global trends toward increased population, greater urbanization, and the rapid development and diffusion of technology, as well as a greater number of regional power centers. With respect to other actors and future challenges in this emerging security environment, U.S. security planning must be equally astute and far-sighted. The Soviet Union's probable goal is that of the renewal and "moral purification" of socialism and a communist renaissance couched in terms of *perestroika* and *glasnost*. These changes do not necessarily mean that the Soviet leadership wishes us well, so U.S. policymakers should therefore continue to focus on the differences between the United States and the Soviet Union, rather than on any perceived commonalities. The Far East/Pacific Rim still lacks a true multilateral security community or framework, and this may delay the advent of a true "Pacific Century." The long-range economic, political, and military trends in the region, however, mandate greater U.S. attention now in order for us to be able to function effectively later. Throughout the world, low-intensity conflict (LIC) will remain a major component of the threat to U.S. interests. Insurgency, counterinsurgency, and other dimensions of LIC will continue to characterize the general state of affairs in the Third World, but the sophistication and complexity of these conflicts will increasingly challenge U.S. preparedness and our ability to prosecute LIC effectively and efficiently. All these issues—and their various subcomponents—will, in a variety of permutations, influence and shape U.S. defense priorities and policy options in the future.

Specifically, advances in military technology will continue to have an enormous impact on the Army, Navy, and Air Force, as well as the emerging military arena of space. The land battlefield of the future may well be one that favors the defense (with a concomitant shift away from offense), due to technological innovations that will make it increasingly likely that key sites will be detected, targeted, and destroyed. The challenge is to realize technology's full potential for the battlefield, and then to focus advances in technology against the adversary's known or perceived weaknesses. Stealth, directed energy, and smart-weapon technologies will also directly affect the U.S. Navy's future Maritime Strategy, creating new requirements for advanced information processing. Advances in space technology are combining with emerging space opportunities and threats to require the United States to view space as a distinct region for military activity. Yet, again, this trend necessitates extending policy, strategy and doctrine in order to encompass "battle space." As some of the authors of this volume point out, while the United States need not strive for space superiority, we presently lack needed space defense and space control capabilities, and must therefore address these deficiencies.

Regarding the strategic balance between the two superpowers, it is crucial to assess Soviet strategic force planning accurately. However, our current process of estimating the strategic balance frequently results in polarized perceptions of Soviet intentions. A non-ideological estimate is therefore ideal, and basic agreement on expectations regarding the Soviet force structure may produce this ideal. With respect to the U.S. force structure per se, American land-based ICBMs are becoming increasingly vulnerable because they are becoming less survivable in the face of the evolving Soviet SLBM threat. The U.S. may be incapable of deploying a survivable ICBM force, in which case a modernized, survivable diad of bombers and submarines may be preferable to a triad that is inherently not survivable. Thus, the matter of finding a survivable deployment mode for land-based missiles—or of recognizing that no such mode exists— requires immediate national attention. With respect to strategic defensive systems, the purpose of SDI or strategic defense seems to have shifted from societal protection to enhanced deterrence; this shift in rationale may signal the ultimate ascendancy of arms control over strategic defense deployment. However, if SDI's purpose reverts to population protection—or enhanced deterrence through real population defense—it could be compatible with arms control and still satisfy important strategic requirements.

The issue of forward defense encompasses the topics of allied burden sharing, coalition warfighting strategies, and forward basing. A balanced perspective on the allied burden-sharing issue means acknowledging that the U.S. does not police the world alone and that our allies contribute substantially to the protection of U.S. interests throughout the world. Moreover, the assumptions underlying the "burden-sharing argument" are invalid when carried to their logical extreme. Burden sharing may be more accurately perceived as evidence of U.S. "deterrence fatigue" and as a tool used by those eager to reduce U.S. involvement abroad. To improve coalition defense, it may be useful to borrow somewhat from the Soviet concept of the operational level of warfare in order to produce innovative operational concepts, which NATO could then employ in such a way as to exploit Warsaw Pact military vulnerabilities. Forward defense also necessarily involves forward deployment or forward basing. In an effort to continue to meet nuclear and conventional power-projection requirements, the United States is experiencing increasing pressures on its existing global basing system. The United States therefore needs to explore alternative strategies for forward basing if it hopes to maintain a "forward deployed" strategy.

The magnitude of the challenges which will confront the United States in the Third World in the next decade will relate directly to U.S. power projection and low-intensity conflict capabilities. The Reagan Doctrine certainly sets a recent precedent (namely, for reviving containment) for the Bush administration, although this doctrine has been both the subject of criticism and a source of lessons learned from unsuccessful performances. Though the Soviets will probably not initiate new Third World ventures soon, there is scant evidence that they will exercise restraint in ongoing conflicts. A central issue is the perception of vacillating resolve on the part of democratic peoples attempting involvement in LIC; misreadings of this resolve by others may lead to testing of U.S. determination and, ultimately, to bloodshed. Thus, any U.S. President trying to establish and maintain the legitimacy (or lack of legitimacy) of any foreign party whom he or she chooses to support or deems it necessary to attack faces a vexing task. Perception is the key variable that one must shape—in U.S. public opinion and in opinion abroad—in order to establish or remove legitimacy in relation to LIC. U.S. forces and security assistance for an unconventional warfare or LIC environment are seen as inadequate, if not ineffective, at present. A more effective U.S. posture in this regard is tied to the need to distinguish sharply between special operations, on the one hand, and revolution and counterrevolution on the other.

The U.S. ability to implement its defense policy and to maintain readiness depends upon its people and their education. Thus, U.S. and allied demographic trends for the 1990s merit serious analysis. Such analysis reveals that, if present trends continue, it will not be possible to man the NATO force structure at current levels throughout the 1990s. However,' the troubles this assessment portends may be offset by unanticipated solutions, such as decreased defense spending leading to force structure cuts (including reductions in personnel). On a related point, one may argue that force readiness must be the basis upon which all U.S. military personnel needs are defined, thereby making the role of women in the U.S. military crucial. Thus, further expansion of the numbers of women in the U.S.military and removal of current combat restrictions may be justified by U.S. requirements for wartime and other global contingencies. In any case, such proposals deserve greater discussion and examination. Also, emerging technologies directly affect personnel requirements, particularly with regard to training and education levels: In point of fact, the demand for highly trained technicians will increase. Furthermore, the integration of emerging technology battlefield systems could offset possible decreases in manpower among frontline combat units so that, in the future, military planners may be able to substitute technology for troops. "Human engineering" must also be considered as high-technology systems enter service, and "user friendly" systems must be given top priority.

Other important aspects of U.S. defense policy include arms control, organization of the national security bureaucracy, and defense procurement. An assessment of current arms control theory reveals that mutual assured destruction is an outmoded theory that is morally wanting. A new arms control paradigm is needed, one which rests upon national consensus. A consensus of opinion is also needed with respect to the advantages and moral soundness of strategic defense within the framework of deterrence and arms control. There is also a vital and pressing need for an arms control compliance policy for the United States, without which treaty enforcement is meaningless. With respect to organizing the policymaking system, the U.S. national security bureaucracy must be responsive to positive presidential control so that it will develop and implement the policies of elected U.S. leaders, not its own. Several remedies outlined in this volume may help to correct the perceived lack of responsiveness to presidential leadership within the bureaucracy, particularly in the areas of arms control and LIC. Finally, the weapons acquisition process, although complex and cumbersome, works reasonably well, produces good results, and is basically sound (despite opinions to the contrary). Nonetheless, room for improvement exists: In particular, Congress needs to rescue itself from the minute details of the process, and true authority must be given back to program managers. Such consensus and organizational structures and procedures could better serve the common U.S. defense. It is important for President Bush to gain control of the debate over the proper direction for U.S. defense policy by emphasizing the complementary themes of strong defense with fiscal responsibility, constancy with flexibility in U.S. policy, the integration of all relevant elements into a national strategy, and alliance cohesion.

While there is broad general agreement on the elements of strategy and its goals, the suggestions on how to improve our strategy formation process have differed. Whether the elements of these several alternative approaches can successfully be combined or whether they are, in fact, mutually exclusive is a topic for informed national debate. As one author argues, a strong case can be made that the United States does not have a clear, coherent, and consistent strategy. U.S. objectives, strategy, and budgets must be integrated, since the (frequently) weak link between strategic planning and fiscal planning breaks down. Moreover, an active national strategy focusing on the long term could help the United States to realize objectives that might otherwise be unattainable. It has been asserted, and it may well be the case, that the U.S. national psyche is inherently ill-suited for strategy-making. Nevertheless, by pursuing the process in a broad-based and integrated fashion (to include broadening the participation in the strategy formation process at the national level), the United States can overcome short-term challenges and squabbles, and concentrate instead on long-term goals and the steps needed to realize them.

Although the various contributors to this volume differ over specific elements of national strategy formulation and how to implement them, they all argue persuasively in support of the need for consensus on national strategy. Reasonable people may disagree over specific policy proposals and initiatives, but the long-term goals of strategy should have broad national support, and, after a reasonable period of debate, the specific means of achieving those goals should be selected and implemented. Among the specific policy recommendations made herein with respect to the various components of national strategy are the following:

- With respect to the emerging global security environment, a rethinking of U.S. strategy to take account of more militarily capable regional actors in the future, along with renewed attention to problems in our LIC infrastructure and the adoption of an integrated approach to the LIC challenge. A more critical appraisal of Soviet long-term objectives, especially with respect to Western Europe, and a better understanding of the Soviet worldview. Recognition of the growing strategic importance of the Asian-Pacific region, and the creation of a genuine multilateral Pacific Rim security community.

- Concerning the nature of future warfare, the United States and its allies must devise a strategy that capitalizes on emerging technologies affecting the tactical, operational, theater-strategic, and strategic nuclear levels of war. Greater attention should be given to various low-observable technologies to challenge Soviet warfighting abilities, and a longer war scenario designed to press the Soviet economy should be worked out. There is an urgent need to develop advanced data handling systems and better communications systems so as better to integrate these emerging technologies. Space will become an arena for conflict in its own right, creating a need for new technologies, weapon systems, and military strategy for dealing with the "space flank."

- Strategic force planning will be shaped by the need for a non-ideological and sober estimate of the strategic balance with the Soviet Union. The survivability problem for the U.S. ICBM force will not go away of its own accord. A choice must be made between various missiles and basing modes, and that choice must be implemented in a timely fashion. Strategic defense has an important role to play in strategic policy, and a more compelling rationale for SDI must be adopted if the United States is serious about deploying defenses.

- With regard to maintaining a forward defense posture, the United States must think through the burden-sharing argument and take a more clear-eyed view of the contributions and capabilities of allies. At the same time, continued effort must be devoted to forging a consensus on NATO military doctrine, to include seeking out innovative approaches to prosecuting true coalition warfare. Improvement in intra-alliance cooperation and consultation should be a continuous process. As to U.S. power projection, policymakers must choose between alternative forward-basing modes and then develop a sound military strategy based in part on that decision.

- The challenge presented by low-intensity conflict is one that mandates a political consensus on a given LIC strategy, as well as a clear rationale for that policy. The issue of legitimacy is critical, and will entail difficult choices over prospective protagonists and antagonists. Special operations and LIC are two different phenomena, and USSO-COM should be restructured in order to take better account of distinctions between them. Ultimately, the U.S. force structure will have to reflect greater attention to LIC, as will military training.

- Demographics will have an important effect on our ability to implement military policy, and current trends (coupled with constricting budgets) may require cutting personnel levels overall and/or removing some troops deployed overseas. The role of women in the armed forces will become increasingly important, requiring a reexamination of at least some restrictions on women in combat positions. Shrinking manpower levels will make it more difficult to maintain a pool of technically trained manpower capable of using new advanced technology systems effectively. We must therefore strive to produce better educated and more technically proficient personnel, while at the same time employing "human engineering" techniques to make advanced technology systems as "user-friendly" as possible.

- Other specific needs include forging a consensus on the objectives of arms control and on the need for strategic defenses in an arms control framework. As treaty verification becomes more important (and verification technology more sophisticated), the need for a credible compliance/enforcement policy will become correspondingly greater. The national security bureaucracy must be made more responsive to presidential leadership, possibly by strengthening the role of the national security advisor and the NSC staff, and by reasserting civilian control over the national security agencies. The greatest need in the acquisition realm is for program stability; two-year budget cycles and less micromanagement would be steps in the right direction. Greater attention should be given to strengthening the industrial base.

• Finally, as steps toward implementing a sound national strategy, the United States must first recognize that it is inherently ill-suited to strategy-making, and then must proceed (cognizant of its handicaps) to formulate a set of policies and forces able to deter, counter, and constrain potential adversaries, principally the Soviet Union. Consideration should be given to moving away from an essentially reactive strategy in favor of a more active and innovative national strategy. In the course of that process, various organizational innovations could be implemented to encourage the development of consensus (such as a presidential council on strategy). Above all, policymakers must make the effort to identify and agree upon long-term goals, and link them to current policy. Effective strategy demands that decision-makers do, in fact, *make decisions*, and have the resolve to follow them through. The United States is entering a complex and challenging era in international affairs. Forming and implementing a sound and integrated long-term strategy will be more important than ever before, but doing so will be increasingly complicated. Attention must be given to *all* elements of strategy—political, military, economic, diplomatic, scientific-technical, and cultural—and to the matter of how best to integrate them given the constraints identified in this volume. Despite the formidable challenges ahead, the United States has the wherewithal to formulate a sound national strategy. Success will depend, in large measure, on the quality of statesmanship, strategic thinking, and resolve displayed by our national leaders in the years ahead.

Abbreviations

AAFCE	Allied Air Forces Central Europe
ABM	antiballistic missile
ACDA	Arms Control and Disarmament Agency
ACE HIGH	Allied Command Europe Communications Network
AFCENT	Allied Forces Central Europe
AFQT	Armed Forces Qualifications Test
AFSATCOM	Air Force satellite communications
ALB	Air-land Battle
ALCM	air-launched cruise missile
ANZUS	Australia, New Zealand, and U.S. (Treaty Organization)
ASAR	advanced synthetic aperture radar
ASAT	antisatellite
ASVAB	armed services vocational aptitude battery
ASW	antisubmarine warfare
ATACMS	Army Tactical Missile System
ATAF	Allied Tactical Air Force
ATGM	antitank guided missile
AUTODIN	automatic digital network
AUTOVON	automated voice network
AVF	All Volunteer Force
AWACS	Airborne Warning and Control System
BMD	ballistic missile defense
BMEWS	ballistic missile early warning system
BTI	balanced technology initiative (DOD)
C^3	command, control, and communications
C^3I	command, control, communications, and intelligence
CENTAG	Central Army Group
CENTO	Central Treaty Organization

CINCENT	Commander-in-Chief Allied Forces Central Europe
COMCENTAG	Commander Central Army Group
COMNORTHAG	Commander Northern Army Group
CONUS	continental United States
CSI	competitive strategies initiative
DCA	defensive counterair
DEW	distant early warning
DF	direction finding
DOD	Department of Defense
DSCS	Defense Satellite Communications System
DSP	Defense Satellite Program
ESF	economic support fund
ET	emerging technology
FAR	Force d'Action Rapide
FBS	forward-based system
FLOT	forward line of own troops
FLTSATCOM	fleet satellite communications
FMS	Foreign Military Sales program
FMSCR	foreign military sales credit (program)
FOFA	Follow-On Forces Attack
FRG	Federal Republic of Germany
FTX	field training exercise
GEODSS	ground-based electro-optical deep-space surveillance
GLCM	ground-launched cruise missile
GNP	gross national product
GNR	General Nuclear Response
GPS	Global Positioning System
HF	high frequency
ICBM	intercontinental ballistic missile
IMET	International Military Education & Training (program)
INF	intermediate-range nuclear forces
JCS	Joint Chiefs of Staff
JSTARS	Joint Surveillance and Target Attack Radar System

LANDSOUTH	Allied Land Forces Southern Europe
LORAN	long-range aid to navigation
MAB	Marine amphibious brigade
MAP	military assistance program
MASF	military assistance service fund
MIRV	multiple independently targetable reentry vehicle
MLRS	multiple launch rocket system
MOS	military occupation specialty
MPTS	manpower, personnel, training, and safety
MTT	military training teams
NATO	North Atlantic Treaty Organization
NAVSTAR	(designation for the U.S. global positioning system)
NCA	National Command Authority
NIE	National Intelligence Estimate
NORTHAG	Northern Army Group
NSC	National Security Council
OCA	offensive counterair
OECD	Organization for Economic Cooperation and Development
OMG	operational maneuver group
OSD	Office of the Secretary of Defense
OSS	Office of Strategic Services
PGM	precision-guided munitions
PLSS	Precision Location Strike System
PRC	People's Republic of China
RAF	Royal Air Force
SAC	Strategic Air Command
SACEUR	Supreme Allied Commander Europe
SALT	Strategic Arms Limitation Talks
SDF	Self-Defense Force (Japanese)
SDI	Strategic Defense Initiative
SDIO	Strategic Defense Initiative Organization
SEATO	Southeast Asian Treaty Organization
SHAPE	Supreme Headquarters Allied Powers Europe
SHF	super high frequency
SIGNIT	signals intelligence

SLBM	submarine-launched ballistic missile
SLCM	sea-launched cruise missile
SNDV	strategic nuclear delivery vehicle
SOF	special operations forces
SOON	Solar Optical Observing Network
SOSUS	sonar surveillance system
SRBM	short-range ballistic missile
SRF	Strategic Rocket Forces (Soviet)
SSBN	subsurface ballistic nuclear
SSN	subsurface nuclear
START	Strategic Arms Reduction Talks
TACAMO	"Take Charge and Move Out"; aircraft for strategic nuclear C³
TRS	tactical reconnaissance system
USD/A	Undersecretary of Defense for Acquisition
USSOCOM	U.S. Special Operations Command
VLF	very low frequency
WAC	Women's Army Corps
WAVE	Navy Women's Reserve
WEU	Western European Union
WTO	Warsaw Treaty Organization

1
The United States
in a Changing World

William F. Burns

T he world is changing in important ways. Perhaps historians will
even look back on this period as a time of transition between the
old postwar era and a new, as yet undefined, era. In any event,
we are certainly entering a more complicated period in foreign affairs, a
period in which the intellectual challenge to those of us who think about
U.S. foreign and defense policies will be substantial.

In particular, we should focus on two questions: first, what kind of
changes are we in fact seeing in world affairs? and second, what do those
changes mean for some of our long-standing policies and approaches?

The Early Postwar Years:
A Clear Threat, a Clear Role

To put things in perspective, it is useful to compare today's world with
the early postwar period. When you go back to the postwar "creation," as
Dean Acheson used to call it, one of the things that stands out is its
comparative simplicity. The threat that we faced was clear, and the role
that we were obligated to assume was equally clear.

The threat was clear because few doubted that the principal challenge
to our security and our way of life came from the Soviet Union. This may
not have been apparent immediately after World War II, and it is true
that for a period we tried to hold the wartime alliance together. But in
time the challenge became evident through a variety of Soviet actions.
Repression of Eastern Europe, opportunism in Iran, the Berlin crisis, the
Soviet acquisition of atomic capability—these things and others confirmed
the primacy of the Soviet threat.

With a clear threat, our central objectives soon became obvious. One
was what George Kennan called the "firm and vigilant containment of

The views expressed herein are solely those of the author and do not necessarily reflect the
views of the Department of Defense or of any other agency of the United States government.

Russian expansive tendencies." We had to contain the expansion of Soviet power and influence around the world. The other objective was nuclear deterrence. With nuclear capability now in Soviet hands, we had to maintain strategic forces of sufficient strength to deter Soviet use.

In these early years, the United State's global role was obvious—not only because we faced an obvious threat, but because we possessed unrivaled power and resources. Our productive capacity accounted for roughly half of global output. Meanwhile, the vital industrial centers of Europe and Asia were weak and vulnerable. It was the kind of vacuum that, without the presence of the United States, might be filled by the Soviet Union.

These simple realities helped to shape U.S. foreign policy. We forged alliances around the world—in Western Europe, in Japan, in South Korea, in the South Pacific. The Truman Doctrine promised to "support free peoples" across the globe. The Marshall Plan took to bankrolling Western Europe's economic recovery. We moved to implement ideas set out in NSC-68, the document that called for an energized commitment to militarily contain and deter Soviet power.

Changes in Power and Ideology

The world of 1988, however, is not the world of 1948. In particular, some of the fundamental premises we once took for granted are beginning to shift. We used to be able to count on at least two things: that there was a palpable Soviet threat, and that American power was unparalleled. But these premises are now being questioned. Mikhail Gorbachev has put a new face on the Soviet Union, and talk of U.S. decline abounds. And so we must ask ourselves just how much things have really changed. Do the old assumptions no longer hold? Or are they simply growing less clear?

Let me explain why I think the latter is the case. One way of thinking about change is to focus on power, ideology, and threat. First, the distribution of power. It is true that our economic position has declined as others have become stronger. This, however, is no great surprise, since our economic standing after World War II was artificially high by virtue of the devastated condition of the Japanese and European economies. As these industrial powers have regained their footing, we have quite naturally seen a relative decline in the U.S. position.

One can exaggerate the extent of decline, however. We experienced relative economic decline from 1950 to 1970, but our share of the global output has remained fairly steady since. So "decline" may not be the right word to describe trends in power; it is quite possible that we are now at a stable plateau. If so, we are by no means destined for second-place status within the world economy. We may be challenged in the years ahead, but we should not assume that we cannot meet that challenge.

Nonetheless, influence is less in an age when power is spread more evenly. Increasing economic interdependence means that, whereas we once exercised significant control over the international economy, today it exercises significant control over us. And in the military arena, we have seen how it is possible for even small countries to make great power intervention a difficult undertaking. And with the threat of intervention reduced, the political leverage exerted by great powers declines accordingly.

Along with changes in power have come more subtle, but by no means unimportant, changes in ideology. Remember that ideas, and not just realities of power, guide the course of global events. Indeed, both the unity of the West and the divide between East and West can be explained, in part, by ideology. We believe in the idea that individuals should live in freedom under democracy. We worry not only about Soviet military capability, but also about the Marxist ideology behind it.

But the struggle over fundamental values is less clear in an age when the ideological divide runs less clearly in parallel with the East-West divide than it used to. There is growing diversity on both sides. The good news is that there is growing diversity among Marxist states. As the economic problems with Marxism have grown apparent, its appeal has declined. Marxism reduces individual incentive, the spark that brings economic dynamism. It requires state control and societal repression, things that are not only politically reprehensible, but in an age of technological innovation and computerization, economically costly. And so we are seeing moves away from the traditional Marxist model. This is occurring not only in the Third World, but in China, in Eastern Europe, and lately in the Soviet Union itself.

Meanwhile, in the West, we have heard increasing talk, particularly in some areas of Western Europe, about the so-called "moral equivalence" of the superpowers. Born after World War II and into the Cold War, some members of younger generations have tended to emphasize peace as a priority, perhaps because they accept freedom as a given. And so, although one superpower protects freedom while the other threatens it, both are blamed equally for propagating the struggle.

It is not clear, however, whether this is a transient phenomenon, peculiar only to the "successor generation" that political scientists have expected will soon come to power, or whether this represents a deeper, longer-term trend away from the United States and the ideas that we stand for. In either case, we may increasingly have to contend, at least for the next decade or two, with a new generation of European leaders that do not share the trans-Atlantic instincts of current leaders.

Changes in Threat: Diversifying Challenges

Is the Soviet threat on the verge of ending forever? This would hardly be a prudent assumption to make. It would be far wiser to assume that, at the very best, that threat may be diminishing. Nonetheless, it is also true that we may be entering an era in which new challenges step up to share priority with the Soviet threat. We may be entering a time in which the challenges we face diversify.

Let me address two such challenges that some have argued merit a central place in our strategic kaleidoscope. One, which I believe does not merit such a place, is the North-South challenge. The less developed countries of the world are certainly important, and it may be that they are growing more important. But I do not believe that they should now be seen as the central strategic concern—that we should shift, as some would urge, from an East-West orientation to a North-South one. Those who argue otherwise point out that, in today's interdependent world, Third World countries can exert greater influence than they once could. But the corollary is also true: the most powerful can also exert greater influence than they once could. And so it must be the most powerful that continue to occupy us.

The current fashion in strategic circles is to talk about the economic challenge that we face, and I happen to believe that there is substance to this fashion. It proceeds from a sound premise: that economic strength is key not only to near-term prosperity, but to long-term power. Putting the economy at the center of our conception of security is not new. President Eisenhower used to speak of what he called the "great equation": the relationship between defense spending, which serves our global purposes, and domestic spending, which serves our economic and social well-being. Too much of one today can undermine the other tomorrow. In an age when serious people see the possibility of a "Pacific Century," we must move to build the economic foundations of our long-term power. We must continue to heed Eisenhower's great equation.

This brings me to the challenge that has preoccupied us for over four decades: the Soviet challenge. It is now clear that important change, and not just the appearance of change, is taking place in the Soviet Union. Gorbachev is cut from a different mold than his predecessors. An economic system that offers greater individual incentive, a bureaucracy reduced in size and power, a society that is more open and expressive— these are all part of Gorbachev's design.

The changes that we are seeing are clearly significant, and they merit our closest attention. The central question is this: do they portend a fundamental transformation of the Soviet state? It is a question that we cannot yet answer. Change may be leading toward a more efficient, but no less dangerous, country. Or, more optimistically, perhaps change will prove to a certain extent irreversible; maybe we are seeing the opening act in a process that ends in fundamental, far-reaching change.

What we *can* say is that far-reaching change is not yet upon us. What we are seeing is ambitious reform, not a fundamental transformation. When Gorbachev speaks, he often seems to suggest that his overarching goal, his guiding star, is a streamlined, restructured economy. *Perestroika* is often treated as the objective, and things like greater openness as necessary to serve this objective. We Americans view freedom as an ultimate end, but Soviet pronouncements seem to view a measure of freedom as a tool by which to achieve material, economic ends. This kind of outlook suggests that Gorbachev and his followers are not closet democrats, but innovative reformers.

Nor can we believe that we are seeing fundamental transformation so long as the apparatus of totalitarianism remains. The Communist party remains the only legitimate political force, and the ruling Politburo is not elected democratically. The Soviet Union continues to be a society controlled from above.

Finally, we cannot say that the Soviets are taking a radically different approach to world politics. The most important positive development is that the Soviets are leaving Afghanistan. The war has become intractable, and they are prudently cutting their losses. But this does not mean that Soviet leaders have forever cast aside visions of expanding their empire. Nor have the Soviets even hinted that they would voluntarily dismantle their empire. Eastern Europe is allowed to emulate Soviet change, but remains under the Soviet thumb. The Iron Curtain still exists. Challenges to the primacy of the Communist Party remain impermissible, and the most basic of human freedoms are curtailed.

All of these things suggest that, while the longer-term is difficult to predict, the near- to mid-term should see a Soviet Union that continues to pursue goals antithetical to our own. It is possible that a period of Soviet self-absorption will mean that these goals will be pursued less ambitiously in the 1990s. Perhaps better said, it is possible that these goals will be pursued with different tools, with an emphasis on political innovation rather than military action. But we cannot assume that the goals themselves are fundamentally changing.

The Implications of Change

In summary, power is shifting, although it is not clear that a shift away from the United States is accelerating or even that it must continue. Shifts in the ideological climate may lead to growing political diversity in East and West. And the Soviet threat to our security and our values still holds, but may grow less apparent as new challenges arise.

What should we do in light of this shifting strategic environment? Let me address this question in the context of our approaches toward the Soviet Union, toward our NATO allies, and toward the Third World generally.

Dealing with the Soviet Union

If my analysis of the Soviet threat is correct—that is, if the threat may diminish but is not likely to soon disappear—then I believe we should avoid major changes in approach. We will have to continue to pay attention to the twin objectives of containment and deterrence.

Deterrence has meant, first and foremost, the deployment and modernization of a robust strategic nuclear force. Arms control can play a modest role in shaping force structures in more stabilizing directions, but arms control is not a panacea, and it often plays at the margins in its impact upon deterrence. Containment, on the other hand, has meant support for allies and friends threatened by the Soviet Union or its proxies. It also means support for democratic elements struggling against totalitarianism.

The kind of approach toward the Soviet Union that best promotes these objectives is the kind of approach that the current Administration has taken. Although we pursued arms control and other areas of mutual interest, we highlighted as most fundamental the need for Soviet change at home and abroad. And so we refused to talk about areas of common interest without spending equal time emphasizing critical differences over regional issues and human rights. In this way, we emphasized rather than overlooked the need for Soviet change. This assured that we put first things first—it kept the differences between East and West at the forefront rather than in the background.

But we are a creative society, a society of problem-solvers, and while this instinctive dynamism is one of our great strengths, it sometimes lends impulse to misguided policies. Today, I notice an impulse to do something—anything—to help bring further Soviet change. And indeed, we must ask ourselves whether a changing Soviet Union now merits a change in our approach toward that country. Perhaps a third objective beyond those of containment and deterrence—the objective of encouraging Soviet transformation—now warrants a more ambitious approach. Perhaps the time has come to forge a closer relationship, despite our regional concerns and human rights objections. There is a case to be made for such a "new detente," and the case is essentially this: it will give us additional levers with which to influence the course of change in the Soviet Union.

I believe such an approach would be misguided for two reasons. The first is that our ability to influence the development of Soviet society would not appear to be great. That development is driven by deep-seated structural forces—historical, geographic, political, cultural—and we should not exaggerate our ability to impact these forces. Our influence is marginal. And, indeed, to the extent that we have it, it may be detrimental. It may be that the best thing we can do to encourage Soviet transformation is to stay relatively uninvolved. By refusing to alleviate the Soviet predicament, we allow the structural forces of change to play out in full.

I find the alternative case—the case for positive influence—weak. It is largely Kremlinological—a matter of helping the right leader look good at the right time. If a new détente can help his economy, or bolster his political prestige, the argument goes, the reformist in power is more likely to stay there. The problem with this view is that it assumes the moment of opportunity to be ephemeral, something that is here today and gone tomorrow. And yet, upon reflection, it seems unwise to view Gorbachev as the last, great hope for peace. Remember that while Gorbachev may be a unique personality, his program is the consequence of root problems that lie at the heart of Soviet society. The leader that follows Gorbachev will face the same problems. And it is those problems, not U.S. fine-tuning, that offer hope for the future.

The second reason a new détente would be misguided is that it will incur tangible risks. Remember that the benefit of the current approach—of emphasizing differences rather than commonalities—is that it puts first things first. Well, we are entering an age when putting first things first will be difficult enough. By existing trends, the Soviet Union will look increasingly friendly, and the West increasingly diverse. The distinction between friends and adversaries will, to many, grow fuzzier. A new détente will only compound this problem. In the 1970s, we used to worry that détente could lull the West into a false sense of security. In the 1990s, a new détente may run the risk not simply of lulling the West, but of guiding its gradual disintegration.

The impulse to forge closer relations is strong, and it is in some ways understandable. But as a means to encourage further change in the Soviet Union, it may not make for wise policy. It is useful to remember that even the détente of the 1970s was not meant to influence internal Soviet change—it was really designed to curb Soviet expansionism. In the wake of Vietnam, America's bag of policy "sticks" was low, and détente's "carrots" were seen as a way to curb Soviet global designs. Unfortunately, those carrots were not sufficient to do so, and in time we came to recognize the merits of a less ambitious approach that placed our important differences, and not the exchange of carrots, at the top of the agenda.

Strengthening the Atlantic Alliance

If a changing Soviet Union and the decline of ideological unity pose one set of challenges to Western cohesion, changes in power and priority pose another. As our allies grow more self-sufficient, and as the United States gives increasing attention to its own economic challenges, the old trans-Atlantic bargain is becoming less tenable.

The United States is shouldering two burdens that we have considered, for some time now, to be excessive. If changes in the distribution of power and subtle shifts in U.S. priorities continue, we can only expect these burdens to grow. At some point, if they are not addressed, the threat to trans-Atlantic solidarity could become real.

One burden is financial. About half of our defense budget goes to NATO. We spend far more than any other NATO country, even though much of the money we spend is dedicated to the direct defense of our allies, territory, not ours. The other, related problem is that we carry an inordinate burden of risk. The United States is committed to defending, with nuclear weapons if necessary, NATO Europe from attack. Introducing this nuclear element obviously incurs a significant risk: we are effectively risking Chicago in order to save Bonn. And so we have always insisted that the nuclear element must be an element of last resort—that a strong conventional defense exist to raise the nuclear threshold. Unfortunately, allied contributions have not been sufficient to provide for such a defense.

If it is true that these burdens are only likely to get worse, the need for increased allied contributions to their own defense will grow stronger. A number of innovations can complement this effort—innovative use of emerging technologies, increasingly integrated procurement policies, perhaps even a conventional arms agreement, although the task of achieving such an agreement should not be underestimated. But the realities of power and economics tell us that changes to the trans-Atlantic bargain are likely to grow in urgency.

I think the changes should involve adjustments within NATO rather than the pursuit of radical alternatives. A radical proposal is entering the debate, however, and we will have to think carefully about its implications. It is a proposal that mainstream figures such as Walter Lippmann and George Kennan entertained in the aftermath of World War II, and that mainstream figures such as Henry Kissinger are resurrecting today. Writing in a recent issue of Newsweek magazine, Kissinger suggests that we begin thinking about the possibility of "a drastic reduction of all outside forces in Europe—including those of the U.S."

To entertain this idea, of course, you have to assume that the Soviets would be willing to do the same, and we have no reason to believe that, at this point, they are. This aside, there are complicating factors that would accompany a full withdrawal of outside forces. One is that we play an important political role in Europe—a role that helps to make us, as one prominent German commentator put it, "Europe's American Pacifier." The U.S. presence probably smooths intra-European rivalries, and thus has helped not only to bring peace in Western Europe, but to push along the process of European integration. Another complicating factor attending the idea of complete withdrawal is that, for both geographic and political reasons, the Soviets would presumably be able to return more quickly than we to the Central Front. Nonetheless, while one can see that radical ideas such as this one have their weaknesses, such ideas are likely to grow in appeal as unhappiness with the current structure of NATO grows.

Growing Equanimity toward the Third World

Let me turn, finally, to the implications of global changes to our policies in the Third World. One should be wary of generalizations here, of course, since our approach necessarily varies between regions and countries. But the central point is this: change augurs an era of increasing equanimity in the U.S. outlook toward Third World developments.

Equanimity should not be confused with complacency. It does not mean that we should disregard developments that threaten important strategic interests, or that we should forgo assistance to forces of freedom in totalitarian states. Rather, it means that we can increasingly afford, and in some cases are increasingly forced, to maintain a calmer disposition toward some of the political twists and turns that have traditionally occurred in less developed regions.

Since I am here discussing defense priorities, let me explain this point in the context of U.S. military intervention. Changes in the world are doing two things to reduce the role of military intervention in the Third World. First, they are making such interventions less strategically advisable. Second, they are making them less strategically necessary.

Why is a highly interventionist foreign policy less advisable? One reason is that it runs counter to military trends. As military power has spread, the prospects of quick, successful intervention have declined. Technology is helping the underdog through highly accurate, portable weapons. The Soviets discovered this in Afghanistan, as we had in Vietnam.

The other reality counseling growing prudence in military interventionism goes to Walter Lippmann's old principle that we must bring ends and means into balance. It is easier to be the world's policeman when you possess unchallenged economic power, when you have the means to pursue ambitious ends. But in an age in which we will be looking to husband resources, the role of global policeman will be less tenable.

Fortunately, intervention is also becoming less strategically necessary. For one, the Soviets may be retrenching, and their opportunism in the Third World may be on the decline. But more fundamentally, our own thinking has evolved. We no longer think that our security is so easily threatened by Third World developments. We used to believe that even small strategic losses could be exceedingly dangerous—that in an era of struggle between communism and democracy, the fall of one anticommunist country might incur, like dominoes, the fall of many. Today we accept that the risk of falling dominoes is not as great because the world has grown increasingly diverse. The Soviets have less influence over, and less to gain from, Third World developments than we once believed.

Finally, the need to intervene declines as the forces of nature take their course. Marxism is proving an economic and political failure, and the trend towards democracy and freedom is gaining in strength. So Soviet influence, whether they like it or not, appears to be on the wane.

We should not pretend, of course, that military intervention is a thing of the past. It is simply both less necessary and less advisable. To a certain extent, other measures can take its place. Security assistance, in particular, is a useful way of promoting our goals prudently and cost-effectively. From time to time we hear that the United States should emphasize political and diplomatic avenues in trying to influence regional events in the Third World, and in many instances we have and should. Nonetheless, we should not exaggerate. Force continues to be a critical variable in determining the outcome of regional conflicts. The UN can play a useful mediating role in resolving those conflicts, but in and of itself the power of the UN is limited. Where U.S. values or interests are suffering, UN mediation and diplomatic overtures cannot be counted on to succeed. There is no substitute for military capability.

Let me conclude this analysis with some questions to ponder:

If Soviet change has brought a decline in the global threat, does that mean that the requirements of containing that threat have lessened? Is there any reason to believe that Soviet change has brought a decline in the nuclear threat?

How can we preserve, and to what extent do we need to preserve, ideological and political cohesion in the West?

How can we increase independence within the Soviet bloc, and to what extent should we try?

If the Pacific rim continues to grow in economic importance, should we restructure our strategic orientation? If so, how?

How can we maintain the forward defense in Europe yet distribute the burdens more equitably?

How can we structure our forces in ways that will allow us to project power with greater success in low-intensity conflicts?

These are some of the questions that we must ask ourselves in this time of domestic and global transition. They are, of course, not easy questions, and we cannot expect that we will find easy answers. But wisdom is never easily found. What it requires, particularly in this complicated age, is that we take to the intellectual challenge, that we think openly and thoroughly. The stakes are too great, after all, to settle for anything less.

2
Major Factors Shaping the Global Security Environment of the 1990s

Robert L. Pfaltzgraff, Jr.

To consider the security environment of the 1990s, the years leading into and even beyond the year 2000, is a complex undertaking in itself. It becomes an even more challenging task if it encompasses an assessment of implications for U.S. defense planning. Such an exercise necessarily includes a delineation of major global and regional security trends affecting U.S. security interests. In the absence of an understanding of those factors shaping the geostrategic setting within which U.S. interests will be identified and defined, however, U.S. military doctrines and force structures would be developed in a vacuum. What is needed, therefore, is an approach that provides a basis for delineating the characteristics of weapons systems that will be required in order to protect U.S. interests within the emerging security environment of the next decade and beyond.

In turn, this type of exercise is fraught with difficulty. As we look to the future, nothing is easier than a straight line projection—casting in terms of the future tense trends that are simply an extrapolation into the future of what we know about the past and the present. Whatever we can say about the future, it will not be simply more of the same. Our task, both as policymakers and policy analysts, in and out of government, must include an ability to discern the elements of continuity and, more importantly, what will be different about the future, and then to be able to determine with some degree of accuracy what all of this means for U.S. defense policy and for force structures.

An assessment of the emerging security environment and its implications for U.S. defense priorities must encompass, but nevertheless extend beyond, the 1990s. It is the capabilities presently in our inventories or those that we have already decided to procure that will be what is available to us in the next decade. Systems that we decided to procure in the present decade are likely only in the 1990s to reach fully the actual procurement and deployment stage. The weapons choices that we make today will only be reflected in actual operational hardware in the form of military capabilities 10 to 15 years from now. Of necessity, therefore, when we decide to build or to acquire a weapons system, we are making, explicitly or implicitly, a series of assumptions about the battlefield environment of the future, the type of armed conflict we will face, and the requirements that we will have for a strategy based on deterrence and the ability actually to engage in armed combat.

Each of our armed services devotes a good deal of time and effort, perhaps never fully adequate but nevertheless substantial, to the discussion of doctrine and the types of battlefield environments in which U.S. forces, as well as those of our major allies and other states, will operate in the years ahead. U.S. military planning, for example, extends into and even beyond the second decade of the twenty-first century. The battlefield of the future, it is suggested, will place a premium on smaller, more lethal combat units, deep operations capability, and increased ability to operate in a high intensity, nighttime and daylight environment. Our force structure will contain units capable of more autonomous operations by smaller formations, with greater mobility, agility, organic firepower, and enhanced command, control, and communications.

It is said that artificial intelligence and robotics will make it possible to place fewer soldiers in the field and that, because of adverse demographic trends and the cost of trained manpower, we will have to devise ways of fighting with fewer soldiers. It should be obvious that a useful point of departure for any analysis of the future international security environment and an assessment of what it portends for force structure would be to find out as much as we can about how the respective military services view the problem. What the services have in common is a growing interest in new technologies at the conventional level. Such an emphasis is understandable in light of the types of conflict that have been fought in the second half of this century, in which nuclear weapons have served to deter war between the possessors of nuclear weapons. At the same time, the global conflict map contains numerous examples of wars of varying intensity levels below the nuclear threshold.

However, the emphasis on new technologies at the conventional level is not confined to U.S. military thought. Soviet military writings give prominence to likely technological developments, such as long-range surveillance, target acquisition, and weapon delivery systems, as well as low observables, including missiles and aircraft. By, or not long after, the end of the first decade of the twenty-first century, it is likely that for the Soviet Union as well as for the United States, emerging technologies will include directed-energy weapons, new families of explosives, earth-penetrating sensors, brilliant information processing, and advanced robotics. Highly accurate strikes, using various types of missiles, will possibly do for conventional military operations what the intercontinental ballistic missile has already done to strategic deterrence and strategic warfare.

For all of the foregoing reasons, it is presumed that the overarching need of the United States will be the development and exploitation of high technology as a means of enhancing our combat capabilities. Therefore, if we are to understand the emerging security environment, it is necessary to forecast technological development both on the basis of on-the-horizon technologies and with some speculation about entirely new types of military capabilities that may come into existence. It is probably safe to assert that, once produced, existing or on-the-horizon technologies will be diffused from the center of origin to a large number of additional possessors. Such is the process by which very expensive technologies can be reproduced much less expensively by larger and larger numbers of groups and even in some cases by individuals. It is instructive to think of the cost of the Manhattan Project that produced the atomic bomb, and how relatively less expensive it is to produce a crude nuclear device today.

New technologies, perhaps exotic systems associated with a defense against ballistic missiles, will be expensive to produce in the first instance. Such systems probably will be available, within the next twenty years or so, principally to the superpowers, although a select number of smaller states such as Israel are likely to acquire defensive systems. For example, the Israeli Arrow system is being heavily financed from SDIO funds. Later there will a process of technology diffusion on a broader scale.

Nevertheless, we must avoid the temptation to assert that the future security environment will only be shaped by the *technologies* that are available at the time. We know that weapons can be used for offense or for defense, for deterrence or for political intimidation. Furthermore, it is political differences that give rise to wars which will be fought with the weapons that are already in the inventories or which can be acquired before the conflict is ended.

Thus, the emerging security environment will be shaped by two dynamic sets of factors: (1) the conflicts of the future in the various regions of the world stemming from political differences, as well as (2) the technologies that will be available to various states and other actors. The conflict map of the world, as we look toward the twenty-first century, will contain a very large number of points of armed confrontation or situations fraught with such potential. Furthermore, the prospect looms large that the process of technology diffusion will continue at an accelerating pace. Many new actors—state and nonstate—will be in the process of acquiring advanced technologies that will confer unprecedented levels of lethality upon them as we move toward and into the twenty-first century.

The emerging security environment is likely to feature a continuing need for the United States to preserve a deterrent force posture toward the

Soviet Union with emphasis on both conventional systems as well as modernization at the nuclear level. Nuclear weapons will remain crucially important to the United States for deterrence against the Soviet Union. Short of a leak-proof defense against ballistic missiles deployed by both superpowers, we will continue to need a force posture that contains such nuclear capabilities in a world in which the Soviet Union will continue to constitute the principal threat to U.S. security. Let us assume for a moment that Gorbachev's *glasnost* and *perestroika* result in an economically strengthened Soviet Union. In this case the Soviet Union will remain a principal competitor to the United States for global influence. The failure of Gorbachev's policies would undoubtedly lead to a successor Soviet leadership determined to retain its grip on power by the possession of major military programs and to enhance its legitimacy by successful foreign policy initiatives, if only to counter the effects of a fundamentally flawed economic system. Hence, an analysis of the future global security environment would be deficient if it did not include the Soviet Union as a factor of importance. However, such an analysis would be inadequate if it was confined to the Soviet Union and neglected the host of emerging issues and threats in a world of many more points of power and conflict from high to mid to low intensity.

Although the technological opportunities available for weapons innovation will increase greatly in the next generation, only the superpowers will be capable of maintaining an inventory of the most advanced weaponry across the full spectrum of capabilities—from the strategic-nuclear to the conventional and lower intensity levels—in light of the vast cost of research and development, as well as production, including the spreading of unit cost over a large number of copies of a specific system. The larger the technological-industrial base devoted to defense, the greater will be the opportunity to develop and maintain a force structure containing a spectrum of capabilities from high- to low-intensity conflict.

At every level, and increasingly at the strategic level, we are likely to see a greater mix of offensive and defensive forces. The unprecedented range, payload and accuracy levels of offensive systems—nuclear and conventional—can be expected to result in intensified efforts to exploit technologies of a defensive nature as well. If targets that can be located are increasingly likely to be destroyed because of the range and accuracy of systems—so-called smart weapons and brilliant munitions—it follows that alternative means for assessing or enhancing defense against such systems will be sought. Such efforts will include, but not be confined to, strategic defense, as well as defense against other types of threats for which an extended air defense of one kind or another will be needed. By the same token, however, the battlefield of the future will feature a variety of offensive systems not easily identifiable—that is, low observables. Thus, there is likely to be a dynamic relationship between technologies of the offense and technologies of the defense.

Space will increase in importance as an environment through which capabilities launched on earth would pass en route to their targets, as with ballistic missiles. Space will gain even greater salience as an arena for reconnaissance and surveillance for target acquisition and for the deployment of component paths of a defensive system against missiles. As we move beyond the 1990s, exploitation of space for national security purposes will continue to grow greatly to support strategic forces, arms control verification, and tactical commanders in terrestrial operations. However, space will become increasingly an environment for conflict in its own right, for we are likely to see the deployment on a permanent basis of a variety of military and civilian assets beyond the earth's gravitational field that themselves would furnish lucrative targets and will therefore become the objects of protection by space powers. The heightened reliance on space-based assets will result in the more extensive use of space, leading to the deployment of various capabilities for space control.

In and especially beyond the 1990s, states other than the United States and the Soviet Union will be in the process of acquiring a growing ability to build and deploy space assets with commercial and military applications. It should be noted that possession of the technological means to place in orbit space hardware will provide an inherent capacity for ballistic missile delivery. Moreover, the growing use of space assets by regional actors will render the battlefield in regional conflicts more transparent and lethal, with important implications for the conduct of warfare by local or regional states as well as intervention by outside powers.

Whatever else we know about the conflict map of the world of the future, we can be certain that it will contain numerous issues, settings, and actors capable of generating armed conflicts of varying levels of intensity. Among the most dramatic changes in the international landscape will be a rise in population and urbanization in the Third World relative to the highly industrialized West. While some countries, notably the Federal Republic of Germany and certain other Western states, will experience an overall decline in population, with obvious effects on personnel availability for military establishments, there will be a huge increase in population in most parts of the Third World in the years leading into the twenty-first century. For example, short of a major conflict or other disaster, by the year 2010 Mexico and India are expected to increase in population by about 40 percent. The total population of Africa may double in the same time period. While the population of advanced industrial countries is aging, most of those living in Third World countries will be very young—below the age of 25. Throughout the Third World there will be a marked movement of population toward cities, with whatever political-social effects such change may portend for patterns of conflict and instability.

The conflict issues of the future, encompassing wars within states, as well as armed conflict between and among states and including nonstate actors, will coincide in time with an unprecedented diffusion of technology, economic capabilities, and military means. It has been estimated that by the year 2010, and perhaps before that time, the combined GNP of four East Asian states (Japan, China, South Korea, and Taiwan) will exceed that of the United States. A large number of states elsewhere, and especially in the Middle East, will be in possession of unprecedented military capabilities, including not only advanced conventional weapons but also the ability to move across the nuclear threshold to become actual possessors of nuclear capabilities if they so choose. Several have already moved as close to acquisition of such systems as possible without actually overtly violating the Non-Proliferation Treaty, of which most are signatories.

Among the major trends that will shape the global security environment will be the proliferation of delivery systems, including missile technologies with a potential for carrying either conventional or nuclear warheads or biological-chemical agents. It remains to be seen whether international agreements, such as the Missile Technology Control Regime unveiled in 1987, will have the intended effect of restricting such proliferation. It is more likely that additional states will acquire their own means for the production of missiles and for the export of such technologies.

In the absence of defensive capabilities, a large number of our military systems, including maritime forces, will be increasingly vulnerable to over-the-horizon attack. The future international security environment will feature short- or long-range delivery systems that will be available to larger numbers of states. They will include both manned aircraft and ballistic missiles and, eventually, highly accurate cruise missiles. Countries such as India, Pakistan, and Israel, already termed de facto nuclear states, will be joined by other threshold powers such as Argentina, South Africa, and Brazil. Such states will have an increasing capability to build their own delivery systems or to acquire necessary technologies from abroad.

Much has been said in recent years about biological and chemical weapons as "the poor man's atomic bomb." Such capabilities can be manufactured in pharmaceutical and chemical factories almost anywhere in the world and made available easily and cheaply. The extent to which they will actually be used remains to be seen. What is evident, however, is the fact that such weapons will be available to larger and larger numbers of states as well as non-state actors in the years ahead.

As a result, the conflict map of the world of the early twenty-first century is likely to contain a host of new actors capable of military operations at a nuclear and non-nuclear level if they choose during or before a conflict to cross the threshold, an act that is now prohibited by the Non-Proliferation Treaty. In any case, delivery systems capable of carrying nuclear warheads can be adapted, with likely reductions in range capability, for the deployment of conventional munitions. Such changes will have potentially profound implications for security in highly volatile regions such as the Middle East or perhaps Southern Africa and South Asia, and even our own hemisphere.

Closely related to weapons diffusion will be the strengthening of a trend that already exists on a large scale. We know that, after the United States, the Soviet Union, Britain, and France there is a lengthening list of exporters of military hardware. These now include Brazil and China, as well as Israel. In the years leading into the next century, we are likely to witness a heightened sophistication in indigenous armaments production in many parts of the world. The broadening diffusion of advanced weapons will be heightened by the ability of such producers to export high-tech military hardware, a phenomenon, incidentally, that is being accelerated by domestically imposed restrictions on U.S. foreign military sales. As the industrial-technological capabilities of other actors outside the United States grow in size and sophistication, there will probably be a heightened tendency for U.S. industry to seek various forms of relationships such as licensing, co-production, and joint ventures and even direct investment.

The diffusion of capabilities that were once the exclusive preserve of the superpowers will undoubtedly weaken substantially the ability of the superpowers, and the United States in particular, to intervene directly in such conflicts. Another direct result will be to create potential security problems for other states in the immediate region who are not the possessors of such advanced military systems. For the latter states, there will undoubtedly be a need to build or otherwise to acquire defensive systems of one kind or another, retaliatory capabilities, or combinations of both. From such an analysis it would be possible to develop and discuss a variety of enabling technologies and weapons characteristics within alternative regional conflict scenarios from Europe to the Asian-Pacific area, from Southwest Asia to Southern Africa, and from South Asia to Central America, from North Africa to South America.

The problems facing the United States will include the need, where our vital interests as well as those of our allies are at stake, to be able to project necessary military power. We will seek to do so in a situation in which systems of unprecedented lethality and accuracy will be available, as already noted, within the various regions and in security environments in which our forward-basing infrastructure will be greatly reduced, if not largely eliminated. It follows that U.S. military assets themselves, in the absence of adequate compensatory measures, will be placed at greater risk in such security environments and that challenges to U.S. security policy will grow in complexity. The task of preserving U.S. interests will be set within a context of expanding foreign policy objectives, pursued by a larger number of increasingly powerful states. Let us assume that our security objective will be to deter the use of regional military forces against U.S. capabilities and thus to exercise whatever political-military leverage we have available to us either to prevent regional conflict or, as in the case of the recent Persian Gulf reflagging operation, to protect vital interests, such as the sea lines of communication. Especially if the regional security environment includes additional possessors of nuclear weapons, together with a variety of conventional systems, it will be necessary both to rethink our conceptions of strategy and the types of weapons systems needed by our allies and other friendly states, and of course by the United States itself. If we come to face a situation in which Third World states have access to nuclear and conventional weapons that could be used for aggression or coercive purposes, the result will be more militarily capable adversaries with threats to U.S. interests coming from multiple sources.

In sum, the emerging global security environment can be expected to have several salient features. They include: continuation of U.S.–Soviet rivalry, but a growing importance in the various regions of actors having unprecedented capabilities; a large number of flashpoints for armed conflict of varying intensity; the existence of a larger number of actors—state and non-state—in a conflict setting providing the potential for wars within and among existing units; and new technologies for the conduct of a spectrum of warfare from the high-intensity nuclear-conventional level to mid- and low-intensity conflict will be available on an unprecedented scale.

There will be a growing indigenization of military production and arms export capabilities to Third World states. Although the Soviet Union will remain a vital focal point of U.S. strategy and force structure, there will be an increasing emphasis in U.S. force planning on Third World contingencies, including low-intensity conflict. In light of the increasing quantity and lethality of weaponry in the hands of states in the various regions, the ability of the United States to project power and thus to influence conflict situations will be diminished in the absence of a rethinking of strategy and means for power projection.

Last but not least, as a result of the foregoing, the problems facing the United States in developing adequate strategies and tactics, as well as necessary weapons systems, will call forth a need continually to monitor and to the greatest extent possible to anticipate such changes both to minimize their adverse impact and, to the extent possible, benefit from them and help shape them in ways consonant with U.S. national interest.

3

"New Thinking" in Soviet Policy?: Assessing the Soviet Threat for the 1990s

Ilana Kass

The purpose of this chapter is to analyze the objective imperatives that drive Soviet strategy at the current stage and set a framework for assessing the implications of that strategy for U.S. national security. The key premise underlying this analysis is that more than three years into the Gorbachev era, the United States has yet to develop a coherent, proactive policy vis-à-vis the Soviet Union. As Mikhail Gorbachev—perhaps the most dynamic and capable Soviet leader since Lenin—leaps from one startling initiative to another, setting the agenda of international discourse and forcing Washington into a reactive posture, the United States appears conceptually unprepared to deal effectively with its key adversary.

The problem is not new. Indeed, a lack of coherence and consistency has been a virtual hallmark of the superpower relationship. It is, however, becoming increasingly acute as euphoria—spawned, in equal measure, by the Soviet "charm offensive" and by our own wishful thinking—sweeps the West away from the moorings of reality.

Several factors—some perennial, some new—combine to account for the problem. First, the United States has always been reluctant to accept as a fact of life that the Soviet Union is and will likely remain an adversary: a nation fundamentally different in its world outlook, goals, and strategy. Our inherent optimism—not to mention self-indulgence—that all societies will sooner or later see the light and adopt democratic standards is now being reinforced by the soothing words and images wafting out of

The views expressed herein are solely those of the author and do not necessarily reflect the views of the Department of Defense or of any other agency of the United States government. This chapter draws upon an earlier paper coauthored with Fred Clark Boli, "Dangerous Terrain: Gorbachev's New Thinking," SIGNAL, Vol. 43, No. 4 (December 1988), pp. 65–71.

the Kremlin. Simply put, Gorbachev looks like a Westerner and speaks like a Westerner. Therefore, conventional wisdom tells us, he cannot help but want to bring his country closer to the West in terms of both its political structure and strategic objectives. The millennial vision of a new era in U.S.–Soviet relations cannot be far behind.

Second, we tend to recast the Soviets in our own image, to assign to them our own values, priorities, goals, methods, and processes of reasoning. What they tell us about themselves that does not conform to our frame of reference we tend to refuse to believe, dismissing it as propaganda, ideological window-dressing, or as largely irrelevant "voices from the past." Our traditional proclivity to mirror-image now thrives on a steady diet of such intrinsically appealing Soviet concepts as "new thinking," "openness," "democratization," and "restructuring"—all widely misinterpreted in the West.

Third, we refuse to treat the Soviet threat holistically and simultaneously in all of its dimensions. As a result, we tend to confuse the transient with the enduring, the marginal with the fundamental, the goals with the assorted means devised to attain them. While such an approach is always fraught with risk, the dangers inherent in misconstruing the nature, directions, and objectives of Soviet strategy increase during periods of dynamic change.

Accordingly, the analysis which follows will set a framework for a sober, precise interpretation of the new directions in Soviet strategy and their implications for the West. This, it is hoped, will help U.S. decisionmakers to develop a proactive policy, capable of fostering potentially beneficial trends, while hedging against complacency and ensuing vulnerability. However, should the euphoria buoyed by wishful thinking and mirror-imaging prevail, the United States might ultimately pursue policies inconsistent with its own interests.

For analytic validity and political utility, any attempt to look beyond the "new thinking" rhetoric and assess the imperatives driving Soviet strategy must begin with a clear statement of assumptions. Making assumptions explicit exposes to scrutiny not only the assessment itself, but also the salience of the data and the rigor of the logic. Further, given the dynamics currently at play in the Soviet Union, these assumptions should be periodically revisited and revalidated.

First and most obvious is the assumption that Gorbachev is a rational politician. As such, he pursues power and seeks to preserve both his own leadership position and the integrity of the regime. The assumption of rationality excludes suicidal tendencies and any intention to preside over the dissolution of the Soviet empire.

A second and related assumption holds that the change currently underway in the Soviet Union is rational and directed, albeit not necessarily precisely calibrated. Indeed, change—any change—tends to generate its own momentum, unleashing forces which might prove difficult to control. Nonetheless, available evidence suggests that, at least from the perspective of the Soviet elite, the change is logical and targeted at specific short-, mid-, and long-range goals. It is these goals—as well as the strategies devised to attain them—which merit attention and a coherent policy response.

Third and last is the assumption that the change is real, not a propaganda sham staged for our benefit. This, however, is not necessarily good news. The fact that Gorbachev is a reformer, genuinely trying to solve the monumental problems facing his nation, does not automatically make him a friend of the West. Indeed, I would argue that a sober look at the goals and motives driving Gorbachev's strategy will make it quite obvious why the Soviets should want *perestroika* to succeed. What is much less clear is why we should help it along.

Gorbachev's regime has demonstrated tremendous acumen in promoting an image of a reforming, introspective, and, therefore, more benign Soviet Union. Most impressive is his ability to present Leninist doctrine and unchanging goals in terms that are appealing both at home and abroad.[1] His strategy is to integrate avant-garde arms-control initiatives with images of systemic change—all orchestrated to the soothing tune of "defensive doctrine" and "reasonable sufficiency." Thereby, the Soviets are setting the terms of *our* national security debate and are well along in their effort to manage the superpower competition through management of Western threat perceptions.

Almost from the very beginning of the Gorbachev era, our attention has been focused on *glasnost* and *perestroika*—the tools of Gorbachev's policy. We have become so fascinated with the nature and scope of the reforms—and the personality of the reformer—that we pay little, if any, attention to the goals these changes are designed to achieve. Viewed, as they should be, however, through the prism of our national security interests, these Soviet goals hold more peril than promise.

Glasnost, Perestroika, and Renewal: A Question of Ends and Means

Glasnost and *perestroika* are fast becoming part of our everyday vocabulary. "Openness" and "restructuring," as the terms are invariably translated, have become symbols of, and synonyms for, Gorbachev's new strategy. Yet, from the very beginning both terms were widely misunderstood in the West. The problem transcends simple semantics or the obvious difficulties involved in translating from one language to another. It has to do with taking words—and the concepts they convey—out of their proper context and imbuing them with political, social, cultural, and ethical connotations which they did not originally have.

Russian dictionaries define *glasnost* as "publicity," i.e., "the business or technique of attracting public attention." If nothing else, *glasnost* certainly has attracted public attention, both within the Soviet Union and abroad. Properly understood, however, the Soviet concept has little to do with "openness" in its broad connotation of candor, freedom of expression, or truthfulness. Deriving, as it does, from the root word *glas*, meaning "voice," the Soviet concept describes the way in which information is transmitted (e.g., loud vice soft, wide vice limited, etc.). In itself, the term says nothing about the *substance* of the information, which could be true, false, or any blend thereof—modulated to suit a specific set of political objectives.

Indeed, Gorbachev himself defines *glasnost* as "a tool to accelerate the movement forward, not a 'game of democracy.' " Further, he asserts that "the essence of *glasnost* is the Party's policy and its sole determining criterion is whether or not it strengthens socialism."[2]

That the Western press and, increasingly, experts in and out of government insist on translating *glasnost* as "openness" is ethnocentric mirror-imaging at its worst. It suggests that the Soviets are becoming just like us, sharing not only our vocabulary but also our moral and ethical values. This, in turn, promotes the image of a more benign, less adversarial Soviet Union. The policy implications are obvious. Little wonder, then, that in addressing Western audiences, Soviet spokesmen play back and, thus, reinforce both the misinterpretation and the ensuing misperception. After all, this is what *glasnost* really is—goal-oriented manipulation of information.

Our misinterpretation of *perestroika*, while less glaring, is equally ominous in its policy implications. Here, the translation is technically correct; the imparted meaning, however, is not. The English word "restructuring" connotes a fundamental, systemic, and total revision. *Perestroika* indicates much less sweeping a change.[3] "Restructuring" suggests rejection of the core structure, i.e., Marxism-Leninism, and its replacement with a brand new system, more akin to Western pluralistic democracy. *Perestroika* lacks this implication.

Misperceptions both feed off and reinforce our enduring hope for systemic convergence and cooperation. Not surprisingly, therefore, Gorbachev's repeated statements that the "fundamental goals remain unchanged" and that "what is needed is more socialism, more efficient socialism" are simply ignored in the West. By the same token, Gorbachev's warnings that "a bitter disappointment awaits those in the West who hope that we will reject socialism, go over to the other camp or build a non-socialist society,"[4] are discounted as lip service to Party troglodytes. That the Soviets intend what they say is evident from the actual meaning of *perestroika*—a change of the methods and procedures through which essentially unchanged goals are pursued. *Perestroika*—just like *glasnost*—is a means to an end, a new strategy to attain traditional objectives.[5]

Gorbachev's stated goal of "renewal and moral purification of socialism"[6] is key to understanding the true direction of his strategy. The calls for a communist renaissance—a return to the "golden age" of communism, wherein the Soviet model commanded broad popular and international appeal—make it clear that Gorbachev's vision of a Soviet Union reborn is hardly a Western-style participatory democracy. Quite the contrary, it is the remaking of a nation in its original, Leninist image—a Soviet Union as it was supposed to be, rather than what it has degenerated into. In Gorbachev's own words:

> Lenin saw the historic mission of socialism in the need to blaze the trail for the transition to communism. . . . We have to impart to socialism a new quality or, as they say, a second wind, and this requires a profound renewal of all aspects of society's life, both material and spiritual. The purpose of *perestroika* is the practical reestablishment of Lenin's conception of socialism.[7]

Today, the USSR is a one-dimensional superpower, whose international stature rests primarily on military might. In all other indices of the "correlation of forces," it is facing a systemic crisis. Gorbachev's efforts, then, are directed at stemming and reversing the tide of economic, political, and social decline. His goal is a more efficient, more competitive, and, therefore, stronger Soviet Union. Thus, the objective imperatives that drive his strategy are not qualitatively different from those that drove every reformer in Russian and Soviet history from Peter the Great through Lenin, Stalin, and Khrushchev—reform on the brink of crisis because "those who fall behind get beaten."

To breathe life into the entire domestic structure, Gorbachev strives to:

> Reactivate public participation in a society where the majority of citizens have become indifferent, if not alienated from and hostile to the regime and its initiatives;

> Discredit, bypass, or otherwise push aside entrenched *apparatchiki*, whose corruption and resistance to change have sapped the Party's credibility as the leading force of society;

> Engage society in a debate which will 1) help release pent-up frustra-

tions born of years of intellectual repression; 2) shake the apathy which has all but stifled creativity and innovation; 3) mobilize the intelligentsia to support leadership policies by giving it a stake in the reform; and, last but not least, 4) create a pool of ideas from which the Party leadership can, at its discretion, draw concepts whose implementation will make the system work;

Revitalize the economy by redirecting resources to capital investments in the industrial and science and technology infrastructure. It is important to point out, however, that the agenda is not simply more butter and fewer guns (although the traditional promise of improving the standard of living is necessary to generate public support), but, rather, fewer off-the-shelf guns now for the sake of more sophisticated guns (and computers!) later.[8]

As indicated above, the long-term goal of this strategy is a communist renaissance. The immediate objective is to avert systemic crisis.

The Soviet Union's foreign policy is designed to facilitate the attainment of these goals. Here the immediate objectives are: 1) slow the opponent down; 2) stabilize the environment; 3) gain time. Time is the critical variable—time to catch up, to rebuild the Soviet economy to the extent that it can effectively compete (or, at least, not trail Japan and other newly industrialized nations). This is not a trivial matter: according to Dr. Abel Aganbegyan, Gorbachev's principal economic advisor, the Soviet Union might need as long as thirty years to bring its economy and science and technology up to competitive levels.[9] Within this framework, the operating assumption seems to be that if the Soviet Union were "to act in such a way as to give nobody grounds for fears, even imagined ones, about their security,"[10] the West would relax its defense posture, giving Moscow the respite it needs.

The concept of respite (or breathing-spell—*peredyshka*) deserves some elaboration. The term was originally coined by Lenin within the context of the 1918 Treaty of Brest-Litovsk, wherein the war-weary Bolsheviks ceded to Germany a third of Russia's population, cultivated land, and industry so as to save the revolution and consolidate the new Soviet state. It came to mean the temporary subordination of long-range goals (in this case, world revolution) to the immediate exigencies of self-preservation—a tactical retreat for the purpose of a later strategic offensive. The concept was skillfully applied in 1921, when, to promote Russia's economic recovery, Lenin instituted the New Economic Policy (NEP), which allowed the revival of free enterprise, relaxed governmental controls on the economy, gave monetary incentives to increase production, welcomed foreign capital and trade, and encouraged artistic freedoms. At the time, Lenin justified the necessary retreat from ideological postulates as "taking a step backward in order to take two steps forward." It is upon this Leninist foundation that Gorbachev's strategy is modeled.[11]

In the interim, two things are needed: 1) ready access to Western technology, capital, and management techniques, preferably applied directly to the Soviet economy through joint ventures, with the attendant relaxation of existing export controls; and 2) stabilization of the arms race. Within this latter category, Moscow seeks to delay, if not eliminate altogether, planned NATO force modernizations and the Strategic Defense Initiative, with its assorted spin-offs.

Given current exigencies, the Soviet Union simply cannot compete across the broad spectrum of technological innovation that has characterized U.S. defense programs in the 1980s. To keep up, it needs to blunt the edge of the competition—to slow its pace, as well as delimit its scope. And, as the experience of earlier détente periods has taught it, one of the most effective ways to get a handle on how the West responds to the threat is through manipulation of how the West perceives the threat.

Given that both the United States and its allies tend to view arms control as a substitute for, rather than an adjunct to, national security policy, Gorbachev's efforts to hobble our defense programs by easing the concerns that fuel them might prove effective, at least in the short term. Already, at least according to recent public opinion polls, the warming of superpower relations is perceived as obviating the need for a strong defense. The confluence of U.S. domestic imperatives—specifically the budget woes—with a diminishing threat perception might undermine support for both large defense budgets and trade restrictions.

Similarly, NATO cohesion might prove vulnerable to continued Soviet pressure on the key elements of the West's nuclear deterrent. For obvious reasons, the rhetoric of "defensive doctrine" and the prospect of Soviet troop reductions carry special appeal in the European context. What is perhaps less obvious are the enduring Soviet objectives of fragmenting NATO, neutralizing Europe, and affecting U.S. withdrawal from the continent which the current strategy seeks to achieve. For example, the current portrayal of a U.S. presence in Europe as both irrelevant (given the diminution of the threat) and detrimental to the goal of a "safe, denuclearized, common European home" is clearly aimed at undermining NATO's very raison d'être.[12] Similarly, the Soviets seek to exploit traditional intra-NATO differences, with the dual purpose of isolating those members who remain wary of Soviet intentions (e.g., Britain), while persuading others to place short-term national interests above those of the alliance as a whole. Here, again, the confluence of internal Western imperatives—from economics to demographics—with the perceived change in the threat environment could redound to the Soviet Union's favor. At least in the near term, concerns over the bottom line might outweigh concerns over the front line.

While pursuing these traditional goals through "new thinking"—that is, by means of "swift changes of form and method, flexibility, unusual solutions and political audacity,"[13]—Moscow seeks more than Western acquiescence. It needs to generate active support for the renewal process; it needs the West to help the strategy succeed. To this end, the program is portrayed as aimed at shared objectives—most notably peace and stability—with its success a vested Western interest. In a truly Orwellian variation on this theme, for example, West German audiences are told that the stronger the Soviet Union is the more secure their nation will be.[14] Similarly, by fostering the perception that *perestroika* and indeed, Gorbachev himself, are vulnerable to a neo-Stalinist backlash, the Soviets strive to persuade the West that unrequited concessions—as well as generous credits and technology transfers—are necessary to protect both the reform and the reformer.

"Reasonable Sufficiency": The Military Dimension of a Holistic Strategy

The essence of the Soviet Union's military agenda stems directly from the domestic and international imperatives analyzed above. Indeed, to be properly understood, the political and military dimensions of Gorbachev's multi-faceted strategy must be assessed holistically, as they are inexorably interlinked.

The "correlation of forces" concept is key to understanding how the Soviets view the interplay among the mutually reinforcing elements of strategy. This uniquely Soviet paradigm stipulates that "the course and outcome of war depend on:

> the correlation of economic strengths of the warring states (or coalitions);
>
> the correlation of the belligerents' scientific and technological potentials;
>
> the correlation of the belligerents' moral-political strengths;
>
> the correlation of the belligerents' military capabilities and mobilization potentials."[15]

In the broadest sense, the "correlation of forces" concept—and the laws of war of which it is part[16]—encapsulates the Soviet leadership's strategic outlook. It reflects the Soviet perception of an ongoing, systemic conflict and of the ensuing need to apply all available tools of statecraft in a concerted, goal-oriented way. Within this integrated context, military power is a major, but not the preeminent, factor.

In practical terms, the "correlation of forces" is a dynamic measure of relative power in peace, crisis, and war—a criterion to judge and be judged by. It shapes strategy insofar as it: 1) facilitates a comprehensive estimate of the situation; 2) diagnoses relative strengths, weaknesses, and vulnerabilities; and 3) sets strategic priorities, thus allowing both concentration of effort (on areas in need of immediate attention) and economy of force (in venues where the line can be held with little risk).

Application of the "correlation of forces" paradigm reveals a dismal picture. It tells the Soviet elite that, thanks to the tremendous effort of the last forty years, the Soviet Union is abreast—perhaps even ahead—militarily, but trailing in all other indices of power. Thus, it is behind in the aggregate. Worse, as the Soviet Minister of Defense has recently acknowledged, further linear growth in the military sphere yields diminishing political returns.[17] In a sense, it has become counterproductive, having spurred the United States to its largest peacetime military buildup in history.

Objectively, the "correlation of forces" estimate leaves the Soviets little choice but to "think anew," stabilize the environment, and devise a better strategy to achieve their enduring goals. Within this framework, holding the line on military growth—even reducing it to levels of "reasonable sufficiency"—while striving to recover in the political, economic, and scientific-technological spheres is both logical and necessary. By the same token, the *relative* nature of the estimate dictates that political efforts be directed at ensuring that the odds stay even and the adversary does not race ahead. Thus, to the Soviets, "sufficiency implies the quantity and quality of armed forces and weapons that can reliably guarantee the defense of the Motherland. The limits of defense sufficiency are conditioned by U.S. and NATO actions."[18]

Where does the current emphasis on the *political* dimension of strategy leave the Soviet military? The short answer is: in a somewhat diminished, but essential role. The following observations will substantiate this conclusion:

As a rational leader, Gorbachev is unlikely to emasculate the military—the sole pillar that gives credibility to his political initiatives and makes his nation a superpower.

Gorbachev and the military might disagree over the pace of weapons acquisition, but not on the fundamental requirement to "guarantee the reliable defense of the Motherland." For, while Soviet policy—or, more precisely, the political side of Soviet doctrine—strives to prevent war, the military still has the task to fight and win should war, nonetheless, break out.[19] Within this framework, the yardstick of sufficiency remains what it has always been: enough to accomplish the mission.

Gorbachev and the military seem to agree that the superpower competition has shifted into the realm of quality, where the West holds a clear advantage. Indeed, the assessment that the Soviet industry is ill-equipped to carry the military into the twenty-first century originated in the Soviet military at least eight years before Gorbachev took power.[20] Consequently, efforts to prevent the West from fielding its technological edge are likely to be endorsed by the military. The same holds for policy and arms-control initiatives that improve the relative security of the Soviet Union, thus making the military's traditional mission easier to accomplish.

Perestroika is compatible with the professional military's assessment of its requirements. The military needs industry to produce the high-tech systems necessary for modern war. It needs society to produce the technologically sophisticated, politically motivated and physically fit citizens who can fight and win on the battlefield. *Perestroika* promises to deliver both, thus responding to long-standing military concerns.[21] This, in turn, leads to the conclusion that, far from being a reluctant victim of the reform, the military stands to gain and emerge stronger. If there is a civil-military discord, it is on the limits of *glasnost*, not on the need for *perestroika*.

The current public emphasis on "defensive doctrine" is not new, although it is much improved. First, Soviet military doctrine has been officially and consistently proclaimed to be defensive at least since 1977.[22] Second, Soviet military thought has never treated offense and defense as an either-or proposition, maintaining, instead, that both the sword and the shield are necessary for victory.[23] The weight attached to defense is clearly reflected in the Soviet Union's investment in air defense, strategic defense, civil defense, and so forth. Third, current Soviet efforts to evolve a better balanced offense-defense mix in both forces and operational concepts go back almost a decade.[24] These ongoing efforts are based on sound military judgments, having little to do with *glasnost* and *perestroika*. Most notably, they reflect the Soviet military's professional assessment that:

1. Current military-technical trends favor the defense, insofar as they increase the defender's ability to strike deep and fast—even preempt

in time and/or place—thus seizing the strategic initiative. Thereby, according to this assessment, defense is acquiring some of the advantages traditionally inherent in the offense;

2. The capabilities vested in such U.S.-NATO concepts as Air-Land Battle, Follow-on Forces Attack (FOFA), SDI, the Maritime Strategy, and so forth, expand the opponent's offensive options. Accordingly, the Soviet Union might have to fight the first battles of World War III on its own territory. (The painful experience of the early period of the Great Patriotic War, with the Red Army totally unprepared for defensive operations, is critical in the context of this worst case scenario); and that

3. In a crisis, the Soviet Union might be politically unwilling or militarily unable to win the mobilization race, preempt on the eve of war, and conduct the high-speed, maneuver warfare it tends to prefer. The prospect of having to gnaw through prepared NATO defenses—facing potentially catastrophic attrition—would, in and of itself, suggest greater attention to defense in both training and force structure.

What is new about "defensive doctrine," then, is the skill with which the Soviets are playing to NATO concerns, the political spin put on basic military prudence, and the strategic capital derived from both. New also is the acumen with which the political and military dimensions of strategy are fused into a synergistic whole. In light of the overarching goals that this integrated strategy seeks to attain, however, granting Gorbachev a free ride is simply not to our advantage.

Notes

1. The only time Gorbachev seems to have overplayed his hand was when, at the Moscow summit, he tried to persuade President Reagan to sign a joint statement proclaiming "peaceful coexistence"—a concept devised by Lenin and perfected by Khrushchev—as the superpowers' common goal. While innocent at first glance, the attempt was quickly perceived as a snare to have the United States sign up to the traditional Soviet goal of managing the East-West competition on terms favorable to Moscow.

2. M.S. Gorbachev, *Perestroika i Novoe Myshlenie,* (Moscow: Politizdat, 1987), pp. 72–78. This book, available in English, should be obligatory reading for U.S. national security professionals. It should be noted, however, that the English-language version is not identical to the Russian.

3. Interestingly, Russian dictionaries offer "restructure, as in a house," "refurbish," "reorganize working procedures," "rearrange the pieces," "remodel," "reform a military unit to meet a new tactical situation," and "switch radio frequencies" as examples of common use of both the noun and the verb.

4. Gorbachev, *Perestroika*, p. 33. See also pp. 55–56.

5. *Pravda*, June 28, 1988, proclaimed in a banner headline: "*Perestroika* is the labor and struggle for the future of socialism." See also Gorbachev, *Perestroika*, pp. 51–55, and Gorbachev's November 2, 1987, speech marking the 70th anniversary of the October Revolution. The speech is available in English through the Novosti Press Agency's publishing house.

6. M.S. Gorbachev, *October and Perestroika: The Revolution Continues*, (Moscow: Novosti Press Agency, 1987), p. 36.

7. Ibid., p. 42.

8. The Soviet General Staff articulated the need to refurbish the industrial and S&T base such as to "prevent the West from gaining the upper hand" well before Gorbachev took power. See, for example, Marshal of the Soviet Union Nikolai Ogarkov, *Vsegda v gotovnosti k zashchite otechestva (Always in Readiness to Defend the Motherland)* (Moscow: Voenizdat, 1982), and subsequent pronouncements, most notably Ogarkov's interview with *Krasnaia zvezda*, May 9, 1984. More recent statements by the Soviet High Command posit that "the meaning of *perestroika* for the Armed Forces is, first and foremost, our readiness for real battle, our ability to attain superiority over a strong, active, well-trained and well-equipped opponent." (*Krasnaia zvezda*, Editorial, November 14, 1987.) For an economist's perspective, see Abel Aganbegyan, *The Challenge of Perestroika*, trans. Pauline M. Tiffen, ed. Michael B. Brown, (London: Century Hutchison, 1988), pp. 226–227.

9. Aganbegyan, *The Challenge of Perestroika*, p. 227.

10. Gorbachev, *Perestroika*, p. 211.

11. Gorbachev, *Perestroika*, pp. 20–21, 34–35. See also Gorbachev, *October and Perestroika*, pp. 14–17. For a balanced Western analysis of the Soviet Union's early years, see Alvin Z. Rubinstein, *Soviet Foreign Policy*, (Boston: Little, Brown, 1985), pp. 3–17.

12. The terminology and slogans of "common security," evident in all major Soviet pronouncements, are borrowed from the vocabulary of the European Left. For a compelling analysis of the dangers to NATO inherent in the Soviet Union's current orientation, see Gerhard Wettig, "New Thinking on Security and East-West Relations," *Problems of Communism* (March–April, 1988): 1–14.

13. The entire statement is worth quoting, since it crystallizes the true thrust of the current strategy: "The very course of Lenin's thought, the entire activity of the Bolsheviks, marked by swift change of form and method, flexibility, unusual tactical solutions, and by political audacity—all this was a vivid example of an anti-dogmatic, truly dialectic, and therefore, new way of thinking. That and only that is how real Marxist-Leninists think and act—especially at times of change, at critical turning points, when the future of the revolution and peace, socialism and progress is at stake." Gorbachev, *October and Perestroika*, p. 10.

14. Professor-doctor Margarita Maksimova, "COCOM and Technological Dependence," *Messemagazine International* (March 1988): 91–102. This dual-language, Russian-German journal is ostensibly intended to promote East-West trade. However, its dominant message is political and overtly anti-U.S. *Messemagazine* has a West German managing editor, a joint editorial board (including, in

addition to the USSR and FRG, representatives from Hungary, Poland, Bulgaria, and Czechoslovakia), and is published in Düsseldorf.

15. Marshal of the Soviet Union N.V. Ogarkov, ed., *Sovetskaia Voennaia Entsiklopediia*, (hereafter SVE), Vol. 3 (Moscow: Voenizdat, 1977), pp. 375–378. For a superb Western analysis see, Michael J. Deane, "The Soviet Concept of the Correlation of World Forces: Implications for American Foreign Policy," *Orbis* (Fall 1976): 625–636. For a more recent operational assessment, see William P. Baxter, *Soviet Airland Battle Tactics* (Novato, CA: Presidio Press, 1986), pp. 6–11.

16. Indeed, the "correlation of forces" *is* the second law of war. In standard formulations it is preceded by the Clausewitzian-Leninist statement that "war depends on its political goals" and followed by the Marxist-Leninist assertion that "victory goes to the side that possesses and uses the capabilities of a new and more progressive social order." As laws, these tenets are outside the subjective realm of personal views and cannot be changed at will. Therefore, they serve as a long-range guide for action in the national security arena.

17. General of the Army D.T. Yazov, "The Qualitative Parameters of Defense Buildup," *Krasnaia zvezda*, August 9, 1988. For an earlier argument along similar lines, see, for example, N.V. Ogarkov, "The Defense of Socialism: The Experience of History and the Contemporary Period," *Krasnaia zvezda*, May 9, 1984.

18. Colonel General Nikolai Chervov, "Mighty Factor for World Peace," *International Affairs* (Moscow, in English), No. 3, March 1988, pp. 9–15, published in JPRS-UMA-88-D14, July 18, 1988, pp. 7–12. See also Yazov, *The Qualitative Parameters of a Defense Building.*"

19. Soviet military doctrine comprises two aspects: the moral-political and the military-technical. Simply put, in political terms, any action taken by the Soviet Union is by definition defensive, because its goal is to *protect* the just interests of the working class. In other words, "defensive" here has little to do with the actual mode of operations. Rather, it is a value judgment, derived from communist morality. It describes the *intent* of the action, not the operational reality. In terms of its political content, Soviet military doctrine has always been defensive, much as the Soviet goal has always been world peace. In military terms, however, a good offense has traditionally been considered the best defense, because it is the offense that brings victory. See Marshal of the Soviet Union S.F. Akhromeev, ed., *Voennoentsiklopedicheski slovar* (hereafter VES) (Moscow: Voenizdat, 1986), p. 240. See also, SVE, Vol. 3, 1977, pp. 225–229.

20. Marshal of the Soviet Union A.A. Grechko, *The Armed Forces of the Soviet State*, (Moscow: Voenizdat, 1975), p. 156. See also Ogarkov, *Always in Readiness*, and Colonel S. Bartnenev, "The Economics of Military Power," *Kommunist Vooruzhennykh Sil*, No. 14 (July 1980): 70.

21. Concerns with the deteriorating moral and physical fitness, as well as educational and technical, skills of Soviet draftees were first voiced by Marshal Ogarkov in "Guarding Peaceful Labor," *Kommunist*, No. 10 (July 1981): 80–91. For recent military assessments of the benefits of *perestroika* see, for example, Yazov, "The Qualitative Parameters of a Defense Buildup." General of the Army A.D. Lizichev, "October and Lenin's Teaching on Defense of the Revolution," *Kommunist*, No. 3 (February 1987); Unsigned lead article, "According to Laws of

High Vigilance," *Zarubezhnoe voennoe obozrenie*, No. 2 (February 1988): 3–6; General of the Army I. Shkadov, "To Shape the Individual," *Krasnaia zvezda*, April 26, 1988.

22. See "Doctrine, military" in SVE, Vol. 3, pp. 225–229 and in VES 1983 and 1986, p. 240.

23. For an in-depth analysis of the relative roles of offense and defense in Soviet strategy, see Michael J. Deane and Ilana Kass, "Why Strategic Defense But Not Defensive Strategy," *SIGNAL* (November 1987): 103–109.

24. By the early 1980s the Soviet General Staff initiated several studies and conferences to explore the role of defensive operations. For a most cogent recent analysis, see Stephen M. Meyer, "The Sources and Prospects of Gorbachev's New Political Thinking on Security," *International Security*, (Fall 1988): 124–163. See also Phillip A. Petersen and Notra Trulock III, "A 'New' Soviet Military Doctrine: Origins and Implications," *Strategic Review* (Summer 1988): 9–24; and Leon Gouré, "A 'New' Soviet Military Doctrine: Reality or Mirage?" *Strategic Review* (Summer 1988): 25–33.

4

Regional Security Environments: Europe and the Pacific Rim

John E. Endicott

The Current Situation

"These are exciting times." This is an ageless introductory phrase used for countless assessments of the Pacific area; however, as worn as it might be, it is an apt manner in which to catch—in the blink of an eye—the dynamism of the Pacific region. From north to south, wherever the Pacific Ocean caresses its far-reaching shores, we see meaningful and unparalled change. The changes occuring are an interesting mixture of political and economic events made possible by the bubbling up of the inherent energies of the area itself, a declining regional reach of the two nuclear-armed superpowers, and the active involvement of Japan, a new kind of economic superpower whose role is only now becoming discernible. Even as this article is put in its final form, Burma, the Rip Van Wrinkle of Asia, is showing increasing signs that it, too, will enter the twenty-first century in far different form than it has maintained for the past generation.

Realizing that the subject of regional security environments and the Pacific Rim is as vast as the Pacific itself, it is my intent to scan the horizon, identify trends, and place those trends into some policy perspective for the United States itself. Using quick glimpses into the domestic scenes of selected states of the Pacific region, I hope to capture some of the nature of this change mentioned above. It is clear from this writer's vantage that opportunities for dramatic and positive change exist in this sector of our national global interests. Rapid and determined political leadership at this important point by the United States could insure a stable future for the continued mutually beneficial economic development of the entire region.

In essence, I am calling for a grand strategy for the Pacific Rim: A strategy that will catch a new consensus on both sides of the Pacific to

The views expressed herein are solely those of the author and do not necessarily reflect the views of the Department of Defense or of any other agency of the United States government.

focus on the long-term process of creating a security community truly deserving of its name, Pacific.

The Philippines

Starting with the Philippines only emphasizes the point that events of the next few years will have a major impact on the shape of deomocracy in this island republic. Over the next decade one of the most important questions will concern the Land Reform Program of the Aquino government, and how responsive generally that government will be to the needs of the Philippine people in order to deny the New People's Army the addherents it needs. The question is, will the land reform be executed in a fair and equitable fashion, or will vested interests get the upper hand and once again thwart the dream of Magsaysay?

In brief, under the land reform program, which has a ten-year implementation period, five hectares are reserved for all land owners, and three for each child; 25 percent of the land value will be provided to owners in cash, and 75 percent in government bonds. This last aspect is copied from historically successful land reform measures such as the Japanese and Taiwanese programs, which used these same techniques to continue to tie those who are losing land to the government through bonds. Other aspects of the Aquino program include a five percent cash incentive for immediate enrollment in the program, rather than delaying over the ten-year period. Of course, one of the major problems is that major incorporated farms are exempt from the reform for ten years; workers, however, are being paid a three percent profit-sharing bonus. Finally, ancestral lands are temporarily excluded from the reform package to lessen the problems that might come from some of the minority communities that seek greater autonomy from central government control.

Politically, relations between the United States and the Philippines have been complicated by several on-going issues directly related to regional security. One is the nuclear restriction act that was introduced into the legislature; the other, of course, was the review of the base rights agreements permitting the United States to station forces in and operate from the Philippines. The anti-nuclear act has already passed the Senate, but will probably not pass the House. This act, if it becomes law, would prohibit nuclear weapons from Philippine territory, defined to include land, sea, and air space. It has produced significant atmospherics useful to the Philippine side in creating an overall environment for the discussion of U.S. base rights. One can expect the issue to remain active and contribute to future events.

Agreement on the base rights issue, that is, the question of U.S. access to its principal bases in Clark and Subic Bay, has been solved temporarily through the review of the U.S. presence that was conducted in Manila between U.S. and Philippine officials. Although this current review was spirited, and the U.S. contribution to continued use significantly increased, it really becomes an issues in 1991, when the United States must depart if asked; however, from the standpoint of the verbal exchanges that took place and the ultimate impact such airing of "dirty linen" had on the bodies politic of both the United States and the Philippines, it is important now. Clearly, some very strong indications of Philippine nationalism were evident.

Of special note was the unique role played in the negotiations by the Philippine foreign minister, Raul Manglapus. He brought a dynamic to the negotiations that was reflected in the daily press in Manila. He also brought a certain informed cynicism to the process that is shown in his personal involvement in a current Manila play called "Yankee Panky," which he scripted and for which he wrote the accompanying music. It is a very successful play; an appropriate follow-up to the "Marcos Follies," another play he wrote. Unfortunately, Americans do not come out too well.

The Foreign Minister spoke publicly about the need for $3 billion for Clark and Subic, and broke off talks on the 28th of July when it was reported in the press that he had reduced his demand to $1.2 billion. However, the gap remained between the $1.2 billion and that which the United States was willing to commit until October 17, 1988, when an agreement was reached which was reported in Manila as an American commitment to pay $1.46 billion to "maintain Subic Naval Base and Clark Air Base until 1991."[1]

The logic of the Philippine argument came from a comparison of U.S. aid to Egypt and Israel, which amounts to roughly $3 billion annually. The Philippine foreign minister asks rhetorically about U.S. bases in these countries, and the number of U.S. personnel stationed there. He drove a point home to us about the Pacific Century and the American dependence on those two bases for carrying out much of our strategy for the South Pacific, South Asia, and Southwest Asia. The location of the Philippines makes an argument that largely speaks for itself.

This argument for a greater U.S. contribution was made even though the American presence brings over $600 million per year in salaries and related income, and even in the face of the U.S. commitment to actively pursue a "Mini Marshall Plan," also known as the Multiateral Aid Initiative (MAI) for the Philippines that could amount to $10 billion in grants and loans from an international consortium. Of course, many factors are at play here, not the least of which is the "special relationship" the United States has with its one-time colony. As we look toward 1991 and a new U.S. administration, the vital importance of these bases needs to be better articulated to the American public, and measures to widen their value to the economy of the Philippines generally should be pursued.

Other challenges to the most recent experiment in Philippine democracy are seen in the continued unease within some elements of the Philippine Armed Forces toward the handling of the Communist insurgency by President Aquino and her civilian advisors. Leadership of such opposition is generally focused in the person of Gregorio Honason, a charismatic colonel who led a coup attempt in August 1987. He was captured, but later escaped with the aid of his navy guards. Rejecting amnesty for this figure who is outspoken in his desire to crush the insurgency militarily, Aquino brings her great popularity with the people of the nation into conflict with a firebrand. In combating this criticism from the Right, Mrs. Aquino has taken to increasing the number of former or retired senior-ranking military in her government. While not an overwhelming practice, it will bring the benefits that come with such incorporation, but also the dangers.

The economy shows a resurgence that is evident in a bustling construction program throughout Manila. The problem, of course, will be to generalize successful economic recovery throughout the island chain, including those areas dominated by one crop, such as sugar. In this regard, land reform on an island-by-island basis might relieve some of the most desperate of situations. On the whole, it appears that the economic community has regained its confidence in the ability of the democracy to survive. It will be up to U.S. policy to aid and nurture such an outcome in conjunction with the other states of the Pacific Rim, especially Japan.

Vietnam

Events in Vietnam are no less dynamic than those just in the Philippines. What is particularly paradoxical is that we now turn to a nation—once the most bitter of foes—that serves as one of the classic failures of the communist economic model. It has squandered precious, already limited, resources on an imperial adventure in Cambodia, cannot adequately feed itself, is in the midst of self-doubt about many of its own party cadre, and faces new economic pressures by a possible realignment of Soviet overseas objectives. This situation calls out for a U.S. response that is creative, innovative, in our self-interest, and productive of regional stability.

The confluence of a number of political, military, and economic factors has led the leadership in Hanoi to announce a significant drawdown in its military posture in Laos and Cambodia. According to Vietnamese accounts, Hanoi has withdrawn 20,000 troops from Laos, practically its entire presence, and has pulled 50,000 troops from the 125,000 now in Cambodia. Remaining forces, according to the Vietnamese, will be placed under command of a Cambodian general, and troops remaining in Cambodia will be pulled back 30 kilometers from the Cambodian-Thai border.

All these developments come at a time when economic needs in Vietnam are increasingly obvious. In an attempt to shore up the economy and bring in foreign capital, joint enterprise opportunities have been forged with Thailand, the United Kingdom, and Hong Kong; limited stock companies have been established to obtain equipment to replace old and inoperable items left from more prosperous times; and a trade delegation from South Korea has even been invited for the December 1988–January 1989 timeframe. These developments, with some doubt expressed as to the continued access to the $2 billion annual Soviet subsidy, reveal a domestic situation in a state of flux.

As if to mirror this dynamism, a new premier, Do Muoi, was elected by the National Assembly in an election characterized by a vocal opposition and some emphasis on the process of *perestroika* currently underway in the Soviet Union. The new leader, known for his conservative communist inclinations, was called on to meet the challenges, especially of food shortages, that his predecessor, Vo Van Kiet, failed to resolve. One of his principal charges will be to get the economy, which has yet to respond to reforms began over a year ago, moving.

The scope of popular dissatisfaction with life in Vietnam continues to be seen in the number of "boat people." Since 1981 over 244,000 Vietnamese have voted with their feet and fled to neighboring states. Over the years, these refugees have changed from the original foes of the regime to individuals who see no economic future in Vietnam. Basically, they have become "migrants escaping Vietnam's economic condition."[2]

Promising improvements in relations with the United States began during the summer of 1987, when Foreign Minister Nguyen Co Thach met with retired Chairman of the Joint Chiefs of Staff, General John W. Vessey, Jr., to discuss outstanding "humanitarian" issues, principaly the resolution of the status of 2,400 U.S. servicemen still listed as "missing." As increased cooperation on this issue began there was also mention of the release of some 10,000 Vietnamese supporters of the old regime from re-education centers and their possible resettlement in the United States.

With reference to Cambodia, Foreign Minister Thach called for the United States and Vietnam to articulate the following common objectives: a withdrawal of Vietnamese forces; no return to Cambodia of the Khmer Rouge leader Pol Pot; a leading role for Sihanouk; and an overall political solution.[3] All this came to an abrupt halt during the first week of August, 1988, with the Vietnamese accusing the United States of following a "hostile policy."[4] Continued pressures on Vietnam forced their reversal of this course only weeks later.

As time passes, it will become clear to the Vietnamese leadership, now obviously engaged in a debate of its own, that resolution of the POW matter and withdrawal from Cambodia are in the interests of their nation, and are not issues for which waiting for a new administration will mean opportunities for a better deal. In the meantime, "reformists" such as Nguyen Van Linh, leader of the Communist Party of Vietnam, will have to look elsewhere for the help necessary to resolve some of Vietnam's fundamental and continuing problems.

The People's Republic of China

Vietnam will not be looking to China for assistance in resolving some of its economic problems; in fact, Vietnam is still smarting over the sinking of several of its patrol boats by the Chinese Navy just off the Spratlys in the South China Sea. However, China's neighbor to the south could certainly spend time profitably by observing the significant changes brought to the Chinese economy by Deng Xiao Ping and his immediate successors. Deng retired from most of his major posts in October 1987, but retains a very important post as Chairman of the Military Commission of the Chinese Communist Party. From that vantage point he remains available as Li Peng, the new Premier, begins to make his own impression.

China continues to follow Deng's policy of the Four Modernizations, by which it is hoped to raise China to the status of a major power by mid-century, or 2050. Under this policy, emphasis is placed on agriculture, the industrial base, and scientific and technical capabilities before the military. The fourth modernization, that of the modernization of the military, has placed the military in the interesting position of using its industrial base for civilian-oriented production. It possibly contributed to the increase in weapon sales to Middle Eastern states, especially Iran, making China one of the five major exporters of weapons in the world.[5] The rapid increase in weapons' exports may be the result of trying to obtain needed hard currency to carry on other aspects of their modernization program.

It is clear that, as a means of social mobility and economic reward, the military is facing keen competition from sectors such as agriculture and small industry that are producing increased profits. Also, military reorganization has reduced the number of personnel in uniform overall, creating some social disruption as disgruntled former military men attempt to make the transition into the civilian economy.[6]

Clearly, as the Deng Reforms continue to fuel annual GNP increases of ten percent or more, disruption and competition may become far more present companions than they have been in the recent past. It has already become apparent in the process of reducing the military that some of the "iron rice howls" of the past will be broken, and that a simple guaranteed level of living will become complicated as the economy generally is brought into the global arena.[7]

While the economic vitality of the PRC dazzles any foreign visitor, and must cause some Chinese to wonder where they are, there are some warning lights that recently have come on. While insignificant when considering the relative scale of the Chinese experiment, they relate to historic indicators of the health of Chinese administration. Local irrigation systems are reported to be "breaking down all over China."[8] Whether this is a resort to hyperbole, or, in fact, 90 percent of the reservoirs of Shandong Province have indeed fallen into disrepair, the importance of the irrigation system from a historic perspective must not be forgotten. It will not be overlooked by the Chinese themselves. With emphasis on profits, it is reasonable to conclude that collective labor needed to sustain the system was not the first thing on the producer's mind; however, reportedly, a new scheme to provide compulsory labor for system maintenance was announced in December 1987.[9]

Another area of concern that accompanies the great release of collective energies associated with the rush into the twenty-first century is the notion that the Chinese people increasingly view their government and party bureaucracies as corrupt. This belief was substantiated somewhat in a survey conducted by the Chinese Academy of Social Sciences, which revealed that 63 percent of cadres interviewed admitted to some kind of corrupt practice.[10] If true, we can see what Mao Tse-tung had in mind when he wished to keep the bureaucracy in a state of almost constant ideological turmoil. Before we cast any stones, however, we should poll our own population about similar questions. Perhaps since the yellow tape appeared in the halls of the Pentagon, we have our own perception gap.

One gap that is not a perception but a reality relates to higher education and its ability to sustain the Chinese drive for technical and scientific competence. During the ten-year Cultural Revolution, the system of higher education suffered incredible excesses. Today China has 1,054 universities, of which approximately 400 are just five years old.[11] Creating educational systems and universities that are more than just physical plants must be one of the greatest challenges facing China, and as the age group most affected by the Cultural Revolution, that is, those now between 34 and 44, begins to assume the leadership roles expected of it, this issue will create challenges and opportunities that may possibly have regional impact.

The success of its economic reforms will give China a new base on which to interact with its immediate neighbors, the Soviet Union, Vietnam, and Japan (as well as Hong Kong, Taiwan, and India). Foreign Minister Qian Qichen has already indicated some flexibility with regard to the Cambodian issue, but it is clear that aid to the Khmer Rouge will continue until Vietnamese forces withdraw.[12] The Soviet Deputy Foreign Minister, Igor Rogachev, visited Beijing to discuss Sino-Soviet relations, which seem to assume a more positive stance daily.[13] And Sino-Japanese affairs, while not the best when it comes to such irritants as the Kyoto dormitory issue and Chinese concerns with revanchist militarism, are robust in the economic shpere. Chinese seeking short-term employment in Japan are crowding visa centers with the hope of temporary but high-paying jobs in Japan.[14]

It is also clear, however, from such events as the Sino-Vietnamese incident over the Spratleys, that China will insist on making its presence in the region very much felt, and will be sensitive to criticism, such as that received from the U.S. Senate in the form of the "Dole Amendment" calling it "unreasonable interference in China's Internal Affairs."[15]

Generally, U.S.-Sino relations reveal a healthy expansion of political and economic interaction, and even some useful on-going contacts in the military sphere. China is now the fifteenth largest trading partner with the United States, running a surplus of approximately $3.5 billion.[16] The fifth round of the U.S.-Chinese talks on disarmament concluded in August, and Secretary of Defense Frank Carlucci visited in September. At the time of this writing, it is too soon to gauge the long-term effects that the violent suppression of the pro-democracy student movement will have on Sino-American relations. Obviously, the events in Beijing, cannot help but have a chilling effect on relations over the near term, but the long-term implications remain to be seen.

The Korean Peninsula

Of all the dynamic states and areas of the Pacific Rim, perhaps the most active if both political and economic achievement are concerned would be this finger-like peninsula jutting out into the Po Hai Gulf and the Sea of Japan. The Chun Doo Hwan succession to Roh Tae Woo of the Democratic Justice Party of South Korea, while made with a high stress factor, was significant in realizing the first peaceful transfer of power on the Korean Peninsula since 1910. Significant also is the responsible opposition of Roh's principal political adversaries Kim Yong Sam, Kim Tae Chung, and Kim Chong Pil. The practice of democracy is often not a clear-cut affair, and can be extremely dysfunctional to those calling for strong leadership and policies of boldness. However, the political progress experienced by South Korea in the last year has been historic.

Similarly, South Korea's economic achievement has been well recorded and recognized worldwide. South Korea is now the seventh largest trading partner with the United States, and enjoys a surplus of approximate $9 billion.[17] The GNP growth rate for 1987 was a fantastic 12.6 percent, but 1988 has been effected by strikes and some disruptive trade disputes with the United States. South Korea, as all the newly industrialized states of Asia are recognizing, will have difficulty maintaining such dramatic economic growth, especially in light of the newly passed U.S. trade legislation, which will address issues such as market access for U.S. business.

South Korean college-age youth have been a major actor in the political and economic sectors. Student unrest, which intensified with the death of Pak Chong Chol, has been an area of concern for many close observers. Of primary concern, however, is the increasingly anti-American current that can be observed among these future leaders of South Korea. Extremely critical of U.S. policy since the Kwangju Incident of 1978, a growing number now believe that the United States has pursued policies to, first, divide Korea in 1946, and, second, continue the separation of the two Koreas since then. In a remarkable revisionism that captures a certain flavor of the state of affairs during Alice's visit to "Wonderland," many college students firmly, and wrongly, believe that the United States is interested only in the continuation of the division of North and South. This has led to a political activism on the part of this vocal group directed toward rapid repair of relations between North and South.

The government of Roh Tae Woo takes the firm position that contacts with North Korea will be through official channels. This flies in the face of desires by students for informal meetings with counterparts at the DMZ. Such pressure, and the overall desire to incorporate North Korea into the Olympic Games, has resulted in a level of contact between the two governments that is unprecedented. Perhaps South Korea's new policy toward the North—to treat it as a younger brother—will change the current state of military threat between the two. Certainly, President Roh Tae Woo's appeal at the U.N. General Assembly calling for an international conference "to end the division of the Korean peninsula" demonstrates the dramatic turn of events in Korea.[18]

The threat from the North is reportedly seen as so severe by the South that it will take until 2005 to gain a posture of "self-reliance." Thus, until that time, the South will seek to retain U.S. forces stationed in Korea. However, action by the U.S. Congress in the 1988 defense budget will certainly not go unnoticed. Although South Korea spends approximately 5 percent of its GNP for defense and contributes some 40 million directly to combined defense projects, the draft of the second defense budget bill passed in 1988 (after a veto) placed a cap on U.S. forces in Korea and called for greater contributions by the Republic of Korea toward defense.[19] While later removed in conference session, a message was sent from some members of Congress to South Korea.

In no uncertain terms, South Korea's future remains tied up in its all-important relationship with its "younger brother to the North." Progress that might be made toward reducing tensions, and eventually toward some form of reunification, will determine in many related ways the kind of future to be experienced on the peninsula and along the Pacific Rim generally.

North Korea

North Korea, the true "Hermit Kingdom," if ever one existed, has followed the leadership of one man since the founding of the communist regime after World War II. Dedicated to the economic self-reliant concepts of Chuche, the dedication to a Korean version of Marxism and Leninism has been North Korea's experience, with only slight moderation. This unique socialist road has yielded a strong military and an austere, almost spartan, way of life for those of the North. As mentioned above, this particular feature, a Korea going it alone and in the face of severe hardship, has captured the imagination of some of the South's college activists—an interesting development that cannot be overlooked.

The North's primary problem, outside the economic sphere, is succession. Superficially, the decision has been made for Kim Chong Il to succeed his father. Whether this will, in fact, occur remains to be seen. A recent report out of Tokyo shows that Kim Hyong-il, the first son of the "great leader's" second wife, can also be considered a serious possibility.[20] He now holds the post of deputy chief of the General Staff Department in the Armed Forces Ministry, and is reportedly popular within the military itself. This report, however, demonstrates one of the major problems in dealing with North Korea: we are dependent on other observers for our planning insights. Perhaps as we, in conjunction with the South Korean leadership, attempt to bring the North into greater contact with the West, this problem will lessen.

Currently, the North is talking past the South on early moves for resolving differences between the two countries. In reply to the U.N. addresss by President Roh Tae Woo, North Korea's spokesman, while turning down all the proposals, did not resort to using the "harsh rhetoric" that is typical of such exchanges.[21] However, back home, a similar statement was denounced as "splittist in nature."[22]

Japan

As has been indicated by inference or direct reference, the role Japan will be expected to play in any regional security concept is already significant, and becoming more so every day. The most recent Defense White Paper reveals a Japan concerned with a continued Soviet military buildup in East Asia in the face of a diplomatic offensive that drives at the very base of support for any democracy—its popular support. The White Paper shows, however, that Japan continues to focus on those areas necessary to the defense of Japan.[23] Three major areas of emphasis were indicated: research and development for the defense forces; recruitment of high quality personnel; and U.S.-Japan defense cooperation.

Budget figures for fiscal year 1989 also indicate continued accomplishment of hardware modernization and force enhancement. Continued acquisition and development of surface-to-surface missiles, aircraft, anti-submarine capability, and so forth, ensures that Japan is heading toward its goal of being able to provide a competent defensive defense for the Japanese home islands. It is clear that by the completion of the next mid-term defense plan in 1995, Japan will be able to defend its northern approaches, mine the straits, and control one thousand miles of sea lanes in and around Japan.

Security is not all defense, however, as the Japanese fully recognize, and their active involvement in the economic assistance area is increasingly, making the difference in the developing world. Prime Minister Takeshita, in carrying out the *kokusaika* (or internationalization) policy, first articulated by former Prime Minister Nakasone, has already pledged Japan to a $50 billion aid package over the next five years, and has made some progress in the total economic restructuring recommended in the Maskawa Report so that by the next century Japan will be an import-oriented society.[24]

While not all is quiet on the U.S.-Japan scene, with such problems as the rice question, patent processing, and the scale of Japanese investments in certain real estate markets in the United States, many of the difficult issues are behind us. Japan has responded to the call that it act responsibly in light of its economic power. In the process, however, there have been some political costs, and a new sensitivity can be seen in the formation of such organizations as the Kokka Kihon Mondai Doshi Kai (Society for the Study of Basic National Problems). It is in the next decade that U.S. policy will have to blend hopes for the future with memories of the past, taking into consideration what the rest of Asia has in mind for the future of Japan also.

The United States and the Need for a New Strategic Consensus

Recently, I had the opportunity to attend a conference on NATO in the fifth decade. There was much attention, I might even say concern, placed on the concept of a Pacific Century. The acceptance of the "reality" of the next century belonging to Pacific powers, with the United States naturally including itself in such a group, was quite surprising. Here I was among scholars, diplomats, and soldiers of the major NATO states who were seemingly ready to accept as an accomplished fact that somehow, some-way, the diverse, non-aligned states of the Pacific Rim would, like magic, turn the economic miracle into a security miracle.

As I have described above, the current situation in this region is one of absolute change and transition. In the Pacific region, even in the face of dynamic change, almost all the security relations are accomplished through bilateral mechanisms. The sixteen member NATO community, by contrast, is reinforced through trade and political organizational institu-tions that form and re-form the various players along meaningful relation-ships. When a security issue confronts the alliance, opportunities such as the NATO Planning Conference abound, allowing the members ready opportunities to sound out others and develop some form of consensus on the pressing problems. With 1992 just around the corner, we can expect a further tightening of the cohesiveness of the European community. Such is not the case in the Pacific Rim; unless some organizational security con-cept is created to fill this void, it is this author's view that the "Pacific Century" may well be the twenty-second century, not the twenty-first.

That is not to say that what can be achieved in the Pacific is less than forward movement. What will be needed, of course, is leadership. To provide that leadership, a road map will be necessary. It will be necesary as today the U.S. national debt stands at $2.8 trillion. The budget deficit is $150 billion; the trade deficit is $170 billion—with three-fifths associ-ated with East Asian nations. Interest payments on the national debt amount to $160 billion per year, and the defense budget stands at approx-imately $300 billion.[25]

While such figures do have shock effect, of even greater importance is the fact that this comes at a time when we as Americans and as leaders of the Free World can declare victory and claim that containment as a grand strategy for our nation has succeeded. What is needed now, and what we are seeking during this transition period, is a new grand consensus that reflects the changes in the international economic order—in both socialist and capitalist camps. Rather than containment as our future strategy, what we may see over the next few years is a policy of active engagement—a policy that will not simply react to Soviet initiatives, but will lead the world, and especially in this instance, the Pacific Rim.

Does my call for a new grand strategy mean that I am unhappy with current U.S. policy? Not in the least! However, as one surveys the Pacific Basin it is clear that above all other considerations, active leadership, in the absence of an integrated organization is absolutely essential. The one nation that all expect, and most hope, to assume this responsibility is the United States. If this is the case, what are those agenda items that will aid in securing our regional security over the next forty to fifty years?

Global Arms Control Regime

To assure continued parity between the two nuclear superpowers in an era of mutual drawdown, an active continuation of the nuclear arms reduction negotiations must be a first priority. However, in terms of security and budgetary outlays, it must be remembered that forty years of Pax Atomica has been purchased at relatively low cost. The security interests of both powers must be recognized, and when nuclear reductions do reach significant percentages, the involvement of regional nuclear powers must be realized.

While the big news is always made in the reduction of nuclear weapons, the big money to be saved is through conventional arms control. This is especially the case in those nations that do not rely on drafts to provide the bulk of their fighting force. Therefore, the reduction of the large standing military forces should be encouraged in line with measures to stabilize regional flash points. In the case of the Pacific Rim, the two peninsulas readily come to mind. A caution here, however, must also be inserted. Rapid reduction in the armed forces of a nation can have very disruptive economic impact if training for such a transition does not carefully precede the actual event. Thus, such manpower reductions must be integrated into regional economic development packages as part of any peace initiative.

Regional Communications

We must develop for the Pacific Rim better, faster, and more routinized means of regional communication. Such meetings as the annual Pacific Basin Symposium conducted by the National Defense University in Hawaii and Washington, D.C., could occur on a regular basis—perhaps every six months—but in different locations throughout the region. A community of scholars, diplomats, military officers, and policy specialists would develop, facilitating frequent and general exchange of information on a variety of important subjects. Better, faster communications are an absolutely essential element in our quest for a regional security community.

Regional Economic Development

Key, absolutely fundamental, to a strategy of active engagement will be support and active advocacy for measures to keep the Pacific economic miracle alive. In this regard, a determination by the United States to "powershare," especially with Japan, is integral to any long-term effort. As efforts by Japan continue, with encouragement by the United States, to increase its responsibility for worldwide involvement in economic assistance, the United States must establish patterns of close cooperation and coordination with its economic partner. As Japan closes the "delta" between its current 1.3 percent contribution to defense and economic assistance and the 3.4 percent weighted average for NATO nations (excluding the United States), its role must be recognized with an appropriate place at the table. The United States will have to be willing to deal with the fact that at some tables, Japan will be in the principal chair.

Priorities for regional development must be established by the principal economic engines of the region to reduce redundancy and waste. As a substantial part of the programs to stabilize the two peninsulas, a fairly high emphasis should be placed on the economic development aspects of such arrangements.

Regional Security Forces

The United States should, in the process of reaching consensus on its grand strategy for the next half-century, commit itself to the concept of forward-deployed forces. Realizing that little if any saving comes from bringing forces back to the continental United States unless they are deactivated, and that much is gained by a U.S. presence in various parts of the region, U.S. forces should remain in strategic locations. However, it should be recognized by the host nations and by the nations of the region as a whole, that these forces are not forward deployed to be captive to one scenario or one nation. They should be viewed as U.S. Expeditionary Forces, and be available for contingencies throughout the region.

With special reference to the U.S. presence on the Korean Peninsula, it might be noted that as confidence grows between North and South Korea, U.S. forces might be drawn back from the DMZ, but retained on the peninsula in some mutually agreeable site. Later, as the confrontation diminishes further, those forces could be relocated to Hawaii or some other compatible host.

Active Engagement

Building on the basic contradictions that still exist within the Soviet Empire, the United States and its Pacific allies should actively draw the Soviet Union into full participation in regional affairs. In fact, without the complete cooperation of the Soviet Union, efforts to stabilize the two peninsulas will be bound to fail. Soviet military assistance to its clients must be minimized; it may be possible to achieve this in a climate of mutual trust.

An active endorsement of efforts to involve the Soviet Far East in the economic activities of the Pacific Rim in a greater measure of interdependency will have the result of pulling the area west of Lake Baikal more toward Vladivostok and less toward Moscow. While not changing the allegience of that area to Moscow, it will have the effect of creating new sensitivities and new dependencies.

In advocating active engagement with the Soviet Union in East Asia— and in other areas as well—I am recognizing that the policy of containment that we followed for the last forty years has succeeded in many ways articulated by its first advocates. We must realize that some of the basic realities of the international system have changed in the past forty years. The grand consensus upon which containment was built was seriously undermined during Vietnam, and since that time changes in worldwide economic relationships and changes internal to the Soviet Union and Eastern Europe underline the need to alter course with a new grand consensus for the next half-century.

Taking advantage of humanity's inherent desire for freedom, a policy that actively brings together the two contesting philosophies will demonstrate the remaining contradictions of the Soviet Empire to its inhabitants; I contend that this is in our national interest and in the interests of regional security for the Pacific Rim.

Notes

1. FBIS-EAS-R8-202, October 19, 1988.
2. *Far Eastern Economic Review (FEER)*, June 23, 1988, p. 27.
3. *FEER*, June 23, 1988, p. 13.
4. *Washington Post*, August 4, 1988, p. 1.
5. *The Military Balance, 1987–1988*, (The International Institute for Strategic Studies: London, 1987), p. 145.
6. See, especially, June Teufel Dreyer, "Deng Xiaoping and Modernization of the Chinese Military," *Armed Forces & Society*, (Winter 1988): 215–231.
7. Don Oberdorfer, "Asia Watch: At the Dawn of the Pacific Century," *Washington Post*, July 31, 1988, p. C4.
8. *FEER*, June 23, 1988.
9. Ibid.
10. *FEER*, June 16, 1988, p. 22.
11. *FEER*, June 16, 1988, p. 31.
12. *Washington Post*, August 12, 1988, p. A20.
13. "Soviet President Gromyko Meets Wu Xiuqian," FBIS-CHI-88-139, July 20, 1988, p. 3, and *Washington Post*, August 5, 1988, p. A31.
14. *Nihon Keizai*, August, 1988.

15. FBIS-CHI-88-151, August 5, 1988, p. 3.

16. "The U.S. and Asia: A Statistical Handbook, 1988 Edition," *Backgrounder*, The Heritage Foundation, July 29, 1988, p. 21.

17. Ibid.

18. *New York Times*, October 19, 1988, p. 1.

19. *Washington Post*, August 12, 1988.

20. *Sankei Shimbun*, September 17, 1988.

21. *Washington Post*, October 19, 1988, p. 1.

22. FBIS-EAS-88-202, October 19, 1988, p. 10.

23. *Sankei Shimbun*, August 24, 1988, p. 2.

24. See *JEI Report*, "Maekawa Report Update," October 1988, for an in-depth review of this report's current status.

25. *FEER*, September 29, 1988, p. 24.

5

Low-Intensity Conflict: Future Challenges and Lessons from the Reagan Years

Richard H. Shultz, Jr.

As the 1970s came to a close American national security specialists began to suggest that the United States was generally unprepared to respond to the more likely kind of violent challenges that threatened its geostrategic interests in the coming decade. These were subsumed under the rubric of low-intensity conflict (LIC).[1] Unconventional in approach and political-military in form, two major varients were identified: one, revolutionary and guerrilla insurgency; two, international terrorism.

In 1981, low-intensity conflict was an important national security theme in the rhetoric of the newly elected Reagan administration. In fact, immediately after assuming office senior officials warned that terrorism and insurgency in the Third World posed both a serious and long-term problem for the United States. Even more worrisome, from the new administration's perspective, was the involvement of the Soviet Union, members of the Warsaw Pact, and Cuba in providing assistance to insurgent, terrorist, and other subversive forces. Moreover, they pointed to countries like Angola, Afghanistan, Ethiopia, South Yemen, Vietnam, Laos, Cambodia, and Nicaragua, where Moscow-supported forces and movements had seized power during the 1970s. To meet these new threats the White House asserted that it intended to develop an integrated policy and the appropriate strategy and capabilities.

Did the Reagan administration achieve its objectives, and is the United States better prepared today to meet the challenge of low-intensity conflict? A review of the record reveals some rather surprising facts. In spite of the appropriation of nearly $2 trillion for defense, many specialists continue to argue that U.S. ability to respond to protracted or low-intensity conflict has improved only marginally since 1981. In fact, a 1987 review of U.S. national security policy by the Commission on Integrated Long-Term Strategy identified several enduring and divisive problems that were not resolved during the last eight years. These include: 1) insufficient coordination among agencies and departments of the Executive Branch involved in this aspect of national security policy; 2) a lack of unifying guidelines and requirements; 3) no consensus on strategy among the key agencies; and 4) most importantly, the absence of a national doctrine for low-intensity conflict. As we shall see in the following section, these problems had an important impact on several policy initiatives.

Policy Initiatives in the 1980s: Dilemmas and Continuing Problems

The Reagan administration's policy for low-intensity conflict can be subsumed into the following categories: 1) assistance to governments threatened by revolutionary insurgent warfare (counterinsurgency); 2) support for resistance movements challenging Soviet-backed regimes in the Third World; and 3) proactive or offensive measures to counter terrorism. However, the approach taken to each during the 1980s can best be described as disjointed and ad hoc.

With respect to counterinsurgency, the United States is still not fully prepared to work with Third World military forces facing revolutionary insurgent threats. The security assistance program remains a major part of the problem. Two factors contribute to this shortcoming: 1) most of the aid goes to five countries (the 1986 budget, for example, reserved 86 percent for Egypt, Israel, Greece, Turkey, and Pakistan); 2) assistance provided to countries facing revolutionary insurgency is generally inappropriate. Standard U.S. military equipment is too complex, too expensive, and often inappropriate for low-intensity conflict. The equipment that is required is different from that which is issued to the conventionally oriented U.S. Army. In addition to materiel, security assistance also includes advisory groups and Military Training Teams (MTT). Here also there is a problem in that MTTs frequently train Third World armed forces facing insurgency to conduct an American-style conventional war. Shortfalls also remain in language skills and regional area and cultural orientation.

The impact on policy can be seen in two specific cases. In 1981 the situation in El Salvador was bleak. The FMLN guerrillas had announced the "final offensive," and it appeared that the government would soon be toppled. Between 1981 and 1984, large quantities of U.S. military equipment, training, and tactical intelligence support helped build the Salvadorian Army on a battalion-size model that forced the FMLN to change its approach to one based on decentralized units using hit-and-run tactics. It appears that the Salvadorian Army has not, in general, been able to adapt to this new environment. As a recently published report by four senior U.S. Army officers points out: "despite ESAF's [Armed Forces of El Salvador] improved battlefield skills, failure to develop a proper framework for counterinsurgency operations led to a deadlock. . . . As of April, 1988, a tough resourceful opponent remains in the field . . . showing no inclination to give up."[2] These developments play into the hands of the FMLN, especially as the political situation in El Salvador polarizes and President Duarte passes from the scene. Recent evidence suggests that FMLN forces are preparing for a major offensive in 1989.

Events in the Philippines during the mid-1980s led the Reagan administration to undertake a dramatic shift in policy with respect to that country. By the end of 1985 U.S. policymakers realized that the twenty-year reign of Ferdinand Marcos had run its course. The United States helped ease Marcos into exile, and Mrs. Aquino assumed the presidency. Although democracy came to the Philippines, the threat of revolutionary insurgent warfare did not subside. Furthermore, neither the Philippine government nor the armed forces appear prepared to cope with it.

The Philippine Communist Party's (CPP) political apparatus controls over 30 percent of the rural villages. It competes with the government in over 60 of the country's 73 provinces. The CPP's military arm, the New Peoples' Army (NPA), has approximately 25,000 well-trained, highly motivated, full-time soldiers. As in El Salvador, the Philippine government has yet to develop a national counterinsurgency plan that integrates military, economic, political, and informational policies. The Philippine Armed Forces (AFP), likewise, is currently unprepared to defeat the NPA in a protracted war. There is insufficent emphasis on the principles of counterinsurgency. Since the departure of Marcos, U.S. security and economic assistance to the Philippines has increased significantly. However, weapons and training have not been tailored to meet the CPP/NPA challenge. The Americanization of the AFP continues, with emphasis on technology and fire power.

A future victory by the insurgent forces in either the Philippines or El Salvador would be a serious geostrategic setback for the Bush administration. While not as serious, other governments friendly to the United States in Central and South America also face incipient insurgent threats. Furthermore, in several of these countries, most notably Columbia and Peru, the insurgents cooperate with narcotic traffickers. As with the Philippines and El Salvador, these situations will be part of the agenda of LIC issues facing President Bush.[3]

In many respects, the conceptual factors that plagued the counterinsurgency policy of the Reagan administration also affected its involvement with anticommunist resistance movements. A major part of the problem can be traced to the fact that the Central Intelligence Agency (CIA) does not possess the kinds of skilled personnel or doctrine necessary to assist these movements to establish an organization and strategy than can achieve political legitimacy and compete for power. In certain cases this was not necessary because the resistance had already achieved it. For example, in Afghanistan the Mujaheddin have their own doctrine of war and politics and only required the military means to carry it out. This also appears to be the case for the forces of Jonas Savimbi in Angola.

However, the same was not true of the Nicaraguan Contras, who required much more than guns and ammunition. However, as General Paul Gorman has noted, the Contras have remained a "largely cross border raiding force, not an unconventional warfare force . . . that [is] capable of defeating the Sandinistas."[4] While they grew rapidly from 5,000 in 1983 to approximately 15,000 in 1986, the resistance forces have not established a political-military infrastructure in-country to take advantage of the situation. With no corps of experts about resistance strategies who also understood the Nicaraguan cultural and physical environment, the United States focused its efforts primarily on providing military assistance.

Additionally, there was disagreement over whether the Department of Defense or the CIA has responsibility for resistance movements. Neither wanted anything to do with it. Indeed, strong institutional opposition was evident among both senior CIA and DOD officials. In light of the political-paramilitary nature of resistance movements the CIA has, in the past, had responsibility for these missions.

Support for anticommunist resistance movements (referred to in the media as the Reagan Doctrine) was a key part of the Reagan administration's policy of countering Soviet bloc and Cuban promotion of insurgency and instability in the Third World. If President Bush decides to follow some variation of the Reagan Doctrine, institutional opposition within the intelligence and defense communities will continue to affect specific initiatives. Congressional doubts about the prudence of such policies will also remain.

In 1982 the Defense Department established the Joint Special Operations Command (JSOC) in response to both the failure of the 1980 Iranian rescue operation and the mounting terrorism problem. Nevertheless, several problems continued to persist. First of all, human intelligence collection has remained inadequate. For example, the Long Commission Report on the bombing of the Marine Corps barracks in Beirut stated that poor intelligence collection was the single most important factor contributing to the disaster. Few specialists disagree that if the United States is to undertake hostage rescue missions or various offensive measures, human intelligence collection programs require a major up-grading. If U.S. intelligence is to be better prepared to operate in diverse and increasingly non-Western societies, personnel selection and training procedures will have to be considerably altered by the Bush administration.[5]

As with the other two aspects of low-intensity conflict, there is little to suggest that international and state-supported terrorist operations directed against the United States will dissipate in the years ahead. Indeed, for states like Iran, Syria, and Libya, it has become an important foreign policy instrument. Consequently, along with the previously discussed issues of counterinsurgency and resistance movements, terrorism will constitute part of the LIC agenda the Bush administration will need to address.

Doctrinal and Bureaucratic Obstacles: The Reagan Years

What obstacles account for the gap between policy objectives and the record of the Reagan years, as highlighted in the previous review? The following three factors stand out: 1) disagreement and confusion among senior officials over the parameters of low-intensity conflict; 2) an inability to develop a coherent political-military doctrine for LIC; and 3) bureaucratic opposition and a lack of interagency coordination.

In shaping LIC policy the Reagan administration had the history of the Kennedy administration and post-Vietnam years to rely upon. This history contains several important lessons.[6] First, an administration requires a clear understanding of the parameters of LIC, which it then must convey to the relevant government agencies and departments. Second, given the contentious nature of low-intensity conflict, reorganization should be seriously considered, especially if bureaucratic opposition impedes effective policy formulation and implementation. Finally, it is essential to form a consensus between the Executive and Legislative branches over foreign policy objectives, the threat, and the ways in which the United States might respond. The Reagan administration appears to have learned little from these historical precedents.

In the first place, it was unable, until 1987, to present a consistent statement on the parameters and interrelationship of the low-intensity threats faced by the United States. Instead, senior administration officials focused on different aspects of this form of warfare, apparently without recognizing that they are all part of the same genre and require an integrated response. For President Reagan, low-intensity conflict was synonymous with assistance to anticommunist guerrillas fighting against Soviet-backed regimes in the Third World.[7] This was likewise of great interest to the late Director of Central Intelligence, William Casey, and UN Ambassador Jeane Kirkpatrick.[8]

At other times, senior administration members focused on counterinsurgency and counterterrorism. The latter was of grave concern to Secretary of State George Shultz and his predecessor, Alexander Haig. At the

Department of Defense, Secretary Weinberger asserted that the problem was "communist inspired wars of national liberation."[9] In fact, well into 1986 senior officials continued to state that defining low-intensity conflict remained an "ambiguous and vexing problem."[10]

This had an important impact on appropriations for special operations and low-intensity conflict capabilities. While appropriations did steadily increase during the 1980s, there was no attempt to create an integrated budget consisting of the appropriate elements from the Departments of Defense and State, the CIA, the Agency for International Development, the U.S. Information Agency, and related agencies.[11]

Finally, while more defense funds have been provided for special operations forces, they have not been concentrated on LIC missions. The focus has been on readiness for conventional wartime preparation, the least likely future mission for special operations forces. Furthermore, by focusing on their conventional role, LIC missions have been accorded a secondary priority.

The inability of the White House to articulate a coherent policy for low-intensity conflict also hindered the development of political-military doctrine. No set of guidelines and principles was established that integrated the non-military and military elements of the national security bureaucracy. Even in the case of the military doctrine, efforts over the last eight years have been plagued by uncertainty and disagreement. This can be seen in the first manual devised for low-intensity conflict and interservice attempts to establish a working definition. The scope of Army FM 100-20 was confined to counterinsurgency missions, with no attention to other aspects of LIC. The interservice definition of low-intensity conflict, on the other hand, covered every conceivable form of competition and conflict below the conventional level of war.[12]

To address this problem, the Joint Chiefs of Staff (JCS) established a Joint Low-Intensity Conflict Project in 1985, and encouraged all services and appropriate civilian agencies to participate. A report was issued in August 1986 that identified the specific LIC missions of most concern to the United States. These included: counterinsurgency, support for resistance movements, counterterrorism, peacetime contingencies (e.g., strike, raid, recovery, demonstration, and related operations), and peacekeeping. This was a significant improvement over the uncertainty and contradictions that had characterized earlier efforts.

The report generated controversy within the Pentagon for several reasons. First, it spelled out mission responsibilities for the services, some of which are anathema to them. Second, it asserted that the U.S. neither understood nor was prepared for this kind of warfare: "Many government departments and agencies . . . fail to comprehend the nature of this type of conflict. They do not understand the special socio-economic environment." Moreover, "conflicting views and varied institutional interests," create "an atmosphere that encourages confusion and inaction at best, mistake and blunder at worst." Finally, the report called for a "comprehensive civil-military strategy," and the replacement of "*ad hoc* organizations with institutionalized organizations."[13] Although the report created a stir in the Pentagon, little change ensued. The authors of the document hoped to engender a constructive dialogue, but the result was silent disregard. As of the summer of 1989 the services are still struggling with this problem. Currently, a revised manual for *Military Operations in Low-Intensity Conflict*, FM 100-20, is still in "final draft" form.[14]

The lack of guidance from the White House had a direct impact on organization, command and control, and interagency coordination. There remained significant opposition in the national security bureaucracy to involvement in low-intensity conflict. Within the armed forces a traditional mindset and conventional approach to war made it exceedingly difficult to develop capabilities and organization for protracted or low-intensity warfare. This is not a new development, for opposition to elite forces and special operations within the American military establishment has existed throughout the post–World War II period. However, following Vietnam it became even more truculent. To remedy the situation the Reagan administration initiated institutional restructuring. This culminated in 1984 with the creation of a Joint Special Operations Agency (JSOA) within the JCS to oversee all military preparation for special operations and low-intensity conflict.[15]

While this was at first seen as a positive step, within the JCS command structure the new agency was severely circumvented. According to its first director, General Wesley Rice, "I had many responsibilities, but I had little authority. . . . As a two-star general I had little clout in a town of three and four-star generals."[16] While Rice may have thought low-intensity conflict was a top priority, others above him believed the principal role for the special operations forces was to support general purpose forces in conventional war. This view is pervasive among senior service officers. For instance, General John Chain, currently Commander of the Strategic Air Command, stated in Congressional testimony that while he "fully supports the existence of special forces," they "should be used only as traditional, behind-the-lines commandos who organize guerrillas and engage in sabotage to support the U.S. military during war."[17] This perspective is not a new one, as the history of the Kennedy administration's attempt to establish a counterinsurgency mission for the military demonstrates.[18]

Opposition to involvement in low-intensity conflict was not confined to the armed services. The Reagan administration also encountered similar antipathy from the CIA. As a result of the end of the Vietnam War, congressional investigations, and Carter administration intelligence policy, the paramilitary assets of the CIA were greatly downgraded.[19] Furthermore, a view developed among senior officers, including the Deputy Director, that this aspect of covert action was no longer a CIA mission.[20] Consequently, when the Reagan administration decided to employ the capability it encountered significant institutional opposition.

The impact on policy was telling, as the CIA's involvement with the Contras reveals. Once the decision was made to provide assistance, the issue of who would do the training and advising had to be addressed. With few assets available at CIA, the administration turned to the Argentine Army. Not surprisingly, they proved to know little about how to nurture a political-military resistance movement that needed to gain legitimacy and popular support inside Nicaragua. Next, veterans of the Vietnam era, guerrilla warfare specialists from other parts of the world, and even private "enterprises" were marshaled to meet the need. All of these efforts appear to have lacked proper perspective. With a few notable exceptions, the CIA had a shortage of specialists who could provide guidance on how to develop a political-military organization and strategy for a protracted conflict in which legitimacy is essential.

Similar opposition to involvement in low-intensity conflict likewise exists in other civilian departments and agencies. This is true of the State Department, the Agency for International Development (AID), and the U.S. Information Agency (USIA), among others. Since no senior coordinating structure existed within the White House to marshal these different bureaucratic elements behind a coherent policy, the result was an ad hoc and disjointed approach that persisted through both presidential terms.

Congressional Reform and Low-Intensity Conflict

During the 1980s, Congress became increasingly involved in the issues of defense organization and military strategy. In 1986 the Congress likewise undertook an extensive examination of the degree to which the United States was organizationally prepared to respond to low-intensity conflict and employ special operations forces.

Members of both houses of Congress were critical of the administration's efforts. Senator William Cohen pointed out: "We are not well prepared for unconventional conflict . . . and it shows." He added that a "new form of warfare has emerged, a form of warfare that we have not properly understood, and that we have not effectively deterred."[21]

During 1986 the Congress carried out a comprehensive review of developments over the first six years of the Reagan presidency. They expressed concern over what had transpired. The investigations centered on interagency coordination, command and control, low-intensity missions, appropriations, and equipment. In an attempt to mollify Congress and head off a new round of military reform legislation, the Department of Defense proposed a series of corrective measures. In the eyes of the Congress, however, the DOD suggestions were seen as cosmetic and inadequate.

In November 1986, a reorganization compromise was worked out between the Senate and House, and attached to the Defense Authorization Bill. It required the creation of a U.S. Special Operations Command (US-SOCOM) to raise the standing and importance of special operations forces within the military hierarchy. Under the direction of a four star flag or general officer, the command would have responsibility for doctrine, training, planning, readiness, acquisition of equipment, and resources. The new Commander-in-Chief of USSOCOM (CINCUSSOCOM) would also participate in the work of the defense resources board to compete at budget time. In effect, special operations forces were taken out of the existing service structure prior to deployment outside the United States. It was hoped that representatives from USSOCOM assigned to each of the regional commands would become more effective advisors to the regional commanders-in-chief (who still will have overall command authority over special operations forces in their area of operation).

The legislation also established the new post of Assistant Secretary of Defense (ASD) for Special Operations and Low-Intensity Conflict (SO/LIC). The purpose was to increase the visibility and importance of these activities within the civilian side of the Pentagon. Congress took the position that low-intensity conflict should not be an "add on" responsibility of the Assistant Secretary of Defense for International Security Affairs.

Since doctrine, strategy, and capabilities for LIC require both military and non-military capabilities, Congress proposed that overall responsibility for setting requirements, planning, and coordination be placed at the National Security Council (NSC). The legislation recommended the creation of a Deputy Assistant to the President for National Security Affairs for Low-Intensity Conflict and creation of a Board for LIC. The Board would be made up of cabinet-level officers, and would establish a single channel for integrating those departments and agencies with LIC responsibilities, including DOD, CIA, State, USIA, AID, and others when appropriate. This aspect of the legislation indicates that Congress views low-intensity conflict as a political-military issue.

As part of the legislation, Congress included accountability, reporting requirements, and a timetable for implementation. Given the procrastination that had characterized the previous six years, Congress apparently felt such measures were necessary. Their suspicions were soon confirmed. A review of how each part of the legislation has been implemented reveals organizational resistance and a series of bureaucratic detours. It also demonstrates the tenacity of Congress in ensuring that its legislation is implemented.

The tenor of the implementation process was set with the decision over where to physically locate the Special Operations Command. Many argued that given the political-military character and interagency nature of its missions, the command should be quartered near Washington, D.C. The Defense Department, however, selected MacDill AFB in Florida. When this was proposed, members of the House Armed Services Committee argued vehemently against MacDill. They observed that the location was "as far away from the rest of the U.S. government as is possible without setting sail out to sea."[22] Nonetheless, the decision stood, and the Special Operations Command was based in Florida.

While it took five months to select the head of the command, staffing started without him. However, the eventual appointment of General James Lindsay was seen as sensible given his considerable experience in special operations. Nevertheless, opposition to the Command continued. For example, when the services were told to cut the Defense budget for 1989 by 10 percent, the Special Operations Command budget was reduced by one third. The arbitrariness of this action led Secretary of Defense Carlucci to restore funding.

The Navy sought to keep the SEALs out of USSOCOM, arguing that they are earmarked for the fleet commanders. But under pressure the Navy agreed to the reorganization, and the SEALs now have two sets of responsibilities, one for the fleet commander and the other for USSOCOM. The Air Force has likewise resisted. There also has been significant opposition from various regional commanders to the Special Operations Command. Some believe that it should be abolished, while others argue that Special Operations Forces assigned to their area of operations belong to them for use in conventional war scenarios.

Finally, during 1988 senior officers began publicly to express opposition to the new command. One member of the JCS stated that the Special Operations Command was not a good idea and that the chiefs will not back it. Another senior JCS officer claimed that a small group of retired zealots forced the legislation through Congress. It was not necessary, and the best thing is for it to go away.

The creation of an Assistant Secretary of Defense for Special Operations and Low-Intensity Conflict (SO/LIC) also generated considerable enmity. According to one official in the Office of the Secretary of Defense (OSD), to support the legislation is to be disloyal to "the Building" (Pentagon). The approach to the nomination of the Assistant Secretary, staffing of the office, and selection of quarters all reflected this attitude. By proposing a series of unqualified and weak candidates over an eighteen-month period, a small group of civilians in the Defense Department stymied the process. The candidates they selected were rejected by Congress even before they were formally nominated.

A second tactic was to argue that until Congress amended Title 10 to authorize twelve Assistant Secretary of Defense positions (only eleven positions were available), the new position could not be filled. In other words, OSD would be above the ceiling, and so the appointment was put on hold. When this issue was raised, the House Armed Services Committee was strongly critical, declaring that it was a "false issue" proposed "to delay, harass, and frustrate successful implementation."[23] When this continued into the spring of 1988 the Congress, in an unprecedented move, assigned the responsibilities of the unappointed Assistant Secretary to the Secretary of the Army. In effect, they made him the acting head of the office. In June the Pentagon finally selected a candidate to nominate formally to Congress, a long-time retired senior State Department officer, who was confirmed.

Congress envisioned a coordinating body at the National Security Council, with parallel structures in all relevant departments and agencies. This was to be the key ingredient for it and would establish a single channel for policy development and integration. The Congress believed that the Deputy Assistant to the President should have a broad understanding of the relevant issues. The White House, however, selected a Navy admiral with no such background. His assistant, an Air Force colonel, also had no relevant experience. The Low-Intensity Conflict Board at NSC has never been convened, and the interagency groups have met sparingly and accomplished little. In fact, not all the relevant agencies are willing to send representatives to the meetings (the CIA has been especially resolute in this respect).

What has been the response of Congress to these developments? In addition to conducting oversight through hearings and other mandated reporting procedures, the Chairman of the Senate Armed Services Committee has requested that the General Accounting Office (GAO) undertake an extensive evaluation of the implementation of the legislation that created the U.S. Special Operations Command. Specifically, GAO has been asked to determine 1) the United States Special Operations Command's progress in integrating the special operations forces of the various services into the new command and 2) the command's plans to assume programming and budgeting responsibilities for all special operations resources. The GAO will also examine implementation of the other aspects of the legislation.

Policy Recommendations
for the New Administration

Will low-intensity conflict continue to threaten U.S. geostrategic interests in the years ahead? As the Reagan era comes to a close, the Commission on Long-Term Integrated Strategy's Regional Conflict Working Group concluded that "to defend its interests the United States will have to take low-intensity conflict much more seriously." In fact, it must become a "permanent addition to the menu of defense planning."[24] Other specialists appear to disagree, and point to several recent international developments as important indicators of a worldwide de-escalation in low-intensity and regional conflict. Perhaps the most significant of these events involves Soviet policy in Afghanistan. These specialists equate that situation with the U.S. defeat in Vietnam, saying that Moscow now realizes that the costs of such adventures outweigh the benefits. The withdrawal from Afghanistan is perceived as the harbinger of a new approach that will take the form of less support for revolutionary insurgent movements and involvement in regional conflicts, and a greater emphasis on cultivating newly industrialized states in the Third World. Other important developments pointing to a decline in low-intensity and regional conflict include the end to the Iran-Iraq war, settlement of the Namibian conflict, progress in negotiations aimed at the withdrawal of the Vietnamese army from Cambodia, Cuban agreement to exit from Angola, and the PLO's rejection of terrorism and recognition of Israel.

While these are all encouraging signs, it would seem premature to suggest that the United States will no longer need to be concerned with threats and challenges at the lower end of the conflict spectrum. Indeed, what has been striking about war and strife in the period since World War II is the extent to which the different kinds of low-intensity or protracted warfare discussed in this study have predominated. While we should be heartened by the recent developments described above, other indicators suggest that the United States will continue to face threats to its interests as a result of low-intensity challenges. LIC is quite likely to remain an important national security issue for the Bush administration.

For instance, while Soviet withdrawal of its forces from Afghanistan is a positive step, one should not equate it with the U.S. departure from Vietnam. In the first place, Moscow has demanded a U.S. guarantee to stop arming the mujahideen as a quid pro quo for the removal of its troops. The Kremlin has said little about its own resupply of the Afghan military, as well as continuing advisory and air support. Its objective appears to be a coalition government composed of some of the mujahideen factions and the current Afghan regime. The latter would dominate key institutions (including the military and intelligence services) in an attempt to ensure Moscow's continued influence over the country. Similarly, the Kremlin has given no signs of lessening its commitment to other Third World regimes like South Yemen, Ethiopia, Angola, Cuba, and Nicaragua, each of which is of geostrategic importance to the Soviet Union. Moscow likewise has not altered its indirect support to revolutionary insurgent movements.

As was noted earlier, the recent accord on Namibia and Angola is unlikely to end Soviet and Cuban involvement in Angola or bring an end to the Civil War. While Havana has agreed to the withdrawal of it formal army, an estimated ten thousand Cuban soldiers will stay behind as "Angolan citizens" joining a large number of East bloc advisors and internationalist forces.

Future low-intensity threats to U.S. interests will not take place solely within an East-West context. For example, Iran, Syria, and Libya have either directly or indirectly used terrorism and other forms of low-intensity conflict against the United States and its Arab allies in the Middle East. For these three regimes terrorism is an instrument of statecraft. Other radical factions and groups have also relied on terrorist tactics in different regions of the globe to undermine U.S. interests and policy.

Finally, during the 1980s, insurgent and terrorist organizations have developed associations with international cartels that smuggle drugs. According to one recent assessment, the cartels "cooperate in certain Third World countries with guerrillas, arms smugglers, terrorists, or other subversives. Among countries so afflicted have been Guatemala, El Salvador, Costa Rica, Columbia, Peru, Bolivia, Lebanon, Iran, India, Burma, Sri Lanka, and the Philippine Republic." Furthermore, the report notes that "in ·Nicaragua and Cuba, the government, at the highest level, [also] cooperates with the traffickers."[25] This new dimension of LIC only adds to the complexity and seriousness of the problem.

In light of these trends there is little to suggest that the Bush administration will be able to avoid the issue of low-intensity conflict. In fact, it is likely to be faced with diverse, urgent, and complex challenges and will have to formulate a national strategy for low-intensity conflict. It took the Reagan administration until 1987, with the enactment of National Security Decision Directive (NSDD) 277, to formulate a concise statement on U.S. policy as it relates to low-intensity conflict. It identified three principal missions: 1) counterterrorism; 2) political, economic, and military assistance to developing nations to prevent or combat insurgent challenges; and 3) support to selected anticommunist resistance movements. This would seem to be a reasonable starting point for the development of an integrated policy and strategy. However, on the third point, assistance might not be confined to anticommunist resistance forces. We should also consider aiding those political coalitions and movements seeking to end authoritarian rule and establish democracy. Panama and Chile would be two obvious examples. An additional mission to consider is assistance to friendly governments in suppressing narcotics trafficking.

However, even if the Bush administration is able to establish the outline of an integrated policy, several other difficulties will have to be addressed. It will inherit a military establishment that, in general, does not understand low-intensity conflict nor take these kinds of challenges very seriously. Moreover, it views special operations forces with suspicion. In addition, the top leadership in the Pentagon, with a few exceptions, feels that the primary, if not the only, role for these forces is as behind-the-lines commandos to support regular U.S. forces during a conventional war in Europe. President Bush will also discover that opposition to this policy is not confined to the Department of Defense. He will certainly encounter it at the CIA, especially in the aftermath of Director Webster's "house cleaning" of several officers who were involved in the Iranian initiative and Contra policy. The message to intelligence professionals is that support for LIC initiatives is not career enhancing. Similar resistance will likewise be found in other civilian departments and agencies that ostensibly have LIC responsibilities. Finally, President Bush will find a Congress in which a bipartisan consensus has been forged over the need to develop policy, strategy, and capabilities to meet protracted or low-intensity conflict challenges. Indeed, if the administration does not act, Congress is likely to set the LIC agenda for it.

Nevertheless, the new administration also has an opportunity to learn from the miscalculations of its predecessor. This means developing an organizational structure that will approach this national security issue in a manner that is neither disjointed nor ad hoc. The first step would be to select a Deputy Assistant to the President for National Security Affairs who has a sophisticated understanding of LIC in all of its political-military dimensions. Second, the new administration must recognize that low-intensity conflict is a "permanent addition to the menu of defense planning," and "to our national security and foreign policy agenda." The next step would be the appointment of the Board for Low-Intensity Conflict at the NSC. However, the level of the Board's membership should be below that recommended by Congress. It might be composed of representatives from each of the appropriate departments and agencies who have the rank of Assistant Secretary or its equivalent. A working group to support the Board should likewise be considered, staffed at the Deputy Assistant Secretary level. Additionally, the Assistant Secretary structure mandated by Congress for the Defense Department might be considered as a prototype—with appropriate modifications where necessary—for these other departments and agencies.

With this kind of professional structure, in conjunction with a small number of professionals on the NSC staff, in place when President Bush is faced with LIC crises, he will have an alternative to what Oliver North described in his Congressional testimony as an "off the shelf, self-sustaining, stand-alone" entity. Ideally, the White House will understand that the Contra policy and the hostages in Lebanon fall within the boundaries of low-intensity conflict. They are a part of a form of warfare that should neither be approached in an ideological manner nor have policy responsibility assigned to zealots (no matter how well intentioned). Low-intensity conflict is a national security policy issue. It should be approached in a systematic and professional manner like other issues on the national security agenda of the United States. While the international arena over the last forty years has been characterized by protracted conflicts, indirect aggression, and other forms of unconventional warfare, the United States has yet to fully understand it. As this study has demonstrated, this continued to be the case during the Reagan years. Hopefully, the Bush years will be different.

Notes

1. Sam Sarkesian, *The New Battlefield: The United States and Unconventional Conflict* (New York: Greenwood Press, 1986). See also Richard Shultz et al., eds., *Guerrilla Warfare and Counterinsurgency: U.S.-Soviet Policy in the Third World* (Lexington, MA: Lexington Books, 1988); *Proceedings of the Low Intensity Warfare Conference* (Washington, DC: Department of Defense, 1986); David Dean, ed., *Low Intensity Conflict and Modern Technology* (Montgomery, AL: Air University Press, 1986).

2. A.J. Bacevich, James D. Hallums, Richard H. White, and Thomas F. Young, *American Military Policy in Small Wars: The Case of El Salvador* (New York: Pergamon-Brassey's, 1988), pp. v–vi.

3. See Regional Conflict Working Group, "A U.S. Strategy for Regional Conflict" a paper produced as one of several addenda to *Discriminate Deterrence: Report of the Commission on Integrated Long-Term Strategy* (Washington, DC: USGPO, 1988).

4. Quoted in James Adams, *Secret Armies* (New York: The Atlantic Monthly Press, 1987), p. 350.

5. Richard Shultz, "Covert Action," in Roy Godson, ed., *Intelligence Requirements for the 1990s* (Lexington, MA: Lexington Books, 1988).

6. On the Kennedy Administration, see Stanley Karnow, *Vietnam: A History* (New York: Viking Press, 1983); Douglas Blaufarb, The Counterinsurgency Era (New York: The Free Press, 1977); Andrew Krepinevich, *The Army and Vietnam* (Baltimore: Johns Hopkins University Press, 1986).

7. For an examination of the Reagan Doctrine see Raymond Copson and Richard Cronin, "The Reagan Doctrine and its Prospects," *Survival* (January/ February, 1987).

8. See the *Report of the Congressional Committees Investigating the Iran-Contra Affair* (Washington, DC: USGPO, 1987). Two examples of such books are Christopher Dickey, *With the Contras* (New York: Simon & Schuster, 1985); Bob Woodward, *Veil: The Secret Wars of the CIA* (New York: Simon & Schuster, 1987).

9. *Proceedings of the Low Intensity Warfare Conference*, p. 7.

10. For the statement by Secretary Shultz, see *Proceedings of the Low-Intensity Conflict Conference*, pp. 9–10. See also statement by Richard L. Armitage, Assistant Secretary of Defense (International Security Affairs) before the Subcommittee on Readiness, Committee on Armed Services, House of Representatives, July 16, 1986.

11. For a discussion, see Regional Conflict Working Group, "A U.S. Strategy for Regional Conflict."

12. U.S. Army Training and Doctrine Command Pamphlet 525-44, *U.S. Army Operational Concept for Low-Intensity Conflict*, (Fort Monroe, VA: Army Training and Doctrine Command, February 10, 1986).

13. Joint Low-Intensity Conflict Project Final Report, *Analytical Review of Low-Intensity Conflict* (Fort Monroe, VA: U.S. Army Training and Doctrine Command, 1986).

14. The office of primary responsibility is the Center for Low-Intensity Conflict at Langley Air Force Base, VA.

15. For a discussion about the Joint Special Operations Agency, see Sarkesian, *The New Battlefield*, and Adams, *Secret Armies*.

16. *New York Times*, (September 6, 1986).

17. *Los Angeles Times*, (November 18, 1984).

18. See Krepinevich, *The Army and Vietnam*.

19. Theodore Shackley, *The Third Option* (New York: Reader's Digest Press, 1981).

20. See Steven Emerson, *Secret Warriors: Inside the Covert Military Operations of the Reagan Era* (New York: G.P. Putnam's Sons, 1988); Adams, *Secret Armies*; Shultz, "Covert Action;" and Woodward, *Veil*.

21. *New York Times*, September 6, 1986; *The Times*-London, August 4, 1986.

22. This statement is from a March 11, 1987, letter to Secretary of Defense Caspar Weinberger from House Armed Services Committee members Earl Hutto, Dan Daniel, and John Kasich.

23. Drawn from the March 11, 1987, letter cited in note 22.

24. See Regional Conflict Working Group, "A U.S. Strategy for Regional Conflict."

25. Ibid.

6

Technology and Battlefields of the Future: Challenges, Opportunities, and Directions

Robert F. Helms II

Technology has been one of the dominant forces shaping the course of military history and can be expected to continue to play a prominent role in establishing parameters within which the future will evolve. The January 1988 Report of The Commission On Integrated Long-Term Strategy projected that "Dramatic developments in military technology appear feasible over the next twenty years."[1] It is not inconceivable that, as advanced technologies revolutionize the conduct of war, victory will in large measure be determined in the laboratories and production lines before battles are even fought.

The Military Potential of Advanced Technologies

Technologies are expanding the battlefield in depth, width, and into the third dimension as space and advanced aviation, to include Army aviation, systems are matured, fielded, and included in operational concepts.[2] The battlefield also increasingly is becoming transparent, making it more difficult, if not impossible, to avoid being detected. Automation is linking target locating systems, data processing, and modern weapon systems to decrease time and distance factors to near real time on modern battlefields. "It is definitely possible . . . by using the edge in technology . . . to go from reconnaissance to target acquisition with real time data relayed to guns with precision munitions."[3] Weapon systems being fielded in the force structure possess greater ranges and improved accuracy. The combination of improved target detection, data processing, weapon systems, and munitions are fueling a potential revolution in the area of indirect fire as capabilities move from requiring multiple rounds for a single hard target kill, through one round-one hard target kill, to one round for multiple

The views expressed herein are solely those of the author and do not necessarily reflect the views of the Department of Defense or of any other agency of the United States government.

hard target kills at greater ranges. One Soviet writer has noted that technology is

> leading to a gradual obliteration of the differences between the efficiency of nuclear means and that of conventional means . . . mainly the result of a radical increase in the accuracy and range of . . . the precision weapon. . . . The equipping of field artillery (conducting indirect fires) with missiles that are self-guiding to the target in the final phase of the flight, and which are also capable of accurately striking individual tanks in motion is having a revolutionary influence on the capabilities and organization of fighting against tanks.[4]

It increasingly will be difficult to avoid being targeted and killed once detected. In the process of this evolution, it is not unreasonable to anticipate battlefield advantages shifting to the defense relative to the offense, perhaps decisively by the twenty-first century. It is possible, perhaps probable, that fires will evolve to a position of dominance not unlike the machine gun in World War I. "The transition will take time and, in the process, shift the balance between fires and maneuver in the direction of fires."[5]

Technologies also are being used in other ways on the battlefield. Robotics are performing many labor-intensive and dangerous battlefield tasks such as mine clearing, reconnaissance by unmanned aircraft, and use of sensors for outposts.[6] This trend can be expected to continue. Logistical organizations also are using technology to become more productive as service organizations infuse advanced systems into support structures. Prognostic diagnostics are expected to enable commanders to predict equipment failures in advance, to permit more efficient preventive maintenance and decrease downtime of key combat systems. Modular repair of major components in field locations is expected to decrease equipment downtime. More efficient fuels and lubricants could improve operations of machines, reducing mechanical failures and fuel requirements. In a similar way, strategic projection capabilities of land forces are becoming more efficient as bulk and weight requirements are reduced with the application of advanced technologies in areas such as fuel, munitions, and communications. Improved capabilities are expected to enable fewer combat systems to perform a greater number of tasks as technology enhancements such as improved munitions impact favorably to increase battlefield capabilities and reduce strategic lift requirements. Technologies also are reported to be available to support fast sea-lift that could transport rapidly large quantities of military materiel over strategic distances. In an era of declining available military manpower, technologies also are being used to reduce personnel requirements through automation of functions wherever possible.[7] The challenge for the United States and its allies is to translate this potential into reality.

Challenges for Realizing Potential of Technology

While advanced technologies offer promising potential to advanced nations, there are a number of challenges that first must be overcome before full advantages can be realized. First, advanced technology "is not an American monopoly."[8] Other nations, both allies and potential adversaries, increasingly are competitors in developing and applying advanced technologies. The U.S. Joint Chiefs of Staff identified twenty basic technology areas considered to have the most "potential for significantly changing the military capability in the next ten to twenty years." Of the twenty, the United States is considered to be ahead in fourteen, but losing ground to the Soviet Union in six; while maintaining its position in seven areas and gaining in only one: computers and software. The United States and Soviet Union are considered relatively equal in the remaining six; however, the United States is thought to be losing in three of these while not gaining in any area.[9] The Commission on Integrated Long-Term Strategy arrived at a similar conclusion:

> the Soviets . . . are producing vastly improved armor for tanks. . . . They have made enormous strides in Submarine technology . . . are sure to stay ahead in . . . chemical weapons. . . . Particularly ominous is the large and rapidly growing Soviet capability for military use of space in support of conventional warfare . . .[10]

Second, development and application of advanced technologies is based on an education system built around hard sciences, which is expensive. The United States seems to be entering an era of flat or declining budgets. It will be necessary, but not easy, to make funds available to reorient the educational system to focus on hard sciences and support research. Neither is there any assurance that U.S. students will accept hard sciences as a preferred career and make the commitment to pursue it as a vocation.

Third, focus is necessary to guide research and development of technologies toward achieving set goals. Scientists understandably prefer letting "a thousand flowers bloom." In a time of plentiful resources and in the absence of a threat, it may be possible to pursue development of technologies across a broad base in the hopes of finding a few "gold nuggets" to mine. This approach reasonably can be expected to take longer, be more costly and generally be less efficient. Noting the unenviable U.S. history for sustaining a stable research and development base, the Commission on Integrated Long-Term Strategy stated that U.S. budgeting for research and development has been constrained and uneven, and from the mid-1960s to the late 1970s, the technology base was substantially eroded. During this same period, from 1965 to 1980, U.S. spending on military research and development declined about 20 percent. In 1965, estimated Soviet spending on military research and development was about 65 percent of the United States's, but by 1980 it had grown to more than 150 percent of U.S. spending. In the 1980s, a turn around for the United States began, but more recently our spending on the technology base has been cut back again.[11]

The inescapable conclusion is that the United States no longer has the luxury of pursuing less efficient options, but must move along those routes promising the greatest potential payoff within an agreed focus to integrate technologies on future battlefields. The Manhattan Project, which produced the atomic bomb; the elimination of polio; and the U.S. space effort, which enabled man to visit and walk on the moon, are three examples of focusing the development of technologies. These examples may provide models of the results that may be possible if a focused framework is provided for directing development and application of technologies on future battlefields.

Framework for Focusing Technologies on Future Battlefields

The potential of shifting the advantage decisively in favor of the defense relative to the offense is a logical framework for the United States and its allies to pursue in developing and applying technologies on future battlefields. NATO is a defense-oriented alliance. The concept for a Forward Defense being pursued within a strategy of Flexible Response inescapably is defensive in orientation. Defensive forces are more economical in terms of structure and budgets required for maintaining them over time. Further, enhancing NATO's defensive capabilities reduces the potential for a Warsaw Pact attack into Western Europe and increases stability in the Central Region of Europe, another desirable goal. Inherent in the defense oriented framework are two additional subordinate areas: 1) Robotics should be developed to perform as many dangerous and labor-intensive tasks as possible and 2) unit productivity should be increased wherever possible to decrease manpower requirements and enable smaller or fewer organizations to perform similar or greater tasks on the battlefield. Priorities should be directed toward capabilities and units whose function contributes directly toward shifting battlefield advantages to the defense.

Focus for Developing
and Integrating Technologies

Several approaches are available for developing and integrating technologies into future battlefields. One approach commonly used for defining military requirements has been to match potential enemies strength for strength, preferably with rough equivalence and built-in safety measures for manpower, equipment, and combat organizations such as corps and divisions. However preferable this approach may be to military strategists and planners, it fails to meet the essential criterion of realism when applied to the U.S.-Soviet relationship. This approach also would be ineffective in establishing enduring advantages, since the Soviet Union absolutely is determined that *"Never Again"* will the Homeland be exposed to potential invaders as a result of military weakness. Moscow repeatedly has demonstrated the determination and willingness to make sacrifices necessary for taking countermeasures within a relatively short period to neutralize U.S. advantages. The net result has been a cycle of actions and counteractions leading to an unproductive arms race. Neither can the United States and its allies expect to match the Soviet Union and other Warsaw Pact members "in every category of weapons systems; e.g., numbers of tanks, aircraft, ships, etc."[12] It is necessary to "recognize the unaffordability and impracticability of trying to match the Soviets plane for plane or tank for tank."[13]

Further, the Soviet Union's growing technological capabilities are enabling Moscow to respond to Western technological advances with effective countermeasures in a relatively short period. This trend can be expected to continue if technological disparities between the two nations disappear, as current trends would seem to indicate. It may be argued that the Soviet Union has even reversed previous roles and assumed the lead in certain areas such as helicopters and advanced armor for tanks. The heretofore successful approach of "outmuscling" the Soviet Union is bankrupt. It now is necessary, more than at any time during the Cold War, to set aside brawn and approach the challenge in a smart way. A more plausible approach is to identify and leverage the strengths of the United States and its allies against enduring the weaknesses of the Soviet Union and other Warsaw Pact nations: "We [NATO nations] have chosen instead to rely on our superior technological capability to produce the force multiplier effects that maintain our deterrent or, if necessary, enable us to fight outnumbered and win."[14]

The process should include identification of weak points within the strengths of potential adversaries to create disutilities in advantages over time, perhaps making critical parts of force structures such as armor-heavy formations, aviation, and fire support obsolete or less efficient.[15] It also may be possible to influence the adversary to divert resources and undertake costly investments to the advantage of the United States and its allies, or adopt less threatening strategies. This approach, when properly applied, provides an appropriate focus to guide the establishment and maintenance of priorities for developing and integrating technologies with the highest battlefield payoff over time and which lead to the most desirable end condition.

Leveraging Technologies Against Enduring Soviet Military Weaknesses

Operational and Tactical Levels of War

It is not possible to develop and defend a set of enduring Soviet strategic military weaknesses in a short paper. However, NATO is a defensive alliance and not likely to initiate an attack into Eastern Europe in the foreseeable future. If war is to occur under existing or foreseeable conditions, it will be necessary for the Soviet Union to assume the initiative and attack NATO nations.[16] It generally is agreed that Soviet military doctrine for land warfare is offensively oriented and dependent on establishing *overwhelming mass* or *combat power* of 5–8 to 1 or greater at the main point of attack for success for the tactical level of war. It logically will be necessary to bring together large numbers of forces, to include air and artillery fires, in a relatively confined area to achieve the minimum 5–8 to 1 force ratio considered necessary for success. This task is achieved using a combination of measures such as maneuvering to bring direct fire weapons to bear on the defender, deception, and surprise, as well as massive fires from air force, helicopter, and artillery systems. It is probable that Warsaw Pact commanders do not expect to achieve more than a two to one favorable force ratio with ground maneuver forces at the main point of attack due to terrain restrictions and prepared fires of the defense.

The Red Army's doctrinal solution has been to use massive numbers of field artillery weapons complemented with fires delivered by air force aircraft and helicopter systems to overcome the 3–5 to 1 force ratio delta necessary for assured success, and establish appropriate force echelons.[17] Follow-on echelons are moved forward to replace leading formations as the latter are depleted in battle. These forces advance according to a carefully prepared movement plan which conforms with doctrinally established and accepted norms. The Soviets also must transport supplies necessary to sustain large offense-oriented armor formations over a *constrained logistics network*. The relatively constrained network of roads and rail could be vulnerable to attack by conventional long-range precision munitions in "missions once assigned to nuclear weapons."[18]

Maintaining tempo at the operational level of war—that is, generating and sustaining favorable combat power ratios at the main point of attack—is essential for the Red Army to maintain the offense over time to achieve objectives deep in NATO's rear area. The components of *tempo* include movement plans and command and control as well as means such as road and rail necessary for moving and sustaining large offense-oriented formations. The complexity of moving large formations over restricted axes of advance requires precision of execution and offers little, if any, opportunity for flexibility. As a result, the Soviet military relies extensively on a *system of centralized command and control* to maintain the *tempo* calculated as necessary to realize conformance with approved plans. This system stifles initiative and basically denies commanders at lower levels flexibility in responding to unexpected events on the battlefield. These systemic faults result in a level of predictability that possibly could be exploited to deny necessary tempo and disrupt approved operation plans. Achieving this state places the Soviet military in the uncomfortable position of reacting in unexpected ways. The Soviet planning system is not easily adaptable and reacts slowly in a cumbersome manner to a rapidly and unexpectedly changing battlefield. Disrupting Warsaw Pact military plans potentially denies the opportunity for a rapid victory.

The *absence of a competent non-commissioned officer corps* to take charge and supervise weapons crews at the tactical level is a product of the Soviet political and social system and a serious weakness that will be difficult to overcome without major systemic changes. The rigidity of the Soviet military at the tactical level of war reflects an attempt to offset the lack of faith in leader initiative at the lower levels of war. In a similar vein, the *unreliability of Warsaw Pact allies* has led the Soviet military to institutionalize safety measures to guard against defections or non-Soviet Warsaw Pact military units possibly turning against Soviet units. The net result is *a level of mistrust* that should be exploited to create possibilities for additional stress between non-Soviet Warsaw Pact nations and the Soviet Union.

Formations moving to the attack inherently are exposed to fires of the defense which has the advantage of fighting on known terrain and from prepared positions. The concentration of forces on the battlefield forecasted to emerge by the end of this century presents a target-rich environment that can be exploited with advanced technologies. NATO can and should take advantage of strengths inherent to the defense by fielding a suite of systems to attack exposed Soviet offensive formations. Follow-on formations should be attacked to weaken the force as well as to disrupt established movement plans to deny tempo required for maintaining overwhelming ratios of combat power at the main point of attack over time. Examples of suitable targets for attack at depth include headquarters of armies and operational fronts, logistical storage sites, critical communication and transportation centers, airfields, and troop concentrations. Successful accomplishment of these tasks should have the effect of delaying the arrival of follow-on formations and logistics in the main battle area, thus isolating lead echelons as adjustments are required in movement plans. Delaying the arrival of follow-on echelons into the main battle area provides NATO forces conducting the Forward Defense additional opportunities for denying required force ratios at the main point of attack. Realizing this condition improves capabilities of the defender to defeat the attacking lead echelon and prepare for battle against follow-on echelons before their arrival in the main battle area. Furthermore, successful attack of follow-on formations keeps these forces from entering the battle without having suffered battle damage.

The suite of systems for attacking follow-on echelons and logistics to deny tempo at the operational level of war should include: 1) target acquisition systems capable of detecting and directing precision munitions onto moving targets such as armor vehicles at depth; 2) automated data processing capable of transmitting essential firing data to firing systems; and 3) weapon systems with precision and brilliant munitions. The term "suite" purposely is used to convey the concept of linkage existing between components necessary to achieve deep attack by fire capabilities. Each element is necessary and must function for the whole to be effective. Conversely, the suite of systems is only as strong as the weakest link. *Technologies should be developed to provide for each of these capabilities with appropriate reliability.*

The attacking force in the Central Region of Europe is confronted with a number of enduring weaknesses. These include: 1) the requirement for establishing and maintainimg superior force ratios at the main point of attack relative to the defender; 2) moving over restrictive terrain, which channels advancing formations into predictable axes of advance; 3) being exposed to prepared fires while moving to the attack, possibly over unfamiliar terrain; and 4) requirements for large quantities of logistical support to sustain offensive operations over time. The attacker enjoys the advantage of selecting the time and place of attack, which traditionally has been subsumed under the principle of war known as "surprise." However, with the emergence of a basically transparent battlefield, the potential of achieving surprise is decreasing. This trend can be expected to continue for the foreseeable future, and it is possible that the advantage of surprise could shift to the defender.

The critical task for NATO to accomplish at the tactical level of war is to deny surprise and the attacker's opportunities to concentrate overwhelming combat power at the main point of attack. Battlefield requirements to be accomplished in performing this task include: 1) knowing in advance the location of the main point of attack; 2) locating and attacking Soviet armor formations at extended ranges; and 3) reducing the effectiveness of enemy fires delivered by both indirect and air means.[19] Inherent in performing these tasks is a capability for tracking and handing off deep operations to forces involved in close operations. Technologies developed to perform these battlefield tasks in the main battle area and to shift the advantage decisively to the defense should include:

1. A suite of indirect fire systems to attack concentrations of advancing Soviet formations. The suite would consist of:
   a. Reconnaissance systems such as sensors and unmanned aerial vehicles to track advancing Warsaw Pact formations and locate targets for indirect fires. These systems should be capable of preprocessing and passing essential information through an automated data system to firing weapons, and then provide guidance to munitions onto designated targets. Further, there is a need for reconnaissance systems used in depth and close operations to be compatible to ensure that a smooth handoff is possible and that gaps in battlefield depth are avoided.
   b. Automated data processing systems capable of passing volumes of information in near real time. The system should include capabilities for rapidly adapting battle plans to take advantage of the enemy wherever possible. Establishing compatibility between reconnaissance and firing weapons is an essential characteristic.
   c. Indirect fire weapons using smart, precision, and brilliant munitions represent a key component of the future battlefield. These systems should be capable of engaging targets at vulnerable location, such as to ranges of 40,000 meters for tanks—with confidence. The menu of munitions available for these systems should include capabilities for multiple kills with single rounds against armor vehicles as well as soft area targets such as personnel and logistics.
2. Advanced antitank weapons capable of being fired from a variety of platforms, including aircraft and helicopers, as well as light vehicles or individual soldiers from concealed positions. The armored vehicle is exposed while moving, and is at a disadvantage relative to the individual soldier armed with advanced antitank weapons in restricted terrain such as woods, mountains, or urban areas. The search for technologies should be expanded to include attacking weapon components such as fire control optics and en-

gines. Examples of possible technologies include microwave and fuel-overpressure explosives. Western nations should capitalize on the advantages derived from the terrain of Central Europe as well as the inherent advantages of the defense to rapidly field a family of antitank weapons with the characteristics described above.

3. Advanced mines capable of being delivered by air or indirect fires. Mines can be used to complement indirect fires and antitank weapons to slow, disrupt, and channelize advancing enemy formations. It may be possible to place mines between leading and follow-on echelons to further separate these formations. This tactic offers promising potential, which should be pursued. Mines also are an excellent means for interdicting logistical lines of communication and making sustainment operations less predictable. Advanced mines should include capabilities for being programmed in advance for activation and deactivation as well as locating specific categories of targets and being triggered from a distance for detonation.

4. Integrated air defense systems using advanced target detection and tracking, missile, electronic warfare, and laser technologies to reduce the utility of Warsaw Pact investments in tactical air and helicopters.[20] The search for technologies for this purpose should be expanded to include degrading the performance of aircraft components such as engines, radars, and optics. Air contaminants using chemicals or microwave technologies could prove useful in realizing these conditions. Use of air defense weapons should be expanded to include proliferation of systems for individual soldiers and on as many military vehicles as possible. Achieving this condition decreases threats to the rear area and denies two categories of fires used to obtain necessary force ratios at the main point of attack. It logically follows that the probability of a successful Forward Defense would be increased significantly as a result of realizing this condition.

5. Electronic warfare systems to attack and disrupt the Soviet centralized command and control. It has been noted that command and control features an enduring weakness in that it lacks flexibility because of the systemic rigidity found in Soviet political and social systems. Electronic warfare systems, which include laser and microwave technologies, seem to offer the most potential for attacking Warsaw Pact command and control capabilities necessary for coordinating the offense and adjusting to unexpected battlefield changes, and should be pursued.

Strategic Level of War

It seems reasonable to assume that Secretary-General Gorbachev is serious in his assertion that "Clausewitz's dictum that war is the continuation of policy by other means . . . has grown hopelessly out of date."[21] "War is not the goal of Soviet strategy; the Soviets prefer to gain their objectives by pacific means—forcing appeasement on the enemy."[22] Accepting that the Soviet strategic objective is to avoid war when possible, it also is reasonable to assume that the objective would shift to not losing and limiting damage to the homeland should war occur for whatever reason. The short war scenario likely is preferred by the Soviet Union for a number of reasons. Conflict extended over time increases the risk that nuclear weapons will be used and provides additional time for Western nations to mobilize and leverage a potentially decisive industrial base as well as to reinforce forward-deployed forces and attack Soviet interests outside Europe. There also is a danger that a long war would create additional tensions within the Warsaw Pact and become a serious problem for the rear operational area. This scenario also could provide opportunities for other nations, such as the People's Republic of China, to settle old scores. Conversely, a relatively short conflict would not stress the rather frail and weak economic system of the Soviet Union, and avoids the potentially destablizing impact that a long war could have on Soviet populations.

Technologies that deny a rapid Warsaw Pact victory at the operational and tactical levels of war contribute to creating a disutility in the Red Army well as eroding the conditions necessary for success at the strategic level. Appropriate technologies would include early warning capabilities to deny opportunities for making strategic preparations necessary to support a surprise attack. Technologies such as fast sea-lift for rapid movement of forces over strategic distances support the reinforcement of forward-deployed forces and should be developed. In a similar vein, technologies that lighten and make the force more combat efficient also contribute to strategic projectability and should be pursued. The West should develop long-range non-nuclear strategic weapons to attack targets such as airfields, rail centers, and power grids deep inside Eastern Europe and the Soviet Union. Technologies that support special operations and psychological warfare inside Eastern Europe and the Soviet Union are desirable and should be developed. Examples of technologies suitable for psychological warfare would include radio and television transmitters.

Summary

Technologies offer the potential for shifting advantages from the offense to the defense by the twenty-first century. The issue is not potential or scientific capability—both exist. The issue is whether the United States and its allies can devise and agree on a strategy that permits capitalizing on the full range of opportunities being offered by technologies. Economic and scientific realities require a combined approach—burden-sharing is appropriate and necessary. There is an urgent need for the Alliance to focus the development of technologies within a framework that shifts battlefield advantages from the offense to the defense at each level of war. The primary foci for developing technologies should be to deny the Warsaw Pact: 1) opportunities for acheiving overwhelming combat power ratios at the tactical level of war; 2) tempo necessary for generating and sustaining necessary combat power ratios at the operational level; and 3) utility of the Red Army at the theater strategic level. Accepting and realizing these foci could be expected to transform military relationships to the advantage of NATO and to increase stability throughout Eurasia. Failure to pursue technologies in the manner described here can be expected to result in NATO's forfeiting an opportunity to capitalize on the Warsaw Pact's weaknesses, which will be to the detriment of the West, perhaps forever.

Notes

1. *Discriminate Deterrence*: Report of The Commission On Integrated Long-Term Strategy, (Washington, DC: USGPO, 1988), p. 8.

2. For example, in World War I, a U.S. division could expect to be responsible for a front of 3,000 to 4,000 meters. The division front increased to 7,000 meters in World War II, to 21,000 meters in Korea, 24,000 meters in the mid-1950s, and is now thought to be between 5,000 and 75,000 meters on the Central Front in Europe.

3. Unpublished speech presented by General Wolfgang Altenburg (FRG), the chairman of the NATO Military Committee, at The Centre For European Policy Studies, Brussels, Belgium, November 13, 1987.

4. Quoted from the U.S. Army Soviet Army Studies Office, January 20, 1987 translation of Colonel Stanislaw Koziej (USSR), *Anticipated Direction for Change in Tactics of Ground Troups*, pp. 2–3 and 4–5.

5. Quoted from Major General (USA) Raphael J. Hallada, "Field Artillery Vision: Master Plan for Fire Support of the Future," *Field Artillery Journal*, (February 1988): 9.

6. See Steven M. Shaker and Alan R. Wise, *War without Men: Robots on the Battlefield* (Washington, DC: Pergamon-Brassey's International Defense Publishers, 1988), pp. 1–3, for discussion of the potential and use for robotics on future battlefields.

7. Examples include the 3 crew members for the M1 Abrams tank, compared to 5 for the M60 series of tanks and 3 for the Multiple Launched Rocket System crew, as compared to the 8-inch howitzer crew of 11 soldiers. Each of these weapons represents a more efficient system capable of achieving better results on the battlefield with fewer men. Other similar manpower savings are being realized throughout the force structure.

8. *Discriminate Deterrence*, p. 8.

9. U.S. Joint Chiefs of Staff, *Military Posture Statement: FY 1988* (Washington, DC: USGPO, 1987), p. 10.

10. *Discriminate Deterrence*, pp. 8–9.

11. Ibid, pp. 46–47.

12. Caspar W. Weinberger, *Annual Report to the Congress: Fiscal Year 1988* (Washington, DC: USGPO), p. 47.

13. Ibid., p. 246.

14. Ibid., pp. 246–247.

15. One of the basic thoughts underlying the U.S. Strategic Defense Initiative is to deny the utility of Soviet investments in land-based ICBMs. A similar effort to identify a weak point and deny Soviet strengths derived from investments in offense-oriented armor formations would be to the advantage of the United States and its allies.

16. In the world of military strategy, the defense enjoys certain enduring advantages relative to the offense. It generally is agreed that the offense requires larger numbers of forces and logistics for success than the defense. In the scenario being described, NATO would have the benefit of these advantages and should capitalize on them.

17. The Soviets also employ electronic systems as a combat multiplier to complement fires of aircraft and field artillery.

18. *Discriminate Deterrence*, p. 8.

19. It should be noted that the Soviet Union plans to use the helicopter in an attempt to reduce the terrain disadvantage confronting the attacker in Central Europe. From the Soviet perspective, the helicopter is, in effect, a "flying tank." As an example, "Drive a tank to an airfield and park it near a military (fighter) aircraft . . . put a helicopter between the tank and the aircraft . . . which does the helicopter resemble more . . . ? Soviet Generals believe that to all intents and purposes the helicopter is a tank . . . one which is capable of high speeds and unrestricted cross-country performance . . . (with) approximately the same firepower as a tank." Victor Suvorov, *Inside the Red Army* (New York: Berkley Books, 1982), p. 224.

20. It is important to note that this condition can also be expected to alter NATO's use of close air support and helicopters, since advanced air defenses reduce the survivability and thus the utility of these systems on advanced battlefields.

21. Mikhail Gorbachev, *Perestroika: New Thinking for our Country and the World* (New York: Harper & Row, 1987), p. 140.

22. Raymond L. Garthoff, *How Russia Makes War* (Boston: Allen & Unwin, 1954), p. 11.

7
Technology and Future Maritime Strategy

E. G. Wylie

I am not a scientist, nor have I worked directly with the application of technology within the Navy. Thus, I cannot provide an articulate discussion of likely technological breakthroughs by the year 2000. I have, however, participated in the development and refinement of the written maritime strategy. From this perspective, I will outline what I see to be the framework surrounding the likely technological advances that will affect the Navy of the near future.

First I must stress that a maritime strategy, developed in written form by the Navy staff in the early 1980's, is not a solo act. By that I mean two things. The writing down of a maritime strategy was an attempt by the Navy to articulate long-held but little-discussed views of the use and place of a Navy within the security and foreign policy complex of the United States. The employment of the U.S. Navy is but one part of our overall national strategy. That national strategy, which includes our historical, economic, security, and cultural interrelationships, is developed as a part of our foreign policy. I state this because much of the recent debate over a maritime strategy has centered on whether or not it was developed as a force-building tool—an attempt by the Navy to obtain more ships, aircraft, submarines, and other weapons systems. While the size of the Navy is certainly fair game in the arenas of public debate, that is not why a maritime strategy was written down.

We developed the written form of a maritime strategy for exactly the opposite reason. We were trying to develop a framework for the weapons systems sponsors to use in deciding the utility of and need for various equipments in a world of finite dollars and personnel constraints. Much as any smart business develops and refines its long-term strategy for the obligation and expenditure of its income, the Navy did the same thing.

The views expressed herein are solely those of the author and do not necessarily reflect the views of the Department of Defense or of any other agency of the United States government. The author gratefully acknowledges the contributions and assistance of Mr. Glenn A. Spaulding and Professor David A. Rosenberg, who helped immeasurably in this effort.

The reason for a written maritime strategy is simple—we have a finite amount of money available to develop, support, and maintain the Navy as a part of our national strategy and in support of our foreign policy. In order to build the best Navy possible, given the internal constraints and the external pressures, we need a framework against which we measure each candidate system or platform. Put another way, we build a Navy that we as U.S. citizens want, need, and are willing to support.

To a large degree how and what we see as our foreign policy needs will influence heavily those technologies we will emphasize in the development of the Navy of the future. Let us look first at the foreign policy milieu of the near future. For example, will we perceive reduced tensions between the superpowers in the potential use of nuclear weapons? I suspect that will be the case, barring unforeseen circumstances. With the INF treaty signed, and the destruction of some weapons already, we may see more treaties to control or even reduce the numbers of other types of nuclear weapons. This, in turn, may affect the numbers of SLBMs, or "boomers," we in the Navy build and deploy.

The collapsed response times needed to utilize effectively enormous amounts of perishable data from satellites and other sources may cause our national planners to look to more SLBMs because of their survivability. They are comparatively less vulnerable than land-based systems. Any move toward greater emphasis on SLBMs will put even more pressure on the continued quieting of submarines. I do not believe we will see anything resembling a "transparent" ocean in the near future, but our abilities to "listen" and "hear" must continue to sharpen if we are to keep our somewhat shrunken but still formidable edge in antisubmarine warfare technology.

Without getting into whether or not reduced nuclear tensions will have the effect of "de-coupling" the United States from Europe, we still ought to assess the future status of the NATO alliance. Will we maintain our leadership role within NATO, or will we see the growth of greater divergent views from the Federal Republic of Germany, France, or the United Kingdom? If the answer to the latter is yes, then what will be our reaction? Do we pick up our marbles and go home? Or do we try harder to fill in the gaps? Will we be persuasive reassuring our allies in the Mediterranean as we move ships to the Persian Gulf, and will NATO help us in "out of area" operations in the future?

And what are our military and economic relationships with the Pacific Rim countries? Do we station more forces in Japan and some forces in places like Australia or Singapore if we end up leaving our bases at Clark Field and Subic Bay in the Philippines? What economic compromises, if any, must be made to accommodate stronger and more complex security relationships with Japan, South Korea, or Malaysia? And let us not forget our long, complicated, and vitally important relationships with the navies of the Latin American nations. As our foreign policy towards Latin America grows more sophisticated, what strategic maritime relationships can or should we develop for the protection of the Western Hemisphere? Each of these geographic areas generates differing relations which, in turn, affect the number and variety of ships deployed, the complexity of our naval involvement, and the employment of those forces.

Now, let's view that situation from the other fellow's perspective. In the near future, how will other nations view us? Will having a part of the United States, in the form of our Navy, nearby be perceived as being an advantage or a detriment? Will other nations, such as Japan, perceive having U.S. forces in and around their waters as a positive in their own foreign policy equations? And what kind of naval forces will they desire or accept? All kinds? Visits only but no facilities? Some minimal facilities such as fuel farms, but no bases? Visits of only non-nuclear ships, as Denmark tried? Or no visits unless we say the ships carry no nuclear weapons at all, as the New Zealanders have said?

As the threat of major superpower conflicts recede, will we likely see conflicts within the Third World arise? Will the United States be a part of those conflicts? Will our foreign interests dictate that we become involved in some of these low-level wars, either because they affect U.S. citizens, U.S. trade, or U.S. allies and friends? In some cases, our involvement will be only logistic support for one or another country or faction. In others, we may see a need to assist with personnel and/or equipment. These changes in the types of threats may indicate the need for new technologies to support unconventional and low-intensity conflicts. I see these "small wars" becoming more numerous and more important to the United States. That, in turn, affects the developments within the Navy. We may need to develop and deploy some number of smaller, low-profile patrol boats capable of delivering a team of unconventional ground forces with highly portable and powerful man-transportable gear. We may also see great utility in conventionally armed cruise missiles, likely of a smaller size and shorter range, deployed on these patrol boats.

And lastly, in our look at the foreign policy milieu of the near future, we need to think about what, if any, foreign basing options we may have. For example, right now we have discussions or negotiations going on with Greece, Spain, Portugal, and the Philippines, among others. If we lose our basing options in any or all of these countries, what effects will that have on our Navy and our foreign policy? We will have to reassess both our own abilities in such an altered world and our allies' and friends' desires for our continued presence? Our foreign policy assessment might include retrenchment to Western Hemisphere waters, or, conversely, a buildup of power projection forces sustainable with fewer overseas bases. If we go this route, our forces will have to be independent of shore facilities for longer periods of time. The proliferation of satellites launched by other nations will undoubtedly include military information-gathering abilities. These in turn will complicate the undetected movement of ships in areas such as the Mediterranean.

I have raised a lot of questions about the foreign policy milieu of the near future. Let me now provide one person's personal views on that future. First, the post–World War II dominance of the free world by the United States is receding. Western Europe is growing rapidly, both economically and militarily. They are fully able to stand tall. I believe a U.S. presence in Western Europe will remain, but likely in an altered state. Some U.S. military presence will be removed, as the NATO allies develop their own military forces at levels they estimate to be adequate and the perceived threat shrinks perceptably. There will be some form of U.S. nuclear weaponry remaining, but the nuclear weapons of the United Kingdom and France will loom increasingly large in protecting the security and stability of Western Europe. After all, collective security is just that—a group of nations cooperating to protect themselves.

Collective security, particularly with submarine-launched nuclear weapons, has to be considered very carefully. As the numbers of, for example, ballistic missile–carrying nuclear propelled submarines are limited or even reduced by treaty, we will likely increase cooperation with the United Kingdom and perhaps even France. The sharing of technologies in this arena is particularly delicate. I predict more combined efforts among these three allies, subject to several difficult hurdles. First, each of us must be sure that the others are not, however unintentionally, conduits for the leakage of extremely sensitive information. Second, we must deal with the technological nationalism natural to each power. Sharing is not easy when one's own industries and jobs are involved.

As European economic strength and cooperation grow, there may well be increased competition for world markets between Western Europe and the United States. While I do not think this economic rivalry will overwhelm us, I do see it as causing periodic re-evaluations of our relationships, especially in the areas of the costs of U.S. military presence in Europe, who pays what percentage of those costs, and what forms those payments may take. As we have had recent disturbances, for example, in our economic relations with an equally prosperous Japan, so I venture we will experience competition with the Western European nations, especially after they eliminate more economic barriers among themselves in 1992. This competition will not diminish our security ties with our allies, but it will test those relationships.

At the same time, we will also be competing on more difficult playing fields with some of the newly industrialized nations of Asia and Latin

America for world markets. Given the American temperment, I suspect that this increased economic competition will cause us to discuss periodically and perhaps loudly for domestic consumption our security arrangements with all of these nations. There will always be Americans who expect a future more akin to their recollections of days past. As we compete and sometimes struggle for world markets, we will go through periods of verbally bashing our friends and allies in order to appeal to domestic audiences. And we are not unique in these reactions, either. Other folks bash us with astonishing regularity.

In the near future, I think we will see a diminution of our overseas basing system. This will most assuredly have an impact on our research and development of naval weapons systems and platforms. If the foreign policy milieu of the near future dictates that we continue a capability for a worldwide presence, and I think that is likely, then we will develop technologies, weapons systems, and platforms which allow these efforts with a reduced basing network. Ships and aircraft with longer ranges, more efficient refuelling-at-sea systems, greater capabilities for weapons loads, and better and more redundant communications systems are just some examples of needed developments in a era of fewer overseas bases. We are becoming a multi-polar world, which will cause a re-evaluation of the ability of our Navy by both the United States and our allies. While nuclear-powered warships are not dependent on refuelling at sea, the majority of our warships and all of our aircraft still depend upon the obtaining and carrying of fossil fuel at sea. Thus we will seek economies in the form of technological breakthroughs allowing greater efficiencies in these areas.

As I said in the beginning, we have a limited number of dollars to apply to the Navy. Of those dollars available for research and development, from which come our technology breakthroughs, we must choose those programs or items we think will be most useful to us for the next thirty to fifty years. The development cycles for major weapons systems run roughly 12 to 15 years. And at any time during those cycles another technological innovation may make obsolete one or more of our partially developed systems.

Additionally, we must decide what portions of those finite R&D dollars we wish to put against technology push or requirements pull. Each has its place, and either could bring forth developments having enormous impact on our maritime strategy. Perhaps another way of saying this is, how much money do we put into basic research and how much into applied research? Further, is this research funded by the Department of Defense, private industry, or educational institutions? As I am sure you recognize, we value academic freedom in our colleges and universities. We need to decide if applied or directed research contravenes this freedom. If research is to be conducted by the government, how do we divide taxpayers' dollars between basic and directed research? These comprise a whole subset of difficult questions which affect the advancement of research and technology. Given limits on dollars and therefore limits on avenues of research, I think our view of the foreign policy milieu will greatly influence the technologies explored in developing the Navy of the future.

Let us look now at some specific weapons systems. We have, on surface ships, guns that can shoot thirteen hundred rounds per minute at anything that penetrates the defensive envelope of that ship. But in the Persian Gulf, do we want to run the risk of blasting a dhow or small fishing boat right out of the water because it accidentally penetrated the defensive envelope? We can develop howitzers with extraordinary ranges, but are they then too heavy and cumbersome for the Marines to move over the beach, and do we need to shoot that far? Within the Navy, the CNO recently announced an all-out push to use electric drive in our future surface ship design. This will certainly change our engineering plants, the amount of space the plants require, the additional power units needed, and the skills the people must have.

Elsewhere in the Navy we are looking at ships without bridges and the greater use of remotely piloted vehicles. We are pursuing the concept of a reduced number of aircraft air frames, with several different "front ends." This type of aircraft technology would allow us to reduce the variety of spare parts, the training needed to maintain the aircraft, and some aspects of pilot training. As the U.S. Navy seeks innovations and economics in weapons development, we also must look at the utility of these designs for our sister services as well as our allies. Joint and combined research dollars permit greater latitude in our technological explorations.

Smart bombs are certainly good from the pilot's perspective, but they may cost so much to develop and stockpile that we can only afford a few of them. Would the reluctance to use expensive ordnance alter our battle tactics or endanger our people? With each platform or weapons system, we must decide if bigger and fewer is better than less complex and more. Each answer has its own set of advantages and detriments. At the risk of commiting heresy, I must ask: Have we made single-seater fighter or attack aircraft so sophisticated that they will shortly out-fly the capabilities of the pilot to handle them? If this is true, we will need to develop dual-seat aircraft, at greater costs in dollars and people. The increased use of computer-generated information in the cockpit may overwhelm a pilot. We must ensure that our technological advances are "user-friendly" for the pilot and for the environment in which he or she operates. And this example applies, of course, to other platforms and weapons systems.

Are there some technologies we do not even want to explore? For example, the international community tried after World War I to outlaw mustard gas because of the horrible consequences of its use. Yet, Iraq now stands accused by the international community of using chemical weapons quite recently. Are we about to face the same sort of situation with the development of lasers for the battlefield? Lasers can be used to blind military personnel, be they ground troops, pilots, or bridge watchstanders. The damage to the eyes can be partial or total. Do we wish to open (or see opened) that particular window of technology? Or should we compromise by saying that lasers are good for aiming and guiding weapons systems such as bombs, missiles, and guns, but cannot be used to disable personnel? If the answer here is yes, then how do we use the detection and communication potential of lasers to enhance our defenses without possibly crippling enemy personnel in the process? Lasers hold enormous promise for augmenting various ordnance and detection systems. They are a key technology which could most assuredly be used as an enhancement to existing systems, but they have an equally significant down side.

On the other hand, other technologies available or almost within our reach fit nicely within our present concepts surrounding the conduct of war. By this I mean that we tend to view war as a defensive or retaliatory necessity, not as an offensive foreign policy tool. We are willing to defend ourselves and our allies, but we do not view the starting of a war as a desirable option. Given this cultural bias, we are unlikely to pursue with any great vigor those technologies clearly viewed as having a "first strike" capability.

Stealth is another superb technology clearly ready to alter the conduct of war. The impact of this low-observable technology will likely be dramatic, especially in aircraft and missiles, and perhaps even ships. On the other hand, this new technology will likely shorten the time between our detection of incoming enemy weapons systems and their destruction. Thus, our defensive capabilities must react ever more quickly. Lasers would be a helpful technological breakthrough here in countering stealth, but will we develop that potentially controversial set of systems? Stealth technology, when it reaches full potential, will certainly require new operational tactics, and perhaps revised battlefield strategies.

Smart weapons, which I mentioned earlier, should be force multipliers, especially for conventional forces. These systems will include self-contained guidance, sensors, and target seekers of astonishing sophistication; and remotely piloted vehicles for air, land, and water use, all coupled with vastly extended ranges. Force-multiplying weapons system allow us to fight better with fewer numbers of people. These weapons will likely be married with improved communications and intelligence gathering. All these may allow us to "see" into the battlefield (ashore or at sea) farther and more clearly than we can now, as we build more sophisticated satellites and earth-based systems. Of all of these emerging technologies, I view those affecting our abilities to gather and process the overwhelming amount of intelligence, as well as to communicate with each other via protected and redundant means, as being the most important. Our capabilities for gathering information bits grow with each new generation of computers. Our ability to assimilate and use those data has not grown so rapidly. We must process more effectively what data we have, and we must get that information to the battlefield in a timely manner. As we have speeded up the weapons of war, so must we now speed up and insure the communciations of war. Without these technologies I think the other breakthroughs will be only partially successful in their impact on the strategies and tactics of the battlefields. I would put significant amounts of those scarce resource dollars into better communications and systems which can more quickly and easily assimilate the vast amounts of information we receive.

We have reviewed the foreign policy milieu; we have recognized some of the near future technology developments affecting maritime warfare and therefore the dynamic maritime strategy. But there are several other factors with which we as citizens must deal—and these are the greatest variables. We must look at the people in the armed forces who are using all these "high-tech" systems, and those in government making the decisions to pursue and purchase such hardware.

The products of our educational system within the United States leave something to be desired. For example, we do not educate enough qualified engineers, scientists, or mathematicians to meet our national needs. We are losing our technological lead in such areas as radar sensors; aerospace propulsion; automated production and manufacturing; light weight, high-strength, and high-temperature materials; and guidance and navigation. Other areas in which we have lost our prior superiority in technology development include conventional warheads and optics.

All these qualitative advantages allowed us in the past to make up for smaller numbers of people and weapons systems. Other nations continue to graduate more hard scientists than the United States while we continue to excel in producing lawyers and MBAs! And the thoughtful analysts of international relations and foreign policy options are scarce at best. Sometimes they are not listened to even when they are available to decision-makers.

These educational considerations affect the Navy in two ways. First, we need scientists who can do the research and develop the technologies this country needs. Second, and equally important, the Navy must have personnel smart enough and educated enough to use and maintain these complex and sophisticated weapons systems. The existing "high-tech" equipments as well as those on the horizon require superior personnel who can read beyond a fifth-grade level and can think beyond the barrel of a gun or the end of the torpedo tube. We have some smart folks in the Navy now, but our schools have to educate for the leading edge of technology—not for the lowest common denominator.

All of this is by way of saying that we, you and I, have hard domestic choices to make in the near future, and that these choices will impact on the development of those technologies available to the Navy in the near future. The impact of technological developments on the future maritime strategy will be enormous. They depend to a great degree, however, on a complex series of factors that involve how we as citizens view the external threats, where in the rest of the world we wish to influence foreign policy, how the other folks view us, and what we are willing to spend in national capital in the form of people, dollars, research and development, and the environment.

None of these decisions is easy. Each has a reaction elsewhere. Each costs us something—none is "free." I cannot predict which technologies will be most useful nor which will fall by the wayside. I have tried to sketch, ever so generally, what the international scene may look like and which areas of technological development hold promise. What I can say is that each of you must become envolved. Each of you must help to make all those hard decisions. Because each of those decisions will affect the development of technology and the future maritime strategy.

8
Technology, Space, and National Security in the 1990s

Horatio W. Turner IV

echnology will have an immense impact on the security dimensions of space during the 1990s. During that period space will truly become a fourth military arena, joining land, sea, and air as a full partner and becoming a battle space in its own right. For purposes of this discussion, the term "battle space" is used to refer to the area in which a military force or a nation may exert violent or deadly influence upon another.

The space systems and space-associated policies, strategies, and tactical doctrine that carry us into the twenty-first century will have a significant impact on land, maritime, and air forces, and will likely foretell the effective balance of military force for deterrence or resolution of armed conflict for many years to come. During the 1990s, the increasing influence of space technology on land, maritime, and air campaigns combined with emerging space opportunities and threats will require us to view space as a distinct region for military activity with the goals of deterrence or successful resolution of conflict.

The notion that space systems are simply alternative means to support terrestrial functions is no longer viable. Decisions that commit nations and military forces to space have already been made by the United States, the Soviet Union, and many other nations. Space options have also been widely selected by the business world, further complicating national security concerns in space.

Technological Imperatives

Technology's application to national security in space is of special importance in the 1990s due to four general factors, which could be termed "space imperatives."

The views expressed herein are solely those of the author and do not necessarily reflect the views of the Department of Defense or of any other agency of the United States government.

Dependence

As a result of steady growth in numbers and performance, our national security space systems—communications, environmental, navigation, early warning, and surveillance—have already become essential elements of U.S. military capability, absolutely necessary to decisionmaking as well as to execution of military operations. About 70 percent of our worldwide military communications are transmitted via space systems. We are placing a high priority on the expanded and more survivable capabilities to be offered by the Defense Satellite Communications System III (DSCS III), Milstar, and UHF Follow-On satellite communications systems for the 1990s. National security communications requirements will continue to increase, much as our commercial satellite communications dependency continues to expand each year.

Technological advances in sea and air transportation have, over the years, expanded our interests and our operating areas to global proportion. As a nation and as military forces we have become dependent upon space observation for weather mapping and prediction. The Defense Meteorological Satellite Program, or DMSP, is essential to worldwide operations on land, at sea, and in the air. This system provides global surveillance of meteorological, oceanographic, and solar-geophysical parameters, with continuous, real-time transmission, as well as storage and retrieval capability.

Similarly, during the 1990s we will come to rely heavily upon the NAVSTAR Global Positioning System (NAVSTAR GPS) for continuous, three-dimensional position information and precise time measurement. These navigation services will be available to all users with no call-up or exchange of data required—a totally passive navigation system with an expected accuracy of one hundred meters for civil and commercial users and sixteen meters for U.S. military users. The NAVSTAR GPS system will include a constellation of twenty-one satellites in three orbital planes, which will provide for continuous support even at or above the poles. Full operational capability should be achieved by late FY 1992.

LANDSAT is a civil land remote sensing system that provides a variety of topographical and environmental perspective information by means of multispectral imagery. Rapid advancements in remote sensing technology and sensor data management now permit the development and transfer of unprecedented quantities of environmental information for immediate application in support of national security requirements. As the civil efforts in this critical space support arena continue, reliance on multispectral imagery for military applications such as terrain, ice, and snow analysis, bathymetry, water analysis, broad area search, and perspective views will become increasingly important.

Other systems provide for detection and rapid warning of ballistic missile launches, for treaty verification, and for a variety of information elements critical to national security analysis and decisionmaking, as well as for direct support of military operations. In fact, the United States has become extremely dependent upon space systems both for obtaining national security information and for the means of rapidly transporting such information. These dependencies will continue to expand.

Opportunity

Progress in a number of space system technologies will in the 1990s allow for the virtual elimination of the horizon as a tactical or strategic barrier to information or force application, in effect making the globe our battle space and the bit stream our most influential projectile. To land, sea, and air lines of communication we have added space lines of communication. Assured use of the space lines of communication, and the ability to deny them to others, are and will be important elements of national security.

If we choose to do so, we possess the technology today to build and deploy a space-based radar system that could watch and report sea, air, and eventually even ground operations all over the earth, regardless of weather, time of day, or national borders. The Soviets have Radar Ocean Reconnaissance Satellites, or RORSATs, operating today and assisting them in tracking U.S. naval forces. We could also build and deploy an infrared, multispectral imagery or other type system for the same purpose, and could use these different technologies together or separately to cross-reference and provide multiple-source confirmation of activities wherever we choose.

Space-based tactical sensor systems such as these could allow a tactical commander to see without being seen, while navigating precisely and receiving continuous information of every sort via satellite downlink. It is possible that late 1990s technology could provide the total tactical picture in a region not only to the on-scene-commander, but also to every command echelon above, all the way to the JCS, the Secretary of Defense, and even to the White House, in near real time, via satellite crosslinks and downlinks. The ability to observe large areas, using a variety of sensors to rapidly process, collate, and transport information, is ours if we choose it, through use of the fourth arena, space.

ASAT Threat

Our dedicated competitor and adversary in space, the Soviet Union, has already challenged us by seizing the initiative in space denial. The Soviets have thereby permanently expanded the battle space, and temporarily flanked the United States and the free world by holding at risk some of our essential space services while we possess no means to threaten theirs. Furthermore, the Soviet antisatellite (ASAT) capability includes a family of systems, the mix of which underscores their policy and provides insight into their intentions for the future.

First, they have a kinetic-kill ASAT interceptor system, which uses a radar sensor and a pellet-type warhead and could be targeted against all current, low-altitude satellites. It is said to have the capability to reach targets as high as five thousand kilometers, and was generally successful in actual tests several years ago. Its SL-11 booster is regularly exercised, as this booster is also used to launch other payloads.

Second, the GALOSH ABM system deployed around Moscow certainly has capability against some low earth-orbit satellites, and third, there is very likely ASAT capability resident in existing lasers at the Sary Shagan Missile Test Center. Although probably limited in range and effect, these lasers and perhaps others in development combine with existing electronic warfare capabilities to suggest a well-rounded first generation family of space denial options for the Soviet Union.

These existing ASAT capabilities serve to underscore Soviet technology and strategy decisions in keeping with their stated policy on space. The Soviet dictionary of basic military terms states that "The main purpose of anti-space defense is to destroy space systems used by the enemy. . . . The principal means of anti-space defenses are special spacecraft and vehicles. . . ." In a speech at Tyuratam in February 1988, General Secretary Gorbachev was quoted as saying: "We do not intend to relax our efforts and lose our vanguard position in the conquest of space." It is reasonable to assume that the Soviet Union will continue to pursue ASAT technologies in the 1990s as a matter of national priority.

Space Weapons Threat

We must accept and plan against the very real possibility of hostile space-based weapons being introduced in the 1990s. Such weapons could be developed and deployed for application against either space or terrestrial/atmospheric targets, and could vary from jammers to directed energy, and from simple pellet projectiles to nuclear weapons. They could be directed and fired by men in space, on board orbiting stations such as MIR, or from small, limited endurance platforms such as the Soviet Space Plane. They could be unmanned, remotely operated systems, launched and long-lived as an overt weapons platform, and could be operated covertly with another apparent (cover) mission, or perhaps even deployed from larger platforms on orbit as space mines.

Since the 1960s the Soviets have been exploring particle beam weapons for space; they spend the equivalent of at least $1 billion U.S. annually in laser weapons research; they may be able to deploy a short-ranged kinetic energy weapon into space during the 1990s. Furthermore, they have designed, built, deployed, and operated small reactor-generator systems in spacecraft, so it is reasonable to assume that they are well along in developing the kinds of power supplies needed for directed-energy weapons in space. Space-to-space directed-energy weapons would not have to contend with difficult atmospheric effects. The possibilities are many, although restricted by technology and resources. But the potential challenges to U.S. national security policy, strategy, technology, and tactical doctrine are significant.

Technology, Policy, and Strategy

Given the technology factors of dependence, opportunity, ASAT threat, and space weapons threat, it seems clear that space emerges as a highly significant dimension of national security for the last decade of this century and indeed for the forseeable future. Rapid advances in many areas require that planners look well ahead as we continually review and update our policies and strategies in light of what technology offers both ourselves and our adversaries in the arena of space. Conversely, we must ensure that we are acting to execute such policies and strategies as we select and apply technologies, and very importantly, as we update our tactics and doctrine and in fact make significant changes in the way we think and operate in all four military arenas: land, sea, air, and space.

In recent years the United States has adhered to a policy of deterrence, maintaining a force able to counter our primary adversary at any level of conflict, while able also to appropriately support and assist allied and friendly nations under a variety of circumstances. These forces have also been used to demonstrably underscore U.S. policies with regard to legal principles such as freedom of navigation and international versus territorial waters and airspace.

Based on a broad range of environmental and geographic factors, the United States has in its recent military strategy generally selected and organized its military forces with emphasis on: high technology, mobility, survivability, and potential for deep or decisive strikes in a forward strategy rather than on massing and attrition on a central front.

Whether our national security policy in the 1990s leans toward mutual assured destruction or assured survival, and whether or not sophisticated ballistic missile defense—specific technologies are successfully deployed in space, it is almost certain that the United States will strive to maintain a viable counterforce, with emphasis on technological advantage for a flexible forward strategy. Space technologies of the 1990s must be pursued as applications of this general strategy. Technology decisions should therefore be made or evaluated in terms of how they fulfill or fall short of these principles. Furthermore, the implications of real and possible space technologies should be examined in terms of how the technologies may influence tactical doctrine.

Where survivability is concerned, our current space systems fall short of our strategy. A review of our communications, navigation, and meteorological satellite planning and programming for the next decade indicates that we acknowledge our dependence upon these space services for support to land, maritime, and air forces, at least for peacetime, crisis, and regional conflict. In the face of the Soviet ASAT threat, we must closely review our ability to sustain critical capabilities should our space systems come under attack. Since U.S. satellite performance has generally exceeded our expectations, it could be argued that maintaining spares of complex, high-performance satellites is an expensive and unnecessary luxury. However, lack of spares for wartime emergencies could have a serious impact on our combat capability and therefore our deterrent influence.

Similarly, where technological advantage is concerned, it is time to press forward. In the area of surveillance, there are no global, wide area, continuous surveillance space systems today dedicated to tactical forces—those land, maritime, and air elements daily fulfilling our forward strategy and facing the superior numbers of adversary forces that constitute the "massing and attrition" orientation of the Soviet Union. Whether defending North America against a transpolar bomber attack, poising to engage incoming Soviet naval air forces in the Greenland-Iceland-Norway gap, or seeking to counter tactical air forces approaching the Central Front from Eastern Europe, U.S. forces, whether on land, at sea, or in the air, by simple arithmetic, require the capability to "shoot the archer, not the arrows." Whether the "archer" is the Soviet Union, and the "arrows" their superior numbers, or the "archer" is a cruise missile carrier and the "arrows" missiles, we require the technological multiplier for success.

These technological multipliers are available. Tactically oriented and responsive surveillance satellite systems, whatever their sensor type or mix, offer the opportunity for standoff detection, identification, targeting, and battle damage assessment. They open the door to standoff weapons for combat engagement. Continuous, all-weather tactical surveillance from space fits well with the principles of technological advantage, mobility, survivability, and a flexible forward strategy.

Standoff surveillance on its own provides local tactical advantage and favors theater and global strategic advantage as well. Long-range standoff weapons and standoff surveillance and targeting together serve to expand your battle space while your adversary's stays the same, translating to deterrence, or victory. The decision to build and dedicate such capable surveillance satellites for direct support to operating forces has not yet been made, but hopefully the most promising technologies and funding availability will permit deployment during the 1990s. The subject of such support is receiving a great deal of attention, but new types of systems will always contend with the tendency to invest in improvement-in-kind rather than improvement-in-concept.

Assuming we take advantage of available tactical surveillance opportunities, the planned U.S. application of technology in space seems to provide for significantly enhanced support to land, maritime, and air forces during the 1990s. That support, however, must still today be qualified as "for peacetime, crisis, and regional conflict," subject to the decisions of our adversary, not ourselves. For our part, the comparable or counterforce is missing in space; thus, there exists a U.S.-Soviet imbalance for deterrence or conflict resolution.

In spite of our significant national security dependence upon space systems, the United States cannot today assure space systems support during all levels of conflict. Our low-earth-orbit satellites are believed to be vulnerable to a variety of Soviet antisatellite options, including hard kill. Our higher altitude systems are probably safe today, although Soviet advances in ASAT systems may threaten them in the 1990s. Our two primary national-DOD launch sites are clearly vulnerable, located close to international waters and, for that matter, adjacent to open highways. One is near a major earthquake fault line, the other in an area threatened annually by severe tropical storms and subject to an exceptionally high incidence of lightning strikes. Currently, U.S. payloads are not easily adaptable to more than one type booster, the numbers of pads and booster/payload buildup and integration facilities are few, and launch preparation times are extensive. Satellite control facilities are likewise few and vulnerable.

Given the importance of space-to-land, maritime, and air force strategies and tactics, and space's own significance as a fourth arena for military operations, our ability to apply counterforce, to protect essential space systems and to assure access to space in the 1990s should become matters of high national priority. During the past twenty years, space systems have steadily increased their influence on national security. Today they are critical to the overall success of our efforts.

Protection of U.S. space capabilities is a complex and challenging task, of which a U.S. ASAT is only one piece. An important part of protection is surveillance, the ability to detect, identify, track, and assess man-made objects, efforts, and intentions in space. Expanding Soviet ASAT capability and the possible introduction of Soviet space-based weapons will determine that this surveillance cannot be accomplished solely from terrestrial sites, but will also require space-based sensors and crosslinks for a full and continuous assessment of hostile activity in space.

Threat-warning sensors may be required on many payloads, and passive as well as active defense capabilities may also be required to protect individual spacecraft. If, for example, destructive electromagnetic weapons are developed and deployed, we may require autonomous protection adjuncts which incorporate onboard sensing, decisionmaking, and countermeasure actions with no man-in-the-loop. If space-based weapons are developed and deployed for purposes of applying force against land, maritime, and air targets, a totally new range of concerns and counterforce requirements will be unleashed. This is unlikely for the 1990s, but is by no means impossible.

For balance in U.S.-Soviet force and capability, a great deal of attention is being paid to development of a U.S. ASAT capability. National and Department of Defense policies dictate achievement of an ASAT capability. But there are a number of technology questions to be answered and choices to be made if we are to field a capable and affordable ASAT system for the 1990s.

To assure our future access to space, a great deal of effort is also being made with respect to future launch and satellite control systems. U.S. Space Command in particular is working hard to underscore the need for approaches that lead to responsive, survivable, combat-adaptive means for launch and control of essential space capabilities. Tradeoffs will have to be made between on-orbit sparing and rapid, survivable launch of ready-stored terrestrial spares for surge, replacement, and reconstitution. If safety and other considerations limit large boosters to current, vulnerable coastal locations, then smaller boosters and comparably down-sized payloads may be required for mobile or at least distributive basing to achieve survivable access to space. In addition to this flexible, survivable approach to launch, a concept for distributive satellite control capability is currently being developed and has widespread support.

Let us assume that the Department of Defense proceeds with development and deployment of its planned communications, navigation, and environmental/weather space systems. And let us assume also that, consistent with our high technology, mobility, survivability, flexible forward strategy and counterforce orientation, we commit to building an ASAT force mix and dedicated tactical surveillance space systems, and that during the same time we develop a combination of launch, satellite-control, and payload-sparing assurances and protective capabilities. How might our 1990s national security space forces affect our tactical doctrine for land, maritime, and air forces? How might we then measure ourselves against the Soviet Union in this expanded battle space?

Technology and Tactical Doctrine

Space technology has major implications for 1990s tactical doctrine in terms of both tactics and rules of engagement, but more importantly, as it relates to the root concepts of military command and responsibility. Tactical surveillance systems, combined with precise, passive navigation and highly directional, high data rate, encrypted communications would tend to support totally covert maneuvering by land, maritime, and air forces. Defensive perimeters represented by platforms such as E-3 AWACS, E-2 Hawkeye, and long-range fighters need not be sustained in great numbers for long periods, but held ready for combat engagement. Adversary movement or redistribution of assets would be known, and hostile forces could be tracked from origin and met at the time and place of advantage without warning to those adversary forces.

Ordnance delivery, by land, sea, or air platforms, can support ground forces with deadly accuracy through precision navigation, positioning, and target plotting data provided by the survivable space-based Global Positioning System. And this same precision system will continue to support friendly forces through reorganization and recovery as search and rescue operations are expedited and the battle area is secured.

Long-range weapons could be launched at significant standoff ranges, alerting their targets only in a terminal guidance phase, if such weapons incorporated a capability for using space-derived targeting and identification information. This might suggest a change, for example, in visual identification criteria for engaging hostile forces to allow for the deeper, more decisive strikes, and for the mobile, survivable, flexible threat to the adversary's flanks. The pressure point is not, after all, where the archer stands, but where he can place his arrow. At what range, then, would a force or unit be considered a threat, and what would constitute a hostile or threatening act? These are difficult questions for our national security leadership.

Similarly, by expanding the tactical battle space through non-organic information support, the technology of 1990s space systems also offers full awareness of the tactical situation to many echelons of command. If the theater commander and his battle staff have all the on-scene commander's information, and the total theater picture as well, who then makes which combat decisions? Who in fact is responsible and accountable for success or failure? Who "owns" the local battle space? For the more mobile and independent forces and units, the comfort of a complete tactical picture could be accompanied by the hindrance of an inability to act independently. Elimination of the horizon will modify the traditional concepts of command and battle space responsibility.

The Challenge

Our measure of confidence and capability vis-à-vis the Soviet Union in the 1990s is potentially dependent upon our relative advantage or disadvantage in exploiting space technology opportunities. If the United States makes a commitment to space superiority in tactical surveillance and targeting and in ASAT capability, and develops assured capability to launch, control, and protect critical national security space capabilities, we will enter the next century with technological advantages that apply to all four military arenas: land, sea, air, and space.

If our challenge were simply to prepare a menu of what technology can provide, and then to select the best, whether fiscally constrained or unconstrained, our task would be relatively simple, and we could concentrate national security space discussions on personal preferences in technology and application. However, developing and deploying space technology is the easy part, something our nation already does well. The greatest national security challenge for the 1990s lies in adjusting the way we conduct the business of national security in the additional battle area of space. Our policy and strategy must thoroughly encompass the space flank. Where treaties and agreements are considered, they must consider all the technology available, as well as the requirements for verification of agreements. Our tactical doctrine will require a thorough appreciation for space technology application, but more importantly, it will demand that individual military personnel come to understand and have confidence in space systems. Both understanding and confidence will have to be earned.

Civil and commercial systems will have to be examined in terms of their suitability to national security purposes in crisis or conflict. Compatibility of such systems is important, as is the question of potentially aiding an adversary with significant security information. This is particularly challenging in that many of these commercial systems will be owned and operated by multinational corporations based in other nations. Some of the commercial imagery and navigation systems may prove more capable and available than we might wish, and will perhaps require adjustments in many areas of policy.

In summary, there is much work to be done in every area of policy, strategy, and tactical doctrine as we face the significant impacts of advancing space technology in the 1990s. It would be difficult enough to stay abreast of technological advances, but we can accept no less than for policy and strategy to lead technology, and in fact to select and drive space technology as a subset of national security planning.

9

The Geostrategy of Space: The View from Space Command

John L. Piotrowski

As we approach the 1990s, we are faced with a growing concern over the deficit and the resulting constraints placed on military expenditures. We are fully embracing arms control on many levels, and we are clearly challenged by a wide variety of difficult and evolving issues. Because it is absolutely essential that national security policy and U.S. military capabilities arc developed based on a realistic appraisal of the actual threat, I shall provide a brief summary of Soviet capabilities in space. After that foundation has been laid, I shall address a few issues that are relevant to policy considerations in the decade ahead.

Thirty-one years ago, the Western world was stunned by the early-morning launch of the world's first satellite—the Soviet *Sputnik*. Prior to the launch of the *Sputnik*, few Western analysts had questioned U.S. technological superiority over the Soviet Union. That launch jarred our complacency, and began the technological evolution that established U.S. superiority in space.

But I would submit that the Soviet Union—despite what we might call technological deficiencies—has developed a superior *operational* strength in space—a strength built on three pivotal characteristics: force structure, readiness, and sustainability.

The Soviet force structure is, from a military perspective, operationally impressive. It includes eight launch vehicles, with a ninth—the SL-X-17—in development. One of their boosters alone, the SL-04, has launched more times than the total number of successful U.S. space launches, and has demonstrated a very high degree of reliability. Their on-orbit assets—over 150 satellites with predominantly military missions—are clearly ready to support their terrestrial forces. Furthermore, these satellite constellations are sustainable. During the Falklands War, for example, they launched twenty-eight times in sixty-nine days—a capability only dreamed of in this country.

The views expressed herein are solely those of the author and do not necessarily reflect the views of the Department of Defense or of any other agency of the United States government.

Many argue that statistical comparisons are not the entire story—that there *are* other considerations—quality, for instance. I agree—when all things are considered, the United States is clearly the peacetime leader in space. But in assigning the U.S. space command missions, the President didn't charge me to coordinate peacetime space requirements—my responsibility is meeting wartime military requirements. I'm not convinced that peacetime leadership necessarily equates to assured mission capability in wartime. The existing U.S. space force structure might not serve the combat needs to the corps, the battle group, or the air wing commander should deterrence fail. In wartime, these commanders would face serious threats from Soviet space systems.

There are two Soviet capabilities that I see as most worrisome and threatening to U.S. military forces. The first of these is their tactical targeting spacecraft—the radar ocean-reconnaissance satellites. These satellites provide real-time targeting data directly to selected deployed forces. Utilizing this space-derived targeting data, Soviet antiship weapons could accurately engage U.S. forces at sea. The second threatening Soviet capability is their antisatellite system—threatening because it could be used to deny our freedom to use space.

The Soviets possess the world's only operational antisatellite system. Their co-orbital antisatellite system is capable of attacking all U.S. and allied low-earth-orbiting satellites, and they have other antisatellite options that can essentially destroy or degrade the majority of the U.S. order of battle. Policymakers and strategists who discount Soviet antisatellite capabilities as crude or nonthreatening have missed the mark. Policy and strategy issues for the next decade must be founded on the knowledge that the Soviets have militarized space, that they have developed doctrine based on the control of space, and that they have acquired the means to achieve that doctrine.

The question, then, is what is to be the U.S. response? How should U.S. space policy and strategy evolve to meet this threat? Should we develop an antisatellite capability? Will the focus of U.S. space activities shift to the operational needs of the field commanders? I will focus briefly on space control and support to the commanders-in-chief of our warfighting commands, but first, I will discuss space control.

Today, U.S. space control posture is, in many respects, similar to our air power posture early in this century. Powered flight was in the development stages, and strategies for employing this infant capability to achieve national objectives had not yet been formulated. At the beginning of World War I, air power was a "gentleman's" activity. Reconnaissance aircraft passed each other en route to reconnoiter the ground activities of the opposing side. The "gentleman pilots" waved greetings to each other as they passed. But, when opposing commanders realized the reconnaissance flights were impacting the outcome of the ground campaigns, the gentleman phase of air power ended, and—well—you know the evolution of air power that followed.

Today space is in the "gentleman phase"—we wave in passing. But like the commanders in World War I, the Soviets long ago realized that the outcome of any future land, sea, or air battle will greatly depend on space. Regrettably, that awareness is just beginning to permeate U.S. military consciousness.

Today, the United States depends on Soviet goodwill—their gentlemanly nature if you will—for our use of space in a conflict. By that I mean that U.S. satellites will only be available in crisis or war *if the* Soviets elect not to employ their several antisatellite capabilities. I believe the Soviets are incapable of such strategic philanthropy. Their doctrine says they will employ antisatellites against opposing satellites, and their systems give them the capability.

Our reliance on space for the functions of communications, navigation, and surveillance creates an incentive for Soviet antisatellite employment. Yet we lack the capability to defend our spacecraft, to replace lost spacecraft, or to remove the advantage an opposing commander would obtain from his spacecraft. In short, the existing U.S. space force structure lacks a space control capability.

Space control is not space supremacy. We don't have to have "space supremacy" to have significant, useful military space capabilities. In my judgment, our strategy for the future need not strive for absolute control of space. Within the bounds of political, technical, and fiscal constraints, that is probably not an achievable strategy, nor is it necesary. But the national command authorities and the theater commanders in chief (CINCs) require support from space, and we must develop strategies and capabilities to ensure continued access to our space lines of commmunications throughout all levels of conflict.

I would suggest a strategy based on offense and defense. Perhaps a passive defense for some satellites—those in geosynchronous orbit—an active defense for others—those threatened by the Soviet co-orbital and direct assent antisatellite systems—and a robust U.S. antisatellite capability. We require a balanced force in space just as we do on the earth.

A fully tested U.S. antisatellite capability will strengthen our deterrent posture by placing an identifiable penalty on Soviet aggression. As with most weapons, knowing a response in kind is possible restrains use. If deterrence fails, an antisatellite capability would give us the wherewithal to interdict Soviet space systems. Some degree of space control is necessary if we are to assure the space support required by the national command authorities and the battle area commanders in time of conflict. Providing this support is also a critical mission of U.S. space command.

The impact of existing and planned space systems on tactical operations is significant. We are fielding precise navigation (GPS) and survivable communications (DSCS) satellites to improve space support to terrestrial military forces. In addition, I believe we *should* field a space-based surveillance system—perhaps a radar/infrared combination—that can detect and track enemy forces from point of origin in all weather conditions. These new systems will certainly improve tactical decisionmaking. And, in the case of a space-based surveillance system, I believe we will find it necesary to revaluate the ground rules used in our dealings with other nations—allies and adversaries alike. A space-based radar will clearly also offer advantages for our allies. How will they participate?

With regard to adversaries, the idea of "plausible denial" will no longer be possible. Preparation and initiation of an attack by one country on another could be observed from space—essentially making the world a fishbowl. To my way of thinking, such a capability is a powerful deterrent. Utilizing the capabilities of a space-based radar involve key policy discussions in the decade ahead. And there are other such issues.

Consider, for example, the increasing number of satellites competing for a finite number of geostationary locations: Will it be necessary to establish boundaries in space? How will we interact with the growing number of our allies who are also competing for those locations? Consider the need for testing—in space—those components necessary for a ballistic missile defense: Is a test range in space necessary? What kind of rules of engagement will we develop if a ballistic missile defense system is deployed? These and other questions will have to be addressed if we are to develop a sound space policy.

In summary, U.S. military forces are, without question, linked to space. Space cannot be separated from our national security. There are many challenges, but there is no doubt that space power *will* become as critical to future military operations as air or sea power is today. It is imperative, therefore, that we have the foresight to develop appropriate doctrine and capabilities so that the United States can function effectively in this vital and rapidly emerging military arena.

10

Offense-Defense in Soviet Strategic Force Planning

G. Paul Holman, Jr.

P erhaps the best way to evaluate Soviet planning for the future of their strategic offensive and defensive forces is to consider four diverse bodies of evidence: Soviet military doctrine, the actual weapon systems that give substance to that doctrine, the military "threat" posed by other countries, and Soviet behavior in a wide range of arms control and disarmament negotiations, both before and after the many innovations of Mikhail Gorbachev. It is my thesis that neither U.S. technological advances, nor Soviet economic reverses, nor improving relations with the West have terminated the old Soviet quest for strategic superiority. Demonstration of this thesis will proceed along three lines: first, a historical summary of force planning in the Soviet Union, stressing Moscow's determination to achieve a proper balance between the strategic offensive and defensive forces; second, a brief review of our past intelligence failures and erroneous estimates concerning the Soviet strategic forces; and third, a "catalogue of expectations" by which we may weigh current Soviet assurances of goodwill against the reality of their offensive and defensive forces.

The Soviet Approach to Force Planning

In the West, the theoretical basis of force planning has not been extensively treated as a serious discipline. This is a curious omission, since most senior officers rarely go to war, have long since delegated troop training to their juniors, and thus, spend their most influential years primarily involved in the planning and acquisition of future forces.[1]

The Soviet approach is very different. Perhaps because of the great power exercised by their General Staff and the many years spent by their senior officers at institutions of higher military education, they go to the

The views expressed herein are solely those of the author and do not necessarily reflect the views of the Department of Defense or of any other agency of the United States government.

opposite extreme. Soviet force planners possess a vast, intensely theoretical, and very sophisticated apparatus for the application of all scientific research and scholarly inquiry to military needs.

This approach does not lack for its own unique problems. Its very size and secrecy assure some waste, sloth, bungling, and bureaucratic fratricide. But when Soviet force planners are compared to their civilian counterparts, they constitute a model of relative sobriety, honesty, and efficiency. Although slow to change internal organization and personnel, they have shown great foresight and consistency in planning both sides of the strategic dialectic between offensive and defensive forces.

The Strategic Nuclear Weapons

The Soviet nuclear weapons program started several years earlier than most Westerners would assume. According to the General Staff journal *Voyennaya mysl'*, Stalin's scientists began the development of Soviet nuclear weapons somewhat before our Manhattan project began. Indeed, it was in the 1930s that academicians A.F. Ioffe, I.V. Kurchatov, L.D. Landau, and "other outstanding Soviet scientists had outlined the main directions in the resolution of the nuclear problem."[2]

Although temporarily distracted by the German invasion in June 1941, nuclear scientists were at work again by the end of 1942. After Hiroshima and Nagasaki, the Central Committee declared that overcoming the American monopoly in nuclear weapons in the shortest period of time was "the primary state task."[3] Knowing what we do of Soviet decisionmaking during Stalin's last decade, there should be little doubt that Soviet planners took that priority seriously. They had more than a little help from the NKVD (the predecessor of today's KGB), Klaus Fuchs, Julius Rosenberg, and the other "atomic spies." Even so, detonating their first nuclear weapon only four years after the United States, especially in view of the astronomical losses suffered by the Soviet industrial base and population over the course of the war, must stand as a major triumph for Soviet offensive force planners.

The Strategic Nuclear Offensive Forces

The first Soviet strategic delivery platforms were, of course, their bombers. As far back as the 1920s, Moscow possessed a large fleet of four-engined attack planes, but the best Soviet aerial strategists died in Stalin's purges. Fairly impressive bombers were produced again during World War II, but Stalin never granted them a mission of strategic bombardment comparable to the extremely ambitious theories germinating in the United States and the United Kingdom.

Strikingly little has changed for the Soviet strategic bomber force over the decades. It has modernized slowly, with dogged persistence, but without the doctrinal importance, high levels of readiness, or numbers of weapons assigned to the U.S. Air Force. Most observers would attribute this lesser status to Soviet history and to Soviet military doctrine, but one may also speculate about interservice tensions and rivalries. The Ground Forces have historically dominated the Soviet General Staff, and the "green suiters" have intriguingly fragmented the power base of their "blue suited" comrades. (For example, the Soviet Air Forces are an entirely separate organization from the Troops of Air Defense, although they wear similar uniforms and fly some of the same aircraft.)

As for the Soviet Navy, Muscovite force planners have given it greater prominence than the Air Forces in strategic offensive missions. Thanks to gradual improvements in the technological quality of the Soviet submarine-launched ballistic missile (SLBM) force, the Navy has been increasingly able to provide a large, secure nuclear reserve. Even so, it ranks last among the services in Soviet protocol and stands far behind the U.S. Navy in its overall contribution to national strategic capabilities.

The Soviet intercontinental ballistic missile (ICBM) force differs sharply from its U.S. equivalent. Its officers trace their lineage to army engineers, artillerists, and combined arms commanders rather than to aviators. And unlike the ICBM portion of our Strategic Air Command, it constitutes an entirely separate and distinct branch of service, the so-called Strategic Rocket Forces. (A better translation would be the Missile Forces of Strategic Designation.)

Created secretly by Khrushchev in 1958, the Strategic Rocket Forces (SRF) have aroused endless controversies among Western analysts. Always punctilious about domestic protocol, Soviet sources officially describe the SRF as the youngest but still the most prestigious branch of service. This honor is supposedly justified by the SRF's combat mission, which would determine the outcome of a putative nuclear world war.

That mission has been variously described by various sources, but never more authoritatively or ambitiously than in Marshal Sokolovsky's *Military Strategy:*

> *Protection of the rear area of the country and groups of armed forces from enemy nuclear attacks* has the aim of preserving the vital functions of the government, of assuring the uninterrupted functioning of the national economy and transportation, and preserving the combat readiness of the armed forces. These aims are achieved mainly by annihilation of the enemy's means of nuclear attack in the regions in which they are based.[4]

Such statements had great importance for Soviet force planners. First printed in 1962, but republished with notable changes in 1963 and 1968, Sokolovsky's book stands as perhaps the most influential and surely the most widely debated book ever written by any member of the Soviet Armed Forces. He enunciated a damage-limiting strategy based upon counterforce strikes, which lay heavy stress upon the need for preemptive attack if war should seem imminent (or at least for quickly regaining the nuclear initiative if the enemy should strike first).

The Strategic Defensive Forces

Sokolovsky's approach to offensive force planning took full account of the need for careful integration with the defensive forces. He stressed that some portion of the enemy bomber force and virtually all of its patrolling SSBNs would survive even a highly successful, counterforce attack against the ICBM fields and bomber bases.

> Therefore, it is necessary to have the necessary forces and means for destroying great masses of enemy aircraft and rockets in the air in order that there be no nuclear attacks against important objectives within the whole territory of the country. This can be done by military operations for protecting the country from attack by enemy aircraft and missles.[5]

Sokolovsky's analysis extended well beyond the capabilities of the 1980s. Not only did he incorporate both antimissile and antisatellite weapons into his strategy, he contended that war in space—high-energy lasers and beam weapons—would all play a role in future combat.

Such optimistic assessments of Soviet capabilities to defend the homeland were entirely consistent with other military writings. General Colonel Lomov expressed the standard Soviet view in 1973, when he remarked that active defense of the country had acquired "state-strategic significance."[6]

Soviet force planners left no doubt that their concept of strategic defense comprised both active (antimissile as well as anti-aircraft) and passive elements. According to Marshal of the Soviet Union Grechko, massive preparations were necessary to protect the leadership of the Communist party, government, population, and industrial base. Civil defense had thus emerged "as a factor of strategic significance in ensuring the vital activities of the state."[7]

Such passages rested upon two clear postulates: that military victory was a meaningful goal for force planners, even in the nuclear era, and that winning such a conflict would require the pre-war achievement of strategic superiority over any potential enemies. These objectives were stated quite strongly throughout the 1960s and early 1970s. All three editions of Sokolovsky's authoritative work declared that "superiority" over the enemy in the qualitative and quantitative measures of modern military power would constitute the "material prerequisites of victory."[8]

American Intelligence Looks at the Threat

After the passage of more than two decades, how much importance can Sokolovsky's book still have? Western observers disagree strongly over this question. Some authorities stress the differences between Soviet and U.S. global objectives. Citing Sokolovsky as their primary evidence, such "hard-liners" see the strategic forces deployed over the 1970s and 1980s as proof of Soviet ambitions for global domination. Other experts detect no great difference between the military objectives of the two superpowers. These "soft-liners" thus dismiss Sokolovsky as unimportant, out-of-date, and unrepresentative of Moscow's "real" desire for nothing more than strategic parity.

Ideology and the National Intelligence Estimates

When it first appeared in 1962, Sokolovsky's book received scant attention from the West. Only a handful of Soviet specialists saw its importance until over a decade had passed. Ironically, at the same time the intelligence community began to analyze Soviet military doctrine more seriously than ever before, the Soviets gradually changed what they were willing to say in public.

After the signing of SALT I in 1972, Soviet spokesmen wrote less and less about victory in nuclear war and strategic superiority. Although they roundly condemned Western concepts of "deterrence" and "mutual assured destruction," they proclaimed parity as their official goal and began referring to nuclear war as unwinnable. Some Westerners took these changes seriously, while others denounced them as deception or "disinformation."[9]

Why do such controversies persist? Never in history has another democratic country devoted such resources to studying its rivals, and our collectors produce astronomical amounts of information. Political bias is rarely a problem in their work, since the sheer volume of their reporting tends to submerge their separate attitudes. We are less fortunate at the pinnacle of the intelligence process, where the millions of raw reports are distilled into thousands of analytical studies and then into a tiny handful of carefully crafted predictions about future threats to U.S. national interests. At each step away from the collectors and toward the decision makers, the biases grow more troublesome.

This problem is most acute (and most newsworthy, all too often) at the very pinnacle of the intelligence process—the National Intelligence Estimates (NIEs). They address all the crises of international relations, ranging from Nicaragua to Iran and terrorism. But, as one scholar has observed, Soviet power has loomed over the entire period as "the prime intelligence subject." Thus the NIEs on Soviet strategic nuclear activities "have been, perhaps, the most vital estimates produced by the intelligence community."[10]

The NIEs provide the president and other key leaders with the best judgments of our most sophisticated observers, who base their findings on the crown jewels of intelligence collection. In theory, the estimators overcome any extremist, alarmist, or parochial positions by dispassionate scrutiny of all available evidence.

The reality is somewhat different. A number of scholarly studies over the past few years have shown that polarized attitudes toward the Soviet Union are deeply rooted in the intelligence community. At the lowest individual level, the analysts array themselves on the familiar spectrum from hawk to dove. At the highest institutional level, each agency tends to espouse positions that best support its missions, budget, and previously declared views.

When newly minted Ph.D.s join the intelligence community, they usually know more about the Soviet government than their own. They are often shocked to discover the ideological bitterness dividing their colleagues. Like their predecessors over the decades of NIEs concerning the Soviet strategic forces, they are likely to witness an intractable rivalry between State Department and the Air Force, with CIA usually supporting State, and the other agencies ranged somewhere in between.

On many topics, this contest causes conceptual gridlock. The estimators shelter themselves in the safety of consensus, and no agency takes an extreme position. At their worst, such noncontroversial estimates may fail to warn the decision maker of emerging military or political disasters. Bureaucratic politics and pap drown the single, dissenting voice who might just happen to be right. Many scholarly assessments have cited Operation Barbarossa, Pearl Harbor, the Yom Kippur War, and the fall of the Shah as examples of such failures in estimative intelligence.

In the opposite case, one or two agencies take an extreme position, dominate the estimative process, and predict an event which obstinately refuses to happen. The Bomber Gap and the Missile Gap stand as the best known examples of such errors.[11]

The "B Team" Affair

During the early 1970s the NIEs aroused severe criticism from many readers. Some condemned them for being too vague, unhelpful, and even

"Talmudic." Others accused them of underestimating the Soviet quest for strategic superiority. The result of all these attacks was surely the best publicized—and perhaps the most innovative—NIE ever attempted on the Soviet strategic forces: the famous "B Team" report of 1976.[12]

It was an experimental effort in "competitive analysis" between two teams of experts. The so-called "A Team" consisted of professional intelligence officers—midlevel civil servants, lieutenant colonels, and commanders from CIA, DIA, State Department, and the military services. Their rivals on the "B Team" included ambassadors, generals, and senior professors at the finest U.S. institutions of higher learning.

According to scholarly accounts of this affair, the final report of the B Team painted a more hawkish view of Soviet intentions and capabilities than did the A Team. The outsiders produced a "scathing critique of U.S. intelligence failure to predict the scope of Soviet developments."[13]

Several members of the B Team then published their own assessments of Soviet strategy in unclassified media.[14] They relied heavily upon Sokolovsky, describing the Soviet goal as a war-fighting, war-winning capability for their strategic offensive and defensive forces. From their perspective, Moscow saw arms control as little more than a handy device to speed the achievement of strategic superiority.

During their final debate, members of the B Team consistently declared their victory over the insiders, but that success may have had less to do with their professional credentials or special insights than with their ideological consistency. The members of the B Team all espoused a hard-line view of the Soviet Union and could thus formulate a consistent, coherent essay from the conservative perspective. The A Team, by contrast, consisted of representatives from both hard-line and soft-line agencies. By all the dreary laws of committee and consensus, they were doomed to produce an unconvincing piece of bureaucratic pabulum.

Implications for the Future

A shrewd consumer of the NIEs would do well to compare the record of the ideological factions within the intelligence community. The political right tends toward "worst case" analysis, in which Soviet capabilities may be maximized and their intentions obscured or even ignored. Such reasoning may be blamed for those two great clichés of intelligence failure, the Bomber Gap and the Missile Gap. One thoughtful observer would go much further, accusing the worst-case advocates of distorting "everything from NATO military strategy to U.S. foreign policy, and from the domestic allocation of resources to attitudes toward arms control."[15] In general, the hard-liners risk exaggerating the speed of modernization, degree of technological quality, and actual impact on the strategic balance of new Soviet weapon systems.

As for the left, its errors have been more subtle but no less significant. Many observers would blame the soft-liners for our failures to anticipate the 1962 introduction of strategic weapons into Cuba, the Soviet invasion of Afghanistan, Polish imposition of martial law, Soviet support for international terrorism, and Soviet willingness to experiment with chemical and toxicological weapons on Third World battlefields. It would appear that the soft-liners tend to minimize Soviet consistency, determination, and deceptiveness, not to mention the periodic brutality of Soviet behavior.[16]

The old debate is very much alive today. Some observers stress the continuity of Soviet strategic force planning from Sokolovsky through Gorbachev. As a result, they suspect Moscow of still seeking military advantage and warn against hasty concessions in foreign trade or arms control. Others see Sokolovsky as utterly out-of-date. They contend that the Soviets have long since adopted Western notions of mutual deterrence, and are thus willing to take Gorbachev's proclamations about "defensive doctrine" and "sufficiency" more or less at face value.

The persistence of this controversy suggests that we may hear renewed criticism of our approach to studying the Soviet strategic offensive and defensive forces. All the old questions and accusations dating from the B Team affair may well resurface. Hard-liners and soft-liners will surely disagree again about which ideological approach best assures our national security. Whatever fruit those discussions may bear, all observers should take care not to suppress heretical—but potentially correct —opinions during this time of unprecedented change in the Soviet system.

Any observer who wishes the American people to comprehend the full range of possibilities facing Gorbachev today would do well to reflect upon the B Team affair of 1976. It still stands as an unsurpassed monument to competitive analysis, albeit flawed in one important sense: no C Team was recruited from the left to provide a third perspective on Soviet long-range intentions. If we could assure full voice to the full spectrum of informed U.S. opinion, it would be difficult to refute the need for more "competitive analysis" in the intelligence community today. One member of the B Team closed his assessment of intelligence requirements for the 1980s with a plea to consider all possible ways of reforming the estimative process:

> There are any number of ways in which this can be done. All need to be studied. In the end it will matter less which of these we choose than it will that we have chosen not to accentuate the present features of our intelligence system which have not served us well.[17]

A Catalogue of Expectations

The uncertainties surrounding Soviet force planning for the 1990s are greater than ever before. *Glasnost* has allowed us unusual glimpses into the Central Committee, but it has not begun to erode the secrecy cloaking the General Staff. Muscovite acceptance of unprecedented and highly intrusive forms of on-site inspection, to verify compliance with the INF Treaty, will shed new light on some dark corners of the Soviet Union. But such positive developments are flagrantly contradicted by Soviet espionage, "active measures," deception, and disinformation, which abuse the openness of Western society.[18]

Whatever the faults, virtues, and trends of Gorbachev's Soviet Union, we will continue to have difficulty explaining him to our own citizens. Our Western combination of simple ignorance and complex misunderstanding is exacerbated by highly partisan, ideological stereotypes of Soviet force planning within the analytical community. Both sides should be encouraged, in my view, to state their positions as trenchantly and as fully as they are able.

I contend that the military objective of the Soviet Strategic Forces is a concept which became banal—deservedly or undeservedly, depending upon one's perspective—through overuse in the early 1970s. That goal is strategic superiority. It would entail the capability to defeat any constellation of rivals upon the Eurasian continent, and at any level of combat. The specific role of the strategic offensive and defensive forces is to dominate the escalatory ladder, ultimately convincing Soviet enemies to choose discretion over valor in the event of a war, which all potential contenders regard as unlikely, unwanted, and potentially disastrous for the entire human race.

At one time—the early 1970s, for example—strategic superiority had little real meaning for the deployed forces. Mere multiplication of the megadeaths on both sides could hardly have constituted victory by any rational definition. For long-range planners and doctrinal specialists, however, that concept never quite lost its importance. In spite of all the familiar constraints of economic stagnation and arms control, the Soviets gradually built the force that Sokolovsky had described twenty years earlier.[19]

But over the past fifteen years, two new factors have begun to upset the deterrent equations and thus to revive the concept of strategic superiority. One was slow, but it was predicted years before it became a reality: namely, Moscow's achievement of militarily useful levels of conventional superiority over NATO. The other was sudden and highly unpredictable in its actual military ramifications: the evolution of both East and West toward drastically greater reliance upon strategic defensive forces.

Few events in the history of force planning seem more ironic than this rehabilitation of the defensive side of the strategic dialectic. Conservatives who once "cried wolf" about Soviet strategic defenses on the grounds that they would destabilize the strategic balance now advocate a far more advanced array of defenses for the West. Liberals who once laughed at strategic defense as a foolish dream now regard it as a nightmare that may delay progress on disarmament, rebuff Gorbachev's peaceful overtures, and radically increase the risk of war.

As for Soviet actions at Geneva, Vladivostok, Vienna, Helsinki, Reykyavik, and all the other hallowed sites of East-West amity, I am the first to admit the existence of Soviet changes, concessions, and compromises which make the actual negotiating record both less malevolent and more complex than my conservative colleagues sometimes like to admit. Even so, I find support for my thesis in some broad conclusions about the Soviet approach to arms control and disarmament negotiations.

With few and trivial exceptions, Soviet force planners have employed negotiations with the West to achieve specific, consistent, and coherent military objectives. Sokolovsky is long gone, but his heirs have so negotiated as to implement, rather than abandon, his declared ambitions. Above all, Soviet negotiators seek to trade current or obsolete Soviet weapons for much newer U.S. programs. In the "best case" from the Soviet perspective, they aspire to impose constraints upon U.S. systems which do not yet even exist.

If my assessment of Soviet strategic offensive and defensive forces is correct, Moscow will not allow the strategic balance to stabilize. The Soviets may accept parity in some areas, but they will maintain or seek superiority in others and tolerate inferiority in few or none. The fate of these predictions should provide a clear, military gauge of Gorbachev's long-term intentions.

To date, all available evidence suggests that there is a high degree of self-serving propaganda in Gorbachev's actions and public image. As the then Director of the U.S. Arms Control and Disarmament Agency, William F. Burns, wrote in November of 1988, Gorbachev is attempting to deprive us of our cherished threat (see chapter 1). That seems a serious matter, since Western force planners need a threat just as soap needs dirt. Indeed, I speculate that Gorbachev may aspire to mutual cuts in defense spending, but at significantly different rates for East and West. Thus he might manage to reduce the crushing military burden upon his own system, while keeping or even widening his advantages in the strategic balance.

If Gorbachev wishes to convince us otherwise, he must undertake a host of changes in the Soviet system. Modest, entirely reversible cuts in the Soviet order of battle will serve only to delude the West, if the broad nature of the Soviet system remains the same. Deep, systemic changes are more thinkable today than at any time since Lenin's death. For those who see *glasnost* as merely the latest device of Soviet deception and disinformation, I urge a closer look at what is happening in the Soviet Union. Even some Western conservatives have asked if we are witnessing the gradual decline of the totalitarian regime. *Glasnost* is having both unintended results that may support our national interests as well as intended consequences that will continue to trouble us.

Being the sort of society that we are, the West will endure protracted controversy over the scale and meaning of Gorbachev's reforms. The very complexity of the facts will make this a heated debate, and past pleas for more "competitive analysis" may well go unnoticed. Thus, I propose a specific "catalogue of expectations" by which we may measure Soviet willingness to stabilize the strategic balance and truly alter the U.S.-Soviet relationship over the long term.[20] If adopted by a broad consensus of informed opinion, such openly declared expectations might allow us to formulate a non-ideological approach to predicting the Soviet future without suppressing divergent views within our ranks. Illustrative examples would include the following:

1. Dismantle the SS-24 and SS-25. These mobile ICBMs could drastically alter the strategic balance in Moscow's favor if not matched or threatened by appropriate U.S. weapons (ranging from the rail garrison Peacekeeper ICBM to the Small ICBM and the B-2).

2. Negotiate the phased deployment by both East and West of space-based defenses against ballistic missile attack. One can envisage no single step by which Moscow could more radically reject Sokolovsky's quest for unilateral Soviet superiority and signal its willingness to consider entirely new approaches to strategic stability.

3. Dismantle the Krasnoyarsk radar without further ado. There are solid grounds for regarding it as a violation of the ABM Treaty, which Gorbachev could cheerfully and truthfully blame on his predecessors (on whom he has already blamed many more important mistakes).

4. Abolish the conscript force. So long as Moscow relies on more or less universal male service, all its neighbors will continue to doubt the benevolence of long-term Soviet intentions.

5. Reduce the military burden on the Soviet economy to no more than is spent by the most militarized member of NATO.

6. Send us fewer spies and tell fewer lies. Espionage and "active measures" perpetuate the worst sort of cold war behavior.

7. Adopt a more constructive attitude toward economic dealings with the

West. Granting due respect to Western patents and copyrights while refraining from the illegal transfer of sensitive technology would drastically enhance the prospects for East-West trade.

8. Remove all foreign communist troops from Angola, Kampuchea, and Ethiopia. The departure of Soviet troops from Afghanistan is quite remarkable, and should be imitated throughout the Soviet empire.

9. Grant federal status to the non-Russian republics of the U.S.S.R. It has been promised by all four of the constitutions the Soviets have propounded, but never honored over the decades.

10. Dismantle the Berlin Wall, defortify the inter-German border, and remove sufficient Soviet troops from Eastern Europe that the non-Soviet members of the Warsaw Pact are left to police their own populations. Many Westerners believe that the "Cold War" began in Eastern Europe, and it is unlikely to end before that region is restored to real independence.

11. Reduce the Soviet military and economic assistance programs to Cuba and Nicaragua to no more than the United States donates to any country bordering the Soviet Union.

Full compliance with all these expectations might be too much for us to ask. Indeed, as General Burns has written, such an embrace by the eagle might cause the death of the bear (see chapter 1). If I were a Soviet citizen, I would surely be troubled by such a possibility. But as an American citizen, I see the need for weighing Soviet rhetoric against Soviet actions and demanding a reasonable price for our concessions. If we do not, I fear that the embrace of the dollar may cause the climax of the ruble.

Notes

1. For an effort to correct this omission, see Richmond M. Lloyd et al., *Foundations of Force Planning: Concepts and Issues, Vol. II: Resources for Defense.* (Newport, RI: Naval War College Press, 1986 and 1988).

2. Major General E. Nikitin and Colonel S. Baranov, "The Revolution in Military Affairs and Measures of the CPSU for Raising the Combat Might of the Armed forces," *Voennaia mysl'* (Military Thought) cited by William T. Lee and Richard F. Staar in *Soviet Military Policy Since World War II* (Stanford, CA: Hoover Institution Press, 1986), p. 11. For this and many other insights, I am indebted to Lee and Staar.

3. Ibid.

4. Marshal of the Soviet Union V.D. Sokolovsky, ed., *Voennaia strategiia*

(Military Strategy), 3rd rev. ed. (Moscow: Voeniz'dat, 1968), p. 359.

5. Ibid.

6. Colonel General N.A. Lomov, ed., *Nauchno-tekhnicheskii progress i revoliutsiia v voennom dele* (Scientific-Technical Progress and the Revolution in Military Affairs) (Moscow: Voeniz'dat, 1973), p. 272.

7. Marshal of the Soviet Union A.A. Grechko, *Vooruzhennye sily sovetskogo gosudarstva*, (The Armed Forces of the Soviet State) 2nd rev. ed. (Moscow: Voeniz'dat, 1975), pp. 107–108.

8. Sokolovsky, *Voennaia strategiia*, 3rd. ed., pp. 253–254.

9. Lee and Staar describe General Secretary Brezhnev as initiating "the current practice of denying that military superiority is a Soviet objective," in 1977. They provide well-documented reasoning to regard such claims as deception. See *Soviet Military Policy Since World War II*, pp. 30–34. Raymond L. Garthoff argues for the opposite view in *Détente and Confrontation: American Soviet Relations from Nixon to Reagan* (Washington, DC: Brookings Institution, 1985).

10. John Prados, *The Soviet Estimate: U.S. Intelligence Analysis and Soviet Strategic Forces* (Princeton, NJ: Princeton University Press), p. xii.

11. For a fuller explanation, see G. Paul Holman, "Estimative Intelligence," in Gerald W. Hoople and Bruce W. Watson, *The Military Intelligence Community* (Boulder, CO: Westview Press, 1986), pp. 129–144.

12. Prados, *Soviet Estimate*, pp. 248–257.

13. Ibid., p. 250.

14. By far the most influential was Richard E. Pipes, "Why the Soviet Union Thinks It Could fight and Win a Nuclear War," *Commentary*, 65, No. 1 (July 1977): 21–34.

15. Michael MccGwire, *Military Objectives in Soviet Foreign Policy* (Washington, DC: Brookings Institution, 1987), p. 368.

16. William R. Kintner argues this position throughout *Soviet Global Strategy* (Fairfax, VA: Hero Books, 1987).

17. Lt. Gen. Daniel O. Graham, U.S. Army (Ret.), "Analysis and Estimates," in Roy Godson, ed., *Intelligence Requirements for the 1980's: Elements of Intelligence* (Washington, DC: National Strategy Information Center, 1979), p. 29.

18. For the most powerful presentation of this thesis, see Richard H. Shultz and Roy Godson, *Dezinformatsia: Active Measures in Soviet Strategy* (Washington, DC: Pergamon-Brassey's, 1984).

19. Lt. Gen. William E. Odom, U.S. Army (Ret.), "Soviet Military Doctrine," *Foreign Affairs*, 67, No. 2, (Winter 1988/89): 114–134, traces a direct line from Sokolovsky's force-building goals of the 1960s to today's Soviet forces.

20. Graham T. Allison, Jr., has persuasively argued the need for such an approach in "Testing Gorbachev," *Foreign Affairs*, 67, No. 1, (Fall 1988): 18–32.

11
U.S. Strategic Forces: Priorities for Modernization and Arms Control

R. James Woolsey

The strategic forces of the United States must be able to survive a Soviet attack and retaliate effectively against the instruments of Soviet state power. These necessary conditions for deterrence—stability through survivability and force effectiveness—mean that U.S. strategic forces will require periodic modernization in order for a deterrent to be maintained.

For at least four reasons, there is good cause to believe that this need to modernize U.S. strategic forces will persist for many years into the future, even in the presence of more cordial U.S.-Soviet relations and arms control agreements. First, much of the U.S. strategic modernization occurred in the 1960s, and systems dating from that period—such as Minuteman ICBMs, B-52 bombers, and Poseidon submarines—must be replaced simply due to their aging if such forces are to be maintained. Second, unless the course of a millennium of Russian history is successfully dammed and the stream permanently diverted in a radically new direction, Moscow spring may be followed by Russian winter. Such has occurred more than once before, and Russian political seasons can change faster than a U.S. deterrent can be modernized. Third, Soviet technology and force improvements—such as improved defenses against bombers and ballistic missiles—will necessitate U.S. force modernization in order for us to continue to be able to hold appropriate targets at risk. Fourth, even the successful negotiation of one or more strategic arms agreements is not likely to have a major strategically relevant impact on the modernization

The original version of this paper was prepared for the Aspen Strategy Group and presented at its conference on August 14–19, 1988; it will be published in *Balancing National Security Objectives in an Uncertain World*, edited by Joseph Nye, Thomas W. Graham, and William J. Perry (Lanham, MD: University Press of America, *forthcoming*). The paper also appears in that more complete form in the Winter 1989 issue of *Washington Quarterly*, vol. 12, no. 1, pp. 69–85. Due to space limitations in this book, the sections Stability and Survivability; Larger Number or Different Design of Ballistic Missile Submarines; Defense Force Programs; and Employment have been significantly condensed. For my complete discussion of these topics, see my contributions to *Balancing National Security Objectives in an Uncertain World* and *Washington Quarterly*, above.

of the Soviet offensive threat to U.S. strategic forces. This is because some parts of U.S. strategic forces are threatened by Soviet conventional force improvements—such as antisubmarine warfare (ASW) capabilities threatening U.S. ballistic missile submarines—that will not be limited by proposed treaties and that will certainly continue to be made. Others are threatened by Soviet strategic force improvements that are nonetheless most unlikely to be constrained by any agreement on strategic weapons— such as quieter Soviet ballistic missile submarines and their more accurate missiles threatening U.S. bombers.

In assessing the needed types of strategic modernization for the United States, however, it is important to take account of both the expense and the framework of likely arms control agreements. Where strategic stability can be enhanced at lower cost, or can be somewhat augmented by some aspects of arms control agreements, the opportunity should be used to save resources and improve stability. In strategic modernization, we are dealing, in a sense, with a major national insurance policy against an admittedly unlikely eventuality. But it is insurance against the most catastrophic of imaginable losses, and it is a curious kind of policy—one where paying the premiums can make the catastrophe less likely. The unlikelihood of strategic nuclear war should incline us to save resources where we can to devote to other national uses. The importance of continuing to have the sorts of nuclear forces that can help deter both nuclear war and general conventional war, however, should also incline us toward care, thoroughness, and hedging our bets.

What follows is an effort, keeping these factors in mind, to suggest *trends* of U.S. strategic modernization that should be set in motion, *not* precise end-points of precisely quantifiable force structures. Such an effort proceeds from a conviction that it is important to view the capabilities of strategic forces in terms of such trends—analogous to the information given by financial profit and loss statements—rather than only in terms of a snapshot of strategic forces at a single point in time—analogous to a single balance sheet. As in financial analysis, both perspectives are necessary. But the proliferation of strategic balance sheets in recent years— whether in the bean-counting bar graphs of popular journalism or in detailed computerized force exchange models—has too often left the impression that the Soviet threats to U.S. strategic forces can be made to stay frozen at a particular point in time. Consequently the implicit judgment is often reached that one specific U.S. force structure, produced as a result of an arms control agreement or whatever, will more or less permanently fix our major strategic problems. This is a false and dangerous assumption. Moreover, the long lead times required to field, or even to modify, major strategic systems means that one must always, and continually, assess long-run trends in both the Soviet threats and our own forces.

Stability and Survivability

Clear survivability is essential for strategic stability. Unfortunately, neither arms control nor cost-driven limitations on Soviet strategic forces are, in the future, likely to limit the threat to the survivability of U.S. strategic forces to any major degree. The Soviet infrastructure that is necessary to put at risk important parts of U.S. strategic forces is already in place and will not be affected in most strategically important ways by the sort of START agreement now being negotiated.

The principal threat to the U.S. submarine force is Soviet antisubmarine warfare capability—the deployment of modern, quiet Soviet attack submarines and Soviet work on advanced antisubmarine warfare techniques. These efforts have always been too intertwined with conventional naval force modernization to be the subject of definable, much less verifiable, arms control constraints.

The U.S. bomber force is threatened in its ability to survive principally by Soviet submarines carrying ballistic or cruise missiles. As has been the case in the past, any numerical constraints placed on submarine-launched ballistic missiles (SLBMs) under an arms control agreement would never be sufficient to constrain the Soviets from having the small number of warheads on station that could attack a few command and control sites and a few bomber bases (in a surprise attack), or even a few tens of bases (if the bombers were dispersed in a crisis).

Only in the case of the U.S. silo-based ICBM force has there been, or is there likely to be, any effort to limit the threat through arms control. That effort has in the past largely failed. Under START the Soviet ability to do two-on-one targeting of U.S. silos with accurate warheads will easily be retained, especially when one adds to the Soviets' accurate SS-18 ICBM warheads the other accurate ICBM and SLBM warheads that will be available to them in the future.

Moreover, as Soviet SLBM warheads become more accurate they create a new problem for U.S. strategic forces. If Soviet boats on patrol carry enough accurate warheads to be able to attack all U.S. ICBMs and bomber bases virtually simultaneously, then the important degree of survivability that our bombers and ICBMs lend to one another, due to Soviet problems in timing an attack, disappears.

Accurate Soviet SLBM warheads effectively eliminate this attack timing problem for Soviet planners, if a sufficient number of warheads can be carried by Soviet boats on patrol to attack with near-simultaneous launch and near-simultaneous detonation all urgent strategic targets in the United States. And we must further face the possibility that with the newer, quieter Soviet ballistic missile submarines, such as the Delta IV and Typhoon, we may have much less accurate locational data than was the case with older boats such as Yankees and Delta Is. We may know that the new boats are on patrol, but not precisely where. A relatively prompt relocation if such modern Soviet boats—such as from the Arctic areas far from the United States to the near-Arctic or from the far side of the mid-Atlantic ridge to the near side—could go undetected for some time. Time is needed to detect such shifts and to prosecute ASW contracts, and such time may not be available.

The survivability problem for U.S. bombers and ICBMs is difficult enough if sufficient numbers of accurate warheads can be launched on standard trajectories from the near-Arctic, with flight times substantially less than half that of ICBMs. But by detonating warheads in such a way as to produce electromagnetic pulse effects, by using depressed trajectories, and by launching from patrol locations close to the United States in the Atlantic and Pacific, the Soviets could make the survivability problem for bombers, and for silo- and garrison-based ICBMs, even harder.

For example, the Soviets have some seven Delta IV submarines in the fleet or under construction. They carry sixteen SS-N-23 missiles, each with eight to ten warheads, according to intelligence estimates made public by DOD. At the Washington summit in December 1987, the United States agreed to count each SS-N-23 as carrying only four warheads. Even at the lower count, the number of Delta IVs that could be on routine patrol in the 1990s in the Arctic, Atlantic, and Pacific (not counting, for example, Soviet Typhoon submarines held in strategic reserve at sea in bastions near the Soviet Union) could well carry enough warheads to cover all strategic targets in the United States, if START constraints lead to a significant reduction in the number of U.S. silos.

Moreover, in September 1988, U.S. Naval Intelligence commented publicly on a doctrinal statement in a new book edited by the father of the modern Soviet Navy, Fleet Admiral Sergei Gorshkov, to the effect that the Soviet Navy was developing a capability to undertake "covert launches from short range" from their SSBNs against U.S. strategic targets. U.S. Naval Intelligence noted that these comments by Gorshkov "highlight the potential importance of recent Soviet SLBM launches to test short-range/short time-of-flight trajectories."

We thus face the realistic possibility that even with a START agreement requiring a 50-percent reduction in accountable warheads—indeed in a small measure *because* of agreement-generated pressures to constrain silo and submarine numbers—the United States will face a new strategic condition in the 1990s. Cost might well have limited the United States in any case to about one thousand ICBMs and about twenty Trident submarines, quite apart from arms control. But START exerts some pressure to stay below those numbers, both because of the ceiling of sixteen hundred strategic nuclear delivery vehicles (SNDVs) covering ICBMs, SLBMs, and heavy bombers, and because of the limit of forty-nine hundred ballistic missile warheads. For these reasons the relatively small number of U.S. bomber bases, silos, C³ nodes, and any garrisons for rail-mobile MX may well be held at risk in the future, even by those Soviet submarines that are on routine patrol in peacetime. If nuclear-armed submarine-launched cruise missiles are prohibited in START and the SNDV and warhead limitations in START encourage a force of Trident submarines of only eighteen or so in number, then the entire inventory of survivable U.S. strategic warheads could well be located in some dozen places at sea. Each such Trident submarine would be, as far as we know now, highly survivable—and such a force would carry some twenty-three hundred warheads. But the prospect of some sort of antisubmarine warfare breakthrough cannot be discounted completely, given the continuing level of Soviet investment in this area. And particularly if survivable U.S. forces are so highly concentrated, the Soviet incentive to pursue antisubmarine warfare efforts is immense.

The importance of maintaining a survivable deterrent mandates a search for, and solid R&D on, some alternatives to this situation toward which we appear to be moving: that is, our survivable strategic forces being concentrated on only a dozen or so platforms at sea.

Offensive Force Programs: Providing One or More
Hedges for the Trident Submarine Force

Larger Number or Different Design of Ballistic-Missile Submarines. Modern quiet ballistic missile submarines—when they can patrol in very large ocean areas and at depths of their choosing—are now, and, for the foreseeable future, are likely to be as difficult to detect and destroy as any military systems in existence. So much depends on the survivability of our ballistic missile submarine force, however, that—for any given number of warheads—it would be prudent to increase the number of boats that the Soviets would have to attack, if such an increased number of platforms can be made affordable.

But there is no specific number of submarines for which survivability is assured or vulnerability worrisome. As in the case of many other military system decisions, it is principally a case of choosing whether or not to pay the added price of spreading a given number of weapons over a greater number of platforms. To further complicate the question, it is not clear that a submarine of smaller size than Trident would be more surviv-able against many types of antisubmarine warfare threats. The threat of nonacoustic detection, for example, obviously increases with the subma-rine's size. But some aspects of acoustic quieting, sonar design, and double hull construction are easier, not harder, if a submarine is relatively large. It is possibly instructive that the newest class of Soviet ballistic missile submarine, and the quietest, is the double-hulled Typhoon—the only sub-marine larger than Trident.

The importance of the U.S. ballistic missile submarine force dictates, above all, that snap decisions not be made about it. Nor is it the type of weapons program for which one should rush to procure enough systems for a fixed force structure and then close down production lines. Since the at-sea portion of the submarine force may for many years provide the only part of U.S. strategic forces that is clearly survivable against a sur-prise attack, its evolution should be managed carefully. Above all, the ballistic missile submarine force should be flexible enough to respond to varying threats over the years and to present as diverse a set of problems as possible to an adversary. The two Trident bases at Kings Bay, Georgia, and Bangor, Washington, could operate on the order of twenty-five sub-marines (counting those normally in overhaul). If ballistic missile subma-rines are built at the rate of one per year and last approximately twenty-five years, a long-run program of constructing one submarine an-nually would sustain a basic force structure for the indefinite future.

Twenty-five Trident boats, however, each fully loaded with twenty-four missiles carrying eight warheads each (the loading for the D-5 Tri-dent II missile negotiated in the START talks) would carry forty-eight hundred warheads—only one hundred fewer than the total ballistic missile warheads allowable under the negotiated START ceiling. To provide some reasonable number of warheads for the ICBM force—under the increas-ingly questionable assumption that an adequately survivable and afforda-ble method of ICBM deployment can both be devised and then be approved by all necessary parts of the U.S. government—there are several ways to reduce this warhead count. First, some two or more boatloads of warheads may be excluded from the SLBM (and added to the number available to the ICBM) count in START by agreeing to exclude subma-rines in overhaul. Second, each boat may be less than fully outfitted with missiles and verifiable steps may be taken to disable some of the missile tubes. Third, one of the four sets of six missile tubes may be physically cut out of any given boat.

There are several means of improving submarine force survivability. (Under START ceilings, of course, any increase in the number of subma-rines would have to be combined with one or more of the above methods of reducing the number of warheads per boat.) Most practically, a method may be available in the relatively near future to combine two already designed submarine classes to improve a very important aspect of the survivability of the individual submarine as well as to reduce size and permit an increase in submarine numbers. The "back end," that is, the propulsion system, for the new SSN-21 Sea Wolf–class attack submarine has already been designed. It has several advantages over the already very quiet Trident propulsion system, the most important being that it can permit a submarine to sustain a much greater quiet speed. "Quiet speed" is a far more important index of submarine survivability than many other measures because a fast quiet speed significantly enhances the area in which a boat can operate within a given time period while operating at minimum noise and listening for enemy submarines. A hybrid submarine that used the propulsion system of the SSN-21, the front end of Trident, and two or three of Trident's four missile sections would be smaller than Trident, carry fewer missiles, and have a much faster patrol speed (and hence a potentially much greater patrol area for a given time period). It might provide a very useful transitional system and help postpone the day by which a far more advanced submarine would have to be funded, designed, and built.

Finally, whichever of the above steps are taken, we must continue vigorous work on our own ASW efforts and on submarine communications. As long as our own general locational ("cueing") data on Soviet attack submarines is as good or better than such Soviet data on our ballistic missile boats, we should have a major ASW advantage in our "bastions," namely, the Atlantic and Pacific, because of the considerable ASW forces available to us and our allies—including aircraft and surface ships as well as submarines. This struggle to retain a cueing advantage is of vital importance, especially given the substantial and growing force of new quiet Soviet attack boats. The only sort of Soviet capability that might even theoretically reverse this advantage, without the Soviets' developing such a cueing advantage, would be some sort of Soviet ASW surveillance system that could not only make the oceans transparent to great depths, but make much of the Atlantic and Pacific, and—if we chose to patrol there—Arctic ice transparent all at once. This would be, to put it mildly, a formidable task for Soviet scientists and engineers to contemplate.

Nuclear Sea-Launched Cruise Missiles (SLCMs). One simple and relatively low-cost way to avoid having all one's survivable strategic eggs in a dozen or so Trident baskets would be simply to refuse to limit sea-launched nuclear cruise missiles in a START agreement. The verification problems of distinguishing nuclear-armed from conventionally-armed cruise missiles, not to speak of the difficulties of defining and verifying cruise missile ranges, are extraordinarily great in any case. If a substantial number of at-sea attack submarines and surface ships carry several nuclear-armed cruise missiles, the Soviet problem in launching an attack against U.S. strategic forces is sharply enhanced. It would be highly unlikely that even substantial improvements in Soviet antisubmarine warfare forces would enable them to put at risk so many targets simultaneously.

As far as arms control is concerned, the certain lack of constraints on Soviet air defenses—warning systems and weapons—offers the Soviets a reasonable approach to countering any perceived SLCM threat. Cruise missiles are, in any case, not destabilizing in the sense that much faster-flying ballistic missiles can be.

Of course nuclear sea-launched cruise missiles serve other, regional interests, such as covering those targets previously covered by ground-based Pershing IIs and GLCMs in Europe. But it should not be forgotten that they also have a potential role in the relatively near future as a hedge against the problem of having our survivable strategic forces located in only a dozen or so Trident boats at sea.

To the extent that U.S. nuclear-armed sea-launched cruise missiles are limited or prohibited in START, the problem of finding some other survivable hedge for the small number of Trident boats is made more salient.

Silo- or Garrison-based ICBMs. In a world in which the Soviet Union is capable of launching, nearly simultaneously, an SLBM attack on U.S. strategic forces from a day-to-day patrol posture and of achieving near-simultaneous detonation of such missiles' warheads on strategic targets in the United States, these sorts of systems do not enhance strategic stability but rather detract from it. A force structure that retains a substantial number of silos under a START agreement by sacrificing far more survivable SLBM tubes may appear to be adequately survivable, but only if it is faced by a threat consisting of Soviet warhead numbers and accuracies that have been artificially frozen in time. And silos are far more vulnerable to Soviet cheating or break-out of an agreement than other, more survivable, basing modes for ICBMs or sea-based systems.

If one looks at the trends—at the increasing vulnerability of silos, at the increasing accuracy of warheads, and at the ease of proliferating warhead numbers by break-out from an agreement or by cheating—then it appears to be extremely unwise to rely on ICBMs in silos or in garrisons to provide stability over time. These trends become troubling even earlier if the number of strategic aim points in the United States is drawn down under a START agreement to a few hundred, and this number of targets can be adequately covered by accurate Soviet SLBM warheads carried by the boats that are normally on patrol. The possibility that the Soviets could rely on more complex attacks oriented toward decapitating the command and control system and utilizing, for example, the effects of electro-magnetic pulse, further enhances the risk.

One major reason it is dangerous to rely on silo- or garrison-based ICBMs is the risk of accidental war. There will be, indeed there has been, a reflexive instinct within the U.S. uniformed command structure to relax the conditions under which such vulnerable weapons may be launched on warning alone—that is, prior to the confirmation of nuclear detonations on U.S. soil. Ultimately, of course, the decision to launch based on warning alone would belong to the National Command Authority. And it enhances our ability to deter war for the Soviets to be assured that we could implement such a policy if we chose. But it is quite another thing to maintain a force, year after year, that can only survive against surprise attack if it is launched on warning without waiting for confirmation of an attack. There is far too much risk that a hair trigger could become an acceptable condition of readiness, and consequently that one day, based on ambiguous warning, the trigger could be inadvertently pulled.

Garrison-based ICBMs (as in the MX rail-garrison basing plan) are even more vulnerable than silos in their day-to-day posture, and equally prone to being placed on a hair trigger. They can gain significant survivability—that is, they can charge a high price to an attacker in terms of attacking throw-weight or percentage of the attacking arsenal—several hours (6 to 12) after being flushed from their bases. But they can do so only if the United States has received strategic warning of an attack, if that warning has been acted upon, and if, after being flushed, the trains containing the missiles are effectively concealed. Thus garrison-based ICBMs are analogous to in-port submarines or non-alert bombers, although slower to escape to security than either of these latter forces if optimally maintained. Advocates of relying on any force of this general sort—a force that requires strategic warning to survive—as a major part of U.S. strategic forces, however, must account for the historic cases of nations have had excellent intelligence about their adversaries and have still failed for one reason or another to take the necessary steps to protect their forces: for example, the United States in 1941, the Soviet Union in 1941, and Israel in 1973. Confidence that one will obtain, recognize, and act upon strategic warning is a highly uncertain basis for deterrence.

Bolts almost never come from the blue, but they do come from the gray. And combinations of clever attackers and uncertain defenders who don't take action, even in such gray periods, have throughout history undercut the logic of relying heavily on strategic warning to maintain stable and survivable forces. Thus, whatever the utility of silo- or garrison-based ICBMs, they do not provide the needed and important survivable hedge for the small number of ballistic missile submarines. Other, more survivable forces can be given the characteristics of accuracy, good communication links, and prompt availability that characterize these sorts of ICBMs. In light of the threat that is coming to be posed to them by MIRVed accurate Soviet SLBMs, in addition to Soviet ICBMs, and the apparent desire of portions of the U.S. bureaucracy not to regard silo- or garrison-based forces as an adjunct but rather to rely exclusively upon them for the entire future U.S. ICBM force, these sorts of ICBM forces should be gradually phased out or, if under development, cancelled.

Multiple-Shelter or Mobile ICBMs. Multiple-shelter systems ("shell games") for ICBMs have always had the major advantage over silo-basing (that is, one shelter per missile) of permitting a nation to create many more targets for the enemy than it must deploy systems of its own. Thus, compared to silo-basing, the cost of a shell game system can be far less for any given number of targets realistically presented to an enemy. The shell game basing system for the MX missile of a decade ago had these advantages in part, but it suffered from two problems that eventually proved to be its undoing. First, the old MX shelters were of only modest hardness and thus needed to be spaced some distance apart. The land requirements consequently necessitated the use of large amounts of government-owned land in Utah and Nevada—land to which the public was to continue to have access, except for a small fenced area around each shelter. This in turn increased the difficulty of maintaining the secrecy of the missiles' location at any given time, and it created serious political problems because of the amount of land use and interaction with the public. Second, the shelters were horizontal, in part to make it simpler for national technical means to verify that there were not more missiles in the shelter system than would have been permitted under an arms control agreement, and each shelter contained expensive communications and other gear to maintain concealment. This was needed partially because public access was permitted up to the fence surrounding each shelter. This all added substantially to the cost of each shelter and thus to the overall cost of the system.

In recent years a very different type of shell game basing mode for an ICBM has been designed; it could conceivably be used for the currently operational Minuteman III. First, close spacing of shelters has become more feasible because one can place a missile in a very hard canister that is inserted into one of several relatively inexpensive vertical shelters. Such a scheme is called "carry-hard." The combination of canister and vertical shelter would be sufficiently hard that close spacing would be possible and thus well under one-tenth the land would be required—one parcel roughly 10 by 25 miles—than under the MX shell game basing mode of a decade ago, which needed over five thousand square miles. The land for a carry-hard shell game both could and should be dedicated land; this substantially simplifies the problem of maintaining the secrecy of the missiles' location and restricting the politically sensitive interaction with the public by making it feasible to secure the entire land area, not just each shelter site. Second, the new Soviet openness to on-site inspection in arms control should make it considerably simpler to design a verification scheme—such as portal monitoring, spot checks, and so forth—that would ensure that any side having such a shell game system using vertical shelters was not exceeding its agreed level of deployed missiles and warheads.

Such a new type of shell-game deployment might well also be designed for existing MX missiles or for a new missile such as a small ICBM—although probably a two-warhead version, since there is no particular reason to avoid multiple warheads in a shell-game deployment, and it is less expensive to buy fewer missiles and fewer canisters.

Mobility in a hard mobile launcher presents another possibility for ICBM survivability. A truly mobile ICBM should be small enough to be capable of being deployed in different locations as different threats materialize—such as on dirt roads in wooded areas. Thus a size and weight approximately that of the thirty-seven thousand pound small ICBM now under design—about half the weight of Minuteman—is most appropriate. Significant cost savings might be made by reducing the number of hard mobile launchers and missiles below the five hundred first considered for the program and equipping each with two warheads. This is practical with the current design for covering most Soviet targets when mobile missiles are deployed in the Northern states—that is, within the fences at Minuteman silo sites. This sort of Minuteman-site deployment for a small ICBM on a hard mobile launcher requires *tactical* warning (that is, warning of a Soviet launch) to survive but, unlike garrison systems, does not require *strategic* warning (that is, several hours' advance notice of a Soviet decision to go to war).

If mobile basing is chosen, it would be important, however, to retain at least a small number single-warhead missiles and to base them in hard mobile launchers on one of the large Southwestern military bases (single warheads are necessary there because the greater distance from the Soviet targets dictates that the missile carry less weight). Properly operated, such a deployment would require neither strategic nor tactical warning to survive. Moreover, a Southwestern deployment of a few (say fifty to one hundred) small mobile ICBMs would provide a base for expansion should the Soviets give evidence of having certain offensive systems (such as fast, depressed-trajectory SLBMs) that could present survivability problems for northern-deployed small mobiles.

If mobility is chosen, there is good reason to maintain hard mobile launchers in order to permit peacetime basing away from the public on military bases. Missiles in hard mobile launchers have high survivability even when kept on such bases; within the time of tactical warning, their ability to move off base a short distance makes them virtually impossible for the Soviets to barrage with any reasonable amount of throw-weight. They are, in a sense, analogous to land-based submarines—able to operate, although not submerged, at least away from the public and in many potential areas if the threat changes. This is quite unlike softer mobile systems, such as small missiles on ordinary trucks or MXs on rail, which must deploy either through or into populated areas either in peacetime or many hours before an attack to achieve reasonable survivability.

Determining the best combination of deployments of shell-game or mobile ICBMs is largely a question of balancing different types of potential Soviet threats and the cost of hedging against them. Some combination of Minuteman III, MX, or two-warhead small ICBMs in a shell-game deployment, or two- and one-warhead small ICBMs in hard mobile launchers should make available five hundred to fifteen hundred highly survivable warheads for the ICBM force. But I must emphasize one point: Should it prove impossible financially or politically for the United States to deploy any of these or any other survivable and stabilizing components of an ICBM force, then we should move away from maintaining ICBM systems and concentrate on keeping sea- and air-based strategic forces solidly survivable and effective. A survivable strategic diad is far less desirable than survivable triad—that is, one in which all three parts of the force have some degree of survivability against surprise attack. But a highly survivable diad is preferable to a triad of which two legs are not properly modernized, while the third leg is vulnerable to surprise attack and kept on a hair trigger.

Bombers and Air-Launched Cruise Missiles (ALCMs). With the advent of stealth, it is plausible that cruise missiles and bombers will be able to penetrate even the very dense air defenses of the Soviet Union and Warsaw Pact. It remains to be seen, however, what aircraft should be given the capability to penetrate Soviet or Warsaw Pact defenses. Several factors are relevant. There is more than one reason to obtain a capability to penetrate such defenses. In a general war in Europe that does not yet involve strategic nuclear exchanges, bombers that can penetrate Warsaw Pact defenses may have a major role. Particularly given the high degree of vulnerability of the European bases for NATO tactical aircraft, strategic missions by long-range bombers—using smart conventional munitions—may be a major way of attacking or interdicting second echelon Warsaw Pact forces. In a war that is in the process of being extended to U.S.-Soviet strategic exchanges, penetrating aircraft may be the best, or only, way to destroy such mobile Soviet targets as command posts, missiles on rail, or Army units out of garrison. U.S. possession of bombers that can penetrate Soviet or Warsaw Pact air space forces the Soviets to spend resources on air defenses rather than on offensive capability. Finally, under the START counting rules, bombers that do not carry long-range cruise missiles count as only one delivery vehicle and one warhead, making them almost free under the potential agreement.

A portion of the B-52s will presumably be kept for some years to carry cruise missiles, but the aging of this venerable force is a problem. B-1s can become cruise missile carriers, but it may be best not to limit them to that role. The B-2 will presumably be much better able to penetrate Soviet air space than the B-1, but if the date of the full operating capability of the B-2 is delayed for cost reasons it may well be desirable to find some way to improve at least a portion of the B-1 force's ability to penetrate Soviet or at least Warsaw Pact defenses in Eastern Europe—by, for example, equipping the B-1 with the newer B-52 electronic countermeasures suite, in light of the well-known problems being experienced by its own.

Survivability against a sudden attack, if aircraft are still located at their main operating bases and not in a high state of alert, is a difficult problem. Escape times of each type of aircraft—B-52, B-1, B-2, and tankers—must be carefully analyzed to consider such threats as launch of SLBMs from the near-Arctic, use of electromagnetic pulse, barrage of bomber escape routes, and so forth. Certainly the development of a Soviet depressed-trajectory SLBM would significantly affect U.S. bomber force on-base survivability, but it is not the only problem.

It is often alleged that, if Soviet submarines pull close to U.S. shores, bombers could easily be placed in a higher state of alert. This response neglects two developments. First, newer Soviet ballistic missile submarines (such as the Delta IV and Typhoon) are considerably quieter than their predecessors, and thus neither precise locational data nor warning of close approach to the United States may be available in a timely manner. Second, some types of attacks launched from within or near what may be regarded as routine Soviet patrol areas (the near-Arctic and the areas off the U.S. Atlantic and Pacific coasts, in which Yankee and earlier classes of Delta submarines regularly patrolled for years until quite recently) can pose serious survivability problems for U.S. bombers. These factors may mean that, in the absence of the *continued* use of high states of alert, U.S. bombers may in the future face serious on-base vulnerabilities against surprise attack, even in the face of normal Soviet patrols by a handful of submarines. If the continued use of high alert conditions proves to be too costly for the bomber force, in terms of both cost and crew stress, then some defensive deployments may be required.

Defensive Force Programs

Some types of limited ground-based ballistic missile defenses could have particular utility in bomber base protection and other missions.

Employment. Although stability and survivability should be our principal concern for strategic forces, there is one important pending force structure question that relates principally to force employment. The nature of Soviet strategic targets is changing. Many more are coming to be mobile (for example, rail-mobile SS-24s and road-mobile SS-25s) and located deeply underground (for example, very deep shelters of the sort located at Sharapovo).

Successful deterrence requires the ability to hold at risk those things that the Soviet leadership most values. The nature of the Soviet state suggests that the Soviet leaders would put the highest such valuation on themselves. This emphasizes the importance of being able to hold at risk deep underground facilities such as that at Sharapovo; this can only effectively be done by an earth-penetrating weapon. Such a weapon should not be employed, however, on any system such as a silo- or garrison-based ICBM that might be used hastily at the beginning of a nuclear exchange—thus destroying initially any party on the other side that might be able to negotiate an end to the war. The most desirable system for deploying earth-penetrating weapons is a mobile or shell game–based ICBM, so that if a war should begin, a surviving National Command Authority could let the Soviets know that it had available at any time, with good command and control, the ability to launch a weapon that could with great certainty arrive at and destroy the most precious Soviet assets. Of chief importance is that such a capability should help deter any nuclear exchange in the first place.

Conclusion

The above suggestions to improve the survivability and the ability to employ U.S. strategic forces concentrate on current and controversial questions, not on overall force decisions. The relative silence about such generally agreed steps as improvements to strategic C^3 should not be taken as a denigration of the importance of such efforts. Moreover, the steps that are recommended emphasize trends that should be set in motion, not the more easily quantifiable end-points of force deployments. They do so with at least one eye on expense and the other on the likely shape of a strategic arms reduction agreement.

This overall approach proceeds from a three-part conviction: first, that U.S. strategic forces are reasonably survivable today—that emergency steps are not needed to help them maintain their ability to deter; second, that, realistically, U.S. strategic forces must be affordable and must be assessed in the context of plausible arms control agreements; third, that deterring general war between East and West is the most important undertaking of this or any government, and that the United States's continued success in this undertaking will require, for the foreseeable future, continued effort and care in the modernization of our strategic nuclear forces.

12

The Role and Phasing of SDI in the Context of START

Keith B. Payne

The role or purpose of the SDI appears to have changed emphasis since it was introduced by President Reagan on March 23, 1983. The President originally envisaged the SDI as a program to render ballistic missiles impotent and obsolete—providing true population protection and an alternative to an "immoral" strategic deterrence policy based solely on threatening nuclear retaliation.[1] Recently, however, official public discussions of SDI's role have focused much more narrowly on the goal of "enhancing deterrence" rather than on population protection. Even at official press conferences intended to signal that "nothing had changed with SDI," the only SDI role identified by White House representatives was to "strengthen deterrence."[2]

Contrary to what SDI critics charge, the identification of deterrence as an SDI objective does *not* represent an ambiguity of purpose or an about-face for the program. Deterrence had been identified as *a goal* of the SDI from its inception. Indeed, prior to the March 1983 announcement, senior members of the relatively new Reagan administration discussed ballistic missile defense (BMD) as an ICBM survivability measure meant to "encourage deterrence."[3]

That the deterrence role for SDI appears to have *eclipsed* population protection, however, is a shift. Such a reorientation should not be too surprising—it was the road of least political and bureaucratic resistance. Deterrence based on an offensive threat has been the traditional framework for strategic force consideration. Moving outside that deterrence framework in an attempt to establish a rationale for BMD was certain to be politically perilous. Nevertheless, there is a universe of difference between an SDI role intended to protect population, and a role intended, as stated in President Reagan's 1988 report, *National Security Strategy of the United States*, to "enhance deterrence by injecting greater uncertainties into Soviet estimates of their ability to achieve their military objectives should they attempt a first strike."[4] These divergent roles are not incompatible, but they do have different implications for strategic and arms control policies. And, most importantly for this discussion, they provide significantly different rationales for BMD deployment. To be specific, the emphasis on SDI's role of enhancing deterrence undermines the *unique* damage-limitation potential of BMD, and consequently probably reduces the prospects for deployment.

Prospects for a Limited Defense: The Past As Prologue?

Conventional wisdom says that a limited BMD system with a limited mission (such as, protection of the National Command Authority [NCA] or against accidents) has a good prospect for deployment.[5] History suggests otherwise. There is a precedent for considering a limited role for U.S. BMD. A brief review of the antiballistic missile (ABM) debate from 1969 through 1973 illustrates the problems SDI will confront in this regard.

The U.S. BMD program introduced by Secretary of Defense Robert S. McNamara in 1967, the *Sentinel* program, was rationalized as a system for light area defense (that is, societal protection) and some protection of U.S. strategic retaliatory capabilities. On March 14, 1969 the Nixon administration revised the mission and the name of the program. It became the *Safeguard* program, intended primarily to provide defense for ICBM and bomber forces and for the NCA in Washington, D.C. With the change from *Sentinel* to *Safeguard*, BMD's role became one of enhancing deterrence by reducing Soviet confidence in first-strike planning.[6]

The intended role for *Safeguard* was precisely that which has become the apparent emphasis for SDI: "enhancing deterrence" by reducing Soviet first-strike confidence. Similarly, the Congressional criticism that then dominated the ABM debate, and ultimately defeated *Safeguard*, also appears to be dominating the current SDI debate. Much of that opposition can, directly or indirectly be traced *to the limited defensive role of enhancing deterrence.*

With SDI's focus now on enhancing deterrence it confronts the same problems that terminated the *Safeguard* program. There is little evidence that those problems have lost their significance. Indeed, the major non-technical difference between the SDI debate and the earlier ABM debate is that the legal and political obstacles to BMD development and deployment are even greater now. A review of the arguments that proved fatal to *Safeguard* demonstrates just how analogous that precedent is for an SDI intended to "enhance deterrence."[7]

In SALT I, "capping" BMD was the price demanded by the Soviets in return for the offensive limitations sought by the United States. In the United States, progress in arms control was thought to require BMD limitation: success in arms control was said to require conceding on BMD. Consequently, the United States ultimately accepted the "grand compromise" of trading away BMD in return for offensive force limitations.

The argument for a grand compromise makes some sense if the role of BMD is simply to enhance the traditional form of offensive deterrence. The reasoning is as follows: If arms control can address the Soviet first-strike threat, *why not* be "flexible" on BMD, secure the agreement necessary to provide survivability for U.S. strategic forces, and conserve all the resources that otherwise would have been devoted to BMD? At the time of SALT I, arms control was seen as the most diplomatic (and least costly) means of ensuring the survivability of the U.S. deterrent—enhancing deterrence. The *Safeguard* program could not compete with the great attractiveness of an arms control alternative that, seemingly, would achieve the same goal.

A repeat of the SALT I "grand compromise" is precisely the course now recommended by SDI critics, arms control enthusiasts, and much of Congress.[8] The Soviets have facilitated the perception that a choice must be made between arms control and BMD deployment, and that another grand compromise can secure the objective of enhancing deterrence—without the political and resource costs of BMD deployment. They have done so by endorsing apparent reductions in heavy ICBMs and linking START success to a restrictive agreement on SDI. The conditions for another grand compromise could not be more attractive.

A repetition of SALT I may not occur, however. The President may be willing to maintain the commitment to SDI and forego success at START, or the Soviets may fall away from their START-SDI linkage. But the prospects for an eventual trade-off seem particularly good because the American public has an uncritical appetite for arms control agreements,[9] and START appears to hold out the prospect for a relatively inexpensive and politically attractive alternative to SDI as a means of enhancing deterrence.

The unfortunate condition that afflicted *Safeguard* now haunts the SDI: arms control and the SDI are seen as incompatible, and arms control appears to be a competitive means for enhancing deterrence. But unlike the earlier *Safeguard* case, this time the administration could offer a reasonable concept for the compatibility of arms control and the SDI—but only while discussions of SDI focused more on its role in population protection. It was relatively easy to understand that the SDI and arms control would have to function synergistically to pursue the goal of societal protection. The administration even developed a conceptual plan, called the "cooperative defense transition," for integrating arms control and BMD deployment.[10]

A defensive transition, as envisaged by the administration, would involve the coordination of negotiated reductions in ballistic missiles and the deployment of ballistic missile defenses. During this process, BMD and arms control would function synergistically to reduce or eliminate the first-strike potential of ballistic missiles and thus enhance stability. The ultimate goal of the transition, however, was societal protection, and BMD would be necessary to achieve that goal. Arms control alone could not be an alternative, if only because BMD would be necessary to "safeguard" an agreement against covert deployments.

According to official discussions, U.S. goals *during* the transition to mutually effective defenses would have been: 1) to strengthen deterrence; and 2) to achieve significant reductions in strategic nuclear arsenals—especially in ballistic missile forces. It often was suggested that deterrence would be strengthened during this transition period because the "destabilizing" military effectiveness of ballistic missiles would be undercut via arms control reductions and the deployment of defensive systems.

Regarding the arms control objective of the transition, it was thought that the deployment of BMD could reduce the value of offensive forces and thereby render deep reductions, particularly in ballistic missiles, more easily attained.[11] Arms control progress was to be one of the principal factors distinguishing a "cooperative" from a "competitive" transition.[12] Arms control was to govern the deployment of defenses, and achieve deep and stabilizing reductions in offensive forces. Deep reductions in MIRVed ballistic missiles would contribute to crisis stability by reducing the warhead-to-launcher ratio.

Eventually, as defensive forces became thicker and offensive forces were reduced, the net effect of defensive deployments and offensive reductions would be to provide "protection" for urban/industrial assets. As then-SDI Chief Scientist, Dr. Gerold Yonas, observed, "You don't get there in one step . . . we start by reducing the military usefulness of offensive weapons [via BMD]. This makes it easier to start reducing the offenses. As the offenses get smaller and the defenses get stronger, you reach a point where the defenses really protect you."[13]

It should be noted in this regard that the administration endorsed the transition goal of mutual defensive capabilities. That is, the transition was not intended to provide a situation wherein the United States could threaten the Soviet Union with ballistic missile attack and defend itself (a condition of considerable strategic advantage); rather, the defensive transition would allow both sides to acquire a defensive capability—U.S. ballistic missile forces would be rendered impotent and obsolete via arms control reductions and Soviet defenses.

The basic thrust of the "defensive transition" concept was as follows:

The U.S. and Soviet Union would agree to deep reductions in their respective arsenals of ballistic missiles—particularly because the value of ICBMs would have been undermined by the approach of effective BMD.

Ballistic missile defenses would be deployed by both sides either during or after the negotiated reduction or elimination of ballistic missiles.

The reduction of ballistic missiles through arms control would ease the defensive task.

The combination of reducing (or eliminating) ballistic missiles and deploying BMD would effectively eliminate their military threat to either the United States or the Soviet Union.

In short, if population protection is BMD's role, SDI and arms control can easily be linked as compatible, even mutually necessary. However, if BMD is intended to enhance deterrence, that compatibility is strained. Indeed, as was the case with *Safeguard*, SDI is now seen as the bargaining chip that must be played to achieve a "stabilizing" START agreement. These conditions proved fatal to the *Safeguard* program, and will cause great political difficulties if the President hopes to fend off another grand compromise. In contrast, the original societal protection role for SDI at least provided a basis for establishing its fundamental compatibility with arms control, a compatibility endorsed even by some fervent arms control enthusiasts.[14]

A second significant factor in the demise of the *Safeguard* program is also instructive. This was the belief that *Safeguard* was unnecessary because a credible U.S. deterrent *did not require* defensive coverage.[15] Alternative means of enhancing deterrence were cited as much more attractive than BMD deployment. The SDI's focus on a deterrence role leads directly to this same problem. If BMD's role is to enhance deterrence by "injecting uncertainties" into Soviet first-strike planning, then BMD must compete with alternative means to satisfy that goal. It does not clearly offer a unique capability.

As discussed above, in the past offensive limitations were pursued as the preferred means of enhancing deterrence, *instead of* BMD. Other alternatives considered preferable to BMD were also highlighted at the time of SALT, particularly, increased reliance on "invulnerable" SLBMs. Other alternatives were also thought possible, including mobile ICBMs, super-hardening, improving the penetrability of U.S. ballistic missile warheads, launch-under-attack tactics, and so forth.[16]

This emphasis on possible alternatives to BMD, which undermined the prospects for *Safeguard*, now affects the SDI—because its role has been shifted to enhance deterrence. For example, the House Democratic Caucus observed in their recent report on SDI that because SDI deployment is for deterrence, it "must therefore be judged against other systems that complicate Soviet attack plans such as mobile intercontinental ballistic missiles, cruise missiles and our nearly invulnerable submarines."[17] This admittedly partisan report goes on to claim that SDI would not be cost-effective compared to the possible alternatives for achieving enhanced deterrence.[18] The director of the Office of Technology Assessment's (OTA) studies of SDI, Thomas Karas, has made much the same point with regard to the cost-effectiveness of BMD's deterrence role: ". . . no one has demonstrated that the $75 billion to $150 billion Phase I BMD system would be the most cost-effective way to address these strategic problems."[19] It should be noted that OTA's earlier pre-SDI examinations of the possible net value of BMD for increasing ICBM survivability have not been sympathetic to the BMD alternative.[20]

The point here is that if SDI's role focuses primarily on complicating Soviet first-strike planning, there are alternatives to BMD to fulfill that role. When factors such as cost-effectiveness, political acceptability, and the effect of Soviet BMD are considered, it is not self-evident that there is a strategically necessary or politically "saleable" role for BMD. With regard to alternatives to BMD deployment, several difficult questions confront SDI: How much "complication" is necessary for deterrence, and how many alternatives are there to BMD for achieving that end? Of the alternatives, which is the most cost-effective and most politically palatable? What would be the impact of BMD, in contrast to other alternatives, on the U.S. offensive deterrent?

A least one set of answers to these questions is: a small mobile ICBM will adequately complicate Soviet targeting plans for deterrence purposes, will be less expensive than BMD deployment, is politically more acceptable because it need not undermine START or the ABM Treaty, and will not degrade the U.S. deterrent by compelling the Soviet Union to deploy its own BMD system. These considerations certainly doomed the prospects for *Safeguard* deployment. Yet, they are virtually irrelevant if population protection is the primary BMD role.

A factor that is new to the current SDI debate is the existence of the ABM Treaty. Anticipation of a treaty from 1969 until 1972 reduced the prospects for *Safeguard*. The ABM Treaty, which now codifies strict limitations on BMD development and deployment, appears to even further reduce the prospects for any BMD role other than a Treaty-compliant defense against very small attacks.[21]

Those who recognize that SALT I did not accomplish (to put it mildly) its intended objectives have called for U.S. withdrawal from the ABM Treaty.[22] However, there is, at this time, insufficient political support even for the implementation of the "broad interpretation" of the ABM Treaty, much less for U.S. withdrawal from the Treaty. For example, the 1989 Defense Authorization Bill, which President Reagan vetoed on August 3, 1988, retained the provision, in effect, banning any tests that would violate the strict interpretation of the ABM Treaty. The current and expected makeup of Congress does not suggest that U.S. Treaty withdrawal is likely. And because the Soviets continue to link maintenance of the Treaty to progress at START, they will be able to use the leverage of U.S. arms control hopes to keep the United States from withdrawal—much as they used such hopes to achieve the ABM Treaty in the first place.

The ABM Treaty now poses a "catch-22" for the SDI. If sufficient Congressional support for its reinterpretation does not exist and shows no sign of emerging, how can withdrawal be considered a realistic option? And if ABM Treaty testing restrictions cannot be eased, there is unlikely to be enough confidence in a proposed system to establish a persuasive rationale for withdrawal and BMD deployment.

The *Safeguard* debate may also be instructive with regard to the prospects for Treaty-compliant BMD intended only for modest NCA defense and/or protection against very limited attacks. Following ratification of the ABM Treaty, the United States had the option of maintaining two BMD sites, including one for the NCA. The rationale presented for this two-site *Safeguard* option was similar to that now heard for very limited SDI deployment.[23] Yet, the program was essentially dismissed by 1973 for being insufficient for useful NCA defense and too costly given the limited protection it would provide against accidental or unauthorized attacks and given the assumed low probability of such attacks.[24] Similar negative arguments are now heard with regard to very limited SDI.[25] There is nothing to suggest that BMD deployment for this very limited role is any more likely now than it was in 1973.

SDI Phasing

As the above discussion suggests, key SDI issues are at least as much a matter of politics, policy, and economics as they are of technical capabilities. If the strategic and arms control environment is hostile to a program, technical credibility will not save it. This is also true with regard to the issue of SDI phasing—although it generally is discussed in terms of what and when certain types of technologies should be emphasized.

There are several non-technical conditions that will determine whether, how, and when the United States will be able to proceed with the deployment of any SDI architecture. These include the following.

First, the U.S. cycle of boom or bust in defense spending is a critical factor for SDI deployment. The SDI had the misfortune of missing out on the most robust years of the Reagan administration's increase in defense spending. Indeed, the Strategic Defense Initiative Organization (SDIO) was established as the Reagan Administration's increases in defense spending began to level off. The efforts to control the federal budget deficit subsequently placed additional pressure on defense spending and led to serious Congressional opposition to the planned increases in the SDI budget. It also exacerbated the view within the military that the SDI was a prospective giant in the competition for scarce funding—and therefore a program to be viewed with skepticism. SDI deployment, in reality, may have to await the next "boom" in the U.S. defense-spending cycle before Congress and the military itself will be less afraid of the squeeze it would place on other parts of the defense budget.

Second, for SDI deployment to be politically possible the President and Congress will have to: 1) be willing to reconsider the continuing validity of the ABM Treaty; and 2) be willing to maintain an SDI development/deployment schedule even at the apparent expense of a new strategic agreement with Moscow. Neither of these conditions appears to pertain to much of the Congress. Indeed, if the Soviets continue to hold START hostage to an agreement restricting BMD, a virtual about-face on the issue of arms control by the majority in Congress will be required to gain sufficient political support for SDI deployment.

Third, U.S. strategic offensive forces and/or defensive potential will have to be so robust that the Joint Chiefs of Staff (JCS) will not be overly concerned that a move toward BMD would rebound to the near-term advantage of the Soviet Union. This JCS concern apparently has been a major impediment to serious reconsideration of the ABM Treaty and SDI deployment.[26]

Finally, as discussed above, the prospects for BMD deployment for the purpose of enhancing deterrence is problematic. However, the prospects for BMD deployment for the role of population protection will also be questionable as long as the U.S. debate over strategic forces is couched solely in the now-traditional terms of stable deterrence. If stable deterrence continues to be defined exclusively in terms of mutual retaliatory threats, it is clear that comprehensive defenses will be inconsistent with basic U.S. deterrence policy. Area protection is intended to help eliminate such deterrent threats.

SDI has the problem that the traditional notion of deterrence does not appear to require BMD, and U.S. strategic forces are considered only within the framework of traditional deterrence—however simplistically. New thinking on the entire subject of deterrence stability and its relationship to strategic defense may be necessary before BMD deployment becomes a possibility. In the past, the United States has chosen offensive-based deterrence over strategic defense, with the two generally being considered incompatible. A new appreciation of the value of strategic defense apart from deterrence considerations may be a necessary prelude to BMD deployment.

Summary

When considering the role of SDI, particularly within the context of START, the history of U.S. BMD programs is instructive. In 1969 the Nixon administration revised the population defense role of *Sentinel* in favor of the *Safeguard* role now attributed to SDI—enhancing deterrence by injecting uncertainties into Soviet offensive targeting plans. This revision of roles rendered the U.S. BMD program politically vulnerable. First, *Safeguard* was seen to be both competitive and incompatible with arms control: Competitive because arms control promised to stabilize deterrence, and incompatible because accepted wisdom was that BMD deployment would destroy the prospects for arms control. SDI, now intended to enhance deterrence, is politically vulnerable to the same problems that doomed *Safeguard*. It is viewed as competitive and incompatible with START.

Second, because *Safeguard's* role was to complicate Soviet targeting, it had to compete with alternative means of achieving the same effect. During the Congressional debate over *Safeguard*, it became clear that alternatives to BMD for this role were preferred on the basis of cost-effectiveness and political acceptability. The same considerations now challenge the SDI. Finally, SDI's phasing will be (at least) as dependent on political/policy conditions as it will be on technological maturity. Those conditions suggest that BMD deployment will require significant progress in strategic thinking on the relationship between defense and arms control and between defense and deterrence. In particular, it will require a greater appreciation for the value of strategic defense apart from deterrence considerations.

Notes

1. See Caspar Weinberger, "Morality Demands the SDI as Only Alternative to U.S.-Soviet Suicide Pact" New York City *Tribune*, January 2, 1986, p. 9; Caspar Weinberger, "Ethics and Public Policy: The Case of SDI," The *Fletcher Forum* (Winter 1986): 1–4; and President Reagan, quoted in, "Keep Space Defense Option," Colorado Springs *Gazette Telegraph*, December 30, 1984.

2. Official White House spokesmen noted that "deterrence is the name of the game," and "our objective is deterrence." Gen. Edward Rowny, "Public Briefing by the White House on SDI," Old Executive Office Building, May, 4, 1988. See also Edward L. Rowny, *SDI: Enhancing Security and Stability*, U.S. State

Department, Current Policy No. 1058, April 1988, p. 2: "It is in our interest to see to it that no Soviet planner could contemplate a first strike under any circumstances with any confidence. This is what enhancing strategic deterrence is all about. SDI contributes to this goal."

3. Secretary of Defense Weinberger appearing on the television program, "Issues and Answers," March 29, 1981.

4. Quoted from, Ronald Reagan, *National Security Strategy of The United States* (Washington, DC: The White House, January 1988), p. 15.

5. As is discussed in Douglas Johnson and Jay Winik, "Scaled-Down Missile Defense Has Merit," *Los Angeles Times*, August 10, 1988, p. 7.

6. See, *inter alia*, the expert and official testimony in: U.S. Senate, Committee on Foreign Relations, Subcommittee on International Organization and Disarmament, *Strategic and Foreign Policy Implications of ABM Systems, Hearings*, Part II, 91st Cong., 1st sess. (Washington, DC: USGPO, 1969); U.S. Senate, Committee on Foreign Relations, Subcommittee on Arms Control, International Law and Organization, *ABM, MIRV, SALT, and the Nuclear Arms Race, Hearings*, 91st Cong., 2nd sess. (Washington, DC: USGPO, 1970); and U.S. Senate, Subcommittee on Appropriations, *Department of Defense Appropriaton for Fiscal Year 1971 Hearings*, Pt. 1, 91st Cong., 2nd sess. (Washington, DC: USGPO, 1970).

7. For a review of the factors that led to *Safeguard*'s demise, see Colin S. Gray, "A New Debate on Ballistic Missile Defense," *Survival* (March/April 1981): 60–72.

8. As best exemplified in: McGeorge Bundy, George Kennan, Robert McNamara, and Gerard Smith, "The Presidents' Choice: Star Wars or Arms Control," *Foreign Affairs* (Winter 1984/85): 264–278. For synopsis of the argument, see Alex Gliksman, "Should SDI Be Part of a 'Grand Compromise': Yes," *The Christian Science Monitor*, August 28, 1986, p. 16.

9. A recent national poll demonstrates that of 14 objectives for the Bush administration, voters view an agreement on nuclear weapons second in importance only to countering the drug problem. See David Broder and Richard Morin, "Bush Will Increase Taxes, Most People Believe," *Washington Post*, November 12, 1988.

10. There were numerous public expressions from the Reagan administration of this notion of integrating deep offensive reductions with defensive deployments. See, for example, Fred Charles Iklé, "Nuclear Strategy: Can There Be a Happy Ending?" *Foreign Affairs* (Spring 1985): 810–826; Ronald Reagan, *National Security Strategy of the United States* (Washington, DC: The White House, January 1987), pp. 19–25; and U.S. Department of State, Bureau of Public Affairs, *The Strategic Defense Initiative*, Special Report No. 129 (Washington, DC: Bureau of Public Affairs, June 1985), pp. 3–5.

11. See, for example, U.S. Department of State, *The Strategic Defense Initiative*, Special Report No. 129 (Washington, DC: Bureau of Public Affairs, June 1985), p. 3.

12. U.S. Department of State, *Strategic Defense Initiative*, Current Policy No. 670 (Washington, DC: Bureau of Public Affairs, March 1985), 2–3.

13. Quoted in Eric Lerner, "The Debate Over Strategic Defense," *Aerospace America* (November 1985): 62–63.

14. As Jonathan Schell, whose book *The Fate of the Earth* was a catalyst for the freeze movement of the early 1980s, states: "Building defenses, depending on what else you do, could make it a lot easier to achieve the abolition [of the nuclear threat]. I think what arms control people are afraid of is that Star Wars is a shield that will allow Reagan to fight a nuclear war. But what if, while you build up the defenses, you reduce the offenses. . . . Then Star Wars isn't a threat at all. If you're afraid of the sword and the shield, OK. But then you should attack the sword—not the shield." Quoted in Gregory A Fossedal, "A Star Wars Caucus in the Freeze Movement," *Wall Street Journal,* February 14, 1985, p 30

15. This oft-repeated point fills the pages of Congressional hearings on *Safeguard*, and is also a mainstay of the critique of the SDI. For the argument as applied to *Safeguard*, see Senator Albert Gore's comments in *Strategic and Foreign Policy Implications of ABM Systems, Hearings,* p. 164, 173.

16. A mobile, small ICBM often is presented as a more attractive means of securing deterrence than a BMD deployment. See, for example, Brent Scowcroft, John Deutch, and R. James Woolsey, "A Small, Survivable, Mobile ICBM," *Washington Post,* December 26, 1986, p. A-23.

17. Quoted in Paul Mann, "Democrats Propose Shift in SDI Research Program to Warhead Upgrades" *Aviation Week and Space Technology,* June 13, 1988, p. 17. Similarly, Thomas Karas states, "There are many potential schemes for ensuring missile survivability—for example, moving the missiles around on land or even moving them to sea." Thomas H. Karas, "Unexamined Questions About SDI," *Issues in Science and Technology* (Fall 1988): 75.

18. House of Representatives, Democratic Caucus, *Strategic Defense, Strategic Choices: Recommendations of the Task Force on the Strategic Defense Initiative,* May 1988 pp. 3, 13–14. The same change is made in, Matthew Bunn, "SDI: Wrong Path for United States," *Defense News,* November 21, 1988, p. 24.

19. Karas, "Unexamined Questions," p. 75.

20. See, for example, U.S. Congress, Office of Technology Assessment, *MX Missile Basing* (Washington, DC: USGPO, September 1981), pp. 15–16, 19–20.

21. As was suggested by Senator Sam Nunn. See Senator Sam Nunn, *Nunn Outlines New Arms Control and Strategic Modernization Agenda,* (U.S. Senate: Office of Senator Sam Nunn, January 16, 1988), pp. 10–13; and Warren Strobel, "White House Ready to Play Chess with Nunn's SDI Plan," *Washington Post,* February 15, 1988, pp. A-1, 11.

22. See, for example, Caspar Weinberger, "It's High Time To Withdraw From ABM Treaty," *Wall Street Journal,* October 12, 1988, p. A-18; and U.S. Senate, Republican Policy Committee, *Soviet Violations and the Future of the ABM Treaty,* October 14, 1988.

23. See the discussion in Charles Murphy, *The Anti-Ballistic Missile Defense of Washington,* Congressional Research Service, Uc-500-USC, February 7, 1973.

24. Even Senator Henry "Scoop" Jackson opposed very limited BMD for costing too much for the minimum protection provided. He referred to such limited defense as "nonsense." See U.S. Senate, Committee on Armed Forces,

Military Implications of the Treaty on the Limitations of Anti-Ballistic Missile Systems and the Interim Agreement on Limitation of Strategic Offensive Arms, Hearings, 92nd Cong., 2nd sess. (Washington, DC: USGPO, 1972), p. 480.

25. See the comments by Professor Al Carnesale, quoted in Warren Strobel, "Teller Backs Limited Anti-Missile System" *Washington Times,* August 31, 1988, p. A-5.

26. As discussed in Republican Policy Committee, *Soviet Violations,* p. 16.

13
Economics, Strategy, and Burden Sharing

Anthony H. Cordesman

T he United States does not police the world alone, or operate in a power vacuum. Its allies provide by far the greater proportion of the land and air defense forces for the West; they contribute to the defense of the Atlantic, Mediterranean, and Pacific; they provide independent nuclear deterrents and many of NATO's delivery systems; they support U.S. forces overseas and provide a substantial portion of the West's sea lift, and they contribute to the protection of American interests throughout the world.

Our European allies now provide 90 percent of NATO's ground forces in Europe, 75 percent of its air power, and 50 percent of its naval assets. Even if one considers all of the forces available to NATO, which includes many U.S. forces that have contingency missions outside the NATO area or that could not deploy to NATO in less than thirty days, our European allies now provide 53 percent of the alliance's peacetime tank strength in Europe, 46 percent of its artillery, 54 percent of its combat aircraft, 83 percent of its combat ships, 58 percent of all active duty personnel, and 80 percent of all reserve personnel. By any objective measure, our European allies contribute far more to the NATO defense effort than non-Soviet Eastern European states contribute to the Warsaw Pact, as Figure 13–1 shows.

The United States often criticizes Japan for its efforts, and not without reason. Nevertheless, Japan is increasing its defense expenditures by roughly 5 percent per year in real terms, and has agreed to break its barrier of spending less than 1 percent of its GNP on defense. Japan has also built up to a force of some 246,000 regulars, 1,800 main battle tanks and other armored vehicles, 15 submarines, 36 destroyers, and 18 frigates. It has some 84 naval combat aircraft, and 389 combat aircraft in its air force. This is a large force by the standard set by many of our NATO allies.

Similarly, the Republic of South Korea maintains a force of some 629,000 men, with an army of more than 24 divisions and 1,300 main

Non-Soviet Warsaw Pact (NSWP) and Non-U.S. NATO Comparisons

A. Total Defense Activities

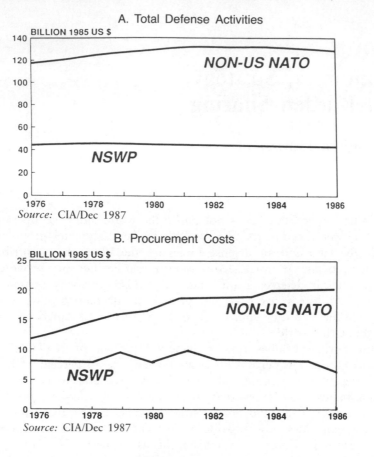

Source: CIA/Dec 1987

B. Procurement Costs

Source: CIA/Dec 1987

Military Burden
(As a percent of GNP)

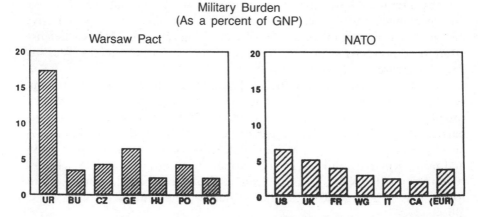

Figure 13–1. The Other Side of Burden Sharing: The Strategic Value of U.S.'s Allies versus Those of the USSR

battle tanks. It has a navy with 32 major surface ships, and an air force with 476 combat aircraft.

If one looks at the comparative trends in defense effort between 1970 and 1987, our NATO allies increased their defense spending by 34 percent in real terms and the United States increased its spending by 15 percent. Our allies increased their per capita defense spending by 21 percent and we cut ours by 3 percent. Finally, our allies cut their active military manpower by 5 percent, but we cut ours by 31 percent.

The United States's present system of alliances is scarcely perfect, but it is the most successful in history. Despite the number of nations the United States depends upon for its status as a "superpower," and their very different political constituencies and national concerns, the U.S. has been able to achieve an unprecedented amount of foreign support in meeting and defending its strategic objectives.

At the same time, however, the United States does pay more for military forces than most of its allies. In 1986, U.S. defense expenditures accounted for 65.3 percent of all the defense spending by NATO countries and Japan. The United States provided 40 percent of all the active military and civilian manpower, 38 percent of all active and reserve manpower, 39 percent of the ground forces, 46 percent of all air force tactical combat airpower, and 63 percent of all naval tonnage.

To put these figures on defense effort into perspective, the United States had 41 percent of the total gross domestic product (GDP) of NATO and Japan in 1986, and 32 percent of the population. It was regularly spending 6–7 percent of its GDP on defense, versus an average of 3.5 percent of GDP for all non-U.S. NATO allies, 5.1 percent of GDP for the United Kingdom, 3.9 percent for France, 3.1 percent for the Federal Republic of Germany, (FRG), and roughly 1 percent for Japan.

While a large part of the U.S. defense effort did not contribute directly to the defense of NATO or Japan, most provided contingency capabilities that were of importance to the West—such as the defense of the West's oil supplies in the Persian Gulf. The United States does, therefore, have a legitimate argument that it is being asked to pay for a disproportionate share of the West's defense.

Allied Recognition of U.S. Arguments
Regarding Burden Sharing

Our major and wealthier allies recognize the merits of these arguments. The United States has long benefited from its efforts to persuade its richer allies to bear more of the burden of the West's defense. During the last two decades, the United States has negotiated arrangements that save it billions of dollars each year and hundreds of thousands of man-years.

The U.S. has reached arrangements with its allies which:

Have led Japan to pay 30 percent of all the costs of stationing U.S. troops in Japan, and Britain and the FRG to pay a steadily increasing amount of all stationing costs.

Have led Japan to increase its real defense spending by 4–5.5 percent per year, to pay roughly $2.5 billion a year in direct and indirect support for U.S. forces for Japan in FY1988, and to buy over $1 billion of U.S. military equipment annually.

Have helped lead Japan to spend some $7.6 billion annually in overseas development aid as an alternative to added military spending.

Have led West Germany alone to agree to provide 93,000 troops in wartime to support U.S. forces in the FRG.

Have led our NATO allies to create a shipping pool of over 4,000 ships, including 450 militarily suitable dry cargo ships, for direct sealift support of NATO.

Have led NATO to sharply increase its infrastructure program over the last fifteen years. The funding for the current five-year sharing period (1985–1990) totals some $11 billion, a 56 percent increase over the prior period. The United States contributes 28 percent of these funds, but gets about 30–40 percent for U.S. or U.S.-user projects.

Have helped persuade our allies to accept a gap in the defense balance of trade that led them to import 2.6 times as much military equipment from the United States as they exported over the period from FY1982 to FY1983—a trade surplus for the United States of $21.3 billion.

In many ways, the United States has been as successful in obtaining allied financial and manpower support for U.S. forces as it has been in obtaining military support. Nevertheless, the United States now faces a major debate over the issue of burden sharing. This debate also shows little concern with whether the United States has already achieved a great deal. It is concerned with whether the United States can achieve the level of additional success that would allow it to achieve radical additional savings, make major cuts in its forces or commitments, or lead to major changes in the West's overall ability to perform given roles and missions.

Several factors have combined to transform burden sharing from a steady ongoing process of negotiation to one of the most popular buzzwords in U.S. discussions of defense. The trade gap, U.S. budget deficits, the rapid growth in the GNP of key allies like the FRG and Japan, and sheer "deterrence fatigue" have all combined to make the idea of increased allied effort seem increasingly necessary.

One result of this popularity is a flood of new studies by the Department of Defense, the Congress, and various research groups. There is a virtual deluge of econometric statistics on the relative defense effort of the major nations in the Western alliance, and of clever new ways in which other nations could spend more on their own forces or help the United States spend less.

Econometrics versus Strategy

At the same time, this flood of studies and statistics has generally ignored the strategic aspects of what the United States should really ask for from its allies. Most burden sharing studies simply assume that more is better, or that the United States should seek some vaguely defined econometric equity. Those few studies which touch on the issue of roles and commitments tend to seek either additive allied efforts or solutions through which the United States can cut its costs, rather than make shifts in its strategic position.

This lack of attention to strategic factors seems to have two primary causes. The first is historical. Since the early 1960s, both the Congress and the Executive have tended to view burden sharing as an exercise in which the United States bargains to reduce its defense spending or achieve increases in allied spending without major changes in roles and missions. In fact, the United States has tended to play a "good guy–bad guy" game with its allies in which the Executive exploits the threat of Congressionally mandated withdrawals to achieve limited annual increases in allied effort. The other cause is the fact that the debate has concentrated heavily on econometrics, and has generally paid remarkably little attention to the comparative capability to generate actual military forces or the ability to meet military commitments and perform given roles and missions.

The Department of Defense, and a few private studies, have begun to rank performance in terms of relative manpower, tanks, divisions, ships, tonnage, and aircraft, but they have spent relatively little time on the meaning of these numbers or the need to examine military effort in terms of the ability to perform given roles and missions.

By and large, most of the U.S. arguments have focused on total national or regional defense spending, and have implied that the West should distribute its military burdens on the basis of econometric equity. While there have been some recent departures from the "equity" thesis, they have tended to use the same econometric arguments to call for "U.S. withdrawal and allied replacement" without going further than comparing the increases in allied economic strength relative to those of the United States.

Costing the Burden

U.S. studies also tend to be rather careless about what they cost. Most simply assume that total national defense effort should be the standard of comparison. The few that actually examine the relative cost of U.S. forces for a given region or mission tend to look solely at the cost of NATO forces, and the authors rarely examine whether the U.S. definition of these costs is particularly meaningful.

This is a major issue, because the U.S. Department of Defense includes a wide mix of forces in the United States in its cost estimates for the U.S. contribution to NATO. It is true that these forces are assigned or earmarked to NATO, but the United States often lacks the sea- and air-lift and sustainability to deploy them. The United States often includes forces in the continental United States (CONUS) more because they do not have an alternative mission than because it has a real-world ability to use them in the vast majority of contingencies that could occur in a NATO–Warsaw Pact conflict.

This kind of statistical gamesmanship is useful—at least from a U.S. perspective—in arguing for more allied effort in terms of support and infrastructure spending, but it has dubious military validity.

"Marginal Value" and "Marginal Cost"

Most of the U.S. arguments relating to burden sharing have also ignored the end result, or "marginal value," of any added allied efforts they have called for. This is comparatively unimportant when allies are being asked to bear the existing costs of U.S. forces, but is a real problem when allies are being asked to spend more on their own forces.

While added defense spending would, by and large, improve the readiness or strength of allied military forces, it would take very large increases in most cases to significantly improve their capabilities to perform roles and missions. For example, a 3 percent real annual increase in defense spending is far larger than our Central Region allies are ever likely to agree to, but even if they did agree to such an increase, it would not materially alter their ability to fight a conventional war in Europe or allow the United States to significantly reduce its forces for NATO.

Increasing Efforts and Diminishing Returns

Finally, the U.S. emphasis on an econometric approach to burden sharing often leads U.S. analysts outside the office of the Secretary of Defense to ignore the problem of diminishing returns. The United States has, after all, been pressuring its allies to help reduce U.S. costs for nearly two decades. It has tacitly or actively posed the threat of U.S. withdrawals ever since the Mansfield Amendment, and the Department of Defense now engages in an almost continuous dialectic with each major ally on why and how it should do more.

At this point in time, it is far from clear why any new econometric argument—or any variation on an old one—should have any serious marginal impact in persuading our allies to do even more. In fact, most of the proposals emanating from outside the administration are so purely econometric, and so devoid of sensitivity to allied needs and politics, that they are more likely to result in a given ally doing less than in that ally doing more.

This kind of counterproductive U.S. effort became all too public during the summer of 1988, when the Senate and House came up with a list of some seventeen burden-sharing measures to add to the FY1989 Defense Appropriations Bill. These measures were drafted at the last minute and tacked onto the bill with only token research. As a result, they threatened to do so much damage to the ongoing burden-sharing negotiations between the United States, the FRG, the United Kingdom, and Japan that the Department of Defense was forced into a major lobbying effort to try to stop the Congress from shooting the U.S. position in the foot.

Roles and Missions: The Strategic Side of Burden Sharing

The United States has little reason to doubt that its allies will continue to do more over time. Its wealthier allies will unquestionably make marginal and symbolic increases in their contribution to burdensharing as long as the United States keeps its demands limited and does not present them in a form that pushes the issue to the level of confrontation or becoming a source of domestic political controversy.

One can also make the argument that the current U.S. debate will—at a minimum—lead to token or marginal increases in allied efforts, which will have political value even if they have little or no meaning in really altering the burden or changing allied military capabilities. Limited amounts of "reverse Danegelt" can have a powerful political impact in the United States in showing the public and the Congress that our allies recognize the importance of our contribution to the common defense, and they can often fund politically controversial programs or expenses.

The real question is whether our allies will do enough to matter in meeting one or more broader strategic objectives: assuming the full cost of the U.S. burden, replacing U.S. forces with allied forces, or making significant enough increases in their forces to make major changes in collective mission capabilities.

Paying for the "Full Cost" of the U.S. Presence

The United States is likely to have the most success in achieving the first strategic objective: persuading its wealthier allies to make major increases in paying for the cost of the U.S. forces on their soil. It is at least possible that if Japan continues to enjoy its present economic growth and trade advantages over the United States, that it will be willing to fund well over 50 percent of these costs.

Japan is also the case where the gap between economic strength and defense spending is most apparent. In 1986, Japan had 20 percent of the total GDP of NATO and Japan, and 16 percent of the population, but only provided 4.6 percent of total defense spending, 3.2 percent of active military and civilian manpower, 2.2 percent of total active and reserve manpower, 3.2 percent of all ground forces, 3.9 percent of all air force tactical combat aircraft, and 3.1 percent of all naval tonnage. While Japanese real defense spending had increased by 139 percent between 1971 and 1986—versus 25 percent for the United States, 48 percent for France, 26 percent for the FRG, and 12 percent for the United Kingdom, the net result still had a very limited impact on Japan's economy. Further, Japanese active military and civilian manpower only increased by 3.3 percent over the same period.

It is important to note, however, that it is extremely unlikely that Japan will ever go to the point of paying for the much larger U.S. force slice that is currently devoted to maintaining the U.S. presence in Asia and for a major share of the U.S. power projection capability in the Gulf. Further, while South Korea is likely to improve its own burden-sharing efforts, these are unlikely to increase quickly, and the net impact of any such effort may well be offset by increased U.S. costs in the Philippines or from relocating outside the Philippines.

The FRG is also likely to be willing to make slow but significant increases in its offset payments. The case for such German action, however, is considerably less clear than with Japan. In 1986, the FRG had 9 percent of the total GNP of NATO and Japan, and 8 percent of the population, and provided 6.4 percent of total defense spending, 8.0 percent of active military manpower, 11.2 percent of total active and reserve manpower, 12.1 percent of all ground forces, 7.0 percent of all air force tactical combat aircraft, and 3.3 percent of all naval tonnage. While the FRG only spent about half the percentage of its GDP on defense that the United States spent, these figures do not imply a major gap between economic strength and military contribution.

The FRG certainly benefits from NATO, but it also has become the West's key "frontline" state. It also makes a contribution to Western defense that is not reflected in its defense spending data or the size of its own forces. The FRG is only about the size of Oregon, but it has 25 percent of the population of the United States. Nevertheless, six nations station some 400,000 troops and 325,000 dependents on its soil. These occupy 800 German military installations, with a value of roughly $30 billion. The FRG also provides exercise facilities for some 5,000 exercises a year, including 85 major field exercises. It also provides air space for some 580,000 sorties, including 110,000 at altitudes below 1,500 feet.

The FRG may well offset more foreign exchange costs for the U.S. presence in the FRG, but it is extremely unlikely to ever pay for all the costs of U.S. forces in West Germany. It would also be very unrealistic to expect it to do so. These U.S. forces are deployed to defend all of NATO, and not the simply the FRG.

As for the other countries in Europe, it is important to note that each makes a very different military contribution and faces very different political and economic constraints. France, for example, has 7.2 percent of the GDP of NATO and Japan and 7.3 percent of its total population. It ranks second to the United States in terms of defense spending as a percent of total NATO and Japan (6.6 percent) and provides 8.3 percent of active military manpower, 8.6 percent of active and reserve manpower, 6.2 percent of all ground forces, 8 percent of all combat aircraft, and 4.3 percent of all naval tonnage.

While France does only spend 3.9 percent of its GDP on defense, it is difficult to argue that its contribution in terms of military forces is out of line with its share of the total defense effort of NATO and Japan. Further, France stands outside the formal structure of the NATO alliance, and is not going to provide direct financial support for the U.S. presence in Europe.

Britain is the only other major U.S. ally which has the mix of wealth and forces to really make a major contribution to burden sharing, and the Thatcher government is probably doing about as much as it can, given the real-world character of its political and economic situation. Britain spent 5.1 percent of its GDP on defense in 1986, or more than five times as much as Japan. Britain also has 5.4 percent of the total GDP of NATO and Japan and 7.4 percent of the population, and provides 6.3 percent of all defense spending, 6.3 percent of active military manpower, 5.3 percent of active and reserve manpower, 4.9 percent of all ground forces, 9 percent of all air force tactical combat aircraft, and 12.1 percent of all naval tonnage. Even if one ignores Britain's economic and political climate, these numbers do not argue that Britain is not doing its share.

As for the smaller NATO nations, Belgium, Denmark, and the Netherlands all have very serious economic and budgetary problems that already impact heavily on their political situation, and face declining real ability to fund their existing level of national military capability, much less fund that of the United States. With luck, they will maintain their existing contribution, but it simply is not realistic to expect them to make significant increases.

The situation is even less promising on the flanks. Italy is the one major exception. It is rapidly overtaking Britain in economic terms, and now has 6 percent of NATO and Japan's GDP and 7.5 percent of its population. It only spends 2.2 percent of its GDP on defense, and provides only 3.1 percent of all defense spending, 7.0 percent of active military manpower, 6.3 percent of active and reserve manpower, 4.9 percent of all ground forces, 5.5 percent of all air force tactical combat aircraft, and 1.9 percent of all naval tonnage. These figures imply that Italy should be able to do more both in terms of offsetting the cost of the U.S. presence in Italy and in defending the Mediterranean—although it is far from clear whether this is politically realistic. Italy may do more in terms of some support and infrastructure costs, but only to a very marginal extent.

As for the other flank countries, Norway faces serious budgetary and revenue problems. Greece, Portugal, Spain, and Turkey are all seeking additional U.S. aid as the price of maintaining current U.S. basing arrangements, and have long received more in terms of NATO-wide funds than they contribute.

The United States is now able to achieve a partial offset for its contingency capabilities in the Gulf in the form of Saudi and Kuwait provision of fuel, transit facilities, arms purchases, and similar indirect support. This support, however, is likely to decline with time as the pressure of the Iran-Iraq War is replaced by a ceasefire, and the financial and political impact of the Saudi decision to buy its arms from Britain impacts on the flow of foreign military sales (FMS) revenues.

It is also important to stress that added U.S. pressure on many allied countries will simply mean that the added payments to the United States will come in the form of trade-offs. With the exception of Japan, our allies are likely to act on the fact that money and manpower are fungible. The United States has often been able to get marginal shifts in allied spending to directly support U.S. forces without such trade-offs in the past, but a close examination of allied defense plans indicates that unless the increase in effort is largely a product of the declining value of the dollar, our allies are simply reprogramming funds within their existing budget.

If Japan is willing to increase both its burden-sharing payments and its defense expenditures, this will be because of its growing sensitivity to its trade gap with the United States, and not because of its interest in changing its capabilities to peform regional roles and missions. Further, any increase in the total Japanese level of burden-sharing and defense spending is likely to be remarkably marginal in terms of its net impact on the econometrics of burden sharing as measured in most U.S. studies.

Replacing U.S. Forces with Allied Forces

Many of the same political and economic forces apply when one examines U.S. ability to achieve its second strategic objective in burden-sharing: replacing U.S. forces with allied forces. It is nice to talk about European defense initiatives, and such discussions may do some exhortative good in persuading individual European countries to maintain their present force levels and their levels of real defense spending. It is important to note, however, that there is no realistic prospect that Europe will either negotiate a major replacement for U.S. forces or react by replacing them if the United States unilaterally withdraws its forces.

To begin with, "Europe" does not exist as a strategic entity. While Italy and France might react to a massive U.S. withdrawal from the Mediterranean on a purely national basis, there is no practical prospect that they would fund anything approaching the capability of a single U.S. carrier task force or that Greece, Portugal, Spain, or Turkey would either fund serious force increases or be willing to develop a common force.

In the case of the northern flank, Britain, Canada, and the Netherlands are already either cutting their present contingency forces for the region or considering such cuts. Even if Norway made major increases in its real defense spending or active manpower—increases as large as 25 percent—it would not materially affect the military balance or furnish a substitute for the kind of amphibious, naval, and air capabilities provided by the United States.

In the case of Central Europe, it is extremely doubtful that Europe would produce the equivalent of one U.S. air wing or full U.S. division slice in reaction to any amount of U.S. political pressure or even a unilateral U.S. withdrawal. At least at this point in time, the FRG would almost certainly take the risk of relying on its improved climate of relations with the Soviet Union—if for no other reason than the inability to obtain the kind of domestic political consensus necessary to fund really major changes in its number of active army combat units and air force. In fact, it might well be pushed into adopting some of the "defensive" force concepts advocated by the more radical Social Democrats.

Denmark would be likely to follow a similar path. Belgium and the Netherlands might spend a little more and increase the readiness of some of their combat units, but would be extremely unlikely to generate the equivalent of more than a single brigade or squadron. France might encourage some form of European defense force on paper, but it would also probably push hard for an increase in dependence on nuclear weapons. Britain would be torn politically between emphasizing nuclear weapons and seeking some kind of conventional force reduction agreement with the Soviet Union.

In short, the United States can always withdraw from Europe, but the only compensation it is likely to get from its European allies is a mix of meetings, good intentions, and political confusion. Unless the United States can cut its forces in Europe in the context of conventional force reductions, it will have no choices other than to either maintain them or cut its forces at the cost of reducing the overall conventional capabilities of the Alliance.

As for other regions, the only two cases where allied substitution for U.S. forces have any practical meaning are Japan and South Korea. In the case of Japan, a major U.S. withdrawal might lead to a significant increase in the role of the Japanese Self-Defense Force, but it is important to understand that even if such an increase took place, it would almost certainly fail to provide any major substitute for U.S. forces.

At a minimum, Japan would probably fail to develop any major power projection forces. It is difficult to see Japan developing the equivalent of carrier task forces in reaction to U.S. force cuts. It is equally difficult to see Japan offering some form of defense guarantee to South Korea or any of its neighbors, or developing any form of nuclear deterrent. It would be far more likely to adopt a posture of enhanced conventional defense of its home territory, and conciliation or some degree of neutralism. At the same time, Japan would almost certainly be thrust into developing a major defense industry and into exporting defense equipment.

Even if Japan followed the opposite course, and did seek to become a regional power, the question arises as to whether this would be acceptable to other pro-Western nations in Asia or desirable from a U.S. perspective. The current slow but steady increase in Japanese homeland defense capabilities is clearly in the U.S. national interest, and has already led the United States to tailor its forces in Asia to support other missions. However, driving Japan into trying to rebuild its former status as a regional superpower raises very serious questions about the resulting impact on long-term Japanese ambitions in the region and U.S. ability to maintain the advantages it draws from its present relationship with the People's Republic of China (PRC).

As for South Korea, the real issue is not whether South Korea can replace the 29,100-man U.S. land force and U.S. infantry division in that country, or the 11,200 men and 168 combat aircraft deployed by the U.S. Air Force. It is rather South Korea's inability to replace the symbolic impact of deploying U.S. conventional and theater nuclear forces near the border with North Korea, and the threat of massive U.S. reinforcement. Further, it is virtually certain that any Korean increases in forces would have a much lower overall level of technology than the present mix of U.S. land and air units.

Threatening to take our marbles and go home unless our friends play the game our way is not a bad negotiating tactic as long as we do not push the tactic too hard. It is not, however, likely to be a successful global strategy. The United States can always cut its forces and commitments, but it is not likely to result in increased allied burden sharing, merely in increased risks.

Making Major Changes in Collective Defense Capability

As for the third strategic objective—making major changes in collective defense capability—four major subsets of military capability are involved:

> strengthening NATO conventional options;
> strengthening nuclear deterrence;
> strengthening the defense of Asia; and
> strengthening the defense of the Persian Gulf.

By and large, the United States is just as unlikely to achieve major changes in any of these mission areas as it is to find replacements for U.S. forces, and for roughly the same reasons.

At the same time, other factors are also at work. In the case of NATO conventional options, the United States faces the practical problem that it would take major amounts of new forces and new weapons to significantly extend NATO's conventional war-fighting capability, and even greater amounts to allow NATO to safely count on conducting a successful conventional defense.

Not only is it unlikely that key allies will pay for these options, it is important to note that the U.S. emphasis on conventional options is not matched by any of its major European allies, and is openly rejected by France. The plain truth is that U.S. allies are satisfied with their current level of conventional capability, and most seriously hope that conventional force reductions will allow them to reduce their present forces. Regardless of buzzwords such as "competitive strategies," "Follow-on Forces Attack (FOFA)," and conventional defense initiatives, it is extremely unlikely that NATO will support the kind of major shift in policy necessary to produce a major shift in conventional war-fighting capability.

The nuclear case is somewhat different. Britain and France are already considering significant improvements in their nuclear capabilities, and many are likely to be funded. The United States can also probably persuade its allies to support the modernization of NATO's theater nuclear forces if the United States can agree on what is to be done. It is very unlikely, however, that the United States can really achieve a major change in the current level of allied and NATO theater nuclear deterrence or in war-fighting capability. If anything, the challenge is to preserve it.

As for Asia, the prospects of major changes in the balance of North and South Korean forces are so negligible that it is unclear that the United States has ever sought such actions—although it is far from clear what can be done to radically change the balance in Asia without changing the balance in Korea. Similarly, even if Japan were to fully assume the responsibility for defense of its home waters, air space, and territory, this would not radically change the overall balance in Northeast Asia and the Pacific. A major change in the balance would require a Japanese fleet that could join the United States in projecting power and fighting a battle of the Pacific with the Soviet surface, attack submarine (SSN), and ballistic missile submarine (SSBN) fleets. Not only is Japan unlikely to support such a new role for its forces, it is also extremely uncertain whether the United States should seek to influence Japan to do so.

The irony of the situation in the Persian Gulf is that the Southern Gulf countries would dearly love to be able to create a much stronger regional deterrent and remove the need for dependence on over-the-horizon reinforcement by the United States, but lack the personnel and human infrastructure to do so. Similarly, it is very unlikely that the United States can preserve, much less increase, all of its present support from states in the region if the Iran-Iraq ceasefire ends in a true peace. The problems created by U.S. ties to Israel are not likely to diminish in the near future.

As for our European allies, they have already done what they are likely to do in any contingency short of a major direct threat to their supplies of oil, and they would then draw down on their forces for NATO. Thus, the practical chances of any ally creating major new power projection forces are nonexistent.

Burdensharing and "Deterrence Fatigue"

There can be no doubt that the United States has, and will continue to benefit from its efforts to use burden-sharing arguments to push its allies to increase or maintain their defense efforts, to subsidize the cost of U.S. deployments overseas, and to provide substitutes for deploying U.S. forces. The United States has saved billions of dollars each year from such efforts.

The problem does not lie in stressing the importance of burden-sharing negotiations, or in attempting to improve their marginal impact and effectiveness. It lies in the assumption that burden sharing will somehow allow the United States to achieve strategic objectives that go far beyond its current successes in negotiating with its allies. It also lies in the assumption that our allies can be treated as one large block, and that econometrics is a valid measure of defense effort.

None of these assumptions is valid. Further, they seem to owe more to "deterrence fatigue" than to strategic reality. They imply a vision of a United States suffering from strain and implied decline, somehow having been unfairly thrust into the position of becoming a global power. They ignore past and present U.S. success in dealing with the Soviet bloc and opportunities like conventional arms reductions. They also ignore the fact that the United States maintains both an extraordinarily stable matrix of deterrents and the ability to play a major role in an increasingly more important Third World, through a structure of alliances in which other nations bear a very large portion of the cost.

In a practical sense, the more extreme advocates of new and stronger burden-sharing methods seem to be committed to a "little America" with very little real-world concern for what this change in the United States's global role would mean. The net result would be to change burden sharing from a highly successful negotiating tool to a means of snatching defeat from the jaws of victory.

14

Coalition Strategy and the Operational Level of Warfare

Phillip A. Karber
Diego A. Ruiz Palmer

"In future warfare, cooperation between tanks and aeroplanes is
likely to prove far more important than cooperation between tanks
and infantry. So important that we may see tanks and aeroplanes
forming one force . . ."
—Major-General J. F. C. Fuller, British Army
*Lectures on F.S.R. III (Operations between
Mechanized Forces)*, 1932

"What we are looking for (rather) is some way to make it possible
to step from the intermediate stage of 'airmobility' to what I call
'airmechanization' . . . The attack helicopter is the forerunner of
the future Airmechanized Main Battle Air Vehicle."
—General Dr. F. von Senger und Etterlin, German Army
New Operational Dimensions, 1983

T here have been numerous attempts to construct a definition of
modern strategy that succinctly captures the essence of the concept. The resulting variety of definitions notwithstanding, modern
military strategy at its heart combines the following five components:

a plan of action,

for the allocation of resources,

based on an anticipated contingency,

specifying the simultaneous and sequential orchestration of military
operations,

for the achievement of a political objective.

The authors wish to express their appreciation to Millard Barger, a senior analyst on the
staff of the NATO Studies Center, at the BDM Corporation, for his assistance in preparing
this paper.

Such a definition implies that there exists some means—concepts of operations—whereby military actions can be "orchestrated" in pursuit of a political objective. This paper will attempt to document the development of operational concepts in NATO and to illuminate their relationship to the evolution of NATO strategy, the maturing Soviet threat, and the rate of technological integration.

Strategy affects operational concepts in two ways: first, as a guide to military action; and second, as a framework for the development of the necessary capabilities to carry out desired operations. The evolution of NATO strategy has reflected both roles with respect to the evolution of operational concepts.

The decade of the 1980s has been a time of unprecedented conceptual innovation in the organization and employment of conventional forces for coalition warfare and in the development of what the Soviets call "operational art" in both NATO and the Warsaw Pact. Both NATO as a whole and its individual member nations have gradually developed a body of doctrine on the command and employment of land, air, and maritime forces at the operational level. Although overshadowed by the publicity accorded the SHAPE (Supreme Headquarters Allied Powers in Europe) "Follow-On Forces Attack" subconcept, other operational concepts and trends in NATO force development—particularly airmobility—merit consideration. Against the background of continuing NATO allegiance to the twin concepts of "Flexible Response" and "Forward Defense," this paper will attempt to review important aspects of the changing operational landscape of coalition strategy.

The Evolution of the Strategic Context

NATO's first strategy, a legacy of the Western Union Defense Organization, called for a defense anchored on the Rhine, strategic bombing of the Soviet Union, and an amphibious invasion to retake the European continent should it be lost. When NATO adopted Military Committee document MC 14/1 in 1949, the Alliance did not then have the forces required for its prosecution. No U.S. nuclear or conventional assets were committed in support of the strategy, and the U.S. Strategic Air Command (SAC) would have been unable to service the targeting requirements had release been given. In addition, the U.S. Air Force in Europe was equipped more for a transportation mission than for a combat role, given that the remnants of the U.S. occupation ground forces were, in the event of hostilities, scheduled to be withdrawn off the continent.

With the advent of the Korean War and the acquisition of convincing intelligence data revealing the existence of a "Stalin Plan" for the invasion of Western Europe, the U.S. military commitment to NATO became a reality with the forward basing of SAC and the return of the U.S. Seventh Army to the continent. As implemented in force goals adopted at Lisbon in 1952, MC 14/1 represented a traditional "Counter-Offensive" doctrine as grandiose in conception as NATO was deficient in its capability to execute it.

Under the MC 14/2 "Sword and Shield" concept, promulgated in 1957, the role of forward-deployed forces was not conventional defense, but political credibility and nuclear capability. After providing a temporary "shield" to determine that an attack was in fact serious and buying time for the uploading and deployment of nuclear assets, they were to participate as one of the avenging "swords" in a large-scale nuclear strike. The scale of strikes was extensive, simultaneously targeted against the maneuver forces of the first echelon and the rear lines of communication supporting the second.

However tenuous the MC 14/2 "tripwire" strategy was as an operational plan, and despite the subsequent criticisms of over-reliance on nuclear escalation, it served remarkably well as a force development guideline, focusing greater attention on the importance of the conventional shield. It was under this strategy that many salient conventional force improvements were made. Most significant was the creation and buildup of the *Bundeswehr* which effectively doubled NATO's conventional strength. As NATO's conventional posture improved, the Alliance converted its operational concept from a delay on the Rhine, to a mobile defense on the Weser, to decisive early engagement at the inner-German border—all within the space of a decade.

In 1967, after an extensive debate, NATO adopted MC 14/3—the strategy of "Flexible Response." While retaining the ultimate sanction of a General Nuclear Response, the primary emphasis of the new strategy was to deploy sufficient conventional forces to provide a Direct Defense against a Warsaw Pact attack. Initial forward defenses were bolstered by an ambiguous threat of Deliberate Escalation in the event they were in danger of being overwhelmed by Soviet reinforcements. This change in NATO strategy was motivated by: the declining credibility of a tripwire nuclear strategy in an approaching era of strategic parity; the realization that mutual possession of tactical nuclear systems negated NATO's previous military advantage; a reappraisal of the conventional balance in Central Europe resulting largely from the completion of the West German rearmament; and an optimistic assessment of NATO's ability to exploit Western technological superiority to produce a robust conventional defense. As a result, NATO focused on the development of conventional force capabilities necessary to implement a successful defense against the Warsaw Pact's first echelon, while retaining nuclear weapon employment options should a direct defense prove unsuccessful.[1]

The Imperative for Forward Defense

Under MC 14/3, the Direct Defense component of Flexible Response was to be a forward defense in recognition of the imperatives implicit in NATO's earlier transition from a concept of a stand on the Rhine to a concept of decisive engagement at the inner-German border (see figure 14–1). The requirements for a forward defense by NATO in Central Europe are many and compelling. A defense predicated on the abandonment of the bulk of West Germany in a space-for-time trade-off would be unacceptable to the Federal Republic, especially given its effort to reconstitute significant military forces and defensive capabilities through the buildup of the Bundeswehr.

Militarily, the need for a forward defense is primarily a function of geography. Considered from the perspective of a theater of military operations, Central Europe is so lacking in strategic depth that a space-for-time approach is simply not viable given the speed of modern combined-arms forces. For every one hundred kilometers given up, NATO loses assets critical to maintaining a coherent coalition defense. Moving back its initial General Defense Plan positions one hundred kilometers from the inner-German border would deprive the Alliance of its most defensible terrain as well as its best opportunity to maximize the force-to-space considerations to its advantage. Beyond this point the terrain allows for greater maneuvering as a result of numerous interconnected routes of approach, which present the attacker with the advantage of flexibility in choosing avenues of advance and rob the defender of force density by forcing him to cover all possibilities rather than concentrate on a few probable potential axes. A defense that cannot hold territory a second one hundred kilometers from the inner-German border would allow an attacker to cross the Rhine and cut the lines of communication between NATO's Northern and Central Army Groups. The loss of territory extending three hundred kilometers from the inner-German border would deprive the Alliance of the bulk of its integrated military infrastructure on the continent as well as the ports and facilities required to receive reinforcements and supplies.

Given this recognition by NATO of the critical importance of a forward defense to its Flexible Response strategy, the Alliance has undertaken a number of measures to enhance its conventional posture. The emphasis has been on the creation of heavily mechanized combined-arms formations integrating main battle tanks, antitank guided missiles

169

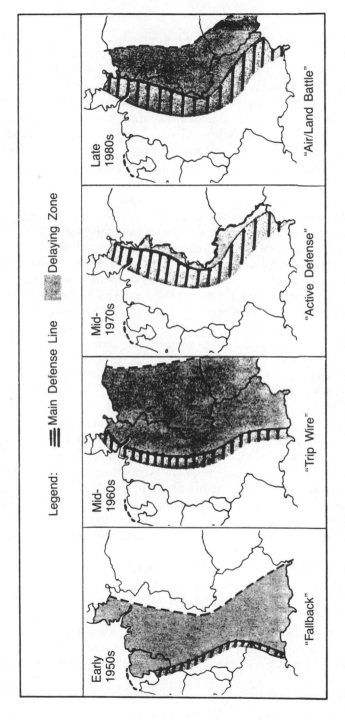

Figure 14–1. Forward Defense: Evolution of a Strategic Concept

Source: Phillip A. Karber, "In Defense of Forward Defense," Armed Forces Journal International (May 1984), p. 28.

(ATGMs) and direct-support artillery. One area of particular focus has been the proliferation throughout all NATO ground forces of man-portable, vehicle-mounted and helicopter-launched ATGMs such as Dragon, Milan, TOW, HOT, and Swingfire. Expansion or relocation forward of fast-consumables and the gradual deployment of improved conventional munitions and precision-guided munitions have also contributed to the increase in NATO's capabilities. The fielding of dedicated close air support aircraft, such as the A-10, Alpha-Jet, and Harrier, was also instrumental in providing a fast-reaction support capability to help stabilize NATO's conventional defense.[2]

The Soviets have striven to undermine the Flexible Response strategy across the range of NATO response options. At the high end of the response spectrum, the Soviets have countered General Nuclear Response by eliminating U.S. superiority in strategic nuclear forces and achieving parity in the 1970s. Regarding Deliberate Escalation, the Soviets have achieved parity with NATO in tactical nuclear weapons, and in the wake of the intermediate-range nuclear forces (INF) agreement have retained a somewhat diminished edge in theater nuclear forces, depriving NATO of escalation dominance and diminishing the military utility and practicality of NATO's first-use option. As for countering the Direct Defense element of the Flexible Response, the Soviets have made progress in two related areas. First, the buildup of Soviet conventional forces over the past twenty years has increased the traditional Soviet quantitative superiority to the point that the Warsaw Pact 55+ division force forward-deployed in Central Europe today is equivalent to the 90 Pact divisions that would have been available after two weeks of mobilization in 1965, a third of which would have had to be reinforcing divisions from the western USSR. Second, this buildup has had not only a quantitative dimension but a qualitative dimension as well. The modernization of Soviet forces with fourth-generation main battle tanks and combat aircraft, the mechanization of its infantry with second-generation armored fighting vehicles, and the wholesale proliferation of self-propelled artillery have allowed the Soviets to achieve combined-arms synergies on a scale suitable for a rapid and decisive theater-level conventional offensive. The Soviet Union has established permanent High Commands of Forces in the various theaters of military operations as a capstone to the maturation of its capability to conduct a theater-strategic operation. In the process, operational art has been given a strategic dimension. Concepts for executing *Front*-level encirclement operations, for conducting air operations with strategic air armies, and for the use of operational maneuver groups (OMGs) have been constantly refined.

Under the long-standing Soviet perception that success in a military confrontation with the West would necessarily require an offensive into the depths of Western Europe, the development of NATO's forward defense concept has not gone unnoticed in the East. Indeed, the Soviets have devoted exceptional effort to formulate concepts and acquire the capabilities required to overcome a "stable" NATO defense. In the view of Soviet military strategists, this can best be accomplished via a "theater-strategic operation" that relies on rapid and deep penetration to envelop, isolate, and eventually destroy NATO military groupings. This emphasis on penetration and encirclement operations stems from the Soviet experience with "mobile groups" and large-scale offensives in the "Great Patriotic War." Of these offensives, according to the former Chief of the Soviet General Staff, Marshal of the Soviet Union Sergey Akhromeyev, "the most effective was the offensive from converging directions which concluded with the encirclement and destruction of large enemy groupings."[3]

Soviet experience in World War II also indicated the critical importance of the breakthrough operation. While such operations are designed to press against the weaker elements of the opposing force groupings, thereby avoiding the cost of attacking enemy strength and maximizing the opportunities for exploiting breakthroughs through the subsequent development of pincer movements, the Soviets also recognize the vulnerability of an offensive in the breakthrough phase to attrition and counterattack by the enemy.

In order to mitigate these vulnerabilities, the Soviets plan to conduct an "air operation" to deny NATO air superiority, exploit NATO's reliance on airpower to offset its ground force imbalance, and preclude the possibility of NATO escalating to nuclear response. The goals of the Soviet air operation, conducted with aircraft as well as surface-to-surface missiles, also include attrition and delay of NATO maneuver units and reinforcing forces to further enhance the possibility of attaining correlations of forces and means more favorable to the attacker.

Drawing on the World War II experience of exploiting weak sectors to enable encirclement of strong sectors, the Soviets currently can avail themselves of the opportunities provided by NATO's "layer cake" defense posture, which assigns responsibility for defense of a continuous front to individual national corps. There are marked differences in the capabilities and posture of the respective NATO forces as well as the challenges facing the various corps themselves. The Soviets have recognized these differences (see figure 14–2) and have planned their operational directions of attack to take advantage of them and to create problems for intra-Alliance command and control. Soviet encirclement strategy calls for fixing attacks against the stronger U.S. (V, VII) and German (I, III) corps, breakthrough operations to be conducted across the weaker Belgian corps sector into the

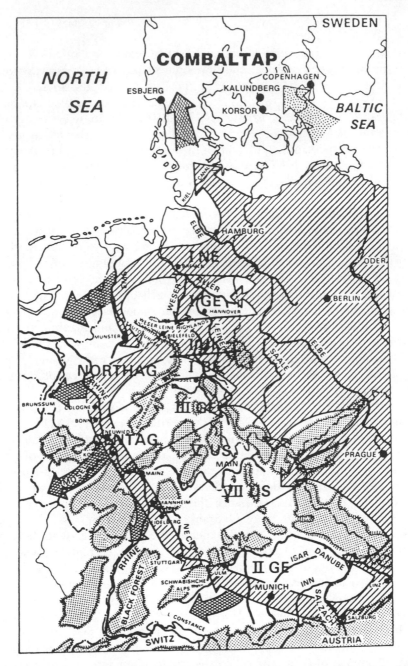

Figure 14–2. Textbook Application of Soviet Encirclement Principles
in NATO Central Region

Source: Phillip A. Petersen, "Italy in Soviet Military Strategy," *The International Spectator, 23* (January–March 1988), p. 21.

British sector, and breakthroughs against the poorly deployed Dutch Corps in NORTHAG and the thin German defense in the large II (GE) Corps area opposite Czechoslovakia and Austria (see figure 14–3).

The exploitation of these breakthroughs by operational maneuver groups would threaten the sustainability of the forward NATO forces by imperiling logistical networks and reinforcement capabilities and open the way for follow-on echelons to complete the envelopment. The combat experience of World War II has convinced Soviet military scientists that swift penetration of defenses coupled with timely commitment of OMGs and other follow-on forces to the engagement and to the breakthrough ensure development of a tactical success into an operational one and create favorable conditions for pursuing the enemy and maneuvering to encircle him.

Encirclement would be considered complete only after creation of a continuous interior and an active exterior front. Distribution of forces between the interior and exterior fronts of envelopment would depend on the assigned missions and composition of the enemy groupings. If the enemy has strong reserves beyond the exterior encirclement, Soviet forces on the exterior encirclement would assume the defense. In conditions where the enemy has no strong reserves in the operational depth, the Soviet forces operating on the exterior front of envelopment would press home the attack in the depth of the defenses.[4]

A Decade of Conceptual Innovation

Until the late 1970s to early 1980s, conceptual thinking in NATO regarding the employment of coalition forces in war, should deterrence fail, was restricted to the strategic and tactical levels. A conceptual vacuum existed in what the Soviets call the operational level, between NATO's strategic concept for the defense of the North Atlantic Treaty area, embodied in MC 14/3, and tactical doctrine developed by individual NATO member nations for application by their own forces. Standardization Agreements and Allied Tactical Publications achieved some level of commonality in tactics and operational procedures, but no NATO "operational art" for waging campaigns emerged until the onset of the U.S. Army's "Air-Land Battle" doctrine.

The Air-Land Battle (ALB) doctrine was originally adopted by the U.S. Army in 1982. It called for U.S. Army corps and lower formations to fight the enemy over an "extended battlefield"—hence, its emphasis on the destruction of Warsaw Pact "follow-on" echelons—in an "integrated" combat environment combining conventional, nuclear, and chemical warfare operations. In contrast with the earlier "Active Defense" doctrine

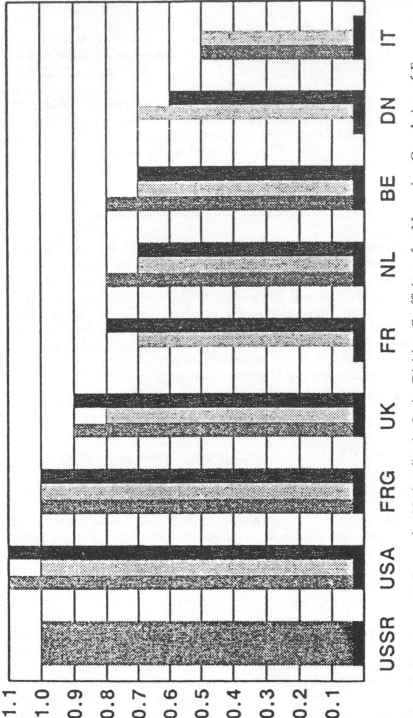

Figure 14–3. K-Factor for Nationality in Soviet Division Coefficients for Measuring Correlation of Forces, 1975, 1979, and 1984

Source: Phillip A. Petersen, "Italy in Soviet Military Strategy," *The International Spectator,* 23 (January–March 1988), p. 18.

instituted in 1976, which was criticized for preemptively conceding the initiative on the battlefield to the enemy by mounting a relatively static, attrition-oriented defense, ALB emphasizes maneuver and seizing the initiative at the operational level from the enemy. In essence, it is intended to "outsmart" the Soviets at their own game of maneuver. Although allied armies deployed on the Central Front would fight NATO's coalition battle using their own nationally developed tactical doctrines, concern was expressed in Europe following the adoption of ALB that its emphasis on "integrated" operations, including the employment of chemical weapons and an "extended battlefield" reaching into the depth of the enemy's deployment in Eastern Europe, might be at odds with the Alliance's defensive character. To assuage those concerns, a revised version of the Air-Land Battle doctrine was promulgated in 1986 that is consistent with Alliance guidance.[5]

In parallel with Air-Land Battle, during his tenure as Supreme Allied Commander Europe (SACEUR), General Bernard Rogers developed a SHAPE subconcept for "Follow-On Forces Attack" (FOFA) based on the doctrinal studies pursued by the U.S. Army Training and Doctrine Command while he was the Army's chief of staff. While ALB and FOFA have many similarities in their approach to the same key objective (that is, to break the momentum of the Pact's offensive in order to keep the ratio of enemy-to-friendly forces in contact at the forward line of own troops (FLOT) at a manageable level), ALB is predominantly a tactical doctrine for the employment of forces at the corps level and lower echelons, whereas FOFA is an operational concept for application by NATO multinational commands at the army group (Northern Army Group [NORTHAG], Central Army Group [CENTAG], Allied Land Forces Southern Europe [LANDSOUTH], and so on) and allied tactical air force (ATAF) levels and higher (Allied Forces Central Europe [AFCENT], Allied Air Forces Central Europe [AAFCE]) headquarters. SACEUR's Long-Term Planning Guideline for Follow-On Forces Attack was approved by the NATO Defense Planning Committee in 1984, and FOFA is now one of the NATO Conceptual Military Framework's Key Mission Components, which guide the Alliance's long-term force requirements.[6]

While ALB and FOFA have received considerable attention in both Western academic literature and Soviet military writings, often being at the origin of controversies over the wisdom of pursuing concepts that allegedly involve offensive or even preemptive operations or imply a de facto conventional retaliatory strategy, other recent initiatives to enhance the ability of allied forces to counter the Soviet/Warsaw Pact theater-strategic offensive at the operational level of war have gone virtually unnoticed. Most prominent among these innovative operational concepts for coalition warfare are the new NORTHAG Concept of Operations, airmobile forces, and the concept of "Composite Air Operations."

NATO Operational Reserves

While NORTHAG has often been derided as a hodgepodge of national contingents suffering from many common deficiencies (maldeployment, low readiness, equipment obsolescence, logistical shortfalls, inadequate training, and so on)—in short, coalition defense at its worst—and British generalship has often been criticized for its lack of imagination, NORTHAG has emerged under the stewardship of two of its recent British commanders, Generals Sagnall and Farndale, as the fulcrum of much innovative thinking at the operational level on the employment of reserves and the conduct of counteroffensive operations.[7]

In the late 1970s, the British Army had grown increasingly dissatisfied with its "positional defense" tactics, in light of the expanding Soviet capability for rapid penetration and envelopment of NATO's antitank defenses, and with the traditional focus of NATO contingency planning on the "corps battle" at the expense of the army group. The conceptual father of the new NORTHAG Concept of Operations, General Sir Nigel Bagnall, defined the challenge before him in the following terms before an audience at the Royal United Services Institute for Defense Studies in London in 1984:

> Let us look at the two major problems as I see them. First of all, developing a broad operational concept within the army group. There has been much talk about a joint Land/Air battle and earnest endeavours have been made to plan for one in the NORTHAG/2ATAF area. However, without an agreed concept of operations, there is inevitably a conflict of ideas and overall priorities cannot be identified while the four in-theatre corps each conduct their own battle independently. Another problem has been what I always describe as an over-literal interpretation of forward defence and the defensive nature of the Alliance. The result is that we tend to try and defend passively and right up to the Inter-German Border (IGB), regardless of whether or not this is feasible.
>
> This inevitably results in a linear deployment and the allocation of resources more or less equally along the entire front, regardless of where the main threat may lie, terrain, or considerations as to capability. Corps are allocated their areas of responsibility and told to fight a corps battle. This in turn leads to a tendency to perpetuate an allocation of territory throughout the chain of command, with divisions, brigades and even BGs being given their areas to defend without any direction as to the overall design for battle."[8]

Hence, the new NORTHAG Concept of Operations, formally adopted in 1986, was developed on the basis of the following ideas:

> that the scope of a Soviet conventional offensive in Europe mandates that NATO's defensive battle be led at the operational level—that is,

by the Army Group and ATAF commanders—and be fought as an integrated land-air battle extending across the somewhat artificial command boundaries of individual national corps sectors;

that an over-literal interpretation of the strategy of Forward Defense had deprived NATO of operational reserves at the army group level with which to counter Soviet encirclement operations and OMGs designed to break through the weaker NATO corps sectors in order to achieve deep penetrations, envelop the stronger NATO corps formations, and ultimately cause a rapid collapse of the Alliance's conventional defenses;

that only an operational-level counterstrike operation, mounted as an army group undertaking, rather than isolated corps-level counterattacks, would achieve the requisite magnitude to defeat a major enemy penetration threatening the cohesion of NATO's forward defense, and wrest the strategic initiative on the battlefield from the Pact;

and that only armored and airmobile formations provide in combination the requisite striking power and maneuverability for an effective use of operational reserves in the counterstrike role.

Under the new NORTHAG concept, individual corps reserves which in the past would have been employed by the Belgian, British, German, and Dutch corps in support of their own operations are henceforth under the control of the army group commander in order to be decisively employed. According to General Farndale, "We now have one powerful reserve. These reserves used to be employed totally by the nations but now we tell the corps that although they are still available, they cannot be employed without my authority."[9] Addressing the implications of the new concept for the use of operational reserves, General Sir Brian Kenny, General Farndale's successor as Commander Northern Army Group (COMNORTHAG), has stated that

> We now fight a much more cohesive battle right across all corps in NORTHAG; we are now all four fighting a NORTHAG concept of operations which we were not some years ago, when we were still fighting our own independent battles, eating off our reserve in the tactical battle. We now in the present concept accept that we have larger reserves for use at operational level to inflict a decisive blow and to regain the initiative under the direction of the Army Group Commander.[10]

General Farndale has identified three alternative options for the employment of army group reserves:

Counter-Penetration. To block an enemy penetration. This however, is entirely defensive and alone will not win. Worse, it will consume the very reserves that might, if used properly, win.

Counter-Attack. This is better. It involves attacking to secure an objective and then to deny it to the enemy. Even if it succeeds it is always limited and alone is unlikely to give the defender the initiative. But it could lead to offensive operations.

Counterstroke. This is the winner if conditions are right. Here the commander sets out, under a broad directive, to destroy the enemy wherever he is, to seize the initiative, get on to the offensive and win. It calls for a high standard of joint all-arms training, good intelligence and high-grade commanders working to a single concept.[11]

Obviously, the counterstrike is the most challenging option, and its success hinges to a large extent on the proper selection of the axis of engagement of the army group reserves, the timing of the operation, and the coordination with the ground forces in contact and the air forces in support (2ATAF, in NORTHAG's instance). The NORTHAG concept of operations is specifically geared to the delivery of the counterstrike by preserving intact the combat potential of the army group reserves through the initial stages of war until the opportunity to seize the initiative from the enemy emerges. But the army group commander's ability to reliably predict the "window of opportunity" and prepare his forces for the execution of the counterstrike is dependent on the timely availability of intelligence on the enemy's force dispositions, anticipated axes of advance, rate of movement, and so forth. The deployment of manned (TR-1, JSTARS, Castor, Orchidee, and so on) and unmanned (RPVs) reconnaissance and battlefield surveillance platforms, as well as the availability of fast, reliable, interoperable, secure, and redundant communications links between the army group command post and the subordinate corps command posts is expected eventually to meet that requirement for near real-time intelligence.

Because the two U.S. and two German corps comprising CENTAG are substantially stronger than the Belgian, British, and Dutch corps in NORTHAG, and the requirement for mutual support among them conceivably less severe in wartime, CENTAG has not followed the lead of NORTHAG in developing an army group–wide concept of operations for the use of operational reserves (see figure 14–4). The difference of approach on this matter between the two army groups was nowhere more evident than in the contrasting formats of REFORGER 87 and RE-FORGER 88. Although field training exercise (FTX) *Certain Strike*, held in September 1987, was a U.S. corps-level exercise involving the employ-

	Operational Focus	Operational Reserves	Interoperability Patterns	Theater Reserves
NORTHAG	Army Group Operations (Army Group reserves compensate for weakness of individual Corps)	Several Armored Divisions	Northern half of NORTHAG: GE-NL-US Southern half of NORTHAG: GE-UK-BE	III (US) Corps
CENTAG	Corps Operations (All Corps, except II (GE) Corps, are strong)	Single Canadian Mechanized Division	Northern half of CENTAG: GE-US Southern half of CENTAG: GE-US-CA	1 (FR) Army and FAR

Figure 14–4. Contrasting Army Group Approaches to Forward Defense

ment in northern Germany of the III (U.S.) Corps as a NORTHAG operational reserve, the exercise was nonetheless directed by COMNORTHAG (General Farndale) to emphasize the army group's preeminence in coordinating the engagement of the U.S. corps with the operations of the four "in-place" corps as part of an overarching army group scheme of maneuver. By comparison, FTX *Certain Challenge*, staged in southern Germany in September 1988, the first ever REFORGER exercise to oppose two U.S. corps (and, hence, theoretically, an army group–scale exercise), focused on corps-level operations and was directed by General Crosbie Saint in his national capacity of Commander-in-Chief, U.S. Army Europe, and not in his NATO capacity as Commander Central Army Group (COMCENTAG).

It is not that CENTAG has ignored the importance of having operational reserves available. The 4th Canadian Mechanized Brigade Group, CENTAG's only ready operational reserve, has recently been expanded to a two-brigade Canadian mechanized division.[12] The First French Army is a potential CENTAG reserve and, in September 1987, France and West Germany staged a large-scale field training exercise, Kecker Spatz-Moineau Hardi, to test procedures for the engagement of the French Army's new Force d'Action Rapide in Bavaria as an operational reserve for the Bundeswehr.[13] However, with strong U.S. and German corps on the front line, CENTAG's emphasis understandably is on effective corps-level operations.

Developments in NATO Airmobility

Concurrently with the "new wave" in conceptual thinking regarding the operational level of command in NATO and the constitution of operational reserves to counter the Soviet encirclement threat, there has been a growing school of thought advocating greater reliance on airmobile forces.

Current interest in NATO for the development of air-mobile forces as army group operational reserves, spearheaded by the creation of France's Force d'Action Rapide (FAR) and the adoption of NORTHAG's new concept of operations, can be traced back to the revolutionary ideas on the use of helicopters at the operational level promoted in the early 1980s by the late General Dr. Ferdinand von Senger und Etterlin, German Army, while serving as NATO's Commander-in-Chief, Allied Forces Central Europe (CINCENT). General von Senger was struck by the fact that while the Alliance lacked operational reserves to counter Soviet penetrations into NATO's forward defenses, member nations with forces in the Central Region (including France) had large helicopter inventories from which to constitute, once pooled, an airmobile reserve corps consisting of eight airmobile divisions (see figure 14–5).[14]

	Scout Helicopters	Antitank Helicopters	Light Transport Helicopters	Medium Transport Helicopters	Heavy Transport Helicopters	Total
Belgium	63 *Alouette* II	on order				63
Canada (in FRG)	13 CH-136 *Kiowa*					13
FRG	148 *Alouette* II 95 BO-105 M	210 PAH-1	187-UH-1D		105 CH-53	745
The Netherlands	64 *Alouette* III 29 BO-105 M	on order				93
U.K.*	30 *Scout* 9 *Alouette* II 159 *Gazelle*	120 *Lynx*		26 *Puma* 28 *Wessex*	27 *Chinook*	399
U.S. (In FRG)	232 OH-58	144 AH-64 48 AH-1S	46 UH-1D	144 UH-60	96 CH-47	710
France*	42 *Alouette* II 67 *Alouette* 67 III 164 *Gazelle* (67 gun-armed)	148 *Gazelle*		135 *Puma*		556
Total	1,115	670	233	333	228	2,579

Figure 14–5. Helicopter Assets in AFCENT

Source: The Military Balance 1988–1989 (London: The International Institute for Strategic Studies, 1988).
*Not all British and French helicopters would necessarily be available for Central European contingencies.

The first NATO member nation to act upon General von Senger's proposals was France, at the initiative of Lieutenant-General Georges Fricaud-Chagnaud. General Fricaud-Chagnaud was Chief of the French Military Mission attached to General von Senger's AFCENT headquarters in The Netherlands. His duties included coordinating with NATO the engagement of French conventional forces alongside the Allies in a contingency should France decide to participate in the common defense. While France has committed to the principle of collective security, as a signatory of the Brussels (1948) and Washington (1949) treaties, her nonparticipation in the Alliance's integrated military structure and the stationing of the First French Army on both sides of the Rhine, at some considerable distance from the Federal Republic of Germany's eastern borders, have effectively precluded a prompt French intervention forward. An Antitank Helicopter Force, because of its inherent mobility and virtually instantaneous striking power, would allow France to rapidly project a conventional force forward into the FRG without the need to station troops on the ground directly opposite Czechoslovakia in peacetime, thereby resolving a political dilemma vis-à-vis NATO.[15] General Fricaud-Chagnaud's concept for an Antitank Helicopter Force eventually provided the impetus for the establishment of a larger formation, the 4th Airmobile Division, as part of the new five-division strong Force d' Action Rapide (see figure 14–6).

Following France's lead, the United Kingdom and the FRG have both been experimenting with the concept of airmobility. In 1983, one of the British Army of the Rhine's eight armored brigades was temporarily converted into an airmobile unit to conduct trials.[16] Once successfully completed in 1987, the brigade was reroled into an armored formation and the airmobile mission given to a motorized infantry brigade stationed in the United Kingdom but assigned to the I British Corps in Germany as a reinforcement. The newly designated 24th Airmobile Brigade conducted its first field exercise in September 1988 before the NATO Military Committee. Despite a growing British interest in airmobile forces, progress has been slowed down somewhat by interservice rivalry between the British Army and the Royal Air Force (RAF) over ownership of medium and heavy transport helicopters. Unlike a U.S. Army corps-level aviation brigade or the FAR's 4th Airmobile Division, both of which operate large complements of antitank helicopters, the British Army's 24th Airmobile Brigade is predominantly an infantry force composed of Milan ATGM teams which are dependent for their mobility and resupply on the battlefield on large transport helicopters operated by the RAF (see figure 14–7).[17]

In the Bundeswehr, airmobile assets in the form of helicopters and airborne infantry have been scattered among the three corps of the Field Army with little opportunity to date for their mass employment in large-

	1981	1982	1983	1984	1985	1986	1987
Concept Development	LTG Fricaud-Chagnaud develops concept of FHAC antitank helicopter force for engagement in Central Europe while head of the French liaison mission attached to CINCENT.		Establishment of FHAC antitank helicopter task force under I (FR) Corps.	Creation of the FAR's 4th Air-mobile Division.	Establishment of air-mobile brigade under 1, (FR) Army.		
Field Testing			FTX *Moselle 83* in eastern France. Exercise tests concept of antitank helicopter task force. First trial of the FHAC.	FTX *Damocles* in eastern France. Exercise is part of larger *Doubs 84* FTX involving the coordination of air-mobile and armored forces.	FTX *Fartel 85* in southeastern France. First full-scale exercise of the FAR. Emphasis on the engagement of the air-mobile division in a simulated Central European environment.		FTX *Kecker Spatz Moineau Hardi* in the FRG. First deployment of the FAR across the Rhine as a "counter-offensive" force. in cooperation with the Bundeswehr.

Figure 14–6. Evolution of the FAR's Air-mobile Concept

FHAC: Force d'Helicopteres Anti-Chars (Antitank Helicopter Force)
FAR: Force d'Action Rapide (Rapid Action Force)

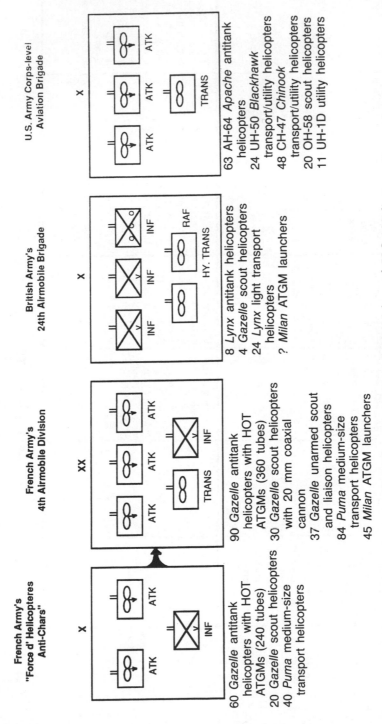

Figure 14–7. Comparative Structure of French, British, and U.S. Helicopter Formations

scale airmobile operations. German Army doctrine essentially calls for the helicopter regiments and airborne infantry brigades to operate as corps reserves in support of the divisions engaged in combat. The Heerstruktur 2000 plan unveiled in February 1988, however, calls for the establishment of two airmobile divisions (one each in NORTHAG and CENTAG), totaling five airmobile brigades (two each in the I and II [GE] Corps, and the remaining one in the III [GE] Corps), by amalgamation of the existing army aviation and airborne units.[18] In view of these developments in the British and German armies, and as a counterpart to the Franco-German brigade, the British and German ministries of defense have reportedly been considering the possibility of creating a joint airmobile division to be employed as a NORTHAG operational reserve.[19] Although the project may be somewhat premature, it has been endorsed by no less than General Sir Nigel Bagnall, presently the British Army's Chief of Staff. Further, at the December 1988 ministerial meeting of the Defense Planning Committee, NATO defense ministers approved a West German proposal to study how such a NORTHAG airmobile division, involving Belgian, British, Dutch, and German forces, might be established.[20]

In developing airmobile forces, NATO is confronted with several challenges. Helicopters have been traditionally associated with the maneuver of the ground forces in a supporting, somewhat secondary role, and rarely employed en masse in independent airmobile operations. In the European theater, experience with the employment of helicopters on a grand scale is limited, and there is no body of standardized doctrine on airmobility. Tactics, employment concepts, missions, and means vary widely from army to army. The compartmentalization by NATO air forces of Central Europe's constricted airspace into various restricted zones and corridors, for purposes of command and control, is not conducive to the flexible use of large formations of rotarywing aircraft. As airmobile forces (or "airmechanized forces" in the future, to use General von Senger's terminology) grow in size and number among NATO armies, and the latter become capable of conducting large-scale airmobile operations across corps sector boundaries, NATO airspace management procedures will have to accommodate such an evolution. Further, airmobile operations may increasingly become disassociated from the maneuver of the ground forces and gradually become part of the air battle.

A NATO Counter-Air Campaign

The flexibility of airpower is inherently conducive to the employment of air forces at the operational level. The Israelis have in many instances employed airpower at the operational level with decisive results at the strategic level (Sinai 1967, Bekaa Valley 1982). Similar expectations seem to drive Soviet planning for an air offensive in Europe. Unlike NATO ground forces, whose conceptual thinking has been driven primarily by the tactical considerations associated with fighting the "corps battle" and have only in the recent past rediscovered the operational dimension of warfare, allied air forces have a long experience in operating in concert, as part of the various NATO allied tactical air forces (ATAFs), across national corps sector boundaries. The establishment of Allied Air Forces Central Europe (AAFCE) in 1974 to harmonize the divergent operational procedures of the British-led 2ATAF and the U.S.-led 4ATAF, and an effort to replicate in the "offensive counter-air" area the level of multinational integration achieved in the "defensive counter-air" area under the aegis of the NATO Integrated Air Defense system, have gradually given rise to a Central Region-wide concept of the "air battle," somewhat akin to the Soviet concept of air and anti-air operations.

In recent years NATO's efforts at formulating an operational concept for a counter-air campaign have focused on joint/combined air raids by multinational force packages. As explained by RAF Air Marshal Sir Patrick Hine, a former commander of NATO's Second Allied Tactical Air Force in northern Germany:

We are now going for combined package formations made up of different types of aircraft for attack, escort, reconnaissance, defence suppression and electronic countermeasures, as the best way of penetrating the more densely defended areas. The Americans used "force packages,"as they were known, quite extensively during their air raids into North Vietnam, but their aircraft flew at medium altitude. A modern package formation would go in either at low altitude or medium altitude, depending on the circumstances. During exercises we have practised bringing together forces with as many as twenty-five or thirty aircraft, including EF-111 electronic countermeasures and F-4 defence suppression aircraft. Sometimes the force package might have to fight its way right through to a well-defended target; at other times it might be sufficient to clear a corridor through the enemy's forward surface-to-air defences.

To put a particularly important airfield out of action for twelve hours or more, my planning staff might decide that the attack force required was twelve Tornadoes. Typically, eight of the Tornadoes might be armed with JP233 airfield denial weapons to crater the runways and taxiways, with the other four aircraft carrying conventional free-fall or parachute-retarded bombs to attack the fuel and bomb storage areas and other vital installations. Supporting this force might be two EF-111 jamming escort aircraft, a flight of four F-4 "Wild Weasel" defence suppression aircraft and perhaps six F-15 escort fighters. The package might also include one or two reconnaissance aircraft, for example Jaguars, to take post-strike photos because we would need to know if the attack had been successful. So a typical force package might comprise about twenty-five aircraft of five different types.[21]

The concept of "Composite Air Operations" or "Joint/Combined Raids," with the attendant difficulties of integrating in flight different types of aircraft from various nationalities, operating from several dispersed home airfields, has been at the center of NATO air training activities for several years.[22] In addition to the *Red Flag* and *Maple Flag* series of air exercises conducted at air combat maneuvering instrumented ranges in the United States and Canada, NATO exercises and competitions continually confront allied air crews with the technical challenges involved in planning and executing multinational air raids, including such issues as timing of the operation and mix of forces, weapons-to-target matching, en-route and target area tactics, and command and control.

The concept of "force packaging" figured prominently in two such events recently, the *Dragon Hammer 87* exercise in May 1987 and the *Tactical Air Meet 88* in June 1988. *Dragon Hammer* is an annual, medium-scale, air-maritime exercise in the Mediterranean designed to test procedures and tactics in all aspects of naval warfare. The 1987 edition focused on the staging of joint combined raids by aircraft operating from airfields in Italy and Turkey and the aircraft carriers *Nimitz* and *Clemenceau*. One such air raid against an Italian airbase involved 23 U.S., French, Italian, and Turkish land-based and carrier-based aircraft. For exercise *Tactical Air Meet 88*, an event held every two years in Central Europe, approximately 80 combat aircraft belonging to nine NATO air forces were organized into five multinational wings (two attack, one electronic countermeasures, one reconnaissance, and one escort) to practice composite air operations (see figure 14–8).

Although the emphasis of "large force packaging" has been on offensive counter-air (OCA) operations, NATO has also addressed the use of force packages for defensive counter-air (DCA) missions in the form of "Mixed Fighter Force" operations involving dedicated air superiority fighters and interceptors, such as a USAF F-15, flying in tandem with less capable combat aircraft, such as a Royal Air Force Hawk or a Luftwaffe Alpha-Jet.[23] According to this concept, in such "high-low" formations the less sophisticated aircraft would benefit from the "beyond visual range" radar detection capabilities of the more capable fighters, attenuating the disparities in relative performance between various aircraft types, both within and among individual NATO air forces, while increasing the interceptor assets available to NATO in a contingency. To be fully effective, however, the Mixed Fighter Force concept is dependent on the existence of a common NATO identification friend-or-foe system, which to date has remained an elusive goal.

Exercise Dragon Hammer 87

Attack
Formations (3)

a) Two A-6 and two A-7 fighter-bombers, escorted by two F-14 fighters, from the *Nimitz.*

b) Six French Navy *Super Etendard* and five Turkish Air Force F-104S fighter-bombers, escorted by two Italian Air Force F-104S interceptors

c) Two USAF B-52 bombers and two U.S. Air National Guard A-7 fighter-bombers

Defense
Formations (3)

d) Two Italian Air Force F-104 S interceptors controlled by a NATO E-3A *Sentry* AWACS

e) Eight F-8E *Crusader* fighters from the *Clemenceau* controlled by a USN E-2 *Hawkeye* AWACS

f) Two USN F-14 and two Italian Air Force F-104S fighters controlled by an Italian NADGE early-warning radar site

Exercise Tactical Air Meet 88

Attack Wing

4 French Air Force *Jaguars*
4 Belgian Air Force *Mirage* 5BA
4 Netherlands Air Force NF-5A
4 Danish Air Force F-35 *Drakens*
8 Canadian Air Force CF-18A

Reconnaissance
Wing

2 French Air Force *Mirage* F-1 CR
2 Belgian Air Force *Mirage* 5 BR
2 Royal Air Force *Jaguars*
2 German Air Force RF-4E

Escort Wing

2 U.S. Air Force F-15 C/D
2 Royal Air Force *Tornados*
2 Royal Air Force *Phantoms*
2 French Air Force *Mirage* 2000 C
2 German Air Force F-4F
2 Belgian Air Force F-16
2 Danish Air Force F-16
3 Italian Air Force F-104S

Figure 14–8. "Composite Air Operations" As Practiced During Two Recent NATO Exercises

Source: Francesco Veltri, "Dragon Hammer 87," *Rivista Aeronautica* (September–October 1987), pp. 26–33; and Jean-Michel Guhl, "TAM 88: Exercice Majeur de l'OTAN, *Air Action* (September 1988), p. 52.

While NATO's limited resources and the Warsaw Pact's dense air defenses cast a doubt on the effectiveness of large air packaging as the instrument of a sustained OCA campaign against the Warsaw Pact's network of 141 main and dispersed operating bases opposite NATO's Center Region, in the absence of unmanned delivery vehicles, such mass air raids represent the best method to optimize the complementary capabilities of the various types of aircraft in service in the Alliance while ensuring the highest level of survivability in hostile airspace. More fundamentally, Composite Air Operations and Joint/Combined Raids reflect a sustained NATO collective effort to counter, at the operational level, the Soviet offensive air threat.

NATO's "Operational Art": Future Prospects?

Given the Alliance's renewed emphasis on a strengthening of conventional defenses, the creation of additional operational reserves and the execution of counter-air operations against Warsaw Pact airfields are topics likely to remain priority areas in U.S. and NATO defense planning for the foreseeable future. NATO efforts to promote operational level initiatives to enhance coalition defense capabilities, however, could be affected in somewhat unpredictable ways by divergent trends in the European strategic environment. Adverse developments might include:

1. A significant scaling-down of the size and frequency of field training exercises (the *Autumn Forge* series in particular) and strategic mobility exercises (REFORGER) as a result of arms control agreements, public opinion pressure in host countries (notably the FRG), and/or U.S. budgetary constraints.[24] In recent years, U.S. and West European field training exercises associated with *Autumn Forge* and REFORGER have increasingly emphasized interoperability among allied forces, combined/joint operations at the operational level, and the employment of operational reserves. While large-scale field exercises are not necessarily conducive to realistic training at the small unit level, given environmental constraints on peacetime exercise activities, they nonetheless provide a unique opportunity for NATO staffs to test, in simulated wartime conditions, the ability of multinational forces to operate in concert as a coalition.

2. Negotiated or unilateral measures linked to the adoption of so-called "defensive defense" postures. While "tank-free zones" and other arms control schemes to reduce the offensive potential associated with armored forces might conceivably enhance NATO's ability to anticipate a Warsaw Pact attack, they will not eliminate the military requirement

to generate an effective forward defense in a contingency. Yet, adoption of defensive postures by individual NATO member nations could undermine the effectiveness of the Alliance's collective defense planning by implying that NATO's pursuit of a counter-offensive capability at the operational level is inconsistent with the intent of such an adoption.[25]

Positive developments, in turn, might include:

1. Sustained commitment by allied nations to continue efforts to improve collective capabilities for coalition defense along the lines of the NORTHAG Concept of Operations, the REFORGER 87 and 88 exercises, the Franco-German brigade, and so forth, at least until fundamental changes in the Warsaw Pact's military posture justify otherwise;
2. Growing interest among the European members of the Alliance in using such mechanisms as bilateral/mixed units (such as the Franco-German brigade, Benelux battalion, hypothetical British-German air-mobile division) and NATO command arrangements (such as NORTHAG and NATO Composite Force for reinforcing Norway) to expand their defense cooperation within NATO and the Western European Union.

Negotiated or unilateral force reductions represent a wild card. The magnitude of the unilateral reductions in Soviet forces forward-deployed in Eastern Europe (6 tank divisions and 5,000 tanks) announced by Soviet Communist Party General Secretary Mikhail Gorbachev on December 7, 1988, suggests that if the reductions are applied predominantly to the Group of Soviet Forces Germany, the Warsaw Pact's surprise attack potential against NORTHAG will be considerably eroded and the threat of early breakthroughs into NATO's forward defenses substantially reduced.[26] However, in the absence of a Conventional Stability Talks agreement in Vienna on mutual, asymmetrical force reductions, the expected positive consequences of the Gorbachev unilateral force reductions could be nullified by untimely unilateral NATO force reductions in either forward-deployed, "in-place" forces or external reinforcement commitments, or both. Such unilateral reductions could be prompted by precipitous reassessments of the balance, calls for NATO to reciprocate, or ever more pressing budgetary constraints. In formulating its own posture of "reasonable sufficiency" for the future, the Alliance will have to keep in balance the legitimate goal of achieving a more stable balance of forces at lower levels with the requirement to preserve the coalition capability necessary for effective forward defense.

Notes

1. For additional detail, see Phillip A. Karber and A.G. Whitley, *Operational Continuity and Change Within the Central European Conventional Arms Competition,* paper prepared for West Point conference on "NATO at Forty," June 4–7, 1987.

2. For a comprehensive analysis of the evolution of NATO's conventional defense posture, see Phillip A. Karber, "In Defense of Forward Defense," *Armed Forces Journal International* (May 1984), pp. 27–80.

3. Quoted in Phillip A. Petersen and Diego A. Ruiz Palmer, *Soviet Encirclement Operations and NATO's Use of Operational Reserves in Central Europe,* paper presented at a conference on "New Technologies and Alliance Security" hosted by the Hanns Seidel Stiftung, Ojen, Spain, June 2–5, 1988.

4. The most authoritative Western analysis of Soviet encirclement operations is John G. Hines, "Soviet Front Operations in Europe—Planning for Encirclement," *Spotlight on the Soviet Union,* A Report from a Conference at Sundvollen, Norway, April 25–27, 1985 (Oslo: Alumni Association of the Norwegian Defense College, 1986). On the nature of the Soviet theater strategic operations, see Phillip A. Petersen and John G. Hines, "The Conventional Offensive in Soviet Theater Strategy," *Orbis,* 27, No. 3 (Fall 1983): 695–739. On the Soviet air offensive in a theater of military operations, see Phillip A. Petersen and John R. Clark, "Soviet Air and Anti-air Operations," *Air University Review,* (March–April 1985): 36–54.

5. On the development of the 1986 version of the U.S. Army's Air-Land Battle doctrine and the differences between the latter and the FOFA subconcept, see General William R. Richardson, "FM 100–5, The Air-Land Battle in 1986," *Military Review* (March 1986): 4–11.

6. On the FOFA subconcept, see General Bernard W. Rogers, "Sword and Shield: ACE Attack of Warsaw Pact Follow-On Forces," *NATO's Sixteen Nations,* 28, No. 1, (February–March 1983): 16–26; and General Bernard W. Rogers, "Follow-On Forces Attack (FOFA): Myths and Realities," *NATO Review* No. 6 (December 1984): 1–9.

7. For an assessment of recent developments in West European thinking regarding the employment of NATO operational reserves, see Diego A. Ruiz Palmer, "Countering Soviet Encirclement Operations—Emerging NATO Concepts," *International Defense Review* (November 1988): 1413–1418.

8. General Sir Nigel Bagnall,"Concepts of Land/Air Operations in the Central Region: 1,"*RUSI Journal* (September 1984): 60.

9. Simon O'Dwyer-Russell, "NORTHAG Concept 'Aims to Win,' " *Jane's Defense Weekly,* July 26, 1986, p. 117.

10. Paolo Valponi, "1st British Corps and British Army Future," *Rivista Militare* (January–February 1988): 4.

11. General Sir Martin Farndale, "The Operational Level of Command," *RUSI Journal* (Autumn 1988): 26.

12. Lieutenant General J. Fox, "The Restructuring of the Canadian Army," *NATO's Sixteen Nations,* 32, No. 6, (October 1988): 20.

13. On the evolving role of the French Army in the defense of West Germany, see Diego A. Ruiz Palmer, "Between the Rhine and the Elbe: France and the Conventional Defense of Central Europe," *Comparative Strategy*, 6, No. 4 (Autumn 1987): 471–512.

14. General Dr. Ferdinand von Senger und Etterlin, "The Airmobile Divisions: Operational Reserves for NATO," *RUSI Journal* (March 1987): 23–30.

15. Georges Fricaud-Chagnaud, "L'Armee de Terre face a ses missions en Europe," *Defense Nationale* (May 1983): 35–44.

16. Simon O'Dwyer-Russell, "Airmobility Proves 'Indispensable' to UK Army," *Jane's Defense Weekly*, August 2, 1986.

17. Charles Miller, "British Army Introduces Fast-Reaction Helicopter Force, Admits Shortcomings," *Defense News*, September 19, 1988, p. 44.

18. " 'Army Structure 2000' for the West German Armed Forces," *International Defense Review*, No. 4, (April 1988): 338.

19. "Anything you can do," *The Economist*, October 22, 1988, p. 24.

20. General Sir Nigel Bagnall, "Airmobile Operations in Northern Army Group," *NATO's Sixteen Nations*, 32, No. 6 (October 1988): 75–79; and Paul L. Montgomery, "NATO is Studying an Airborne Force," *New York Times*, December 2, 1988.

21. Alfred Price, *Air Battle Central Europe* (New York: The Free Press, 1986), pp. 11–12.

22. On the concept of "Composite Air Operations," see Lt. Colonel James F. Clavenna, USAF, and Lt. Colonel Perry G. Elphik, CAF, "The Evolution and History of the Tactical Air Meet," *NATO's Sixteen Nations*, 33, No. 3 (June 1988) (TAM Supplement p. 23).

23. See Squadron Leader Gus A. B. Crockatt, RAF, "Mixed Fighter Force Operations," *NATO's Sixteen Nations*, 33, No. 3 (June 1988) (TAM Supplement p. 57).

24. Peter Almond, "NATO Officers Expect Slashes in U.S. Forces," *Washington Post*, September 21, 1988.

25. "Don't hit me, I can't hit back," *The Economist*, September 20, 1986, p. 54.

26. For an assessment of the implications of the Soviet unilateral reductions announced by Mr. Gorbachev, see Phillip A. Karber, "The Military Impact of the Gorbachev Reductions," *Armed Forces Journal International* (January 1989): 54–64.

15
Forward Deployment: Basing Needs, Emerging Constraints, and Alternative Solutions

Robert E. Harkavy

Recent years have witnessed increasing pressures on the once more elaborate U.S. global basing system; indeed, this has been reflected in the mounting attention devoted to this subject in the popular press and in journals.[1] Access has been lost in some places (Vietnam, Madagascar, Malta, Ethiopia), and greatly restricted in others (Spain, New Zealand, Thailand, Seychelles, Greece); variously, because of political upheavals, the breakup or withering of alliances, increased sensitivities about infringements on sovereignty and national pride, anti-Americanism, nuclear environmental pressures and, generally, a lessened shared sense of convergent national security interests. Elsewhere, the dollar cost of access (in the form of security assistance or economic aid used in effect as "rent," howsoever rarely defined as such) has risen as some well-leveraged nations (Turkey, Greece, Philippines, Portugal, Spain) have taken advantage of United States's lack of easy alternative options in some key places, while increasingly denying the relevance of U.S. bases for their own security.

Also, U.S. access in some circumstances has become increasingly contingent or ad hoc, as in the uncertainty about the use of Portugal's Azores for possible arms resupply operations on behalf of Israel, Spain's refusal to allow U.S. staging of aircraft to Egypt, and the denial of access to air space over France and Spain for the U.S. raid against Libya mounted from the United Kingdom. These trends may accelerate. There is even talk of extensive U.S. withdrawal from Europe, which could in turn seriously jeopardize access to facilities important to the U.S. nuclear strategic posture.[2]

The Historical Context

The modern period—here somewhat arbitrarily defined as that since the close of World War I—has seen three more or less identifiable phases of global access diplomacy, albeit somewhat telescoped and hence not altogether discrete:

1. the colonial period, from 1919 up to and beyond World War II;
2. the early postwar period, characterized by a tight bipolar, ideologically based alliance structure.
3. the most recent period, characterized by greater multipolarity, ideological diffusion, proliferation of independent sovereignties, and the changing basis of North-South relations.[3]

The interwar period—as an extension of the pre–World War I global system—saw most of what is now referred to as the Third World remain under colonial control. Thus, basing networks, in a relative sense, were mostly a function of the scope of rival empires. Britain had by far the largest basing system, followed in turn by France, Spain, Portugal, the Netherlands, Italy, Japan, and the United States. The Soviet Union had virtually none; neither had defeated Germany. Hence, in contrast to the present, there was little congruence between the overall facts of relative military power and the extent of basing access.

Further, the interwar period was characterized by shifting, relatively impermanent alliances (less clearly ideologically based than would later be the case), and there was no pre–World War II equivalent to the later highly structured and durable North Atlantic Treaty Organization (NATO) and Warsaw Treaty Organization (WTO). Hence, there was little if any stationing of forces by major powers on their allies' soil—that applied to naval and air bases as well as to ground force deployments. Also lacking by comparison with the present period was a nexus of arms sales to granting of basing access—the arms trade of that period was still conducted on a "free market" basis, that is, it was removed from governmental licensing restrictions. Nowadays, that relationship has become a hallmark of contemporary diplomacy.

The early postwar period saw the retention of most prewar colonial holdings by the Western powers, which gradually were reduced and eliminated over the next thirty years. But of greater importance, the West— underwritten by massive U.S. military and economic aid—was able to fashion an elaborate system of formal alliances around the Eurasian rimland, as primarily embodied in the NATO, Central Treaty Organization (CENTO), and Southeast Asian Treaty Organization (SEATO) alliances, and supplemented by Washington's bilateral or otherwise multilateral security ties to Japan, South Korea, Taiwan, and the ANZUS (Australia, New Zealand and United States) Treaty powers.[4]

During this period, which preceded the partial unravelling of Pax Americana beginning in the 1960s, there was assumed a convergence of security interests between the United States and most of its allies and clients, so that access was usually freely granted and was not normally the subject of grudging negotiations over quid pro quo, nor over "status of forces," that is, contingent restriction of access.

The more recent period—since the 1960s—has seen gradual but cumulatively profound changes, resulting in a qualitatively different pattern of access and associated diplomacy. Increasingly, indeed, the United States has found it difficult to persuade many of its erstwhile clients that their security interests, are convergent with its own. The result in many cases has been a move towards decoupling, resulting variously in full denial of access, the imposition of more restrictive terms of access or, in combination, the imposition of higher costs in the form of rent, increased security assistance and economic aid, political quid pro quo, and so on.

There is now a somewhat altered diplomacy of access. It is no longer so automatically granted to hegemonic alliance leaders on the basis of past friendship, gratitude for liberation in World War II, or mere ideological congruence on one side or the other of the great power divide. Access must now be bargained for, and the reciprocal balance of leverage involved appears in many cases more symmetrical than in the past. Primarily, the instrument of arms supplies (or more broadly, security assistance) has become the foremost item of exchange. Many U.S. clients—Greece, Morocco, the Philippines, Portugal, Somalia, Spain, and Turkey, among others—have sought and obtained large annual assistance packages (in actual fact a form of rent) ranging close to U.S. $1 billion per year.

By the late 1980s, these trends had been extended to the point at which one might speculate as to whether a distinct, fourth phase of basing diplomacy could be discerned. Difficult to label, it might be characterized as one in which basing diplomacy had, to a degree, become depoliticized (in an ideological sense) and placed, increasingly, on an almost crass commercial basis. Greece, for instance, appeared to abjure expelling the U.S. presence seemingly only because it needed the rent.

The Current State of U.S. Access to Bases: A Quick Review

The United States now utilizes some 750 separate base sites distributed among some 38 nations around the globe.[5] During World War II, it had twice as many in more than twice as many countries. Nearly half, however, are in West Germany (FRG), and together the FRG, Italy, United Kingdom, South Korea, and Japan account for some three-quarters of U.S. base sites overseas.

These bases (some of which involve colocation of two or more at one site) can be broken down into the following categories: airfields, naval bases, ground force installations, missile sites, communications and intelligence facilities, space-related facilities, and those involving research, environmental, and logistical functions.

These categories in turn can be regrouped along more "functional" lines. Perhaps the most obviously appropriate dividing line, however, is that between conventional and nuclear military operations; or short of actual combat, deployment for the eventuality of such contingencies. In the conventional realm, one can discuss the U.S. basing structure as it is configured to support global power projection activities. On the nuclear side, there is a basing infrastructure designed for "normal" peacetime deterrence, but also for various levels of alerts (involving dispersion, higher levels of readiness) during crises or even during hypothetical protracted conventional phases of superpower war. Some overseas facilities will, of course, be configured for both conventional and nuclear purposes, for instance, satellite surveillance systems' ground downlinks, various communications facilities, air tanker bases, and so forth.

Strategic Nuclear-Related Basing Structure

The United States is now reliant on overseas basing hosts for a plethora of strategic nuclear-related facilities, stretching across the various categories of air, naval, communications, intelligence bases, and so on. This structure has been fairly stable for a long time, evolving only slowly, so that U.S. dependence on these facilities is not likely to be greatly altered during the 1990s. But, there are political and technological alternatives, as well as the option of absorbing some loss of redundancy or of important but not utterly crucial capabilities.

Following is a summary of the various types of nuclear-related facilities.[6]

SSBN and SSN bases (Holy Loch, La Maddalena);

Bases for nuclear-armed aircraft carriers;

Forward bases for fighter-attack aircraft: F-4, F-16, F-104, F-111, and so forth;

Forward bases for short-range nuclear missiles, such as Lance

Staging points for P-3 (ASW) aircraft

Intelligence and space related: early warning radars (BMEWS), DEW/ North Warning System, space detection and tracking systems (Baker-Nunn cameras and GEODSS), downlinks for DSP early warning satellites, satellite control and receiver stations for SIGINT, ocean reconnaissance, navigation, meteorological satellites, HF/DF ocean surveillance facilities, SOSUS (for ASW), nuclear detection (seismic arrays), SIGINT ground stations, and so forth;

Communications: a spectrum from VLF to SHF, LORAN C/D, TACAMO aircraft, ground stations for DSCS, AFSATCOM, FLTSATCOM, NAVSTAR, AUTOVON, ACE HIGH microwave, and so forth;

Bases for reconnaissance and SIGINT aircraft: U-2, SR-71, TR-1, EC-135, RC-135, and so forth;

Research and environmental facilities in connection with missile test ranges, nuclear testing, monitoring of solar flare emissions, weather stations, and so forth.

Some countries are more important than most others for the U.S. nuclear posture, for instance, the United Kingdom, West Germany, Japan, and the Philippines. But Turkey, Greece, Italy, Spain, Iceland, Greenland, Norway, the Azores, Diego Garcia, Singapore, South Korea, and Australia also are vital.

Norway, with its critical location on NATO's northern flank and its near proximity to the Soviet cluster of naval and air bases in the Kola Peninsula area, hosts a variety of important nuclear-related facilities: bases for P-3 ASW aircraft, SIGINT and nuclear detection facilities, VLF communications and a forward base for AWACs.

The United Kingdom, not surprisingly, hosts a profuse variety of nuclear-related facilities, with a not unexpected close integration of U.S. and British forces and bases.[7] There are F-111E bomber bases, SAC standby bases, and those for ground-launched cruise missiles, and the important Poseidon SSBN base at Holy Loch. There are air bases and nuclear storage sites for P-3 ASW craft, other bases for EF-111 "Raven" electronic warfare and command and control aircraft, and for tankers and TACAMO aircraft. And, there is a profusion of C³I and space-related facilities: SOSUS, Giant Talk/Scope Signal transmitters for SAC, nuclear test detection stations, LORAN-C, BMEWS, AUTODIN, a satellite control facility, and weather intercept control units.

West Germany, of course, while hosting the large U.S. Seventh Army and its associated facilities, is also vital to the U.S. nuclear posture. It hosts numerous nuclear-armed strike aircraft (the Pershing II missiles and GLCMs are now being removed); also numerous tactical and battlefield nuclear systems, such as, Lance missiles, nuclear-capable howitzers, and so on. There are also vital SIGINT and communications facilities, the early warning satellite down-link at Kapaun, bases for AWACs and U-2s, LORAN-C, and a host of important headquarters and command centers.

The several U.S. NATO allies in the southern flank/Mediterranean area (Spain, Portugal, Italy, Greece, Turkey) all host crucial U.S. facilities, albeit perhaps with a degree of (actual or potential) redundancy now threatened by political problems militating towards decoupling, particularly in the cases of Spain and Greece, but still potentially with Portugal and perhaps Italy.

Spain provides important air bases for KC-135 tankers and for SAC bomber recovery, and for P-3 ASW operations. It also provides facilities for naval HF and for SAC's "fail-safe" communications, weather intercepts, nuclear bombing practice, nuclear detection, and satellite communications' control centers.

Portugal's mainland provides only a part-time P-3 rotational base, but its Azores Islands host a number of crucial nuclear facilities: SOSUS, missile tracking, satellite control, P-3s, and HF transmitters. Crucial are the functions related to ASW and ocean surveillance, for obvious geographical reasons paralleled by other islands such as Diego Garcia, Ascension, and Bermuda.

Italy is a crucial hub of U.S./NAT0 nuclear activities. This involves Lance missiles, nuclear artillery, F-16 rotational bases and nuclear storage, a vital attack submarine base on Sardinia, another for P-3 and other ASW aircraft, a variety of communications and surveillance functions, LORAN-C, a SOON observatory, and a home port for the U.S. Sixth Fleet's carrier battle group along with that fleet's headquarters.

Greece, although somewhat politically estranged from the United States under its present regime, still provides NATO and the United States access to vital nuclear facilities. There are tactical fighters armed with two-key nuclear weapons, though the Nike-Hercules and Honest John missiles have been phased out. Vital are a P-3 aircraft rotational base, a NATO missile training range, HF and LF naval transmitters (some used for submarines), facilities for KC-135 tankers and strategic reconnaissance aircraft, weather intercepts, an AWACs forward base, and some headquarters functions. Rival Turkey is equally if not more important: five bases for nuclear-armed strike aircraft, a DSCS satellite communications downlink, Giant Talk/Scope Signal III, an AWACs forward base, critical SIGINT stations and radars vital for missile telemetry and satellite tracking, early warning radars and NADGE tactical radars, nuclear detection, and LORAN-C. Incirlik is a crucial air staging base for U.S. Middle Eastern operations as well as a communications hub, and Pirinçlik is critical for monitoring Soviet missile tests.

In the Asia-Pacific area, Australia, the Philippines, and Japan—and to a lesser degree South Korea—are crucial to various aspects of the U.S.

nuclear posture. Australia hosts the critical satellite-related facilities at Nurrungar (DSP early warning) and Pine Gap (SIGINT and reconnaissance satellite downlinks);[8] allows B-52 transits through Darwin, and also provides access for an important VLF transmitter, Omega, seismic detectors, a SOON laboratory, P-3 flights, and FLTSATCOM and DSCS facilities. Japan provides major naval and tactical fighter air bases, important communications and satellite-related facilities (including B-52 fail-safe communications, VLF/HF transmitters, AFSATCOM ground terminals), nuclear detection, LORAN-C/D, Omega, Clarinet Pilgrim, P-3 and TA-CAMO bases, SOSUS terminals, and an air base on Okinawa where tankers, SR-71s, RC-135s, and P-3s are deployed. The Phillippines hosts the major bases at Subic and Clark, plus the whole gamut of technical facilities: fail-safe communications, SIGINT, nuclear detection, strategic-related radars, HF and LF facilities, a SOON facility, weather intercept control, a DSCS satellite operation, and so forth.[9] In South Korea, there are bases for nuclear-armed strike aircraft that can reach the Soviet Union, plus LORAN C/D, a GEODSS facility, nuclear test detection, storage sites for army-related nuclear weapons, and a variety of nuclear-related communications facilities.

Bases for Conventional Power Projection

Rivalling in importance the U.S. basing network for nuclear-strategic purposes is that related to global conventional power projection. Indeed, some bases are or can be used for both purposes (for instance, tanker refueling facilities, those utilized for a variety of communications, ocean surveillance facilities, and so on). But generally speaking, several related kinds of purposes are involved in conventional power projection, as follows:

possible actual U.S. military interventions involving numerous possible scenarios; hence, importantly involving stockpiled or pre-positioned materiel;

contingent U.S. access to bases in order to deter Soviet conventional military operations outside Europe, such as in Southwest Asia;

air staging and overflight rights in relation to arms resupply of U.S. clients involved in conflict;

the movement of "surrogate" or "proxy" forces to Third World conflicts, and related logistics;

coercive diplomacy—the use of bases for various manifestations of gunboat diplomacy, or for subtler but similar forms of deterrence;

"presence"—naval and other visits, for "showing the flag," as an aspect of ongoing diplomatic competition.

The recent use of bases in the United Kingdom for mounting an air raid on Libya was one salient example of the use of foreign bases for out-of-area military invention, one which saw U.S. access to en route overhead airspace denied by U.S. allies in France and Spain. Much earlier, the 1958 U.S. intervention in Lebanon, which operationalized the Eisenhower Doctrine, was mounted from bases in West Germany, utilizing en route staging access to Turkey. The U.S. hostage raid in Iran was publicly known to have involved access to facilities in Egypt and Oman; presumably use was made of some European facilities as well in marshaling men and materiel for the operation.

Regarding arms resupply operations, the airlift to Israel in 1973 was the classic case, at a time most European nations denied the U.S. access under pressure from Arab OPEC states. But the U.S. had important staging access to Lajes Air Base in Portugal's Azores Islands; is rumored secretly to have operated tankers out of air bases in Spain during the crisis,[10] and is also reported to have moved materiel to Israel from U.S. Seventh Army stocks in Germany, governmental denials notwithstanding.[11] It was also then alleged by the Egyptians that U.S. SR-71 reconnaissance aircraft based on Cyprus had provided intelligence information to Israel used to plan the latter's crossing of the Suez Canal during the latter stages of that war.[12] U.S. aircraft based in Europe helped ferry Belgian, French, and Moroccan troops (and their materiel) to Zaire in crises during the late 1970s, utilizing en route access to airfields in Senegal and Liberia.[13] And the United States has had some earlier diplomatic imbroglios with Spain over the ferrying of fighter aircraft to nations in the Middle East other than Israel.[14]

Regarding coercive diplomacy, one may note the use of the Sixth Fleet—based in the Mediterranean—for deterring a Syrian invasion of Jordan in 1970, one instance in which U.S. and Israeli interests and actions dovetailed. And more recently, U.S. AWACs aircraft based in Europe have been moved to Sudan as a warning to Libya about aggression against Chad and Sudan; and to Egypt for similar purposes.[15]

Regarding conventional deterrence of the Soviet Union, to the extent separable from nuclear deterrence, one salient example is that of U.S. access to some half-dozen air bases in eastern Turkey, which is intended to help deter a Soviet invasion of Iran and on into the Persian Gulf area. This access to Turkey was expanded at the time the United States was developing its Rapid Deployment Force (now designated as the Central

Command), which involved expanded access to Oman, Egypt, Somalia, Kenya, Diego Garcia, and Morocco, in particular.

Finally, it is noted that the United States has moved in recent years towards forward pre-positioning of materiel (in Norway, the Mediterranean, and the Indian Ocean) and has also formed several MABs (Marine Amphibious Brigades) to marry up with this materiel in the case of conflict. These deployments in Norway pertain solely to the eventuality of a central war with the Soviet Union; those in Diego Garcia are geared to Southwest Asian contingencies. But the pre-positioning and forward shipboard stationing of Marines in the Mediterranean are, obviously, related to possible "out-of-area" conflicts in North Africa or Southwest Asia.

For the future, the trends in the U.S. requirements for bases in connection with the foregoing various aspects of conventional power projection are somewhat indeterminate. Much depends on emerging political developments.

It is, of course, unclear as to whether the seeming current warming of U.S.-Soviet relations will lead to lessened rivalry in the Third World. Currently, the Soviet Union seems to be drawing in its horns in that vast region, among other things, involving fewer ship-days for the Soviet navy in far-flung waters. And even if that is so, it is not clear that it will translate into a reduced U.S. need for facilities needed for interventions or for assistance to clients in Third World wars. Much depends on the number of such future wars, their locales, and the level of U.S. interest. That, in turn, affects the need for air staging bases and overflight rights, in particular.

Much is now being said about the decreasing importance of the Southwest Asia/Persian Gulf region in response to falling oil prices, the end of the Iran-Iraq war, and the Soviet withdrawal from Afghanistan. If that is so, U.S. dependence on the string of bases from Morocco to Egypt and on to Oman, Kenya, Somalia, and Sudan may decrease.

One specter for U.S. defense planning is that of reduced access to European bases (in the Mediterranean, but also in Western Europe) for "out-of-area" operations, something now widely discussed in the wake of the U.S. raid on Libya, which saw only reluctant (and perhaps regretted) British cooperation. This trend may be enhanced by U.S. withdrawal (if only partial) from Europe, by tightened European integration, and by a reduced Soviet threat if that should increase European independence from the United States. For Middle Eastern operations, that may drive a bigger U.S. effort at acquiring staging facilities and overflight rights in Morocco and Egypt, and perhaps Tunisia and Israel.

Areas other than Southwest Asia could become focal points of security concerns, for instance, Central America or even some parts of South America, or the islands of the central and southwestern Pacific. That would focus attention on new staging routes and access requirements, perhaps in Central America, the Galapagos Islands, New Zealand, and so on. An explosion in southern Africa and concomitant en route basing requirements is another possibility.

Evolving Political Changes: Macro-Political Trends and Basing

The preceding review of historical phases in basing diplomacy leads into the broader questions of emerging political trends which, in a fundamental way, impact on U.S. basing access. This is a highly speculative matter, one also subject to the dangers of overreliance on mere extrapolation from seeming present trends. And, too, there is a spectrum running from macro- to micro-level trends. In the former category, one can look at long-range shifts in relative national power, in turn impelled by GNP growth, demographics, and so forth. But then, there are questions such as those about the future of the Soviet leadership—only weakly linked to macro-trends—which can also heavily affect the principles of U.S. basing diplomacy, as translated through the question of the future state of super-power relations.

Following are some of the issue areas that appear to be most relevant to an analysis of emerging macro-political trends.

1. Broad changes in the global political "climate" for big-power basing, involving a complex web of essentially subjective, psychological factors revolving around issues of sovereignty, national dignity/humiliation, and so forth.

2. Shifting conditions of international economics, involving North-South, East-West, intra-OECD (Organization for Economic Co-operation and Development) dimensions: trade, investment, raw materials.

3. Changing global political structure, involving such factors as polarity (bipolarity versus trends towards multipolarity), the continued role of ideology in determining alignments, propensities towards or against neutralism on the part not only of Third World countries but also of nations now firmly within the Western or Eastern military blocs.

4. The future of arms control, centrally involving SALT/START, test bans, and outer space but, as it applies to basing, also potentially involving arms transfers, nuclear weapon-free zones, nuclear non-proliferation, and perhaps conventional arms control in Central Europe.

5. The remnant "decolonialization" of the Third World, for instance,

how many and what additional new nations might be created from still non-independent island groups.

6. Trends in intra–Third World warfare: how many wars, what types (conventional or unconventional), the extent of big power involvement, and so forth.

7. Trends in conventional weapon developments, and the relationship to arms transfers and warfare in the Third World.

8. Changes in the extent of nuclear proliferation, such as, a possible large-scale expansion of the number of nuclear-armed states.

Generally, regarding the "climate" for big-power access, it is clear that recent years have seen an increasingly less permissive environment for foreign access. A foreign presence is, for obvious reasons, almost nowhere welcome, except where it can be construed as contributing directly and visibly to protection. Indeed, almost everywhere, both in the Third World and within the U.S. orbit of Western democracies, governments are subject to pressures regarding a foreign presence. Bruised dignities and compromised sovereignties are involved. In Western countries, and in U.S. clients in the Third World, the Soviet Union conducts a daily onslaught of propaganda designed to unhinge U.S. basing access—the United States in turn is engaged in various base denial activities directed at Soviet access.

Further, there is now a great deal of "lateral" pressure among Third World countries involving superpower basing presences, echoed in UN resolutions and, for instance, such manifestations as the Iraqi Charter, floated several years ago, which called on all Third World countries to eliminate foreign bases.[16] Some of these pressures are global; some regional (such as, discussions among Indian Ocean littoral countries about demilitarization of that region—in reality, specifically directed against Diego Garcia; and intra-Arab pressures linking U.S. bases in such countries as Oman and Morocco to the Israeli issue).

Additionally, recent years have witnessed the spread of antinuclear and environmental movements throughout the Western world and elsewhere, generally associated with the radical left. The recent U.S. problems in New Zealand well illustrate how such factors can constrain U.S. basing access even in connection with an old U.S. ally, and one rather remote from the cold war front lines.[17]

It might be said that the present seeming trend towards "decoupling" of the major powers' basing access could be disaggregated into largely distinct nuclear and conventional components. On the one hand, numerous clients and basing hosts of the major powers have come to fear the consequences of hosting nuclear-related facilities if war should erupt. Hence, scenarios such as that in Tom Clancy's *Red Storm Rising* (reflective of reported war games and other projections in Washington) have U.S. allies making secret deals with the Soviet Union, or simply closing down U.S. access when push comes to shove—fear and intimidation come to outweigh paper alliance commitments when the balloon really does go up.[18]

On a distinct plane, however, are such phenomena as France's refusal to allow U.S. aircraft overflights en route to the Libya bombing raid, or Kuwait's refusal to allow access for U.S. helicopters operating over the tense Persian Gulf. These actions represent not so much the duress of imminent destruction or involvement in an unwanted war as they do narrow, pragmatic political calculations which carefully weigh the economic and political trade-offs where competing interests are involved.

Any of a number of possible broad structural changes in the international system could affect basing structure. Though it is unlikely, Western Europe and the United States could split, perhaps dramatically (this could, of course, involve partial split-offs). West Germany's Ostpolitik could be pushed much further, perhaps even to a "second Rapallo." The People's Republic of China (PRC) could become more closely aligned with the United States; contrariwise one might envision a revival of the Sino-Soviet alliance. Historically, long-term, stable, ideologically based alliances have been more conducive to basing access; multipolar global systems with more rapidly shifting alignments less so. There seems to be now an overall trend towards alliance decoupling—if so, access will presumably become more precarious and tenuous, or at least more costly, all round. Alliances based on "pragmatic" (hence, also probably more unstable) rather than ideological grounds are probably less conducive to access.

The overall future of arms control is, at the time of writing, very unclear, both generally and with respect to specific arms control domains. It is also presumably subject to volatile short-term as well as long-term political shifts within the United States and the Soviet Union. Whether the (until recently) frozen "SALT structure" will survive or be transformed by a new START treaty is unclear, as are the futures of test ban treaties and those possibly pertaining to antisatellite (ASAT) weapons. The outcomes could affect basing requirements in response to changing (that is, allowed) weapon deployments; for instance, ground and/or space-based laser weapons, cruise missile deployments, missile-launching facilities, command, control, communications, and intelligence (C^3I) installations connected to ballistic missile defense, numbers of externally based nuclear-powered ballistic missile submarines (SSBNs), seismological stations, and so on. And certain arms control arrangements which may be envisioned for Central Europe—conventional force reductions, nuclear weapon-free zones—may also critically affect basing issues, for instance by re-opening the question of U.S. forward-based systems (FBS) in Central Europe and/or the Mediterranean in the wake of the INF Treaty.

The future of arms transfer diplomacy—related to the above—will be important, both generally and with reference to specific cases, to the future of basing diplomacy. As indicated, arms transfers—modified by the ideological component of alignments—have become, overwhelmingly, the major coin of basing diplomacy. There are few cases indeed where significant basing access has been granted either superpower without a significant arms transfer relationship, though the reverse of this proposition does not necessarily hold—that is, arms transfers do not always or automatically translate into access, as witness the recent U.S. experience in and around the Persian Gulf. Overall leverage here is critical.

Future Options

In a recent study by the Hudson Institute, four general options were set forth as possible U.S. responses to a decline in access to bases: 1) an attempt to maintain the existing base structure (or at least the more valuable portions of it) by paying higher permit or access costs; 2) accelerate technologies that can compensate for continued base constriction; 3) change current U.S. strategy; and 4) recreate greater redundancy in U.S. overseas base sites.[19]

These are, of course, general strategies deemed applicable on a global basis. But, regarding future options, there are also more specific problems related to the contingency of loss of access to particular nations or of specific crucial facilities. What, for instance, can the U.S. do if it loses access to the Lajes air base in the Azores? Or to Keflavik in Iceland? Or to air bases in eastern Turkey? What if it loses access to the DSP East satellite downlink at Nurrungar in Australia? To the air and naval bases in Oman and/or Somalia? The scenarios are, of course, almost open-ended.

A review of the most recent *Congressional Presentation for Security Assistance* (Fiscal Year 1988) provides an approximate picture of the current costs (that is, rents) for the U.S. overseas basing structure. That document actually divides up the security assistance budget according to several basic purposes, as follows: 1) promote Middle East peace; 2) enhance cooperative defense and security; 3) deter and combat aggression; 4) promote regional stability; 5) promote key interests through foreign military cash sales/commercial exports; and 6) promote profession military relationships through grant training. Cutting across these categories, assistance is provided other nations through such formal program categories as a) economic support; b) concessionary FMS financing; c) MAP grants; and d) IMET grants. The bulk of the assistance more or less explicitly intended as "rents" for basing access falls under "enhance cooperative defense and security," with the following total figures obtaining in the FY 1988 budget.

Several points stand out here. First, the bulk of the rents go to five countries: Greece, Philippines, Portugal, Spain, and Turkey. Second, the total involved—some $2.3 billion—might be said to be a rather small figure relative to the overall defense budget, indeed, relative to the some $5 billion worth of annual assistance that goes to Israel and Egypt to underwrite the Camp David accords. Even in the present climate of budgetary stringency, there clearly remains the option of increasing the rental costs needed to maintain the U.S. overseas basing structure. (That part related to the Rapid Deployment Force involving Oman, Somalia, Kenya, Morocco, and Sudan, adds up only to about $200 million, far less than the cost of maintaining bases in the Mediterranean.)

There are some cases falling under the other categories of "deter and combat aggression," "promote regional stability," "promote key interests through foreign military cash sales," where basing access is involved, if only in a subsidiary way. Pakistan and Thailand fall under the former category, involving a total cost of some $600 million annually, most of it to Pakistan in connection with the (now ended) Afghanistan war and the U.S. hope of forestalling Islamabad's thrust toward nuclear weapons sta-

Table 15–1
The Security Assistance Budget, FY88, by Purpose

Country	1	2	3	4	5	6	Total
Djbouti	3,000	0	0	2,000	135	0	5,135
Greece	0	0	435,000	0	1,250	0	436,250
Kenya	17,000	0	0	19,000	1,600	0	37,600
Liberia	17,000	0	0	3,000	900	0	20,900
Morocco	20,000	0	0	50,000	1,450	0	71,450
Oman	20,000	0	5,150	0	150	0	25,300
Panama	10,000	0	0	3,000	600	0	13,600
Philippines	124,000	0	0	110,000	2,600	0	236,600
Portugal	80,000	0	40,000	85,000	2,550	0	207,550
Somalia	23,000	0	0	22,000	1,250	0	46,250
Spain	12,000	0	265,000	0	3,000	0	280,000
Sudan	18,000	0	0	10,000	1,000	0	29,000
Turkey	125,000	0	235,000	550,000	3,500	0	913,000
Total	469,000	0	980,150	854,000	19,985	0	2,323,135

Source: *Congressional Presentation for Security Assistance Programs, Fiscal Year 1988* (Washington: USGPO).

Note: Purposes are enumerated in the text.

tus. But some access is provided by both these nations, and both could provide expanded access in key areas. In the "regional stability" category are several nations which provide the United States some access—Antigua, Cyprus, Senegal, Seychelles—but only very limited costs are involved.

There are other areas in which, if only indirectly, the United States uses aid as a quid pro quo to acquire or maintain basing access. This involves everything from PL 480 food programs, to anti-narcotics assistance to the Peace Corps. But again, the amounts are small. The overall rental cost of the U.S. basing system appears now around $3 billion total. If what is involved is so crucial, larger payments may well have to be borne.

Regarding technological change, one main point needs be made at the outset. The rate of that change, at least as it is applicable to basing requirements, tends to be very slow.

As noted earlier, technology can often substitute for bases by providing the same or higher levels of military output from fewer bases or more sparsely distributed bases. Historically, this has usually been accomplished by introducing military systems that can reduce the constraints of time and distance. Increased efficiency on the part of some systems has likewise paid off in less dependency on bases in the past.

In the future, a number of improvements can be anticipated, if not from dramatic new technologies, certainly from the incremental improvements that are bound to occur by the turn of the century and from the increasing number of transport systems that will enter the inventory. Additional C-5s, KC-10s, and the new C-17, completing the maritime prepositioning ship program, expanding the ready reserve forces and continual purchases of equipment to unload ships in austere or damaged ports will all have an impact, improving the ability to meet logistics requirements between now and the mid-1990s (assuming that the existing base structure remains intact).[20]

Regarding more dramatic and less incremental developments, the Hudson study discusses artificial islands (studied extensively by RAND in the 1970s),[21] space platforms as basing surrogates, and prefabrication of base sites (presumably to eliminate the normal use of bases outside of crisis periods).

Satellites have taken over some functions previously performed solely or predominantly by land facilities: communications relays, navigation and accurate positioning of submarines, nuclear detection, various aspects of SIGINT, among others. An extension of these trends provides, perhaps, the most promising route to mitigating the political vulnerabilities associated with land bases. In particular, the use of satellites to relay data through space for programs such as DSP and Rhyolite appears promising. But then, there is the offsetting problem of the vulnerability of satellites to

ASAT interdiction during warfare, which may then re-focus attention on external land bases.

The United States may, of course, resolve the problem of its declining basing structure by adjusting its strategy/strategies. Needless to say, however, there are numerous other considerations which feed into grand strategy, and the United States would not want to see such strategy driven by a lack of access to bases. Otherwise, however, it might be argued that heretofore, the United States has had redundant access in some areas, and that it could absorb some reduction of that access to support its strategy.

Recently, as Hudson points out, U.S. defense planning—and associated basing requirements—has been focused on three areas: NATO, Northeast Asia, and Southwest Asia. Hence, "the basing structure tends to reflect these priorities as well, and therefore changes in the relative strategic priority of these areas could modify the strategic significance of some bases, perhaps to the extent that dismantling them would be of little importance."[22]

A declined importance of Southwest Asia (easing of oil problem, end of Soviet occupation of Afghanistan, end of Iran-Iraq war) would lessen the importance of U.S. access to Morocco, Egypt, Oman, Bahrain, Somalia, Sudan, Djibouti, Kenya, Pakistan, and so forth. And, of course, there is much talk about a (partial or full) U.S. withdrawal from Europe.

The final "strategy" adumbrated by Hudson is that falling under the heading of "redundancy." More a tactic than a strategy, it involves dealing with the increased demands for rent by the Philippines, Spain, Greece, Turkey, Portugal, and so forth, by achieving access in other nations which do not now provide the U.S. access (or which provide limited access which might be expanded). In so doing, the United States would achieve increased leverage over its existing base hosts.

Hudson suggests attempting to implement this strategy of proliferation in Morocco, Liberia, Israel, Singapore, and Taiwan, all of which now provide some access for U.S. forces. The obvious problem, of course, is that of the countervailing political problems, particularly in the cases of Israel and Taiwan, that is, the impact on relations with the Arab world and with China. Liberia would, indeed, also have a problem with the remainder of Black Africa if it expanded U.S. access. Morocco too must take into account its image elsewhere in the Arab world. But, this is not necessarily an exhaustive list. Senegal? Gabon? Ivory Coast? Egypt? Sri Lanka? Brazil? Chile?

Generally speaking, however, the short-to-medium term focus will, presumably, be on the U.S. effort to retain some degree of access to key basing hosts: Spain, Portugal, Turkey, Iceland, Australia, Philippines, and Japan. At present, the overall prognosis is merely fair.

Notes

1. See, for instance "Shrinking Power: Network of U.S. Bases Overseas Is Unraveling as Need for It Grows," *Wall Street Journal*, December 29, 1987, p. 1; and "When the Stepping Stones of Power Are Rocky Bases," *U.S. News and World Report*, November 23, 1987, pp. 30–31.

2. See the forthcoming works, one edited by Jane Sharp and the other authored by Simon Duke, both Oxford University Press, 1989, under the auspices of SIPRI. See also R. Rudney and L. Reychler, eds., *European Security Beyond the Year 2000* (New York: Praeger, 1988).

3. An elaboration on these themes is in R. E. Harkavy, *Great Power Competition for Overseas Bases: The Geopolitics of Access Diplomacy* (New York: Pergamon, 1982), esp. chap. 1.

4. R. Paul, *American Military Commitments Abroad* (New Brunswick, NJ: Rutgers University Press, 1973); and U.S. Senate, Committee on Foreign Relations, *United States Security Agreements and Commitments Abroad*, Hearings Before the Sub-Committee on U.S. Security Agreements and Commitments Abroad, 91st Cong., Volumes I and II (Washington, DC: USGPO, 1971).

5. J.R. Blaker, S.J. Tsagronis, and K.T. Walter, *U.S. Global Basing: U.S. Basing Options*, Report for the U.S. Department of Defense, HI-3916-RR, (Alexandria, VA: Hudson Institute, October 1987), p. 5.

6. The subsequent discussion is greatly elaborated upon in R.E. Harkavy, *Bases Abroad: The Global Foreign Military Presence* (Oxford: Oxford University Press, 1989). Other recent works in this area, particularly as pertains to intelligence, communications, and space-related facilities, are: W.M. Arkin and R. Fieldhouse, *Nuclear Battlefields* (Cambridge, MA: Ballinger, 1985); J. Bamford, *The Puzzle Palace* (Boston: Houghton-Mifflin, 1982); B. Blair, *Strategic Command and Control* (Washington, DC: Brookings Institution, 1985); P. Bracken, *The Command and Control of Nuclear Forces* (New Haven: Yale University Press, 1983); W. Burrows, *Deep Black* (New York: Random House, 1985); B. Dismukes and J. McConnell, eds., *Soviet Naval Diplomacy* (New York: Pergamon, 1979); D. Ford, *The Button* (New York: Simon & Schuster, 1985); J.T. Richelson and D. Ball, *The Ties That Bind* (Boston: Allen and Unwin, 1985); J.T. Richelson, *Sword and Shield* (Cambridge, MA: Ballinger, 1986); J.T. Richelson, *The U.S. Intelligence Community* (Cambridge, MA: Ballinger, 1985); and P. Stares, *Space and National Security* (Washington, DC: Brookings Institution, 1987).

7. D. Campbell, *The Unsinkable Aircraft Carrier: American Military Power in Britain* (London: Paladin, 1986).

8. D. Ball, *A Base for Debate: The U.S. Satellite Station at Nurrungar* (Sydney: Allen and Unwin, 1987).

9. A.J. Gregor and V. Aganon, *The Philippines Bases: U.S. Security at Risk* (Washington, DC: Ethics and Public Policy Center, 1987).

10. "Spain Reportedly Urges U.S. to Quit Air Base Near Madrid," *International Herald Tribune*, February 25, 1975; "Secret U.S.-Spain Airlift Accord Told," *Washington Post*, October 11, 1976, p. A24; and "No Secret Pact on Bases, Spain Says," *Washington Post*, October 14, 1976, p. A25.

11. W. Laqueur, *Confrontation: The Middle East and World Politics* (New York: Quadrangle/The New York Times Book Co., 1974).

12. Lt. Gen. S. El Shazli, *The Crossing of the Suez* (San Francisco: American Mideast Research, 1980); and M. Heikal, *The Road to Ramadan* (London: Collins, 1975).

13. "U.S. Role in Zaire Grows with Gabon, Senegal Airlift," *Washington Post*, June 7, 1978, p. A21.

14. "Use of Bases May Become Thorny Issue for U.S., Spain," *Washington Post*, January 30, 1979; "Spain Tosses a Wrench into U.S. F-15 Plans," *Baltimore Sun*, January 12, 1979, p. 2; "Spain Bars Refueling of U.S. Planes," *Baltimore Sun*, August 8, 1980, p. 2.

15. C. Kupchan, *The Persian Gulf and the West* (Boston: Allen and Unwin, 1987), p. 132; and "U.S. Calls Back AWACs Planes from Chad War," *International Herald Tribune*, August 24, 1983.

16. R. Weinland, "Superpower Access to Support Facilities in the Third World: Effects and Their Causes," paper delivered at meeting of International Studies Association, Philadelphia, March 18–21, 1981.

17. D. Alves, *Anti-Nuclear Attitudes in New Zealand and Australia* (Washington, DC: National Defense University Press, 1985).

18. T. Clancy, *Resd Storm Rising* (New York: G.P. Putnam's Sons, 1986).

19. Blaker, Tsagronis, and Walter, *U.S. Global Basing*.

20. *Ibid.*, p. 54.

21. J.H. Hayes, "Alternative to Overseas Bases," Santa Monica, CA, RAND Corp., August 1985.

22. Blaker, Tsagronis, and Walter, *U.S. Global Basing*, p. 55.

16
The Reagan Doctrine: Implications and Opportunities for the Next Administration

Jeffrey Salmon

> Around the world, in Afghanistan, Angola, Cambodia and, yes, Central America, the United States stands today with those who would fight for freedom. We stand with ordinary people who have the courage to take up arms against the communist tyranny. This stand is at the core of what some have called the Reagan doctrine.[1]

Along with the Strategic Defense Initiative, the Reagan Doctrine represents a genuine policy innovation and captures the essential thrust of Reagan administration's understanding of the U.S. role in world politics.[2] As with SDI, the Reagan Doctrine is an idea that the President himself championed: Both ideas present fundamental challenges to the received orthodoxy of U.S. foreign relations and both represent a critical test to vital elements of Soviet power—its reliance on first-strike missiles and its success with Third World revolutionary movements.

Indeed, both SDI and the Reagan Doctrine represent strategic thrusts at potential Soviet vulnerabilities. As SDI seeks to neutralize the Kremlin's heavy investment in ICBMs, aid to anticommunist insurgents takes advantage of possible Soviet overextension in the Third World. In short, each seeks to put the United States on the strategic offensive.

Perhaps most obvious, both policies generated enormous controversy in part because of the rhetorical point the President put on these policies. On the one hand, the President spoke of making missiles impotent and obsolete, and on the other, he spoke of a universal obligation to freedom fighters. These notions were bound to draw fire, and it was fire that unnecessarily directed the debate away from more central issues.

Finally, the future of each of these policy innovations after Reagan is much in doubt. In fact, if there is any future for the Reagan Doctrine it

The views expressed herein are solely those of the author and do not necessarily reflect the views of the Department of Defense or of any other agency of the United States government.

will come only from a clear-eyed view of its strengths and weaknesses and an assessment of the politics that have shaped this doctrine's execution. As the new administration defines its foreign policy agenda, it is an appropriate time to survey the origins of the Reagan Doctrine, examine its primary critics, and to note briefly what lessons the new administration can learn from the doctrine's execution.

Containment and the Reagan Doctrine

The most arresting aspect of the Reagan Doctrine's history is how short many people think that history has been. Within a little over three years of the President's first making a general statement on aid to "freedom fighters," conservatives were arguing that the doctrine had been largely abandoned by the administration and that in truth the policy was dead.[3] In this, as other things, the Reagan Doctrine shares the fate of the Truman Doctrine, which was declared lifeless by *The New Republic* in January 1950.[4] In each case, the obituary was premature, for both doctrines make significant clarifications to U.S. containment policy. Our understanding of containment is, therefore, permanently altered, for the policy options suggested by these doctrines have become a part of U.S. foreign policy debate.

There are important differences, however, between the Truman and Reagan doctrines, differences that owe a great deal to the circumstances of the late 1970s. The role defined by the Truman Doctrine was that of defender of the status quo against antigovernment insurgencies. Rollback, liberation, and the like were explicitly not Truman's intention.[5]

But today, as several observers have pointed out, the wheel has turned. The Soviet Union is now compelled to support a host of client states embroiled in counter-insurgency warfare. One set of critics has written that the Reagan Doctrine "is aimed to change the rules of the game. Suddenly the Soviet Union seemed locked in fixed positions that it had to protect, while the United States had gained a greater freedom to pick the terrain on which to challenge Moscow."[6] Circumstances seemed to have joined with a more assertive administration to restructure our understanding of U.S. foreign policy toward the Third World.

As Robert Osgood wrote just one year into the Reagan presidency, "the dominate theme of President Reagan's foreign policy, to which all major policies were subordinated, was revitalizing the containment of Soviet expansion."[7] Osgood noted that there were no "pretensions of an all-embracing grand design or even intimations of a Reagan Doctrine" in the administration's rethinking of containment.[8] That seems to have come much later.

Put most simply, the Reagan Doctrine was the administration's codicil to containment. It was not a wholesale rejection of containment as static and defensive, nor did it announce a crusade against communism everywhere. Rather, it combined strategic opportunity, the willingness to create the means to seize that opportunity, and Ronald Reagan's belief in America's obligation to the future of democracy. There is a common belief, however, that the Reagan Doctrine is really a return to the rollback of John Foster Dulles or the liberation of James Burnham.[9]

Rollback, however, was merely bravado, since we had no intention of making a serious effort to liberate Eastern Europe.[10] But liberation is a different matter, at least so far as it can be applied to the Third World.

In one of the earliest and most detailed criticisms of containment, James Burnham argued that George Kennan's formulation as expressed in the famous "X" article was ineffective against the "typical modes of Soviet expansion." According to Burnham,

> [Containment] does not indicate what to do when a thrust is carried out not by Soviet military forces in their own name, but by non-Soviet communist formations or by nationalist, labor or other groups who may be under unadmitted Soviet control. Furthermore, it does not explain how to counter a communist advance that proceeds by political rather than territorial stages.[11]

While Burnham may be correct that Kennan's theory fails to account for Soviet indirect strategy, it is nonetheless clear that practice has generally proved containment to be a durable policy. One need only consider U.S. overt and covert activities in Europe against Soviet subversion in the late 1940s to see that there was at least nothing in containment to prevent the United States from countering Soviet political subversion.

Still, Burnham does have a point, since in the Third World, especially in the decade of the 1970s, the Soviets have proved themselves skilled, if not flawless, manipulators of political change. They have done this in ways perfectly consistent with Burnham's analysis, and our response has been about as effective as Burnham would have predicted. As Fred Iklé has noted, our "grand strategy" of containment has been a success in the so-called first world; Europe, Japan, and Korea have been held. But Iklé questions the adequacy of containment in the Third World, where we have undoubtedly lost considerable ground, and where low-intensity conflict puts unusual demands on U.S. defense policy.[12]

Of course, the Reagan administration's reflections on containment did not take place in a vacuum. The administration's response to Soviet exposure in the Third World was structured by Vietnam in much the same way that Nixon responded to Vietnam with the Nixon Doctrine. As one high Reagan administration official put it, "the Nixon Doctrine used surrogate countries, the Reagan Doctrine used surrogate forces."[13] Indeed, for former Secretary of Defense Caspar Weinberger, the essence of the Reagan Doctrine, was the idea of not having to send U.S. troops to faraway lands.[14] For all the talk of the aggressive nature of this doctrine, the fact remains that it is grounded on the nearly unquestioned premise that we must get others to do the fighting for us.

The Reagan Doctrine, therefore, is the consequence of the Reagan administration's willingness to take advantage of Soviet vulnerabilities in the Third World by expanding our understanding of containment. While it is certainly true that this expansion of containment has aggressive aspects, this is probably the case because our definition of what is an aggressive foreign policy has changed considerably since Vietnam.

The Reagan Doctrine and Its Critics

Had the Reagan Doctrine come down to nothing more than strategic common sense, the debate surrounding it would have a far different character. The controversy would surely be as intense, owing to the depth of disagreement over funding for the Contras in Nicaragua. It would not, however, have inspired the sheer bitterness that accompanies intellectual disputes. For the administration's overall justification for aiding anticommunist rebel groups, a justification that came only after much of the policy was in place, did not rest on *realpolitik*. Rather, its argument was grounded on the United States's fundamental obligation to foster the growth of freedom.[15]

None of this should have come as any surprise. President Reagan has never been shy about expressing the view that democracy is a superior form of government, nor in insisting that the United States had a responsibility beyond its own narrow national interest. In his speech accepting the Republican nomination for President in 1980, Reagan noted that "the United States has an obligation to its citizens and to the people of the world never to let those who would destroy freedom dictate the future course of human life on this planet."

The full force of this message was revealed to the British Parliament in 1982, when the President argued that the corrupt and failed totalitarian ideology of Marxism was in crisis around the world, and that the future lay with democracy and pluralism. This future, however, was not self-enforcing. "If the rest of this century is to witness the gradual growth of freedom and democratic ideals," the President said, "we must take actions to assist the campaign for democracy." The most immediate consequence of this speech was the formation of the National Endowment for Democracy, although it clearly set forth the outlines for a theoretical defense of a more activist policy of containment.[16]

With this as a background, it is curious that it took until the President's second term for the themes of democracy and foreign obligations to become a part of the administration's ongoing effort to support anticommunist resistance forces. It was not enough for the President to justify assistance to UNITA, the Contras, or the mujahideen on grounds of self-interest, let alone bleeding the opposition. Rather, borrowing from the principled defense of democracy worked out early in the administration, the President argued that aid makes possible "the growth and expansion of freedom" and that insurgent forces were in fact "freedom fighters."[17] Anyone who argues that the Reagan Doctrine is really a cynical maneuver to bleed the Soviets in the Third World has simply not understood the President's real intention. For Ronald Reagan, at least, that our moral obligation to democracy supported prudent strategy was a happy coincidence.[18]

What the President had done, of course, was give new life to the continuing debate in U.S. foreign policy over U.S. exceptionalism and the limits of containment. Harkening back to the early criticism of containment by Walter Lippman, modern commentators saw in Reagan's moral basis of international action an alarming lack of limits and no recognition between core and peripheral interests, in short, an imprudent call for the universal spread of democracy at the hands of U.S. military power. Typical of this criticism is Christopher Laynes's conservative isolationism:

> Global containment—recast as the Reagan Doctrine—commits the United States to resisting Soviet and Soviet-supported aggression wherever it arises; to building American-style democracies in third world countries; and to rolling back communism by aiding anticommunist insurgencies. The Reagan Doctrine aims to create an ideologically congenial world, and it assumes that America's security requires nothing less.[19]

In this criticism, Layne joins Left-multilaterialist writers such as Thomas Hughes in a total rejection of not only the Reagan Doctrine, but virtually any assertion of U.S. power.[20]

What this debate comes down to is the question of U.S. exceptionalism. Indeed, Layne and Hughes's real dispute is not with the Reagan Doctrine, but the Declaration of Independence and the principled traditions of U.S. foreign policy. Like it or not, the United States is founded on the idea of universal natural rights. Consequently, our interests are not like those of other nations. Does this mean the United States is at war with every regime that denies inalienable rights? Of course not. How could this be, since at the time of its founding the United States could hardly take care of its own affairs, let alone those of other nations? The question for U.S. foreign policy has always been one of mixing prudence with our principled dedication to individual rights.[21]

While critics from the Left and Right seem to agree that the United States has no business in ventures to spread democracy, they tend to diverge on the issue of the principled nature of foreign policy. While Layne believes our foreign relations should rest purely on the cornerstone of self-interest, Hughes argues that the United States does in fact have a strong obligation to principle. In his view, our obligation is to the global community, an obligation that can only be fulfilled through multilateral cooperation.[22]

The Reagan Doctrine, of course, rejects both narrow self-interest and the vague desire to turn its foreign policy over to the complex interdependence of the global community. As such, it remains well within the tradition of U.S. foreign policy, which recognized our principled dedication to fostering adherence of natural rights.

It must be admitted, however, that the rhetoric of the Reagan Doctrine is poorly honed. Using the term "freedom fighters" to describe the Mujahideen or other rebel groups was bound to produce ridicule and convince some that the administration's concern with democracy was purely cynical. Moreover, this rhetoric obscured the deeper and more important argument that the administration was trying to make with respect to the benefits of self-determination and of a world less dominated by Marxist ideology. Indeed, it would have been better to have put more stress on encouraging pluralism and self-determination as the principled basis for Reagan Doctrine assistance.

The debate over the principled or moral ground of the Reagan Doctrine raised concern for the policy of assisting anti-Marxist forces above the level of practical considerations, and made it one over the definition of the goals of U.S. foreign policy. Below the level of that debate, the lines between pro– and anti–Reagan Doctrine forces become blurred. For not only is there bipartisan support for funding the Mujahideen and (noncommunist) Cambodian rebels, but in some cases the political drive behind a funding operation has come from Congress, not the administration. Admitting that in some special cases aid to rebel forces is legitimate, the critics attempt to restrict the application of the Reagan Doctrine by setting up criteria that must be met if aid is to be granted.

In fact, these criteria for assistance to anticommunist rebel groups have the same ex post facto character as the Reagan Doctrine itself. On the one hand, a theoretical justification is announced; on the other, restrictive criteria are set forth to justify aid already agreed to, or already rejected. In both cases, strategic common sense led to decisions that required explanation. In the case of the criteria, however, the thinly disguised purpose was to justify denying aid to the Contras.

Among critics who accept the legitimacy in principle of aid to insurgent forces, but seek to define explicit limits to its application, the most vocal and articulate is Stephen Solarz. Solarz regards the universal aspects of the President's rhetoric "a manifest absurdity" since, he argues, it is not in our interest to support every anticommunist resistance.[23] In place of the Reagan administration's principles of promoting freedom and self-determination, Solarz substitutes rules for intervention. Self-interest is the guide for Solarz, and this will seldom be served if the following items come into play.

1. If support undermines a negotiated settlement.
2. If our friends in the region oppose aid.
3. If the established government is legitimate (that is, not a puppet).
4. If the resistance forces do not seem capable of victory.[24]

Given the political problems that often follow in the train of a decision to aid guerrilla forces, it is quite proper that the burden of proof rest with those who favor assistance. And it is undeniable that each of Solarz's rules should be taken into account when decisionmaking time comes around. This list and indeed any list of criteria tends to focus a debate rather than conclude it. Indeed, it is possible for such criteria to set up a burden of proof so great that it would be impossible to meet. For example, it is always feasible to argue that military support can undermine a negotiated settlement, since at least half the responsibility for such a settlement rests with the forces that oppose aid. Calls that we have to give diplomacy "another try," or that military aid shuts the door on negotiations, are a common retort to claims that assistance of any kind is necessary. Moreover, what is the criteria we are to use to determine if a guerilla movement is capable of winning? In fact, we are very poor judges of this, as the case of the Mujahideen proves. If strictly applied, Solarz's rules would have prevented aid to those rebels, aid Solarz himself supported.

Solarz finds two cases that fit, if somewhat uneasily, into his criteria—Cambodia and Afghanistan. To make these cases fit and at the same time exclude others (mainly the Contras) takes some sophistry. In fact, what seems to separate Cambodia and Afghanistan from the other cases is the fact of an outright invasion and the presence of foreign troops. In the case where there was no invasion, but where foreign troops are present—Angola—there has also been relatively wide support for assistance.

The lesson here seems to be that if you have a combination of invasion and occupation, the way seems open for bipartisan backing of aid to rebel groups. If there are foreign troops, but no outright invasion, support is less likely, but still possible. Naturally, specific political issues surrounding a particular case always complicate easy formulations In Angola, for example, the South African connection as well as the promise of a regional settlement consistently complicated the political debate over aid to Jonas Savimbi.

The difficulty, however, with the true Solarz criteria, that is, support only in the case of invasion, is that it fails to meet the Burnham criticism of containment. In other words, restricting assistance to cases in which invasions have taken place ignores the most common method employed by the Soviets to gain control or dominate influence in the Third World—armed insurgencies supported by Moscow or political subversion. While Solarz recognizes the defect in a containment that is wholly passive in the Third World, he does not suggest policy that can deal adequately with the majority of cases that might be considered by the Reagan Doctrine.

Solarz could, no doubt, respond that diplomacy is the alternative to the Reagan Doctrine, and that some limiting criteria is necessary to keep the policy from becoming unchecked interventionism. The call for diplomacy, however, has become in many cases mere ritual, since it is often unconnected to any real ability on the part of the forces we support to affect the outcome. Nicaragua is the most striking example of this insistence upon diplomacy untied to power. Criteria such as that set down by Solarz too easily comes down to an excuse for doing nothing.

The Future of the Reagan Doctrine

The future of the Reagan Doctrine is cloudy for all the normal reasons connected to a change in administration, even one that does not entail a change in political party. Added to this dynamic, however, is the pervasive idea that peace is breaking out in the world and that the Soviet Union is undergoing a fundamental transformation that signals a far less aggressive foreign policy. In some cases the former dynamic is seen to result from the latter.

However, the notion that peace is at hand in Afghanistan, Angola, and Nicaragua, as well as in other areas, is objected to strongly by conservative circles in the United States.[25] In their view, Reagan's support for anticommunist rebel groups has been undermined by the hope that negotiations and accords will bring about peace and better relations with the Soviet Union.[26]

Even granting the conservative's argument on the Reagan administration's recent execution of the rebel support program, it is no more correct to call the policy dead than it was to declare the Truman Doctrine dead after the United States chose not to continue support for the Kuomintang.

Reagan's codicil to containment is now a permanent part of the U.S. foreign policy arsenal.

Nevertheless, skepticism with respect to favorable outcomes in a host of regional conflicts is certainly wise. The withdrawal of Soviet troops from Afghanistan has been recently called into question; a positive settlement in Angola depends upon the departure of over fifty thousand Cuban troops, a departure that is not clearly in Cuba's interest and so not at all certain; and the possibility of an outcome in Nicaragua consistent with U.S. interests is, at best, in doubt.

So far as the Soviet Union and the Third World are concerned, there is no evidence that General Secretary Gorbachev is willing to give up any of the gains the Kremlin made in the 1970s despite the enormous costs. As Francis Fukuyama has pointed out, while it is unlikely that Moscow will take on any new expensive projects in the Third World, such as Nicaragua or Angola, it is doubtful that the Soviets will turn their back on any of their current expensive projects.[27] Far from it in fact. According to Fukuyama, ". . . under Gorbachev the Soviets have demonstrated a renewed willingness to expend resources and to take tough measures to back up important clients like Angola, Afghanistan, Ethiopia and Libya."[28]

There is no real indication, then, that we can expect early solutions to regional conflicts or that we can rely simply on the Soviets to ease tensions in areas of interest to the Reagan Doctrine. The problem of regional conflicts will remain for the next president and, in some cases, particularly Nicaragua, those problems are very serious.

Dealing with these dilemmas will require a dispassionate appraisal of the Reagan administration's policy in the Third World, especially policies surrounding the Reagan Doctrine. Three areas would be of particular importance in this review—the question of public and Congressional support; bureaucratic and organizational issues; and U.S.-Soviet relations and the problem of regional conflict.

Public Support

Having made the initial overarching argument for backing anticommunist resistance groups, the Reagan administration left to its successor the task of refining and enlarging the initial justification. As noted earlier, the principled defense of the policy should point out the contribution it can make to pluralism and self-determination and our hope for an increase in respect for individual rights.

But, in fact, the decision on what to say is probably not as difficult as the decision to articulate fully the policy on support for anticommunist insurgency. Such a statement was never made by the Reagan administration owing, one suspects, to its desire to retain flexibility. "We are not eager to see [the anticommunist resistance policy] labelled as a doctrine," one administration official said, "because the cases are complex and no rigid set of answers or mechanical formula can be applied."[29] Flexibility is certainly desirable, but the cat is out of the bag and it is clearly time to offer a detailed rationale for continued support of resistance forces.

This rationale would have several benefits. First, the exercise of writing a complete justification for continued support of rebel forces would compel the Bush administration to hammer out a fully coordinated policy. This would be of particular importance with respect to Nicaragua and Afghanistan. Second, it could put the Bush administration in control of the terms of the debate over the case-by-case issues, where the important decision will have to be made with Congress. Finally, it would send a strong and much-needed signal to the world that the new administration is not going to abandon those the United States had supported in the previous administration.

Bureaucratic and Organizational Issues

The Report by the Regional Conflict Working Group submitted to the Commission on Integrated Long-Term Strategy provides a detailed examination of the ways, means, and ends of a comprehensive strategy for the Third World. Its recommendations should be given serious consideration by the Bush administration. Several general points, however, can be stressed with respect to the specific issue of funding resistance forces.

Former Secretary Weinberger was particularly sensitive to the defense department becoming the controlling force in paramilitary operations. At the same time, it was reported that former CIA Director William Casey was more than willing to take that task under his wing. This division of labor should be reconsidered. The Office of the Assistant Secretary of Defense for Special Operations and Low-Intensity Conflict should become a key participant in this area. There should, however, be added stress put on political support for resistance forces. This would include a vigorous public diplomacy campaign headed by the State Department, as well as assistance with political operations within the rebel group.

U.S.-Soviet Relations

Regional conflict issues should be put at the top of the U.S.-Soviet agenda. It is reported that during the Moscow summit these issues ranked far below arms control, and were never the focus of the two leaders' conversations.

It would be a mistake, nevertheless, to personalize our relations with the Soviets to the extent that our policy reflects a desire to assist Gorbachev in managing his domestic crisis. Not only are we poor judges of what exactly will "help" a Soviet leader, but it is a mistake to assume that Gorbachev's success would spell easy sailing for the West. While reforms within the Soviet Union will no doubt benefit the Soviet people, our concern must focus on the Kremlin's foreign policy.

In terms of the Reagan Doctrine, this means continuing or increasing support for anticommunist resistance. Indeed, the Bush administration should make clear that such support is not necessarily restricted to those groups currently receiving our help. The administration should continually assess our interest in giving aid to insurgents that are not as yet a part of the Reagan Doctrine.

Conclusion

If the Bush administration chooses to follow the policy innovation now known as the Reagan Doctrine, it must keep in mind the greatest risk of such a policy. That risk is not, as the critics often say, "another Vietnam." As noted, the Reagan Doctrine was shaped precisely to avoid the use of U.S. combat troops—it is truly a post-Vietnam doctrine. In truth, the primary risk of this policy is connected to the great difficult of a democratic foreign policy—remaining consistent and making your intentions understood.

Nicaragua is the case in point. Given the erratic and confused nature of our support for the Contras, it is reasonable to conclude that the United States is not serious about its interests in Central America, or at least that it is simply incapable of building a consensus around one course of action. Half-hearted action, as in 1962 in the Bay of Pigs, is easily misread by the Soviets as a fundamental lack of will, and a lack of will that is worth a test.

It is hard to see how a continued absence of consensus on funding for the Contras can help but convince our enemies that the United States will turn a blind eye toward continued communist subversion in the region. The great test of leadership for the Bush administration will be creating a consensus on policy toward Central America in order to convince the Soviets that we intend to defend our southern flank.

Clarity and consistency of policy is the first and in some ways most difficult requirement for a democratic nations. For the failure to make ourselves understood in the world is to invite the dangerous, indeed perilous, thought that we are either incapable or unwilling to defend our security.

Notes

1. From a speech by President Ronald Reagan, quoted in Lou Cannon, "Reagan Lauds Bush's Role in Grenada," *Washington Post*, October 26, 1988, p. A4.

2. Jeremy R. Azreal and Stephen Sestanovich, "Superpower Balancing Acts," *Foreign Affairs* (America and the World, 1985), 479. Here SDI and the Reagan Doctrine are called the "distinctive elements of Ronald Reagan's diplomacy." See also Charles Krauthammer, "The Reagan Doctrine," in Robert W. Tucker, *Intervention and the Reagan Doctrine* (New York: Council on Religion and International Affairs, 1985), p. 19.

3. See, for example, "Death of the Reagan Doctrine," editorial, *Washington Times*, October 19, 1988. For a detailed examination of the internal working of the Reagan Doctrine, see Constantine Menges, *Inside the National Security Council* (New York: Simon & Schuster, forthcoming).

4. "The Truman Doctrine is Dead," *The New Republic*, January 23, 1950, p. 5.

5. Daniel Yergin, *Shattered Peace: The Origins of the National Security State* (Boston: Houghton-Mifflin, 1977), p. 295.

6. Azeal and Sestanovich, "Superpower Balancing Acts," p. 485.

7. Robert Osgood, "The Revitalization of Containment," *Foreign Affairs*, (America and the World, 1981), p. 472.

8. Ibid., p. 473.

9. William LeoGrande, "Rollback or Containment? The United States, Nicaragua and the Search for Peace in Central America," *International Security 11* (Fall 1986), pp. 89–120.

10. Krauthammer, "The Reagan Doctrine," p. 19.

11. James Burnham, *Containment or Liberation? An Inquiry into the Aims of United States Foreign Policy*, (New York: John Day, 1952), p. 27.

12. Fred Iklé, Forward to Charles Wolf, Jr., and Katharine Wathkins Webb, eds., *Developing Cooperative Forces in the Third World*, (Lexington, MA: Lexington Books, 1987), p. vii. See also *Discriminate Deterrence, Report on the Commission of Long-Term Strategy*, January 1988, p. 13–17.

13. Interview with Assistant Secretary of State Elliot Abrams, October 31, 1988.

14. Interview with Former Secretary of Defense Caspar Weinberger, November 1, 1988.

15. Access to this question of America's positive obligation to freedom as it applies to Reagan foreign policy can be found in the ongoing debate between Charles Krauthammer and Robert W. Tucker. See, for example, Charles Krauthammer: "Isolationism, Left and Right," *The New Republic*, March 4, 1985, pp. 18–26; "The Multilateral Fallacy," *The New Republic*, December 9, 1985, pp. 7–20; "The Poverty of Realism," *The New Republic*, February 17, 1986, pp. 14–24; "Morality and the Reagan Doctrine," *The New Republic*, September 8, 1986, pp. 17–26; "Isolationism: A Riposte," *The National Interest* (Winter 1985/86), pp. 115–118; and Robert W. Tucker: "Isolationism and Intervention," *The National*

Interest (Fall 1985), pp. 16–26; *Intervention and the Reagan Doctrine* (New York: The Council on Religion and International Affairs, 1985); "Exemplar or Crusader? Reflections on America's Role," *The National Interest* (Fall 1986), pp. 64–76.

16. The president of the Endowment, an organization enjoying wide bipartisan support, is at pains to distinguish his effort from that of the Reagan Doctrine. Justification of both efforts, however, must involve America's right to intervene in the affairs of other states. Interview with Carl Gershman, September 14, 1988.

17. President Ronald Reagan, State of the Union Address, February 6, 1985. See also President Ronald Reagan, "Remarks at Conservative Political Action Conference," *Weekly Compilation of Presidential Documents*, Vol. 21, No. 10. See also Menges, *Inside the National Security Council*, p. 243.

18. See, for example, LeoGrande, "Rollback or Containment," and Selig S. Harrison, "Inside the Afghan Talks," *Foreign Policy*, 72 (Fall, 1988), pp. 31–61.

19. Christopher Layne, "The Real Conservative Agenda," *Foreign* Policy, 61 (Winter 1985/86): 73, and Russell F. Sizemore, "The Prudent Cold Warrior," *Ethics and International Affairs* No. 2 (1988). For a full discussion of the orgins of the Reagan Doctrine in Congress and an argument against the ideological aspects of the policy see, Stephen Rosenfeld, "The Guns of July," *Foreign Affairs* (Spring 1986), pp. 698–714.

20. Thomas Hughes, "The Twilight of Internationalism," *Foreign* Policy, 61 (Winter 1985/86), pp. 25–49.

21. Nathan Tarcov, "Principles and Prudence in Foreign Policy: The Founders' Perspective," *The Public Interest*, 76 (Summer 1984), pp. 45–60.

22. Hughes, "The Twilight of Internationalism."

23. Stephen Solarz, in Christopher C. DeMuth, et. al., eds., *The Reagan Doctrine and Beyond* (Washington, DC: The American Enterprise Institute, 1988), p. 7.

24. Stephen Solarz, "When To Intervene," Foreign Policy, 63 (Summer 1986): 2.

25. See, for example, Angelo Codevilla, "The Reagan Doctrine (As Yet) a Declaratory Policy," *Strategic Review* (Summer 1986), pp. 17–26.

26. Rowland Evans and Robert Novak, "Schultz's Final Days," *The Washington Post*, November 9, 1988, p. A15.

27. Francis Fukuyama, "Gorbachev's New Politics," reprinted from Problems of Communism in *Current* (June, 1988): 15; and Francis Fukuyama, "Gorbachev and the Third World," *Foreign Affairs* (Spring, 1986): 716.

28. Ibid.

29. Quoted in Raymond W. Copson and Richard P. Cronin, "The 'Reagan Doctrine' and its Prospects," *Survival* (January/February 1987): 45.

17
Designing U.S. Forces and Security Assistance for a Low-Intensity Conflict Environment

Sam C. Sarkesian

The post-INF period has witnessed a renewed interest in U.S. conventional force posture and has revitalized examination of conventional strategies and operational capabilities. At the same time, it has drawn a variety of politicians, policymakers, and interest groups into the debates over force posture, burden sharing, and budgetary issues, among other things. Almost lost among these visible and seemingly more pressing issues is the U.S. posture for unconventional conflicts or what are officially referred to as "low-intensity conflicts." There are some excellent reports and studies on U.S. policy and strategy that include some attention to such conflicts, but even in these cases, the major interest rests heavily on conventional military instruments and nuclear comparisons. The irony is that the least likely wars are those that have attracted the most attention and resources, while the most likely wars—unconventional ones—are those that have attracted the least attention and resources.

There may be a number of reasons for this. But a close study suggests that not only is unconventional conflict incompatible with the U.S. way of war, but also at a more fundamental level, it is not understood by most Americans. Many who have struggled with the "lessons" of Vietnam are the first to admit the complexity of such conflicts and the dilemmas they pose to U.S. policy and strategy.

In coming to grips with specific issues of unconventional conflicts, therefore, we are faced at the outset with problems of concepts and terminology. Compounding these issues is the fact that many of those who study unconventional conflicts dismiss concepts and approaches as abstractions with little utility. They argue for "getting on with it" and a "can do" mentality. It is difficult to understand how policy strategy, and operational implementation can be designed effectively, if there is little agreement and much misunderstanding on what it is the United States must respond to. Yet, we have "answers," partly based on security assistance programs and U.S. forces designed for low-intensity conflicts.

These answers and the issues they raise form the focus of this chapter.

The analysis to follow examines U.S. security assistance and force structure to determine the effectiveness of the U.S. posture for unconventional conflicts. There are two complementary purposes. First, to formulate a conceptual base for understanding unconventional conflicts. Second, to analyze U.S. response (answer) to unconventional conflict and how to make that response more effective in terms of security assistance and force design. The argument is based on the premise that unconventional conflicts are likely to characterize the security environment over the next decade. Further, many of these conflicts are likely to challenge long-range U.S. national interests.

A Preliminary Conclusion

The central focus of this study and its importance in the analysis to follow warrant a preliminary conclusion. The current U.S. capability in unconventional conflicts is inadequate and, by and large, ineffective.[1] This is primarily a consequence of a conceptual and strategic view stemming from a misreading of the fundamental question, what kind of conflict is unconventional? This is true with respect to the broader issues relating to policy and strategy, as well as with security assistance and force design. While security assistance and force design for unconventional conflicts have been the focus of some attention at the national level, a great deal remains to be done in providing the substance and capability to effectively implement strategy at the operational level. In brief, there is a mismatch between policy, strategy, and operational implementation. Projections into the next decade offer little hope for change.

A number of conceptual and strategic realities reinforce these observations. First, the second U.S. counterinsurgency era has become mired in conceptual confusion and technical jargon, obscuring the essence of unconventional conflict. Second, the design of special operations units is being fashioned by conventional dogma, reflecting the conceptual problem in defining the nature of the new battlefield. Third, the fact that most unconventional conflicts are endemic to the Third World has compounded the problems of conceptual clarity and relevant force design by obscuring the distinction between the inherent instability associated with change and modernization and unconventional conflicts. Fourth, the problems of political change and development in states in the Third World are likely to continue, exposing them to major power involvement and making them vulnerable to political violence. Fifth, and finally, U.S. security assistance to Third World states is unbalanced and inadequate, compounding the problems of effective response to unconventional conflicts.

An authoritative study on the lessons of Vietnam best sums up these realities:

> While the next U.S. major military involvement undoubtedly will be in a Third World region, our forces remain structured almost exclusively for the war that will not be. Low-intensity conflict, the offspring of the Vietnam War, seems no better understood by U.S. officials, military or civilian, than the American war in Vietnam.[2]

Security assistance and U.S. force design are parts of the larger issue of Third World environment and policy and strategy for unconventional conflicts. The primary concern here is not on these broader questions. Yet, without some reference to the larger issues, the analysis of security assistance and U.S. forces would lack contextual references and border on the abstract.

The Third World

There are a variety of excellent studies on Third World politics, change, and development that describe and analyze the complexities and ambiguities of the Third World environment.[3] There is no substitute for the serious reading of such studies. But, for our purposes, it is sufficient to outline several important considerations.

In brief, the move from a traditionally based political and economic system to one based on a more secular and modern value system is often characterized by internal struggles within a state and among contending elites.[4] Even a change from one traditional group of leaders to another is often accompanied by internal struggles.

More than two decades ago, one scholar identified and described the major directions of Third World change and development. Among other things, he stated,

> Economic development is not primarily an economic but a political and social process. The political and social changes required for economic development are apt to be revolutionary in nature. . . . Economic development is not a process which breeds social contentment. . . . The price of development is apt to be political and economic authoritarianism.[5]

Although some of these judgments need to be qualified in the decade of the 1980s, much remains as true today as they were when those words were written. In simple terms, instability is inherent in development and change. In more specific terms, the primary problems facing many states in the Third World revolve around ideological relevancy and cohesion, effective governing systems, economic growth, law and order, and personal security. Effective response to these problems does not necessarily engender democracy.

Moreover, regardless of the new U.S.-USSR relationships and the era of *glasnost* and *perestroika*, the two superpowers remain serious competitors in Third World areas. While the Soviet Union has undergone some important changes in its view of the Third World, there is little to suggest that it is in *retreat*. Rather, it appears that the policy and strategy of consolidation and retrenchment is the more accurate description, with a recognition that the Soviet Union is placing less emphasis on visible military presence and more on political and psychological means. These new perspectives, posture, and a more pragmatic and opportunistic policy make the Soviet Union a formidable adversary in the Third World, perhaps even more so than in the past.

In sum, in the drive for modernization and change, a revolutionary environment develops in many Third World states. Such an environment has its roots in complex political-social and structural dynamics that rarely lend themselves to democratic solutions, at least at the outset.[6] Additionally, in such situations, states are exposed to external forces and influence. It is this kind of environment that sparks and nurtures unconventional conflict.

What Kind of Conflict?

According to the Report by the Commission on Integrated Long-Term Strategy, "In the past forty years all the wars in which the United States has been involved have occurred in the Third World."[7] Virtually all of these wars have been unconventional.

In assessing U.S. national interests, the President stated in 1988: ". . . low intensity conflicts continue to pose a variety of threats to the achievement of important U.S. objectives. . . . These conflicts, generally in the Third World, can have both regional and global implications for our national security interests."[8]

It seems clear, therefore, that U.S. capability to respond to unconventional conflicts must be based on an understanding of and sensitivity to Third World change, development, and culture; an understanding of the "essence" of unconventional conflicts; and knowledge of the linkages between such conflicts and the Third World.

One of the most basic issues in coming to grips with such matters is to make some sense out of the multitude of labels and confusing descriptions for what many term low-intensity conflict and special operations.

This charge has been made on a number of occasions. Yet, the problems and confusion associated with concepts and terminology continues to grow.

Without repeating the litany of arguments regarding these issues, the following is offered:

> Unconventional conflicts are political-military struggles involving two or more groups ruled by indigenous elites, aimed at taking or maintaining control of the existing system. These are struggles violently contesting control of the indigenous political-social system and are framed primarily in political-psychological terms rooted in the indigenous culture. Such struggles, more often than not, are contests in a no-holds-barred environment, usually taking place in Third World areas.[9]

The characteristics of unconventional conflicts rest primarily on revolution, counterrevolution, and terrorism that evolves from such conflicts.[10] While these conflicts have their military dimensions, they are primarily rooted in the problems facing Third World states evolving from change and development, as discussed earlier. To limit U.S. policy and strategy, therefore, to military considerations is simply to focus on the symptoms rather than the cause and the cure. Effective response to unconventional conflict cannot be designed on a piecemeal basis, with bits and pieces of strategy and operations being parceled out to various agencies and institutions as an end in themselves.

> There exists today no persistent, direct, high-level emphasis for the development of an interdepartmental approach to the problem of foreign internal defense. . . . With a structural void such as that which exists today comes a scarcity of the resources and/or incentives necessary to motivate the Army to overcome its institutional bias and inertia and develop a true capability for FID contingencies.[11]

The complexity of such conflicts is compounded by the fact that the United States may need to support revolutions to further its national objectives. The problems associated with support of existing systems—that is, counterrevolution—while applicable in broad terms, need to be considerably reshaped and redesigned to support revolutions at the operational level.

The Contemporary View

An important part of the current U.S. efforts in unconventional conflicts is in security assistance and forces designed for special operations and low-intensity conflict. A brief overview of these two components is important for our analysis, recognizing that we will only touch on some of the more prominent characteristics, rather than providing a comprehensive review.

Security Assistance: An Overview

U.S. strategy for unconventional conflicts was spelled out by the President's 1988 annual strategy statement:

> . . . the most appropriate application of U.S. military power is usually indirect through security assistance—training, advisory help, logistics support, and the supply of essential military equipment. Recipients of such assistance bear the principal responsibility for promoting their own security interests with the U.S. aid provided.[12]

In his statement a year earlier, the President noted that the role of the U.S. military was a supportive one, but that the armed forces had to be prepared to take a more direct role if necessary. And finally, he made it clear that the commitment of U.S. combat forces in a low-intensity conflict would occur only as a last resort when U.S. vital interests are at stake.[13]

In official terms, the objectives of U.S. security assistance:

> . . . are to assist countries struggling to preserve their independence and enhance their democratic processes . . . ; engage local armed forces in the process of civic action and nation building as opposed to political infighting; encourage small countries to pool their resources in collective security arrangements; and ease potential burdens on U.S. armed forces.[14]

Security assistance includes a variety of programs:

> The major components of security assistance are the Foreign Military Sales (FMS) Program, the FMS Credit (FMSCR) Program, the Military Assistance Program (MAP), the International Military Education and Training (IMET) Program, the Economic Support Fund (ESF), and peacekeeping operations.[15]

From time-to-time, a variety of complimentary programs were designed to provide some flexibility in security assistance, including, for example, the special military assistance service fund (MASF) channeled through the Department of Defense. This provided additional assistance to Vietnam and other countries in Southeast Asia from 1966 to 1975.[16] A number of other programs add to security assistance efforts. These range from assignment of military advisors and military training teams (MTT) to combined training exercises with indigenous forces and host in-country training of U.S. forces (the National Guard in Honduras). In a larger sense, therefore, security assistance can be seen as the total U.S. effort to assist a particular country in its security effort, both internally and externally.

At the present time, there seems to be considerable imbalance in the planning and implementation of U.S. security assistance programs.[17] Not only does security assistance appear to be inadequate in such vital areas as Central and South America (with perhaps the exception of El Salvador), but budget cutting has limited funding.[18] According to the Military Posture Statement:

> Beginning in FY 1985 and continuing in FY 1988, the political momentum for a balanced budget was one of several factors causing security assistance funding for friendly nations to level off and then significantly decrease. The FY 1987 and 1988 budgets reflected congressional cuts to the President's proposed security assistance program combined with heavy earmarking for two countries, Israel and Egypt.[19]

In light of the increasing concern with the federal budget deficit and the budget cutting syndrome in Congress, it does not appear likely that security assistance funds will see any dramatic increase over the coming decade. As will be shown later, however, improvement in security assistance requires more than legislation and financial resources.

While the policy statements and program objectives articulated at the national level may appear coherent and clear, they have not been sustained by appropriate resources and legislative flexibility. But perhaps more important, they have not been translated into operational effectiveness. These flaws have been recognized by others, and are important considerations in the conceptual and strategic realities addressed earlier.[20]

Most of the problems associated with security assistance, its objectives, and support (or lack thereof) by political leaders and national policymakers can be traced to the lack of understanding of the question, what kind of conflict? In turn, the lack of clear conflict criteria, the nature and character of Third World states for which the major effort of security assistance should be designed, and charges of U.S. "intervention" in Third World states, in the aggregate, have politicized the strategy. This has lead to caution, hesitancy, and indeed, reluctance on the part of many political leaders and policymakers to support any form of U.S. involvement in unconventional conflicts. Lacking a politically effective constituency, there are few in political circles advocating innovative and long-range policy and strategy focused on security assistance and unconventional conflicts. Compounding the politics is the tendency for many Americans to link security assistance, U.S. armed forces, and foreign involvement, raising the fear of another Vietnam.

Moreover, for many military men and women, security assistance is not a career-enhancing assignment, nor is it considered to be an important element in military capability and effectiveness. The fact is that U.S. military efforts and, to a lesser, but still important, degree, political economic efforts, are rooted in "mainstream" command and staff channels and their civilian equivalents. In sum, the professional military ethos is primarily driven by conventional thought and major battle mentality. These, in turn, direct policies, strategies, and resources to concentrate on the European-type battlefield.

U.S. Force Design

One of the most simple yet most difficult parts of U.S. response to unconventional conflicts is shaping an effective military instrument. The primary military instrument for U.S. response to unconventional conflicts is the United States Special Operations Command.

> The United States Special Operations Command (USSOCOM) was established on 16 April 1986 to unify all CONUS-based Special Operations Forces (SOF) under one commander responsible for preparing SOF to carry out assigned missions. The command consists of Army, Navy, and Air Force Component which has about forty thousand active and reserve personnel organized to accomplish the following missions:
>
> Provide combat ready SOF to rapidly reinforce the other unified commands.
>
> Plan and conduct selected special operations as directed by the National Command Authority (NCA). . . .[21]

The prevailing view of conflicts shaping the organization and training of SOF is subsumed under special operations and low-intensity conflict. There is evidence that the current organizational structure and operational guidelines reflect a conventional perspective of the "unconventional," reflecting patterns paralleling security assistance efforts.[22]

At the present time, the design of special operations forces does not realistically account for the distinction between special operations and low-intensity conflict. This is reflected, for example, in the fact that Special Forces traces its lineage to the First Special Service Unit of World War II fame—a unit organized to conduct a special conventional-type operation. However, Special Forces should trace its lineage to the Office of Strategic Services (OSS) and all this suggests with respect to training, operations, and doctrine.

Moreover, even for many who see unconventional conflicts as threats to long-range U.S. national interests, such conflicts are usually perceived in terms of special operations. Accordingly, ranger/commando–type forces and contingencies in support of conventional operations weigh heavily in the special operations/low-intensity conflict equation. Since such operations are more attuned to conventional mind-sets and conventional contingencies, they are less difficult to "digest" within mainstream military perspectives and doctrines. Increasingly, as resources and command and control systems, among other considerations, become institutionalized, there is a great likelihood that special operations will totally subsume the low-intensity conflict dimensions, or as conceptualized here, unconventional conflicts.

Compounding the problems of U.S. capability in unconventional conflicts are the lack of clear lines of authority and a cumbersome bureaucratic structure.

> The single greatest impediment to the management and effective use of SOF, whether against protracted insurgent threats or against terrorism, is the endless bureaucracy which overlards these forces. . . . The hallowed bureaucratic prerogative known as "peeing on the bush"—each later demanding an acknowledgement of its own authority before it is willing to concede that the national interest can be served—has left its deleterious mark on every U.S. military exertion from Vietnam forward.[23]

An even more caustic criticism is offered by an authority on special operations.

> The condition of U.S. Special Operations Forces is poor in spite of billions of dollars spent in 1980. . . . None of the services gave up money to USSOCOM. Now that there is a push for USSOCOM to do the things stated by law, it will discover that it does not have a budget department manned, trained, or equipped to participate in the complex DoD budget process. . . . The resistance within the JCS and DoD is so strong that it appears the answer must lie outside that structure. The blatant lack of support and continuing malicious implementation make the best argument for a separate agency.[24]

Equally damaging to U.S. capability in unconventional conflicts is the fact that between the option of committing U.S. combat forces and the option of security assistance there is almost a vacuum in terms of strategy, doctrine, and force capability.

U.S. involvement in El Salvador provides operational credence to many of the criticisms and problems of the U.S. effort addressed here. According to an authoritative study:

> U.S. policy toward El Salvador represents an attempt to formulate a new approach to a painfully familiar military problem. The essence of that approach has been to provide a besieged ally with weapons, ammunition,

and other equipment, economic aid, intelligence support, strategic counsel, and tactical training—while preserving the principle that the war remains ultimately theirs to win or lose. This principle has precluded any consideration of committing U.S. troops to combat. More broadly, it has restricted the human component of American assistance, both in numbers and in the activities permitted to the few Americans deployed to the war zone.[25]

The authors conclude that in El Salvador, "American officials have yet to devise adequate mechanisms to achieve" the aim of winning popular support. American officials appear ". . . more comfortable giving advice on the minor tactics of counterinsurgency, they allowed themselves in El Salvador to drift into what one official termed 'a band-aid approach' to fighting the 'other war.' "[26]

What Needs To Be Done?

As stated earlier, the three parts composing the main focus of this analysis are strategic distinctions regarding the Third World, restructuring and redesigning security assistance and U.S. forces for the unconventional conflict environment, and education and rethinking. In each of these parts, the primary concern is to develop a more effective capability, based on the problems identified earlier, for unconventional conflicts.

Strategic Distinctions, the Third World, and Security Assistance

U.S. strategy must make a distinction between internal instability associated with modernization and unconventional conflict. Instability in Third World states does not necessarily lead to unconventional conflicts. All systems, regardless of degree of development, have some degree of internal conflict. The need is to clarify when internal instability broadens into unconventional conflict, and when such conflicts are a threat to U.S. national interests.

An important step in strategy, therefore, is to make a reasonable distinction between such "expected" instabilities and those that cross the line into unconventional conflicts (as defined earlier).[27] In the former case, where the primary purpose is prevention (preventive phase), traditional diplomacy, aid, and assistance are the appropriate instruments. This should be (and in the main, is) a civilian directed and implemented strategy, with the Department of State serving as the "lead" agency. In such circumstances, the military performs a supportive but subordinate role—

oftentimes a passive role. In this respect, the role of intelligence is critical. Further, a variety of private U.S. corporations and organizations can play an important role in Third World development (preventive phase). While there may be a great deal of private activity, there is a great deal of potential that has yet to be exploited, including a serious look at "privatization" of security assistance.[28]

The objectives of U.S. security assistance are pertinent to the preventive phase and are part and parcel of unconventional conflicts. In the preventive phase, security assistance should be in place *prior* to the emergence of unconventional conflict. To be sure, security assistance needs to continue after the emergence of unconventional conflict, but it is extremely important to try to *prevent* such conflicts from developing in the first place.

Once it is determined that internal instability has gone beyond the preventive phase and into unconventional conflict, the United States must determine whether such a conflict in a particular state is a serious threat to U.S. national interests. Further, important strategic guidelines need to be established before a determination is made regarding U.S. involvement beyond the preventive phase, including the importance to U.S. national interests and the potential of the existing system or group to govern effectively and, in the long run, its compatibility with U.S. national interests.

The main point is that all Third World instability is not a case of unconventional conflict. All unconventional conflicts do not demand U.S. involvement. Only some unconventional conflicts may be serious threats to U.S. national interests.

Once unconventional conflicts occur, security assistance becomes an important part of the overall U.S. effort. Further, assistance in an unconventional environment must be reshaped to respond to direct challenges raised by revolutionary forces. At the same time, security assistance must also be directed at long-range objectives in their own right. This means that it must be part of a broadly coordinated effort, combining security assistance with U.S. forces designed to engage in unconventional conflicts.

Security assistance in any phase cannot succeed without an effort evolving from an integrated and coordinated political-military structure addressing not only the military, but the broader political and psychological dimensions as well. Piecemeal efforts at specific military issues without coordination and integration through political channels and channels unique to the indigenous culture cannot succeed, and may serve merely to provide grist for the adversary's mill. For example, some of the most important elements of security assistance are police functions and those performed by government bureaucracies at both national and local levels.

There are a variety of institutional means to integrate and coordinate political, psychological, and military efforts. These can begin with a revitalization of the Country Team concept (in-country) and its equivalent at the national security planning levels, including a combined Department of State/Department of Defense/CIA Country Team system. A number of interdepartmental committees and senior level committees can also be created for security assistance purposes. If it is used properly and is functioning effectively, the Assistant Secretary of Defense for Special Operations and Low-Intensity Conflict can serve as the central point for all these efforts. The major need is to bring together the variety of agencies involved in some part of the U.S. effort in any particular Third World state. Underpinning any structure, however, is the need to acquire acceptance by individuals and agencies, as well as by Congress, of the need for central control and coordination of the security assistance effort. Add to this a need to view security assistance beyond the "security" horizon—that is, there is a need to develop a strategy and programs to assist governments to "govern effectively," with a view towards developing a more open system.

Redesign of U.S. Forces

A more realistic view of the conflict spectrum is needed before any redesign of U.S. forces is considered. This realism must distinguish between special operations and low-intensity conflict. The more accurate terminology is unconventional conflicts, divided into two dimensions.[29] One dimension is special operations, which are primarily highly focused conventional operations by units skilled in small-unit actions and vanguard contingencies. These are conceived as unconventional because they are, in the main, beyond the capability of standard conventional units.

Another dimension is low-intensity conflict. This term is used here simply to retain some continuity from existing literature and planning, and not necessarily because it is the most appropriate term. This type of conflict is primarily revolution, counterrevolution, and the terrorism that evolves from such conflicts. These are likely to be protracted conflicts, characterized by a variety of "unconventional" operations ranging from ambushes, assassinations, and hit-and-run raids to terror, and focused on the political-social milieu of society. By and large, U.S. military involvement must be conceived on a long-term basis stemming from political will and staying power, as part of the larger political-military effort.

It is in low-intensity conflicts, as distinct from special operations, that the following guidelines apply:

1. U.S. involvement must be channeled through the existing indigenous system and leadership.

2. U.S. presence must have low visibility to insure that the indigenous system and leadership remain in control of the effort (or are perceived as such).
3. U.S. involvement must be shaped to function as a force multiplier and political-economic reinforcement to the indigenous system.
4. U.S. combat forces must not be deployed into the conflict arena unless there is no alternative but defeat of the indigenous system and the issue is vital to U.S. national interests.
5. U.S. involvement must be part of an overall strategy designed to foster U.S. national interests.

At the operational level, doctrine should include a number of "teachings" that are generally neglected in much of the current thinking. These teachings, for example, need to foster a sense of self-reliance in indigenous leaders and organizations and establish trust and confidence at all levels between U.S. and indigenous personnel.[30]

Combining doctrine and operational guidelines with the essence of unconventional conflicts, a basic change may be needed in the command system. The U.S. Special Operations Command must reflect the differences in the two dimensions of unconventional conflicts and establish two autonomous commands within the Special Operations Command.[31] This is not a call for another military bureaucracy. Rather, these subordinate commands should be lean operational commands, with the bulk of the administrative and logistical effort retained by USSOCOM. A more effective approach may be to designate the whole structure the Unified Unconventional Conflict Command (UUCC).[32] As I have written elsewhere:

> Special operations and low-intensity conflicts differ in substance and purpose. The template for unconventional conflicts, while overarching and encompassing both dimensions, must also make clear distinctions between the two, conceptually, doctrinally, as well as organizationally.[33]

Another dimension of U.S. force design is the light infantry concept. While the importance of this dimension is recognized, it will only be noted here with respect to several major conceptual considerations. The study of light infantry and its applicability to unconventional conflicts must first redefine the unconventional conflict environment. The commitment of light infantry forces suggests a qualitative difference in the conflict—that it has shifted against the existing system in favor of the revolutionary forces. Further, the commitment of light infantry forces also suggests a "last resort" contingency, recognizing the expanded scope of the conflict and a broader U.S. involvement. Moreover, there is considerable debate regarding the proper role, function, and organization of light infantry forces.[34] It is a debate, it might be added, whose horizons are considerably beyond a light infantry mission in an unconventional conflict.

The main thrust seems to be on tactical contingencies associated with conventional conflicts. Much attention is given to light infantry involvement in what some military men call mid- and high-intensity conflicts, overshadowing the low-intensity dimension. Moreover, most of the operational orientation of light infantry forces have their roots in conventional operations. According to one authority, in low-intensity conflicts:

> Clearly, light infantry operations . . . are inherently more demanding and difficult than those in mid- to high-intensity wars. While politically derived restrictions on the use of force hinder all military operations to a significant degree, in low-intensity conflicts, they are especially straining. In addition, light forces have the disadvantage that their enemy is hard to identify, while they, themselves, are always identifiable. In low-intensity conflicts, a higher degree cf cooperation between civil, military, and police organizations is necessary for success, yet is more difficult to obtain.[35]

Another important consideration is doctrinal development for deploying light infantry forces in small units to serve as force multipliers for indigenous forces in countering revolutions. Little attention has been placed on such a contingency.

For the reasons outlined here, the light infantry concept deserves a separate study in its own right, particularly since the concept encompasses commitment of such forces to any type of conflict in any geographic area. Implicit in such a perspective is the view that individuals trained for any type of conventional conflict can readily be committed to an unconventional conflict. It is the contention here that the commitment of such forces to an unconventional conflict requires special training not readily part of the standard infantry structure.

Finally, the overall problem of security assistance and U.S. force design may not be so much with the existing structure, as it is with the problems of coordination and control of the variety of military and nonmilitary inputs required for any successful response to unconventional conflicts. This is not solely a responsibility of the Department of State, the CIA, or the Department of Defense. From the strategic point of view, it is a responsibility shared by all of these primary departments and agencies. While the creation of the Office of the Assistant Secretary of Defense for Special Operations and Low-Intensity Conflict may not resolve all of the problems, at the least it provides a central point for coordination and control, as well as a point of departure for senior level task forces. The key is that the person occupying the office understands the meaning of unconventional conflicts and the multidimensional nature of successful

U.S. response. Based on this understanding, the occupant must exercise leadership, bureaucratic skills, and staying power.

Education and Rethinking
about Unconventional Conflicts

It seems clear from this analysis that an essential part of an improved U.S. effort is a more sophisticated and realistic view of the Third World and unconventional conflicts. There must be some common conceptual base from which can flow strategic coherency and operational guidelines that are relevant to the characteristics of the Third World and the unconventional conflict environment.

In brief, education must be broadened, as well as focused, to insure that U.S. policy, strategy, and doctrine are attuned to Third World realities. Equally important, U.S. personnel must be educated to adapt to the Third World environment and, at the same time, develop the knowledge and skills to deal with unconventional conflicts. The essentials of such education must include a serious study of subjects such as non-Western value systems, the psychological make-up of those in non-Western cultures, goals and aspirations of individuals in Third World systems, the political-psychological driving force of indigenous leaders, and causes and outcomes of revolutions. The importance of language training is a foregone conclusion.

The major purpose is to produce people who know how to realistically assist indigenous individuals, groups, and systems in achieving goals appropriate to their own particular state, without "Americanizing" the environment. At the same time, U.S. personnel must also be able to reconcile indigenous efforts to the larger issues of U.S. national interests. Much has been written about such matters. It would seem that further comments are unnecessary. Yet, there is a need to constantly repeat what has been implicit and explicit in this study because of the fact that conventional mind-sets, convoluted perceptions, and mainstream dogmatism persist in fashioning concepts and analyses of the unconventional through conventional lenses. Such perspectives continue to be the major influence on strategy and doctrine. Unfortunately, some of the most flagrant intellectual and conceptual distortions are committed by those who should know better.[36]

An important starting point for rethinking the U.S effort in unconventional conflicts is to establish a new or different set of premises—premises that are not bound or directed by U.S. cultural considerations or the U.S. way of war. Such premises must begin with attention to the needs of the indigenous system or group to establish effective governing structures, legitimacy, and a close linkage between the needs of the people and their aspirations and the ideology of the system. In brief, premises need to be based on the environment from the indigenous perspective. Rethinking is closely linked to the quality and sophistication of the education to be provided about the Third World and unconventional conflicts.

One of the most difficult aspects of education and the rethinking process is developing a *serious* commitment within the U.S. military to respond to unconventional conflicts. While there may be a great deal of rhetoric and bureaucratic posturing on the subject, the prevailing view seems to be that unconventional conflict contingencies can be met by existing forces and doctrine. According to this view, forces organized and trained for NATO contingencies are equally prepared for unconventional conflict contingencies. In most simple terms, mainstream military thought and postures relegate "elite" or special units and unconventional conflict response to the periphery of military professionalism.[37]

Conclusions

From the preliminary conclusion offered earlier there flows a number of complementary ones. These are, by and large, a reflection of continuing and persistent conceptual incoherency, conventional mind-sets, and imposition of mainstream military doctrine. There is a close relationship between these and the way security assistance is conceived and implemented, as well as how U.S. forces are structured.

In brief, the United States must rethink its security assistance strategy, develop a more sophisticated (and realistic) view of the Third World and unconventional conflicts, and redesign strategy and operational guidelines accordingly. Further, the training and education of U.S. personnel in the field of security assistance and of U.S. forces designed for unconventional conflict must be relevant to the Third World environment and to the characteristics of unconventional conflicts. Finally, U.S. strategy, operational implementation, and doctrine must be flexible enough to adapt to specific and unique situations.

At the national level, U.S. policy and strategy must take care not to make "unconventional conflicts" a catch-all for anything and everything that cannot be categorized into mainstream military thought and conventional structures. Serious attention ought to be given to just where contingencies such as drug trafficking, immigration controls, and peacekeeping enter into U.S. military response. Should these be part of unconventional conflicts? Such a "delicatessen" approach does little to sharpen U.S. effectiveness in unconventional conflicts. In this respect, personnel trained in conventional contingencies and in a mainstream military environment are not necessarily prepared to engage in unconventional conflicts. It may also be true that no amount of preparation suits military units for involvement in drug abatement operations and immigration control. Civil authorities with effective police and intelligence systems, provided with effective communications and transportation, may be the most effective approach to the "police" dimensions of U.S. assistance.

Even though some important structures and career incentives have been created for unconventional conflicts (Special Forces designated as a branch), serious loyalty of most military professionals to this area appears to be lacking. Similarly, the broader policy and strategy issues of unconventional conflicts seem wrought with political considerations, making it difficult to specify with any degree of clarity when and if forces for unconventional conflicts will be used—if ever.

Underpinning the problems identified in this study is the fact that the U.S. military is performance-oriented: It is inclined to operate according to the "can do" approach to contingencies. Time for reflection and conceptualization is rare. Thus, terminology, structures, and operations are heavily shaped by the drive to perform effectively and efficiently. There is a long-term problem associated with this approach, which is rarely acknowledged, even by those who applaud the progress made by the United States in preparing for unconventional conflicts. Once organizational orientation, structural design, and ways of doing things become institutionalized, they tend to develop a rationale of their own. Training, planning, operational perspectives, and mind-sets become driven by the "posture-in-being." This makes it extremely difficult to incorporate new concepts and organizational designs and hinders flexibility and resilience. The present design of U.S. forces for unconventional conflicts reflects the can-do mentality.

Having said all of this, it may well be that we need to pause and allow (and urge) the whole matter of security assistance and U.S. force design to flow into the U.S. political-military bloodstream. The present posture for unconventional conflict needs to be energized by intellectual attention, professional commitment, and substantive muscle. Equally important, Third World realities must replace a number of prevailing assumptions.

Yet, even if the United States did everything right, there is no assurance of success. There are limits to what the United States can reasonably accomplish without resorting to major war. This may well be a subtle yet important factor in shaping the views of many Americans—the view that U.S. involvement in the Third World, at more than a minimal level, will lead to another Vietnam. Thus, the United States should not be involved, according to this view, unless the issues and objectives are clear and there is certainty that the United States will win. Given the nature of the Third World environment and the character of unconventional conflicts, adopting such a view leaves the field to our adversaries.

Notes

1. See Sam C. Sarkesian, "The Myth of U.S. Capability in Unconventional Conflicts," *Military Review* (September 1988): 2–17.

2. Lawrence E. Grinter and Peter M. Dunn, eds., *The American War in Vietnam: Lessons, Legacies, and Implications for Future Conflicts* (Westport, CT: Greenwood Press, 1987), p. 147.

3. See, for example, Monte Palmer, *Dilemmas of Political Development,* 3rd. ed. (Itasca, IL: F.E. Peacock, 1985); Charles K. Wilber, ed., *The Political Economy of Development and Under-Development,* 4th ed. (New York: Random House, 1988); Joseph Weatherby, Jr., et al., *The Other World: Issues and Politics in the Third World* (New York: Macmillan, 1987); and Jerry F. Hough, *The Struggle for the Third World: Soviet Debates and American Options* (Washington, DC: The Brookings Institution, 1986). I recognize that the label "Third World" is not accurate, since it lumps all states in the Southern Hemisphere into one category. It is obvious that Nigeria, for example, is quite different from Chad, and that India differs from Burma. The term is used here in its broadest perspective and as a convenient tool for categorizing general characteristics of the environment.

4. This is not to suggest that development necessarily means adoption of "Western" values.

5. Robert L. Heilbroner, *The Great Ascent: The Struggle for Economic Development in our Time* (New York: Harper Torchbooks, 1963), pp. 16–18, 20.

6. For an analysis of the complexities and ambiguities of revolutionary theory and a critique, see Theda Skopcol, *States and Social Revolutions: A Comparative Analysis of France, Russia, and China* (Cambridge: Cambridge University Press, 1979).

7. *Discriminate Deterrence,* Report of the Commission on Integrated Long-Term Strategy (Washington, DC: USGPO, January, 1988), p. 13.

8. President Ronald Reagan, *National Security Strategy of the United States* (Washington, DC: The White House, January 1988), p. 34.

9. Sarkesian, "The Myth of U.S. Capability in Unconventional Conflicts," p. 12.

10. See Sam C. Sarkesian, *The New Battlefield: The United States and Unconventional Conflicts* (Westport, CT: Greenwood Press, 1986), pp. 44–50. See also Bernard Fall, *Street without Joy: Insurgency in Indo-china, 1946–63,* 3rd rev. ed. (Harrisburg, PA: Stackpole, 1963), pp. 356–357.

11. Andrew F. Krepinevich, Jr., *The Army in Vietnam* (Baltimore, MD: The Johns Hopkins University Press, 1986), p. 275.

12. Reagan, *National Security Strategy of the United States,* 1988, p. 35.

13. President Ronald Reagan, *National Security Strategy of the United States,* (Washington, DC: The White House, January 1987), pp. 33–34.

14. *United States Military Posture FY 1989,* prepared by the Joint Staff, p. 33.

15. Ibid., pp. 33–34.

16. See, for example, Richard F. Grimmett, "The Role of Security Assistance in Historical Perspective, " in Ernest Graves and Steven A. Hildreth, eds. *U.S.*

Security Assistance: The Political Process (Lexington, MA: Lexington Books, 1985), pp. 23–24. Other studies of security assistance include: Richard L. Hough, *Economic Assistance and Security: Rethinking U.S. Policy* (Washington, DC: National Defense University Press, 1982) and Howard D. Graves, "U.S. Capabilities for Military Intervention," in Sam C. Sarkesian and William L. Scully, eds., *U.S. Policy and Low-Intensity Conflicts: Potentials for Military Struggles in the 1980s* (New Brunswick: Transaction Books, 1981), pp. 69–94. See also Franklin D. Kramer, "The Government's Approach to Security Assistance Decisions," in Graves and Hildreth, p. 102.

17. See, for example, *United States Military Posture FY 1989*, pp. 33–38. See also Steven A. Hildreth, "Perceptions of U.S. Security Assistance, 1959–1983: The Public Record," in Graves and Hildreth, pp. 79–89 and *Discriminate Deterrence*, pp. 13—22.

18. See Brooks Larmer, "Backsliding to the Bad Old Days" *Christian Science Monitor*, October 18, 1988, p. 14. The author writes, "For a country the size of Massachusetts, the transfusion of $3 billion has been staggering. El Salvador is now the fifth largest recipient of U.S. aid in the world."

19. *United States Military Posture*, p. 36. See also *Discriminate Deterrence*, p. 17.

20. See, for example, Larry E. Cable, *Conflict of Myths: The Development of American Counterinsurgency Doctrine and the Vietnam War* (New York: New York University Press, 1986); Grinter and Dunn, *The American War in Vietnam*, Sarkesian, *The New Battlefield*, and Maj. Eric M. Petersen, USAF, "Providing Tools for Victory in the Third World," *Armed Forces Journal International*, (September 1988): 108–113.

21. *Military Posture Statement*, pp. 84–85. Pages 69–70 show a listing of units assigned to the Unified Special Operations Command.

22. This matter is discussed at length in Sarkesian, *The New Battlefield*, pp. 101–126.

23. Noel Koch, "Special Operations Forces: Tidying Up the Lines" *Armed Forces Journal International*, (October 1988): 110.

24. Stephan Oliver Foster, "Pentagon Slow-Rollers Stymie SOF Improvements" *Armed Forces Journal International*, (October 1988): 102.

25. A.J. Bacevich, James D. Hallums, Richard H. White, and Thomas F. Young, *American Military Policy in Small Wars: The Case of El Salvador*, Special Report (Washington, DC: Pergamon-Brassey's, 1988), p. v.

26. Ibid., p. 45.

27. Sarkesian, "The Myth of U.S. Capability in Unconventional Conflicts," p. 12.

28. See, for example, a paper prepared by George T. Talbot, "Security Assistance in the Low-Intensity Conflict Environment: A Case for Privatization," June 1988, Washington, DC.

29. The point here is that special operations and low-intensity conflict should be two distinct parts of unconventional conflicts. See Sarkesian, "The Myth of U.S. Capability in Unconventional Conflicts."

30. This approach is reflected in the experience of Edward Lansdale in the Philippines during the Huk campaigns. See Major Lawrence M. Greenberg, *The*

Hukbalahap Insurrection: A Case Study of a Successful Anti-Insurgency Operation in the Philippines, 1946–1955 (Washington, DC: USGPO, 1987), particularly page 149.

31. See Sarkesian, "The Myth of U.S. Capability in Unconventional Conflicts."

32. Sarkesian, "The Myth of U.S. Capability in Unconventional Conflicts," p. 16.

33. Ibid., p. 16.

34. See, for example, Major Scott R. McMichael, *A Historical Perspective on Light Infantry*, Research Survey No. 6, Combat Studies Institute, U.S. Army Command and General Staff College (Washington, DC: USGPO, September 1987). The author writes:

> What is the precise meaning of the term "light infantry"? How does light infantry differ from regular or conventional infantry? . . . Do light forces have utility in low-, mid-, and high-intensity conflict? . . . These questions and others have occupied the attention of planners and trainers in the U.S. since 1983 when the Chief of Staff of the Army decided to introduce light infantry divisions into the force structure. Four years later, most of these questions remain unanswered. (p. xi)

35. McMichael, *A Historical Perspective on Light Infantry*, p. 231.

36. This is particularly true in the academic profession, where many consider U.S. involvement in anything but support of "liberal" regimes to be immoral. The naiveté of such perspectives is translated into sharp criticism of anything that assesses and analyzes other options and concepts. Such political biases and prejudices do little to advance the cause of scholarship. Other misconceptions include, for example, the view that there is little use in studying U.S. domestic politics and political leadership in the context of U.S. involvement in unconventional conflicts, revealing an ignorance of the very meaning of such conflicts. Perhaps one of the most distorted and convoluted perspectives is that which sees a systematic analysis of unconventional conflicts as "potpourri." Such views can only come from those whose mind-sets are shaped by narrow conventional dogmatism and whose understanding of unconventional conflicts rarely goes beyond the front page of the local newspaper.

37. See, for example, the comment made by a commander of a U.S. armored battalion of an officer's request for transfer to a special forces assignment, as quoted in *Armed Forces Journal International* (August 1988): 105.

> I approve this request only because I want to support my officer's career objectives no matter how ill-advised they may be. However, I believe that the Army leadership must stop this erosion of its top junior talent into Special Forces Branch which is at best a current fad, and in the long term, a pitiful sideshow from the mainstream Army.

18
Toward Legitimacy: Building Government Support Amid Conflict

P.F. Gorman

O ne of the last acts of the frayed survivors in former President
Reagan's Department of Defense was to mail out to some ill-
defined constituency three papers that had been prepared earlier
this year for the Commission on Integrated Long-Term Strategy. One was
an assessment of sources of change in the future security environment, and
the other two dealt specifically with that genre of political violence known
to the administration, Congress, and the framers of this conference as
low-intensity conflict.[1]

I was one author of those latter two papers, and as such have had
more occasion than some to consider the implications for U.S. national
strategy of the likelihood that a future president will support, as his or her
predecessors have supported, a friendly government afflicted with politically motivated sabotage, terrorism, armed subversion, or more open
forms of insurgency. I have thought about the possibility that said future
president might see fit to support a foreign faction in arms against its
government, through what is loosely referred to as covert action, or other
means. And I have also considered the prospect of that president directing
the limited use of U.S. armed forces abroad. Among the most challenging,
and assuredly vexatious, tasks facing that president's administration in
acting upon such policy choices will be to establish and maintain the
legitimacy of any foreign party the president chooses to support, both here
in the United States and in the country of interest, or in justifying U.S.
attack by deprecating the legitimacy of the target. U.S. policies which turn
upon legitimacy are the subject of this paper.

In other fora I have urged my listeners to interpret the acronym
LIC—pronounced "lick" in Washington—as "Lawyer-Intensive Conflict,"
for I certainly found myself enmeshed by lawyers throughout my experience with it in Central America. But I am no John Norton Moore, and I
have construed for our purposes here "legitimacy" not as a legal, but as
an operative term. I propose to discuss it as an element in executing
national security policy.

My usage is close to that of the armed services. This past June, the U.S. Army and the U.S. Air Force collaborated in publishing a draft manual entitled *Military Operations in Low-Intensity Conflict*, which offered this definition:

> Legitimacy is the willing acceptance of the right of a government to govern or of a group or agency to make or enforce decisions. Legitimacy is not tangible, nor easily quantifiable. Popular votes do not always confer or reflect legitimacy. Legitimacy derives from the perception that authority is genuine and effective and uses proper agencies for reasonable purposes. No group or force can create legitimacy for itself, but it can encourage and sustain legitimacy by its actions. Legitimacy is the central concern of all parties directly involved in a conflict. It is also important to other parties who may be involved even indirectly.[2]

I agree that the nub of this issue of "legitimacy" is *perception*, public opinion here, and public opinion abroad. There are those who suppose that, if this be the case, then the policy imperative for the president's men is to manipulate the media. I think that the record would indicate that more often than not, the media will do the manipulating. But I also believe that in recent years opinion has been influenced less by the media, or by what the Reagan administration called "public diplomacy," than by realities. While media hype, ill-conceived editorial policies, or reportorial amateurism might mislead public opinion in the shortrun, the recourse to violence for political purposes we have under consideration is only rarely short-lived, and ultimately some approximation of the truth will become evident to the public. It would certainly be difficult, if not impossible, for any administration to sustain over a long period of time claims of legitimacy for any government or group that lacked acceptance among its own people, or that persisted in practices abhorrent to the American public. It might be possible for an administration to use U.S. forces for a quick, sharp, military action, and even fence that from the media to some extent, but eventually the enduring issues of legitimacy will be fully vented.

Hence, the planners for any administration would be well advised to appraise carefully their prospective protagonist or antagonist. Those we support must, as a matter of foremost importance, be patently legitimate, or agree to undertake measures to establish legitimacy as a condition for U.S. support. Those we attack must have truly forfeited legitimacy. The foregoing phrases obscure immense difficulties, but the eight examples from President Reagan's experience outlined in figure 18–1 may help illuminate the future president's choices.

Afghanistan and Nicaragua

The first two cases both involve U.S. support for a foreign insurgency, with dramatically different outcomes. In both instances, the United States

Nation	Legitimacy Issues	Legitimacy "Lessons"
Afghanistan	Kabul government; USSR invaders Pakistani, Chinese, U.S. support	• Higher principle: "containment" justifies all • International consensus in favor
Nicaragua	Sandinista government; Contras; U.S. support	• Doomed by dollars
El Salvador	GOES; rule of Sandinistas; U.S. support	• Reform breeds legitimacy • Centrality of military
Grenada	Grenadan government; Cuban role	• Allies can help; regional threat forestalled
Libya	Libyan-sponsored terrorism	• Pariah dog should not bite
Philippines	Marcos's rigidity; U.S. support for opposition	
Haiti	Duvalier's autocracy; U.S. support for opposition	• Corruption can foster democratic revolution • Centrality of military
Panama	Noriega's venality; U.S. support for opposition	

Figure 18–1. Legitimacy: Empirical Examples During the Reagan Administration

supported guerrilla forces attacking a government we recognized diplomatically, and with which we maintained relations. In the case of the Afghanistan mujahideen, there was almost no attention paid to legitimacy in Washington. In the case of the Nicaraguan resistance, however, the rival claims to legitimacy of the Sandinista government and its opposition became matters of intense debate.

Conditioned as we Americans are to accepting the strategic doctrine of containment, few of us questioned the legitimacy of the Afghan resistance, or of U.S. aid to it. President Reagan's characterization of the mujahadeen as "Freedom Fighters" went largely unchallenged, although most Americans sensed that the Afghan tribesmen probably entertained few political ideas close to Jeffersonian democracy, and that their notions of human rights probably would not jibe well with ours. For members of Congress, and for most of their constituents, it was enough to believe that the Soviets had invaded Afghanistan in 1979 on a flimsy pretext of protecting their communist puppet government, and that the full weight of the Red Army had been exerted to crush primitive tribesmen fighting for their homes and families. Few knew of the years of training for Afghan guerrilla leaders in Pakistan during the 1970s, or of the aid from Pakistan and China for the guerrillas, or the extent to which the guerrillas controlled Afghanistan when the Soviets intervened. What mattered was that the Red Army had rolled beyond its Yalta-demarcated line for the first time since its invasion of Iran in 1945, and that any measures to force them back were therefore justified, that is, rendered "legitimate."

Yet, many Americans did question President Reagan's belief that those who took up arms against the Sandinistas in Nicaragua also merited U.S. support. Some Congressional figures have held that, because the United States recognized the government in Managua and maintained a U.S. Embassy there, the armed resistance (Contras) could therefore have no claim to legitimacy. I have heard statements in Congress that the administration, if it wanted aid for the Contras to pressure the Sandinistas toward a negotiated settlement of regional and internal strife, should break diplomatic relations with Managua and apply to Congress for a declaration of war. Some members deprecated the thousands of young men and women who rallied to one or another of the insurgent groups as remnants of Somoza's National Guard, although most of them must have been under ten years of age when Somoza was deposed, and many were Indians. As many saw it, the Sandinistas were the legitimate authority in Nicaragua, and the U.S. administration had no right to intervene in events there, not even to the limited extent of encouraging domestic political demonstrations against a repressive government.

What is important for this discussion is not who is right, the President or his critics in Congress, but that this division over legitimacy at the highest levels of the U.S. government well illustrates the ambiguity that enfolds most internal wars, and our lack of consensus on what legitimacy is, or by what criteria to judge it. Since the administration and the Congress were divided, the issue was resolved by well-publicized debates and votes in both bodies of Congress not over the issues of legitimacy, but over the amounts of money to be paid to the Nicaraguan rebels, and whether the sum could be spent for "lethal" or "non-lethal" purposes. By its actions, even when it did approve support, Congress stigmatized all who took up arms against the Sandinistas as mercenaries, and fatally detracted from their legitimacy among their own people and within Central America.[3]

It is quite possible that the administration would have found more understanding and support for its policies in Nicaragua if the insurgency had been better managed, and therefore more successful in pressuring the Sandinistas. Guerrillas who could stretch and test the Sandinista Army would have been perceptibly more legitimate than CIA Director Casey's cross-border raiders. The bipartisan Commission on Integrated Long-Term

Strategy, with both the success of the Afghanistan case and the fumbles in Central America in mind, concluded:

> In carefully selected situations, where important U.S. objectives would be served and U.S. support might favorably affect outcomes, the United States should help anti-Communist [sic] insurgencies, especially those against regimes threatening their neighbors.
>
> Supporting such rebels is usually difficult and demanding. Many of those we support will be ill-trained, unlike their Soviet-supported enemies, and will be primitive in their strategies, inept in their tactics and logistics. They will badly need help with intelligence and strategy, and with tactics, communications, intelligence operations, and routine field operations.
>
> If the U.S. support for these insurgents is a large and continuing effort, it is bound to be referred to in the press. Nevertheless, neighboring countries that provide access to or bases for the freedom fighters often prefer that the U.S. Government role not be officially acknowledged. By designating the U.S. support as a "Special Activity" (also known as a "covert action") the U.S. Government can maintain official silence. The laws governing "Special Activities" provide for a great deal of flexibility. They make it possible to assign the task of supporting the insurgents to a military command, under cognizance of the commander-in-chief of the U.S. combatant command in whose region the insurgency is located.
>
> Military management of this kind may have advantages if the support operation involves extensive training and supplies. In any event, the issue is not whether the operation can be kept secret, or whether the CIA should be involved. The President has the flexibility to have "Special Activities" managed by any government department, for example by the Departments of State or Defense. And the activity does not necessarily have to be kept secret in each and every aspect any more than other military operations that involve both classified and open matters. Given Congressional support, the organizational problems can readily be solved.[4]

(Had USSOUTHCOM been assigned the mission of aiding the organizing, training, and equipping the Nicaraguan rebels, and had it brought to those tasks the techniques it applied successfully with the Salvadorans, the rebellion might have been significantly more influential politically. The reactions of the Sandinistas themselves would then have done much to establish the legitimacy of their opposition. But that baton was not passed, and at the moment, the rebellion is virtually at an end.)

Having deposed Somoza, the revolutionary government in Managua was accorded legitimacy by most Americans, and that perception of legitimacy withstood doubts occasioned not only by the mere existence of thousands of "Contras," but also by the Sandinista role in supporting insurgencies in neighboring countries and in intimidating the same neigh-

bors with a regionally unprecedented military buildup and periodic brand-
ishing of advanced Soviet weapons.

Many members of Congress have hesitated to be critical of the Sandinista military extravaganza; short of Nicaragua's providing bases for
Soviet bombers or Cuban fighters, they acknowledge its legitimate right of
self-defense, and some have held that much of its buildup was an understandable reaction to new levels of American military activity in the region. However, almost all profess to believe that the Sandinistas have no
right to intervene in the war in El Salvador, or to introduce arms into any
other country. But in this respect, many disbelieve the administration's
contention that Managua has been broadly involved not only with command and control of Salvadoran guerrillas, but also in training, equipping,
and supplying them. They have demanded that the administration "produce a smoking gun," that is, prove Sandinista complicity by adducing
just one documented case of infiltrators from Nicaragua caught in the act,
and point to the absence of such conclusive evidence as proof of Sandinista innocence.

One influential Senator recently stated that it was his belief that the
Reagan administration had fabricated out of whole cloth the story that
Nicaragua has been involved militarily outside its borders. He contended
that the administration did so to justify U.S. intervention in El Salvador
and its support for the "Contras." Moreover, he maintained that it was
the United States, not the Sandinistas, who had shipped arms to the
guerrillas: U.S. Security Assistance supplied the Salvadoran armed forces,
who then sold arms and munitions to the insurgents, or abandoned same
to them on the battlefields. He cited the Jesuit Rector of the University of
San Salvador as his source for his information. Here is my reply, based
upon my experience as Commander in Chief of USSOUTHCOM and as a
participant in the work of the President's Commission on Integrated Long-
Term Strategy:

> Both Ambassador Pickering and I resolved to test the thesis advanced by
> the rector of the university. In August, 1984, I presented to the Select
> Committee on Intelligence of the Senate the results of that investigation.
> We sent people into the countryside to buy arms. We made every effort
> through the El Salvadoran armed forces to collect documents which con-
> tained in them references to arms in possession of the guerrillas. We
> examined weapons taken from the battlefields. We collected in all over
> 500 [examples of] weapons which had serial numbers on them which
> could be traced. 70 percent of those weapons were shipped from the
> United States to the Republic of Vietnam during the Vietnam War, and
> in our view, could only have entered El Salvador via the communist
> infiltration system. Over 20 percent of the weapons we had no records
> of. We had very good records of the weapons we had shipped to El
> Salvador. So my conclusion at the time was that the rector was simply
> wrong.

Now he may have been right in the sense that in 1983 no weapons were coming in because weapons were already there, and what was coming in was cryptologic material, people who had been trained on the outside, ammunition, et cetera.

I did report to your Committee, you will recall, a specific instance where, while we did not get a smoking gun, we did come very close to doing so, and in the ensuing battle picked up on the battlefield three rocket launchers of Chinese manufacture, the serial numbers of which were identical, that is to say in the same series, as those found in a warehouse in Grenada in the previous months.

So my conclusion is quite contrary to yours, sir. I think the Nicaraguans were complicit in moving arms into El Salvador.[5]

The rules of evidence for presenting the administration's case in such issues are not clear, although it is plain that they are demanding. None of the several White Papers produced by the Department of State in the Kennedy and Johnson administrations to document North Vietnam's invasion of South Vietnam as justification for U.S. intervention in Southeast Asia met the test. Scholars and the media demolished them at the time, although their representations of what North Vietnam did were modest in comparison to the claims advanced in recent years by the North Vietnamese themselves. The State Department White Paper on El Salvador produced early in the Reagan years was similarly hooted down: the "evidence" of Nicaraguan malfeasance cited (largely based on watered-down intelligence reports) failed to meet courtroom rigor, and was widely disbelieved.

The fact is, of course, that the highly trained subversives who manage such forms of indirect aggression are masters at concealing their undertakings. Thirty years ago the Rockefeller Commission warned that "concealed wars" would be among the most serious strategic challenges of our era:

These conflicts raise issues with which in terms of our preconceptions and the structure of our forces we are least prepared to deal. The gradual subversion of a government by concealed foreign penetration is difficult to deal with from the outside, even though the fate of millions may depend upon it. . . . Our security and that of the rest of the non-Communist world will hinge importantly on our willingness to support friendly governments in situations which fit neither the soldier's classic concept of war nor the diplomat's traditional concept of aggression.[6]

El Salvador

The U.S support for El Salvador was originally justified—by the State Department's White Paper, for example—as a case of U.S. aid to a country in exactly the situation just described: a classic case of subversive aggression, in which with Soviet and Cuban backing, the Sandinistas actively sought to install a Leninist government in San Salvador compatible with their own. Subsequently, the administration's emphasis shifted to depicting U.S. aid as shielding a nascent democracy from both internal and external foes, and the comparative visibility of that aid made the U.S. stance more credible. A concerted effort was made by both the United States and the Salvadoran government to make the latter legitimately a democracy in form and substance. Nothing less was involved than reforming the entire government, a reform—more successful in the armed forces than in other branches —which eventuated in two well-supervised, countrywide elections with excellent voter turnout, and the election of José Napoleon Duarte to the Presidency. Eventually, legitimacy came to rest on arguments over the nature and extent of the reform itself, and in particular over the role of the military, which Duarte always identified as wielding pivotal influence over the future of democracy in his country.

The fog of war settles over low-intensity conflict no less than over classical battlefields. Both parties to efforts for reform-under-fire are often quite ill informed, and U.S. advisors are almost certain to commend actions that are distasteful or painful to the advised, and perhaps actually dysfunctional in aiding the latter's legitimacy. Despite nearly a century of involvement in foreign domestic politics, the United States has only an inchoate doctrine for responding to low-intensity conflict.[7] Usually neither side has much choice save to endure the other and to proceed with the hope that over time the other will learn.

The foremost consideration for the U.S. side will usually be the claim of the other to the right to govern or to represent the people—that is, legitimacy. In the political turbulence of most countries, constitutionality is problematic, and political infrastructure immature. One government follows another more often by force or default than by any prescribed succession process. However, exposing U.S. political and military advisors to scholarly recitations of the history of political turnovers in any country is less useful, given recent advances in media outreach, than imparting to them an appreciation of the current extent of popular awareness of the central government, and current popular expectations for it. In El Salvador, as is the case even in some of the most archaic and traditional societies of the world, there is evident a yearning for democracy. The U.S. advisor must make it clear that a popularly supported government, legitimated by honest elections, may be the sine qua non for a coherent, long-term U.S. aid program. A militarized government may be expedient amid conflict, but the repeated governmental failures of soldier-dominated regimes, and their severe disadvantages with the U.S. Congress and the American public, will lead U.S. spokesmen to press for genuinely civil rule, if not immediately, then at a date certain in the foreseeable future. The other side, for its part, will probably speak of a "state of emergency" or a "state of siege" that requires suspending "politics," and giving priority to achieving military objectives.

Each instance of such a dialogue is certain to be so highly particularized as to negate much generalization from one country to another, but the Salvadoran example shows that the U.S. side is likely to emphasize respect for human rights, the rule of law, and limits on the use of force, and the other country the kinds, amounts, and timing of U.S. fiscal and material help. They are quite unlikely to understand any American reference to low-intensity conflict, for usually the conflict afflicting them is, in their view, already intolerably intense. They are probably predisposed to talk about "total war" rather than military restraint. They are likely to assert that there are compelling strategic priorities for military action, and that they must defer looking after human rights and referring the perpetrators of violence to their courts to the day when their armed forces have eliminated armed opposition. The U.S. side will have to convince them that no significant aid will flow unless they pursue all three goals simultaneously. Counter-intuitive as that advice may be, whether U.S. aid flows or not, they would indeed be better off devising a strategy that served all three goals.

El Salvador is one of several instances of low-intensity conflict with which I am personally familiar that have had in common a central role for native armed forces. In all these cases, legitimacy turned in large measure on the behavior of those forces. Regardless of the nature of the central authority, an armed force that isolates itself from its people, treats the recruits it draws from them with disdain, acts toward the populace arrogantly and viciously, actually contributes to the insecurity of its sponsor, induces violent responses to its authority, and plays into the hands of subversives and professional revolutionaries. Conversely, an armed force that identifies itself with the populace, sees itself as the protector of the people, and acts toward them judiciously, communicating good will and genuine respect, is likely to elicit reciprocal sentiments that are readily translated into internal security for the central government. Clearly the latter force is more likely than the former to be able to assess and to promote legitimacy. It is also in a much better position to perform its military mission, whether that be acting to foil saboteurs, terrorists, subversives, or insurgents, or to eject invaders.

Let me describe a syndrome of difficulties which besets armed forces that lack legitimacy. Such forces have difficulty recruiting, and they often treat new members brutally. Little attention and few resources are devoted to the welfare of anyone other than officers; for example, there are only the most rudimentary provisions for housing, clothing, morale, or medical care for lower ranks (even if wounded in battle). Military casualty rates are high, and mortality rates are exorbitant. Leadership and decision-making (and usually access to ill-gotten wealth) are held tightly by officers of the upper echelons. Little or no attention is paid to training junior leaders, and initiative among them is thoroughly discouraged. Senior officers are openly scornful of the people, regard them as part of the threat to national security, and negligently accept extensive collateral damage and casualties among civilians as a concomitant of military operations. Typically, the people hate or fear the armed forces, and within such forces members have as low an opinion of themselves and their units as do the people. Such forces can operate successfully only in large formations, and suffer often from ambushes and from frequent attacks on encampments and facilities.

There are cures for this syndrome. They involve, first and foremost, obtaining the commitment of both civil and military leaders of the top echelons to military reform, and to weeding out systematically any military officer, however prominent, who is not prepared to agree that a lack of civic consciousness is militarily dysfunctional. The entire military hierarchy must be brought to demand strict adherence to high standards for conduct in the presence of civilians, particularly discrimination in the use of firepower, and to require subordinate commanders to build mutual respect between troop units and the communities within which they operate, to train junior leaders for independent tactical operations, and to encourage them to innovate, within the foregoing guidance. Commanders must learn to praise and reward successful tactical leaders and to sanction poor performers. They must be led to review and critique operations as a training method, capitalizing on defeats to identify ameliorative action and on victories to encourage emulation. For the force as a whole, troop information programs must aim at instilling pride in their service and in their unit. Public information programs must convey the genuine resolve of the armed forces to act as the people's security shield. From outside the armed forces, the civil authorities must implement corresponding information programs promoting the image of the armed forces as the shield of the people, and foster, as best they can, civil-military cooperation. Beyond that, they must provide for sound public administration in areas secured by the military forces, and that administration must be judicious, caring, and patently beneficial.

To quote the judgment of the Commission on Integrated Long-Term Strategy as to why U.S. prescriptions and aid worked in El Salvador:

> The transformation in large measure reflects ideas that are applicable elsewhere. American technology gave the Salvadorans a new tactical intelligence capability, which became a prod to action for the military (while also giving it constant feedback on its operations). The war also

became a model of sorts for cooperative efforts: under American leadership, other Latin American countries proved willing to offer military training and some economic aid of their own to El Salvador. Our security assistance program helped the Salvadorans to acquire weapon systems that made possible more discriminate attacks on enemy troops and reduced civilian casualties. We also did a lot for the morale of our allies by introducing medical programs that drastically reduced death rates among wounded Salvadoran troops (from around 45% to around 5%).[8]

Obviously, nothing like the foregoing changes is likely to occur in a matter of weeks or even months. As in El Salvador, reform probably will occur only under pressure, and then it is likely to progress slowly, through stages of promises without performance, grudging moves under duress, and then creeping adaptation as civil and military leaders grasp the advantages of the new mandates. Often, as was the case there, the United States will have to undertake to train native trainers, or junior leaders, before tactical proficiency is possible. Sometimes modest U.S. aid—such as help with tactical intelligence and communications, boots, rations, and medical services can make major differences in military morale and efficiency. Sometimes the United States can assist by providing more discriminate weapons and fire control instruments and more responsive command and control. Usually U.S. aid will also be needed with public administration, especially with the system of criminal justice.

In any event, it helps when the United States can obtain the cooperation of friends and allies in its efforts to reform and upgrade, as was the case in El Salvador. A main contributor was Honduras, who set aside ancient enmity to become particularly helpful, and while its internal politics militated against its maintaining its support for much more than nine months, its provision of training areas for entire Salvadoran battalions came at a crucial time in the combined U.S.-Salvadoran upgrade undertaking.

However, international support for U.S. friends or allies is not always and everywhere helpful. I had to demur from suggestions from Washington that the United States inveigle an Asian or a Middle Eastern ally to take over primary responsibility for advising and assisting El Salvador with intelligence and other aspects of military training, both on the grounds that "they really know how to do that better than we Americans," and that their participation would help the legitimacy of the assisted nation. I am dubious on both counts. Asian or Middle Eastern ideas on counterterrorism, intelligence, and counterintelligence, and the treatment of civilians are often markedly different from our own, and quite inconsistent with U.S. notions of "reasonable purpose." I have observed that their concepts can prompt clumsy thuggery by agents of a supported government, which severely detracts from its legitimacy. My criticism might properly be directed less to the advisors than to the recipients of their advice, who tend to proceed on their own to sorcerer's apprentice versions of recommended operational techniques. But the upshot has often been sordid media coverage and a setback for perceptions of the aided government both in its own country and here.

Overall, the sheer tedium of reform occasions doubts of legitimacy. The length of time involved in bootstrapping, its unevenness, and its vulnerability to frequent setback is unlikely to evoke sympathetic treatment from "minute bite" U.S. media representatives or their editors, or from impatient officials in Washington. But the El Salvador experience shows that if the U.S representatives on scene and the native authorities persist in their progress toward mutually agreed goals, legitimacy can be significantly advanced within a year or two, even amid extensive conflict.

Grenada and Libya

Legitimacy is a two-edged concept, and within the highest councils of our government the violent involvement of the United States in Grenada and Libya was justified to some extent by perceptions that government leaders in both those countries had forfeited legitimacy. And it helps if foreigners share U.S. perceptions. Past U.S. administrations have found it helpful with the Congress and the public to be able to point to support from other nations for its policies and its deeds, or for those of a government or group we have chosen to support. José Napoleon Duarte's well-received swing through Europe in 1984, appealing in particular to his fellow Christian Democrats, assuredly helped the U.S. administration in mustering support for him politically. Similarly, President Reagan's cause against Grenada in 1983 gained legitimacy in the condemnation of the Grenadan government by its island neighbors and by their endorsement and support of the U.S. invasion. The subsequent detailing by the U.S. government of the captured material and documentary evidence of Grenadan-Cuban collusion for aggression helped resolve remaining doubts about the overthrowing of an established government.

The U.S. premonitory attack on Libya was a case in which the United States acted without much support from Libya's neighbors, and the refusal of friends like France and Spain to allow overflight severely complicated the operation. But Libya was an international outcast, involved in a recent case of international terrorism, and the administration acted with some confidence that its attack would be seen in a favorable light by the American people and by friends of the United States worldwide, and would have a powerfully deterrent effect on Libyans and other states that sponsored terrorism against Americans—a judgment subsequently proved to be well founded.

The Philippines, Haiti, and Panama

There is at least one egregious error in the recent report of the Commission on Integrated Long-Term Strategy, *Discriminate Deterrence*.⁹ The Commissioners endorse selective U.S. support for "anti-Communist insurgencies," although I know they were thoroughly supportive of U.S. backing for democratic uprisings within Marcos's Philippines, Duvalier's Haiti, and Noriega's Panama.

The United States could scarcely have abstained from intervention in any of these three instances. The destinies of all three countries have been inextricably intertwined with that of our own. Throughout the twentieth century, Panama and the Philippines have been closest of the Third World nations to the United States. Haiti, geographically an even closer neighbor, has extensive ties with us through immigration, and increasing commercial linkages. Corrupt and inept governments in all three eventually evoked popular revulsion, and in all three, the political opposition needed, and received, U.S. understanding and support. In all, the native military establishment became the arbiter of the political destiny of three governments which had lost their legitimacy: military cooperation with reformers led to the ejection of Marcos and Duvalier, and military opposition to the first genuine middle-class political movement in Panama's history has so far stymied attempts to unseat General Noriega. All three nations are in the midst of profound change, change in which the United States will be unavoidably involved. President Bush will most likely face tough decisions in all three.

In the instance of the Philippines, the apolitical stance of General Ramos deserves applause; the military performance of his officer corps and troops do not. The Philippine armed forces continue to be plagued with difficulties in their long struggle against armed communists, prominent among which are lack of popular confidence and trust. Reforms not unlike those undertaken with the El Salvadoran armed forces appear to be needed. The legitimacy of President Aquino's government hangs in the balance.

In Haiti, Duvalier's flight has precipitated a succession of military coups, punctuated by terrorism and riotous violence. But, in that pitiably impoverished and politically immature country, only the military seems to have the power, the organization, and the cohesion for public administration. The challenge for the United States, and other nations interested in the emergence of democratic civil rules, is to aid and guide the uniformed leaders into constructive and supportive roles, and above all to prevent the emergence of a Noriega-like general dominating an entrenched militarized government.

The frustration of U.S. and Panamanian aspirations for legitimate democratic government in Panama can reasonably be described as a product of U.S. neglect as much as a failure of U.S. intelligence, for despite our years of living cheek-by-jowl with the Panamanian military establishment, its organizational dynamics, wiles, and ways—especially those rooted in corruption and venality—were considered relatively unimportant, and were therefore largely ignored by senior U.S. commanders and ambassadors. It is true also that they were largely uninvestigated by U.S. military intelligence. But both failings contributed to our standing by while the obdurate and amoral Noriega seized commanding political ground from which he could defy outraged public opinion in Panama and the United States, the determined efforts of the Department of State and the CIA to unseat him, and an order for extradition handed down by a U.S. Federal Court. Noriega is both a nineteenth-century *caudillo,* and a twenty-first century political renegade, an unlettered and unprincipled opportunist prepared, in the name of Panamanian nationalism, to form leagues with narcotics traffickers, with the Cubans, and with any other source of support for the perpetuation of his power. He, and the political progress he has blocked, will assuredly be high on the political agenda of President Bush, and probably of his successor. In my view, legitimacy depends upon stripping the Panamanian Defense Forces of their civil authorities—which assuredly means removing *El Sapo*[10] and his toadies—and capitalizing upon the new political energy of the middle class to reform the Panamanian government. I am optimistic that the job can done—but I will readily admit that it seems as daunting as the task in El Salvador did in 1983.

Notes

1. Future Environment Working Group, "Sources of Change in the Future Security Environment," paper submitted to the Commission on Integrated Long-Term Strategy, April 1988. Regional Conflict Working Group, "Commitment to Freedom—Security Assistance as a U.S. Policy Instrument in the Third World," paper submitted to the Commission on Integrated Long-Term Strategy, May 1988. Regional Conflict Working Group, "Supporting U.S. Strategy for Third World Conflict," report to the Commission on Integrated Long-Term Strategy, June 1988. These papers each bear this notation: "The Report of the Commission on Integrated Long-Term Strategy, *Discriminate Deterrence,* was published in January 1988 and is available for sale by the Superintendent of Documents, U.S. Government Printing Office, Washington, DC 20402 for $6.50."

"Working Group reports and other separate papers which were prepared in support of the Commission on Integrated Long-Term Strategy are being printed in limited numbers by the Department of Defense. There are no restrictions on further reproduction of these Working Group reports and other papers."

2. Headquarters, Department of the Army, Department of the Air Force, *Military Operations in Low Intensity Conflict,* FM 100–20, AFM 2-XY, Final Draft, June 24, 1988, pp. 1–9,10. "Legitimacy" is cited as one of five imperatives

for success in Low-Intensity Conflict, together with "political dominance," "unity of effort," "adaptability," and "patience."

3. One Central American President recently told the author that President Reagan had no right to expect support from any government in the region for policies which were being debated within the United States in terms of whether or not to continue financial support for armed mercenaries, and whether or not a judge in Florida should summon to trial the head of a foreign army.

4. *Discriminate Deterrence*, pp. 16–17.

5. Testimony before the Senate Committee on Foreign Relations, Subcommittee on International Narcotics Trafficking, February 8, 1988.

6. Quoted in "Supporting U.S. Strategy for Third World Conflict," p. 6.

7. See, for example, A.J. Bacevich, J.D. Hallums, R.H. White, and T.F. Young, *American Military Policy in Small Wars: The Case of El Salvador*, (Washington, DC: Pergammon-Brassey's, 1988). The authors, a group of U.S. Army lieutenant colonels at Harvard, characterize the Reagan administration's policies in El Salvador as expedient for the short run, but unsuccessful for the long-term in that the insurgency persists and the Salvadorans have no strategy for terminating it. They perceive a distinction between the military struggle and the "other war," possibly of itself an explanation for the failure of U.S. Salvadoran planning.

8. *Discriminate Deterrence*, p. 15.

9. *Discriminate Deterrence*, p. 16. See the quote in the section on Afghanistan and Nicaragua, above.

10. Manuel Antonio Noriega was known within the Guardia National as "The Toad," a physiognomic reference to his propensity for laying back in the political weeds, his bulging, unblinking eyes watching for the opportune moment to strike.

19

The Demographics of Defense: Implications for U.S. and Allied Force Needs in the 1990s

William J. Taylor, Jr.

We will begin our analysis of the demographics of defense with the case of the United States, and then proceed to examine the situations in relation to our allies in NATO, Japan, and the Republic of Korea for the 1990s.

United States

Those concerned with military manpower planning for the United States have long been aware of the demographic problems with which we have been confronted in the late 1980s, problems which will be more severe in the 1990s.[1] The main problem is that by 1996, the 18- to 24-year-old male cohort will have declined by some 3.34 million men—a decline of 22 percent (see table 19–1). Yet, the Department of Defense (DOD) forecasts little difficulty in manning the force at current levels. This is partly because women, who compose 10 percent of the force structure, help to compress the raw number of males required for military service, thereby reducing the percentage of non–prior service males who must be recruited. Indeed, in 1996 only 6.6 percent of the 11.8 million man cohort must be recruited to meet projected accession goals—a percentage less than when the All-Volunteer Force (AVF) was begun in 1974. Yet DOD's optimism is fueled to a great extent by some critical assumptions concerning the willingness of Congress to fund the costs associated with attracting and maintaining military manpower; the absence of any significant decline in current rates of youth unemployment; and the ability of the services themselves to recruit and retain the requisite numbers of personnel.

The rate of employment is an important variable. Consider the current picture. Since 1982, the youth labor market has strengthened greatly. Between 1980 and 1987, the youth population declined by 10.4 percent, but the improved economy created 92,000 more youth jobs—thereby offering young men and women additional economic options. Over the same

Table 19–1
Demographic Constraints on Military Manpower Planning

Country	Male Population Aged 18–22, (thousands)				Change, 1987 to 2000		Change, 1987 to 2010	
	1987	1990	2000	2010	(thousands)	(percent)	(thousands)	(percent)
Bulgaria	312	326	323	291	11	3.5%	−21	−6.7%
Czechoslovakia	547	561	644	550	97	17.7	3	0.5
East Germany	649	582	582	547	−67	−10.3	−102	−15.7
Hungary	355	376	387	321	32	9.0	−34	−9.6
Poland	1,279	1,312	1,670	1,504	391	10.6	225	17.6
Romania	938	1,107	964	919	26	2.8	−19	−2.0
East Europe	4,080	4,264	4,570	4,132	490	12.0	52	1.3
USSR	10,459	10,476	12,184	12,882	1,725	16.5	2,423	23.2
Warsaw Pact	14,539	14,740	16,754	17,014	2,215	15.2	2,475	17.0
West Germany	2,626	2,221	1,524	1,698	1,102	−42.0	−928	−35.3
France	2,214	2,179	1,900	1,898	−314	−14.2	−316	−14.3
UK	2,394	2,229	1,788	1,926	−606	−25.3	−468	−19.5
Belgium	381	360	310	302	−71	−18.6	−79	−20.7
Netherlands	634	617	455	481	−179	−28.2	−153	−24.1
Denmark	208	190	149	148	−59	−28.4	−60	−28.8
Norway	171	170	132	135	−39	−22.8	−36	−21.1
NATO Europe	8,628	7,966	6,258	6,588	−2,370	−27.5	−2,040	−23.6
United States	9,650	9,522	9,329	9,831	−321	−3.3	101	1.9
NATO Total	18,278	17,488	15,587	16,419	−2,691	−14.7	−1,059	−10.2
Japan*	4,928	—	4,857	—	−71	−1.4	—	—
Korea*	2,770	—	2,540	—	−230	−8.3	—	—

Sources: Peter A. Wilson, *A Review of General Purpose Force Issues for the 1990s* (Washington, DC: The Washington Defense Research Group, December 1987), p. 5; *World Demographic Estimates and Projections, 1950–2025* (United Nations, 1988); *World Population Prospects: Estimates and Projections as Assessed in 1984* (United Nations, 1984); *World Population Profile: 1987* (U.S. Bureau of the Census, 1987).

*Figures for Japan and Korea are for ages 18–23 and are based on author's estimates using total population and male:female ratios.

period, military pay, as measured by the Employment Cost Index (ECI), has lagged a full 11 percent behind private sector growth. As a result of the interaction of these variables, the number of *quality* recruits accessed into the services has declined steadily since 1987. Increased retention rates reduced the total DOD recruiting goal for the first quarter of FY88 by 14,600, but the services accessed 11,200 fewer high school graduates—an overall decline of 16 percent. A similar drop took place in Armed Forces Qualifications Test (AFQT) scores as all of the services experienced in-creased difficulty in attracting high-quality volunteers. This trend probably will continue, and the percentage of lower quality recruits will increase over time, unless Congress funds military pay, educational programs, and the recruiting effort at requisite levels.

In recent years, the decline in enlistment supply created by the erosion of military compensation and a decline in the youth cohort has been offset by an intensification of the recruiting effort; however, the services now appear to have reached the point of diminishing returns. Congressional inaction will impact upon the services' ability to attract sufficient quantities of high-quality recruits at a time when all of the services require greater numbers of high-quality personnel than ever before.

The impact of modern technology over the past generation has been exponential in its demand for high-quality personnel to man increasingly complex battlefield systems. Indeed, eight out of the ten DOD occupational groups with the largest percentage of male enlisted personnel in AFQT categories I and II in 1984 did not even exist in 1956.[2] And the increase in the services' technological rate of growth continues at an accelerated pace. From 1984 to 1990, the percentage of technical ratings in the Navy will have increased by 17 percent.[3] Between 1984 and the year 2000, the Air Force will have experienced a 33 percent increase in 1984 requirements for airmen with a high degree of electronic aptitude,[4] and the Army has been undergoing similar expansion as it reconfigures to fight on the battlefield of the future. As stated in the FY 88 Army Long-Range Planning Guidance: ". . . reduced manpower pool and advances in technology are likely to result in smaller but more effective army units in the future. Units will be organized to exploit technology incorporated into newly fielded systems . . ."[5] In this regard, the recent decline in high-quality accessions does not augur well for the future. It is significant to note that even if the Army reverses the trend and continues to field a force which, by AFQT standards, is 96 percent average to above average in intelligence, the demand for soldiers at the upper end of the intelligence spectrum may soon exceed the realistic market share available. Since 1983, the Army has increased its Combat Support Base (primarily Signal and Military Intelligence) at the rate of 1 percent a year while experiencing a net decrease in that percentage of the force which comprises the

Combat Arms.[6] In quantitative and qualitative terms this has meant an increase of approximately 4,000 Signal positions, which require a relatively high score of 95 or better on the electronic component of the Armed Services Vocational Aptitude Battery (ASVAB), and the addition of over 3,000 military intelligence positions, which require a score of 120 or better on the ASVAB's electronic and skill technical components. Average is good, but average may no longer be good enough, as the Army and the other services move into a high-tech operational environment on all levels of the battlefield.

Minorities, primarily blacks and Hispanics, account for 17.8 percent of the 18- to 24-year-old youth cohort, but they represent a full 27 percent of all DOD accessions and 30 percent of the Army's enlistments.[7] They also tend to re-enlist at a rate that far surpasses that of their white counterparts. Hence, although minorities account for only 13.6 percent of the civilian labor force, they provide 29.4 percent of the total active DOD enlisted force and 38 percent of all active Army enlisted personnel.[8] These figures will undoubtedly increase throughout the next decade due to the interaction of two variables. The first of these is that the percentage of minority youth in the total eligible population will actually increase by two percentage points from 1989 through 1996—despite the fact that the youth cohort as a whole is on the decline.[9] This phenomenon occurs because the black youth cohort will not decrease to the extent experienced by the Caucasian cohort and because other portions of the minority population will increase in size by almost 18 percent.[10]

The second variable is unemployment. Although the total youth unemployment rate is only 16 percent, it is almost twice as high among minorities. Barring an unforeseen miracle in the domestic sector, high rates of minority unemployment and the demographic composition of the 1990s youth cohort will combine to produce even higher percentages of minority military participation than those experienced today. By the mid-1990s, it is not inconceivable that a full 45 percent of the army will be minorities. This figure, though significant, obscures the fact that certain career fields will have even higher levels of minority participation due to historically low minority scores on those components of the ASVAB that govern entry into the more technical career fields. The Army has a disproportionate level of minority participation at the lower end of the technological spectrum (such as combat arms, supply, and administration) and an overrepresentation of Caucasian personnel at the upper end of that spectrum (such as military and signal intelligence)—a phenomenon that exists in all of the services.

The technological explosion that has engulfed the services confronts us with a visible inequity in our social economics. The point is that a large minority population wants to participate in military service but is academically unprepared to serve in the technical sectors experiencing the most growth and in which the post-service employment payoff is greatest. There is another large issue embedded in this analysis; that a significant majority of male racial minorities will be found in the combat arms units, which experience disproportionate casualties on the battlefield. This can lead to an issue of social injustice.

These are likely to be serious social issues which must be addressed as the total force evolves toward the twenty-first century. Coupled with shortfalls in the services' ability to man the force, these issues will lead us inexorably to a reopened debate on the merits and demerits of the All Volunteer Force versus some alternative, such as a system of Universal Military Service.

Western Europe

The qualitative military manpower problems faced by the United States also confront our European allies. But for the latter, the main problem is a sheer lack of numbers. While some European nations, such as traditionally Catholic Spain, Portugal, and Ireland, will experience positive population growth, five key NATO nations—West Germany, France, the United Kingdom, the Netherlands, and Belgium—will undergo a population decline well into the twenty-first century. This phenomenon reflects a fundamental change in traditional lifestyles: young men and women want more, and they want it at an earlier age. This rise in expectations, coupled with the impact of women's movements, has created a situation in which people marry at a later age, have fewer children, and divorce more often.

The situation in the key five countries is projected to be as acute as in Denmark—where the decline in the male population has been so severe that the Danes have taken the unprecedented step of integrating women into combat units.[11] Nonetheless, the problems facing the members of the Western European Union (WEU) are serious.

West Germany

If the population projections for West Germany appear shocking, they are more so when one realizes that these figures include a sizable percentage of non-German laborers (primarily Turks), whose birth rates greatly exceed that of the population as a whole. With 1.28 children per family, the ethnic German population has had the lowest birth rate in Europe for the past fifteen years. By the year 2050, only three of every four German residents will be of Germanic descent. More important, the 18- to 24-year-old male cohort will have declined from 3.6 million in 1988 to a mere 1.8 million—and only 1.35 million of these will be ethnic Germans.[12] Clearly there is a manpower problem, even if the Federal Republic finds a way to tap into its pool of foreign laborers for some type of national service. Actually, the squeeze is already being felt, and the government has begun to initiate measures designed to provide short-term relief.

With an authorized strength ceiling of 500,000 the Bundeswehr has traditionally attempted to maintain an active duty force of 495,000 and a balance of roughly 55 percent volunteers and 45 percent conscripts in a total force that includes 800,000 reserve component personnel.[13] Since there are cultural and legal constraints regarding the employment of women in the armed forces, maintaining adequate forces has become an increasingly difficult task given the continued decline in the male youth cohort—a cohort that must provide 250,000 conscripts a year just to maintain the status quo.[14] Indeed, by 1985 the situation was so acute that force planners projected a shortfall of 100,000 men a year by the year 2000, unless extraordinary measures were taken.[15] To bridge this gap, the government has:

Extended military service from 15 to 18 months,

Lowered entry requirements,

Reduced the full-time active force to 456,000,

Increased conscript pay by 12.5 percent, and

Begun drafting more males at the upper end of the age eligibility spectrum.[16]

What the government has not yet done is to enact legislation permitting the integration of women into the armed forces. Until this is accomplished, the FRG will not solve the long-term problem. If only 10 percent of the Bundeswehr were manned by women, an additional forty-five thousand men—the equivalent of an army corps-could be made available for combat-related duties.

Can West Germany pay the personnel, equipment, and modernization costs associated with a 500,000-man Bundeswehr? Yes, but Bonn has placed its priorities elsewhere. From 1960 through the early 1980s, the Federal Republic did increase its share of NATO's total expenses from 5 percent to 10.4 percent, but, in terms of the percentage of GNP spent on defense, it still ranks seventh in NATO.[17] Perhaps more significant, the FRG has consistently failed to meet its commitment for an annual 3 percent real increase in defense spending—a commitment imposed by the NATO agreement of 1977. Since 1977, West Germany has increased real defense spending at a rate of 2.1 percent per year; however, social spending has increased at a real rate of 4 percent per year.[18] Clearly, Bonn could do more in the area of defense if it chose to do so. Unfortunately, it appears that Bonn may be moving in the other direction, as the Federal Republic enters an era of reduced economic growth. Indeed, faced with the prospect of limited economic growth and burdened with the demand for increased social spending imposed by an aging population,[19] the Bundestag cut the Kohl defense budget by $244.8 million in FY 1987.[20]

The United Kingdom

Britain's 18- to 24-year-old male cohort will decline from 2.4 to 1.7 million by the year 2000, but this decline probably will not adversely affect Britain's ability to man its comparatively small force of 326,000 men and women. High unemployment rates generated by economic stagnation, coupled with civilian and military pay comparability, ensure that Britain will not face a manpower problem for the foreseeable future. But, the same factors that support an adequate military manpower pool have produced significant economic constraints on both the size and the quality of the British defense establishment.

The discovery of North Sea oil and the resultant expectation of wealth led the UK to sign up for NATO's 1977 "3 percent solution," and the UK attempted to meet that obligation through the mid-1980s. From 1978 to 1982, Britain achieved an average real increase in defense spending of 2.9 percent per year,[21] and in 1983 Britain ranked third in NATO in the percentage of GDP spent on defense.[22] But this growth did not keep pace with the costs associated with maintaining an all-volunteer force and the tremendous costs imposed by Britain's choice to develop many of its own military systems while also attempting to develop and maintain an independent nuclear capability.[23] Indeed, the UK spent more to buy less in a quantitative sense. To state the problem more succinctly, Great Britain today has half the planes and surface escorts that it had 20 years ago.[24] Meanwhile, oil revenues have not reached expected levels; the economy has declined; and Britain faces a situation in which it must make some difficult choices in the defense area. The UK can no longer afford to fund all of its programs. The question is where—if anywhere—Britain can absorb defense cuts without reducing its commitment to NATO. Indeed, former Prime Minister Callaghan called for a reduction in the 55,000-man British Army of the Rhine and either the elimination or reallocation of those spaces elsewhere in the defense community.[25]

France

Despite de Gaulle's removal of French forces from NATO military control, France remains a member of the North Atlantic Council, and France maintains an army corps in West Germany under the terms of its bilateral agreement with the Federal Republic.

France has a population of 55 million, an active duty defense establishment of 471,000, a balanced nuclear capability, a power projection capability, and modern, diversified forces. France shows no sign of decline in its overall military capabilities for either demographic or economic reasons. The pool of 18- to 24-year-old males will decrease by 14 percent by the year 2000; however, that pool will still contain 1.9 million young men, a number more than sufficient to meet current force requirements while still providing room for expansion if required.

This is not to say that France can afford to expand its military capabilities to any great extent, only that there are no economic indicators pointing toward a decline. The French have continued to average the 3-percent annual spending increases required to modernize the force, and France ranks among the top three nations in Europe in terms of the percentage of gross domestic product (GDP) spent on defense.[26] In a post-INF environment requiring that Europe assume a greater responsibility for its conventional defense, France alone among the WEU nations is capable of providing the manpower to bridge the gap.

The Netherlands

Between 1987 and 2000, the 18- to 22-year-old male cohort will decline by about 28 percent, from 634,000 to 450,000, thus making it increasingly difficult to maintain the existing 97,000-man force. It was this realization, coupled perhaps with the example of Nordic models and with a desire to drive down personnel costs, that led the Netherlands to reject the concept of an all-volunteer force in favor of a force that is 70 percent conscript. It also led the Dutch to make compulsory military service more palatable by implementing a unique unit-manning system that reduced the amount of time a draftee spends on active duty while emphasizing the role of reserve component unit augmentation.[27] Thus far, the Dutch have made the system work, but the future is doubtful given the large decline in the manpower base.

Meanwhile, the Dutch face an economic environment that is unlikely to allow further increases in military spending. In recent years, the Netherlands has experienced budget deficits, despite the existence of a favorable balance of payments. To a great extent this is attributable to the very large sums the Dutch allocate to social security and welfare programs—programs that consume almost 40 percent of the total annual budget as opposed to the 5 percent allocated to defense.[28] The Netherlands may face personnel constraints in the leaner years, but the Dutch clearly have the economic capacity to do more in the defense arena. But, like the West Germans, they have chosen not to do so.

Belgium

With an active duty force of ninety-one thousand, Belgium faces a decline in the 18 to 24-year-old male cohort similar to that of Great Britain. By the year 2000 there will be seventy-one thousand fewer males available for military service—a decline of 18.6 percent. Unique to Belgium is the ethnic cleavage between the Flemish and the Walloons, which permeates all aspects of Belgian life. Hence, in addition to worrying about manpower in a general sense, the Belgians must ensure that a fragile ethnic balance is maintained within the military establishment. In this regard, it is significant that the manpower problem is already sufficiently acute that the government is considering revisions to the communal balance rule, which would allow the military to recruit more heavily in Walloonia, an area of high unemployment, than in Flanders, a more prosperous region of the country where the military has less appeal.

The government is further attempting to ensure the availability of military manpower by implementing a series of measures designed to fill the ranks of its mixed conscript and volunteer force. Some of the measures include:

Increasing conscript pay by 50 percent,

Eliminating various categories of draft exemptions, and

Lengthening the period of conscript service.[29]

Thus far, the government has not expanded the participation of women beyond the 6 percent level; however, this is an option which clearly will have to be pursued in the years ahead.

From 1978 to 1981, Belgium achieved a 3 percent increase in annual defense spending, but the bottom fell out in 1982 when the rate of increase dropped to 0.2 percent.[30] Since that time, a series of economic problems fueled by a stagnant economy have caused decreased defense outlays; in 1987, the annual defense budget decreased by 3.5 percent. Unfortunately, significant economic growth is not in sight, and if current budget trends continue, Belgium will only be able to afford half of its military equipment needs over the next decade.[31]

Japan

A glance at the demographic data for both men and women (see table 19–1) suggests a problem in manning the volunteer Japanese Self-Defense Force (SDF). The force is authorized for 272,768, but presently manned at 244,422, a manning rate of 89.6 percent.[32] That percentage may or may not be worrisome, depending on where the 10.4 percent shortfalls occur. However

> ... a growing number of the young people, who are the source of fresh SDF personnel, are opting to higher education in college or university and their values are being diversified. It is now anticipated that the population eligible for recruitment for the SDF uniformed personnel (over the age of 18 and under 25) will be on the decline year after year from 1993 and onwards.[33]

In full comprehension of this situation, the Japanese have instituted a number of measures to alleviate the problem. They have:

Established fifty SDF regional liaison offices across the country to work with prefect governors, mayors, boards of education, schools, and even private recruiting counselors.

Assured pay balanced with that of civil servants, given the relatively demanding nature of assignments on isolated islands or remote places and 24-hour, on-call work.

Continued efforts to improve living conditions in barracks and aboard ships for enlisted personnel and to increase the number of officers' quarters.

Improved military medical care.

Attended to the problems of reemployment in the civilian sector for 2–3-year-service enlisted personnel and for professional military retirees.

Whether these measures will be sufficient to man an SDF with expanding missions remains to be seen. But with a 10.4 percent shortfall now in meeting the recruitment and retention goals to maintain the force currently authorized, and with a large decrease in eligible volunteers over the horizon, the future does not look bright for a force committed to defend its territory, airspace and vital sea lines of communication out to one thousand miles.

The Republic of Korea

The ROK has no demographic problem related to its military manpower, unless it is the declining average age of its population. Sixty percent of the population is under age thirty and have no memory of the Korean War. Their perception of threats and their sense of sacrifice in the cause of national security may be different from their elders. This could eventually lead to rejection of military conscription.

The pool of eligible males will be adequate to man the active armed forces, currently at 629,000, assuming continuation of conscription. The terms of conscripted military service of thirty to thirty-six months have long been accepted as a legitimate responsibility to the nation, given the imminent threat from the North and a thoroughly enforced conscription system.

The technical requirements of ROK military systems have been increasing steadily. The development of South Korean industry has been part of a national plan for building the ROK into an industrial power fully capable of defending itself as well as providing a high standard of living for its people. In addition to the acquisition of sophisticated U.S.-manufactured systems such as the F-16 fighter aircraft, the ROK is producing its own high-technology systems. For example, in producing the indigenous XK-1 tank the ROK has taken full advantage of all the technology leading up to the production of the U.S. M-1 tank and has adopted proven components from France and the FRG as well. And, the ROK and the United States are now considering the most ambitious project of defense industrial cooperation in the history of the alliance—the Korean FX advanced fighter aircraft.[34]

There is every reason to believe that the ROK military manpower base will be up to the technological challenge. With one of the most rigorous school systems in the world, South Korea now has 98 percent literacy and one million college students. Education, especially technical education, is highly prized in the booming ROK economy. Competition for admission to the nation's premier universities, Seoul National and Yongsei, is fierce.

Most projections show that the military capability of South Korea will surpass that of the North by the mid-1990s.[35] And despite overtures by both South and North for reunification of the Korean peninsula, threat perception of the military capabilities and intentions of the North should be sufficient to undergird the ROK conscription system for the foreseeable future.

Implications

It is stating the obvious to say that, other things being equal, demographics show that U.S. alliances are confronted with serious military manpower problems—both quantitative and qualitative—in the future. But usual in political-military affairs, other things are not equal.

First, the United States probably will have to reduce military manpower significantly in the foreseeable future. Confronted by a huge cumulative federal debt of $2.6 trillion, under an administration continuing the

Republican pledge not to raise taxes and with a Democratic Congress not predisposed to reduce entitlements, the United States must reduce defense spending. Planned forces in the Five-Year Defense Plan (FYDP) 1990–1994 may be as much as 25 to 30 percent larger than planned budgets can sustain—a gap of approximately $300 billion (estimates range from $200–$400 billion). In essence, current plans presume we will be buying five years' worth of forces with four years' worth of budgets. Defense budgets have been declining since 1985, from $345 billion to about $290 billion today in real terms. Military spending in the early 1990s might dip to $250 billion or less; thus, at least $300 billion must already be cut over the next five years.[36]

The greatest potential savings are in force structure, and it is highly probable that significant cuts will have to be made in this area as they were in the FY89 budget, when Secretary Carlucci had to cut $40 billion. The Army alone had to absorb end strength reductions of eighty-five hundred soldiers.[37] Ironically, these and future manpower reductions over FYDP 1990–1994 would help relieve the current U.S. manpower squeeze and get us through to the mid-1990s when the decline in the draft-eligible male cohort is projected to end. Additionally, there is no inviolable gospel dictating that there must be 2.1 million in the active force and 1.2 million in the National Guard and Reserves. As some have argued, it is time to take a closer look at the strategic dimension of military manpower.[38]

Second, there is a legitimate debate over burden sharing in NATO, and in the mutual security arrangements with Japan and the Republic of Korea. There are many models for calculating these relationships—relative percentages of GNP expended on defense; the burdens of conscription; the burdens of financial and social costs of hosting foreign military formations; balance of trade, and so on. But it is possible to argue that the United States has been carrying an excessive burden in each of these alliance relationships and that our partners should do more. The unpersuasive U.S. arguments of the past will become much more convincing as the United States confronts the FYDP 1990–94.[39]

There have been loud arguments for years that the United States could drive down manpower costs by moving via technology to a more capital-intensive armed force. However, only a few new systems have been introduced into the inventory that provide the same or greater capability with significantly reduced manpower. A case in point is the Army's main battle tank, which requires the same crew of four required in World War II tanks, even though the M1A1 is approaching $3 million each. Perhaps U.S. budgetary and demographic problems will force the eventual realization of past technological promise. In other words, the budgetary squeeze may force our manpower planners to do what they should have been doing all along, before they were "saved" by the enormous budget increases of 1981–85—that is, start working closely with strategic and R&D planners.

Alternatively, some say the current momentum toward conventional force reductions in the Warsaw Pact and NATO may produce treaties which permit significant military manpower savings. That may be, but the negotiations involved are so complex that it may be many years before such agreements can be reached. This alternative provides no relief to the near-term budget/manpower problems with which we are confronted.

But U.S. manpower problems pale in significance compared to those of our Central and Northern European allies in NATO, except France. Even if they could afford the costs of larger conventional force commitments, they will lack both the requisite military manpower and the political will to do so. The individual West European nations will no longer have the resources with which to purchase traditional, balanced defense establishments while simultaneously satisfying NATO's conventional requirements. If NATO is to remain viable, there must be a more precise delineation of national responsibilities and some degree of role specialization. Hence the potential importance of the Western European Union (WEU), the "European Pillar of NATO." Despite the obstacles along the march toward Europe 1992 and U.S. concerns about economic competition (to include the arms industry), there is potential for European political and economic union to expand into the defense sector. Indeed, under the umbrella of the WEU, role specialization coupled with intensively managed military manpower programs could provide partial solutions to the demographic and economic obstacles that exist today.

Role specialization for the Europeans has another dimension which involves the United States. The Europeans should be prepared to assume a greater share of the heavy ground unit missions in NATO Europe. This is because the United States will likely be confronted increasingly with "out of area," "low-intensity conflict" missions, which its European allies either cannot or will not support. Many of these missions will require U.S. light forces, which do not exist now in appropriate configurations. Arguably, the United States should consider selling or even giving away, for use by the FRG reserves, the heavy unit POMCUS stocks now prepositioned in Europe. This does not mean that the U.S. ground forces would be withdrawn from Europe; rather, it means increasing numbers (not all) of U.S. units would assume "light unit" missions in NATO Europe and be available for deployment in Third World contingencies. They could also form part of possible reductions of U.S. troops stationed in NATO in the event that the Congress finds European burden sharing unacceptable at some future date or in the event that conventional arms reductions negotiations proceed to agreement faster than most now anticipate.

The U.S. defense budget crunch for FY90–94, combined with demographic factors, will also have an impact on our two major East Asian alliances. It is almost certain that the United States will press even more vigorously on Japan's military capability to fulfill its security obligations. That certainly is the trend. As Secretary of Defense Carlucci has said, "Achieving a greater self-defense capability will require significantly more effort by Japan in the 1990s. We encourage the Japanese government to pursue these efforts."[40]

Chafing at the large trade deficit with Japan, concerned about increasing Japanese investments in the United States (despite the fact that this helps carry the huge U.S. federal deficit), and irked that the average annual increase in real defense outlays for Japan had been on the decline consistently until 1988 (see table 19–2), many Americans feel that Japan is not carrying its fair share of the defense burden.[41] At a time when the U.S. defense budget will be squeezed severely, one can expect increasing tensions in U.S.-Japanese relations, including a reexamination of the need to keep all fifty thousand U.S. troops stationed in Japan.

Table 19–2
Average Annual Increase in Real Defense Outlays for NATO Countries and Japan, 1975–1987 (Percent)

Country	1975–77	1978–80	1981–83	1984–87
Belgium	5.9	3.6	0.1	1.0
Canada	3.3	1.3	5.3	3.1
Denmark	1.6	2.8	0.4	0.5
France	4.3	3.9	2.7	0.9
Germany	−0.6	2.0	1.2	−0.2
Greece	20.0	−2.6	4.5	2.4
Italy	0.3	3.0	1.7	2.4
Luxembourg	3.6	9.3	4.0	4.4
Netherlands	4.6	−0.9	2.3	1.5
Norway	2.4	3.8	3.6	3.3
Portugal	−18.5	4.5	−0.5	0.6
Spain	4.8	5.7	3.0	1.0
Turkey	28.4	1.5	0.7	8.2
United Kingdom	−0.2	1.7	2.6	−0.1
United States	−1.8	3.0	6.5	4.8
Non-US NATO Total				
Excluding Spain	1.8	2.3	2.2	0.9
Including Spain	1.9	2.5	2.2	0.9
NATO Total				
Excluding Spain	−0.5	2.8	4.9	3.5
Including Spain	−0.4	2.8	4.9	3.5
Japan	8.5	6.1	5.4	5.1

Source: Frank C. Carlucci, *Report on Allied Contributions to the Common Defense* (Washington, DC: USGPO, April 1988), p. 52.

Despite (or perhaps because of) the twin economic and political miracles that have occurred in the ROK (such as, 10 percent annual GNP growth and a huge balance of trade surplus; 1987 free elections for the presidency and 1988 elections for the National Assembly), South Korean nationalism is accelerating rapidly and freedom of expression is, relatively speaking, "running rampant." Anti-Americanism, now openly aired, is growing for many reasons: two-way protectionism, command and control disagreements, resentment of the large U.S. military presence (and property holdings) in Seoul, and revisionist history taught in the universities, blaming the United States for the division of the Korean peninsula.

On the U.S. side, the size of the U.S. military presence in the ROK (43,000 troops) has come under increasing scrutiny in the 1980s. At the heart of the criticism is burden sharing. Some estimate that the U.S. total price tag for the ROK is nearly $25 billion.[42] As the U.S. economy suffers from deficit anxiety and meager gains in productivity, South Korea continues as one of the "Four Tigers" of the East.

The principal concern in U.S.-ROK relations is not demographic; it is a combination of the U.S. trade deficit with the ROK ($6.26 billion in 1987); the U.S. federal deficit, and defense burden sharing. In the context of force structure cuts in general, it is probable that there will be a special focus on the rationale for the large number of U.S. troops stationed in the ROK. The coming dispute surrounding the U.S. military presence in Korea will not disappear in the 1990s as quickly as it did in the 1970s; the economic and political realities are different.

On balance, the demographics combined with the other factors listed above tell us that there are significant alliance problems on the horizon. There are always routine alliance problems to be managed, but the problems of the 1990s are not likely to be routine. The political character of the Soviet Union and the perceived threats that it presents, which has formed the basis for many of these alliances, is no longer routine. The solutions to these problems will require extraordinary leadership in all alliance quarters.

Notes

1. See, for example, Robert B. Pirie, Jr., "An Overview: Manpower into the 1980s," in William J. Taylor, Jr., et al., eds., *Defense Manpower Planning: Issues for the 1980s* (New York Pergamon, 1981), p. vx.

2. See Mark Eitelberg, *Manpower for Military Occupation* (Alexandria, VA: HUMRRO, April 1988), p. 39.

3. See Robert J. Murray, "Technology and Manpower: Navy Perspective" in *The All-Volunteer Force After a Decade*, (Washington, DC: Pergamon-Brassey's International Defense Publishers, 1986), p. 141.

4. See John M. Roberts, "Technology and Manpower: Air Force Perspective" in *The All-Volunteer Force After a Decade*, p. 152.

5. See *U.S. Army Long-Range Planning Guidance* (Washington, DC: Department of the Army, July 1988), p. 14.

6. See William E. De Puy, "Technology and Manpower: An Army Perspective" in *The All-Volunteer Force After a Decade*, p. 126. Note especially De Puy's data on TOW gunners for a case in point.

7. See *Population Representation in the Military Services, Fiscal Year 1986* (Washington, DC: U.S. Department of Defense, 1986), pp. 11–27.

8. Ibid., p. III-6.

9. See Martin Binkin and Mark J. Eitelberg, "Women and Minorities in the All-Volunteer Force," in *The All-Volunteer Force After a Decade*, p. 90.

10. Ibid.

11. See Julian Isherwood, "Denmark in Historic First, Opens Combat Jobs to Women" *Armed Forces Journal International* (July 1988): 25.

12. See unclassified U.S. Embassy Bonn message "FRG Population Developments: Trends to 2030," 171013Z, January 1988.

13. See Richard R. Nyrop, ed., *Federal Republic of Germany: A Country Study* (Washington, DC: Emerson University Press, 1983), pp. 347-348.

14. Ibid. This figure also includes 25,000 conscripts required to maintain the Border Guard, Police, Disaster Control Service, and the Development Aid Service.

15. See *The Future of NATO Ground Forces in the Year 2000* (Washington, DC: The Institute for Foreign Policy Analysis, June 1987), pp. 14–44.

16. Ibid., pp. 16–17.

17. See James R. Golden, "Alliance Burden Sharing," a draft paper prepared for the CSIS conference on Defense Economics for the 1990s, Washington, DC, October 31–November 1, 1988, figure 1, cited with permission of the author.

18. Ibid.

19. The retiree-to-worker ratio is 45 percent. See *The Future of NATO Ground Forces in the Year 2000*, p. 22.

20. Ibid., p. 30.

21. See James R. Golden, *NATO Burden Sharing: Risks and Opportunities* (Washington, DC: Praeger, 1984), p. 51.

22. Ibid., p. 32.

23. An example of the costs associated with such a course of action may be found in the Nimrod Airborne Early Warning System, which cost the British government $1.62 billion before the project was cancelled. *The Future of NATO Ground Forces in the Year 2000*, p. 40.

24. Ibid., p. 48.

25. Ibid., p. 50.

26. See Golden, *NATO Burden Sharing*, p. 51.

27. For a discussion of the Dutch reserve system, see *The Future of NATO Ground Forces in the Year 2000*, pp. 73–74.

28. Ibid., p. 68.

29. See Golden, *NATO Burden Sharing*, p. 51.

30. See *The Future of NATO Ground Forces in the Year 2000*, p. 63.

31. Ibid., p. 133.

32. See *Defense of Japan, 1987*, White Paper (Defense Agency of Japan, 1987), p. 289.

33. See Golden, *NATO Burden Sharing*, pp. 5–7.

34. Ernest Graves, "Republic of Korea–United States of America Security Cooperation: Current Status," draft paper for the KIDA/U.S. Conference on The Future of ROK-U.S. Security Relations, Seoul, Korea, September 11–13, 1988. Cited with permission of the author.

35. See, for example, Council on Foreign Relations, *Korea at the Crossroads* (New York: CFR, 1987), p. 38.

36. For recent analyses, see William W. Kaufmann, "Defense Options, Fiscal 1990–1994," pp. 3–8 and Leonard Sullivan, Jr., "Major Defense Options," pp. 14–20, both draft papers prepared for the CSIS conference on Defense Economics for the 1990s, Washington, DC, October 31–November 1, 1988.

37. See Lt. Gen. Allen K. Ono, "Personnel: An Army Tightens up Its Belt," *Army*, 38, No. 10 (October 1988): 158.

38. See Alan Ned Sabrosky, William J. Taylor, Jr., and Greg Foster, "The Strategy-Manpower Interface" in William J. Taylor, Jr., et al., eds., *The Strategic Dimension of Military Manpower* (Cambridge, MA: Ballinger, 1987), pp. 211–24.

39. See Golden, *NATO Burden Sharing*, pp. 22–23.

40. See Secretary of Defense Frank C. Carlucci, *Annual Report to the Congress: Fiscal Year 1989* (Washington, DC: USGPO, February 18, 1988), p. 84.

41. See Golden, *NATO Burden Sharing*, pp. 5–7.

42. See Doug Bandow, "Korea: The Case for Disengagement," CATO Institute for Policy Analyses, No. 96 December 8, 1987.

20
The Role of Women in the U.S. Military

Jacquelyn K. Davis

In the 1980s, women serve in all branches of the U.S. Armed Forces, from work in the more "traditional" administrative and medical areas to jobs in the "nontraditional" service sectors, such as machinists, tool-dye casters, pilots, weapons loaders, civil engineers, and communications specialists. Women repair planes and stand watch in ICBM silos, serve on missile launch crews, and operate Army air defense assets, including the *Patriot* air defense system. The extent to which women are integrated into military job categories varies among the services, although on average women in 1988 comprised approximately 10 percent of the personnel component of U.S. active duty forces. With a 10.2 percent officer and 10.5 percent enlisted proportion of Army personnel accounted for by women; a 10.1 percent officer and 9.0 percent enlisted percentage in the Navy; and a 11.3 percent officer and 12.3 percent enlisted percentage in the Air Force, the capacity of the services to meet their respective mission assignments is increasingly dependent on the job performance of female personnel. In fact, of growing importance is the question of whether the military forces of the United States can perform their respective assigned peacetime duties and wartime missions without reliance on their female service members.

Even in the Marine Corps, which has a lower percentage of female service members—3.2 percent officer and 5.2 percent enlisted—in its force structure mix, reliance on women marines to perform in critical job areas has increased over the years. The end-strength of women marines has grown four-fold since 1970, with duty assignments expanding to include overseas commands in Okinawa and Iwakuni, Japan.[1] This should not be surprising since, with the decision in the early 1970s to adopt the All-Volunteer Force concept, the ability of the services to attract and retain

---

This paper does not specifically address the issue of women in the Coast Guard, although it should be noted that the Department of Transportation allows women to compete for all positions in that Service. For Coast Guard women, however, major restrictions on their assignment flow from the wartime assignment of the Coast Guard to the Navy.

qualified males suffered from competition with the civilian sector, which increasingly was able to offer more attractive pay and benefits programs to a shrinking cohort pool of 18–25 year olds.[2] In addition, at this time in the history of our nation military service was viewed from a clouded prism, in part due to the Vietnam War, but also because of a diminished threat perception of the Soviet Union. As the decade wore on, the tendency of more and more women choosing the military as a career option grew, perhaps because, traditionally, the U.S. Armed Forces had proven to be more progressive than, and on the leading edge of, the civilian community when it came to providing opportunities for minorities, including women.

The use of women in the U.S. military is not, however, a recent phenomenon. Since the 1850s women have provided critically needed support for the U.S. military, even though their roles were and have been limited to support functions—principally in the administrative and medical areas. From service in the Civil War, where Dorothea Dix formed a corps of nurses to serve with the Union Army; to the Spanish-American War, during which time Congress authorized the use of women nurses (under civilian contract),[3] to World War I, when the Navy permitted the enrollment of women in the Naval Reserve in certain essential ratings (yeoman, radio, etc.) and Army and Navy nurses served with distinction; military planners increasingly recognized a need for consideration of women in the U.S. military establishment. World War II represented "breakthrough" years for women in the military.[4] After the attack on Pearl Harbor and amid skirmishes in Congress over the structure and role of women in the Armed Forces, the Women's Army Corps (WAC) was established in June 1943 with full military status. A Navy Women's Reserve (WAVE) was established to release men for duty with the Fleet and to "man" forward bases. A Marine reserve of women (MCWR) was also authorized in 1942, again out of the practical need to release men for combat duty. During the war, women served in occupations far beyond those initially envisaged for them. In 1942 the services had assumed that women would be assigned to only three or four job specialities. However, as the war progressed and personnel demands increased, operational requirements dictated the utilization of women in a growing variety of military skills, including assignment to LORAN (Long-Range Aid to Navigation) stations and the *Manhattan* project. Thus, dating from the World War II period onward, American women served in all sorts of logistical and service support roles, including piloting and crewing non-combatant ferrying missions across the Atlantic.

Perhaps more importantly, the great influx of women into the services during the World War II period served to challenge traditional views of the roles of females in society and provide the basis for fundamental change in the military institutions themselves. In 1948, as part of Public Law 30-625, The Women's Armed Services Integration Act, women were made a permanent part of the American military establishment, although Congressional restrictions on their capacity to engage in combat created the basis for an institutional barrier to their full integration into the Services force structures.[5] This law, which effectively brought women permanently into the U.S. Armed Services structure on both a regular, active duty and reserve basis, also placed a 2 percent ceiling on the number of enlisted women who could be brought into the military, and restricted them to service at the highest rank of Lieutenant Colonel/Lieutenant Commander.[6] Both of these restrictions were subsequently lifted by passage of Public Law 91-30 in 1967.

The combat restrictions provisions embodied in U.S. Code Title 10, Sections 6015 for the Navy and Marine Corps; 8549 for the Air Force; and 3012, which determines the Army policy for assignment of women to military occupation specialties (MOS), remain in force today.[7] By law, the Air Force, Navy, and Marine Corps cannot assign women to aircraft engaged in combat missions, and the Navy and Marine Corps cannot assign women to naval vessels having combat missions. The Air Force further restricts women from serving in positions that are likely to cause "capture" of its personnel, based upon a policy interpretation of the combat restriction law. The Marine Corps defines its combat in terms of its personnel requirements (to provide two Marine Expeditionary Brigades in each of the three marine Expeditionary Forces formed by the Fleet Marine Forces), while the Army, by policy, does not assign women to positions identified as the most likely to engage in direct combat. Each service's definition of combat allows for further restrictions of mission assignments for women based on war casually replacement requirements, sea-shore rotation (in the Navy) and personnel needs to offensive forces. A recent Government Accounting Office (GAO) study concluded that: "the combat exclusion statutes and Service policies implementing those statutes prohibit women from serving in about 675,000 combat jobs," and from 375,000 noncombat jobs designed to meet the program needs created by the existence of combat restrictions.[8]

Combat Exclusion

It is this issue of combat exclusion that goes to the heart of the current debate regarding women in the military. The combat-related restrictions embodied in U.S. Code Title 10 prohibit women from engaging in direct combat with enemy forces and dictate that women may not be assigned to duty on vessels or aircraft platforms that may be engaged in combat missions, except for temporary duty. There are exceptions to this, however, and women serving in job categories such as medical, dental, or religious (chaplain) professionals are exempt from the law's combat restrictions. Moreover, by a quirk of the law, the Army is not directly restricted from assigning women to all job categories, although the Secretary of the Army may determine which job categories are not appropriate for the assignment of women in accordance with his interpretation of the intent of Public Law 80-625 and Title 10 of the U.S. Code. One of the problems resulting from the absence of a direct restriction on the Army's utilization and assignment of women is a lack of consistency across the services in their respective policy interpretations of U.S. Code Title 10. To get at this inconsistency as well as to answer increasing complaints from women service members themselves, (then) Secretary of Defense Caspar Weinberger issued a memorandum in July 1983 to the Service Secretaries in which he stressed that all women be "provided full and equal opportunity with men to pursue appropriate military careers for which they can qualify. This means that military women can and should be utilized in all roles except those explicitly prohibited by combat exclusion statutes and related policy . . ."

While Weinberger's directive provided much-needed reinforcement for military women, for all practical purposes its self-proclaimed objective of ensuring the broadest possible utilization of female service members was doomed to failure because the latitude for change still resided with the Services themselves, the leadership of which, in some cases, adamently opposed changes to existing policy restrictions. In most instances, subjective assessment of "the intent of the law" continued to drive service policies directing the assignment of women. Exceptions, however, have been apparent. Air Force Secretary Verne Orr and Navy Secretary Jim Webb participated in decisions that were to open significant and new opportunities for women in the military. But this piecemeal approach to resolving the dilemma posed by the Combat Restriction law was in many instances not enough to foster change in the attitudes, perceptions, and behaviors of many males, who saw women as "second-class" service personnel and a threat to their ability to get CONUS (or shore-based) assignments. From this mentality arose a desire to limit not just the opportunities (for advancement) of women in the services, but, more fundamentally, the number of women under arms. There was a tendency in the Reagan administration to support a ceiling on the number of women in the military and a resistance to Congressionally imposed quotas on accession rates for women. As one analyst characterized it, the problem is that "once women are excluded from the prime work of the military—fighting—other restrictions follow logically. Certainly non-fighters can fill only a limited number of spots in the armed forces whose purpose is to fight wars, and since no women can fight, the number of women must be restricted."[9] Increasingly, however, the premises underlying the combat exclusion of women are being questioned by a growing number of military and civilian personnel policy analysts. For them, the issue comes down to the question of whether the combat exclusion policy is legitimate in light of changes that have taken place in the global strategic environment and in view of the force structure needs of the U.S. Armed Services in an All-Volunteer Force environment.

If we only examine the potential for conflict in the European theater it is clear that female service members will, at the outset, be engaged in combat and can be expected to have to perform defensive missions. Women service personnel assigned to Western Europe, especially those stationed in the Federal Republic of Germany, will be faced in the earliest hours of a war with enemy fire and forced to defend themselves and their units from hostile activities. In NATO Europe, women are predominantly stationed in headquarters and other areas (such as *Patriot* air defense units) that promise to be high value targets that Soviet and Warsaw Pact planners would certainly (according to Soviet military doctrine) seek to destroy in the earliest stages of a European theater operation. Likewise, women deployed onboard a Boeing E-3A airborne early warning aircraft (AWACS) or on submarine and ship tenders in the U.S. Navy would be subject to the threat of interdiction as part of a Soviet campaign to destroy NATO's critically important logistical infrastructure. These two brief examples suffice to illustrate a dilemma that the American public and Congress now must face: namely, how well prepared do we want our military women to be in the event of conflict; and, more fundamentally, given the adverse demographic trends facing the United States (and other Western industrialized nations) can we afford not to expand the opportunities of women in the military services, especially in light of the current constrained defense budget environment, which is likely to continue in the 1990s?

Public Attitudes and Women in the Military

As regards the changing nature of the global security environment, the issue is not, as it is often conceptualized, whether or not we wish to see women in combat; but rather, how to utilize more effectively and efficiently the resources that the military has already invested in its female personnel. In a global security environment in which women and men face the same risks associated with the threat of nuclear war at one extreme of the conflict spectrum, and terrorist activity at the other, the question of combat exclusion increasingly appears to have less and less relevance. This is not to say that there may be mission responsibilities in each of the services for which women, because of physical limitations, may not, over-all, be optimal personnel candidates. It is to suggest, however, that women who, in most instances, volunteer for the same risks and opportunities as their male counterparts should not be denied the chance to work in any area where they can fully compete with males. Those who support the current policy of restricting the mission assignments of women systemati-cally evoke public attitudes and the "will of the American people" as evidence of the need to sustain the status quo. To be sure, public attitudes and opinion on this issue are divided, although public opinion and polling data increasingly indicate that the American public, by and large, is less traditional on this issue than our legislators would have us believe." A poll conducted in August of 1986 by NBC News found that 52 percent of the public supported women in combat support roles, and 77 percent were comfortable with the current policy that military women will not be evacuated in a military conflict."[10] These statistics compare favorably with the results of an earlier poll conducted by the National Opinion Research Center in 1982. This poll measured an 84 percent approval rate of the American public for keeping or increasing the number of women in the services, and a 93 percent (93.7%) approval rate for the stationing of women (nurses) in combat zone sectors.[11] Ours is an ever changing society with evolving socialization experiences which, over the last three decades, have nurtured a decidedly different view of the role of women in Ameri-can society than what was prevalent as recently as the 1950s. This has led to public acceptance of women in "nontraditional" occupations in the civilian sector, including as firefighters, police officers, and intelligence operatives.[12] Before exploring in greater detail some of the issues attendant upon the question of a combat exclusion policy and the role of women in the U.S. military, it behooves U.S. policymakers and the American public to understand that the issue of combat restrictions does not mean that women will not be in combat in virtually any of the conflict scenarios that can be realistically discussed in relation to the potential employment of U.S. forces. In the closing years of the twentieth century we can be under no illusion; women *will* be involved in the conflict contingencies for which U.S. forces prepare, and they will suffer casualties along with our men under arms.

The extent to which women have been integrated into the fabric of the U.S. force posture is not generally appreciated by the U.S. public. At the time of the 1983 invasion of Grenada, Army women were deployed to that island on the second day of hostilities while Air Force women served under fire in aerial support squadrons and in other Service support capacities. During the 1986 raid against Libya, American Air Force women flew as part of the tanker crews that supported the F-111 mission and female Navy pilots performed carrier landings on ships stationed in the region. More recently, in the Persian Gulf arena, the support ship *Acadia* was deployed to repair the *Stark*. Women sailors accounted for twenty-five percent of the *Acadia*'s crew.

Deployment of women in crisis situations and to combat regions raises questions about their capacity to perform in a conflict situation. While the empirical evidence is thin because of past restrictions on the military utilization of women, existing data suggest that the reactions of women in combat would not be dissimilar from those of their male counterparts. Some can be expected to "freeze," but a majority of women would likely perform their mission assignments with courage and competence.

A more disconcerting issue underlies much of the resistance, especially from males, to expanding the military opportunities of women. This is the perceived fear of the reaction of women as "prisoners of war." The disturbing vision of women being held prisoner and threatened with torture brings to the forefront of this debate an emotionalism that is not logically or easily countered. While none of us as individuals is able to predict how long or under what circumstances we would be able to endure pain under capture, allegedly the psychological traits that are associated with the female of the species leads to the judgment that women would be more susceptible to pain and therefore more likely "to break" under pressure than males. The meager evidence that we have from past conflict situations (for instance, female agents and nurses in World War II) indicates that this may not be the case. But whatever the truth of the allegation, such arguments may be a red herring in the debate on women in the military. The real issue may relate more to the type of contingencies that the United States may face in coming years. Indeed, it may be the case, with the greater sophistication of weapons technologies and the broad diffusion of power globally, that future engagements of U.S. military forces may result in diminished opportunities for the taking of prisoners on the battlefield. Certainly the greater lethality of future battlefield environments may mean that casualties will be higher and so fewer, if any, prisoners will be taken, at least in high- to mid-intensity conflict environments as predicted in the European theater, the Middle East, and a Korean Peninsula contingency. In low-intensity conflict environments the situation may be different but, then again, given the sparseness of psychological evidence on how women would perform in those environments, the question must turn on force structure needs and mission responsibilities.

Personnel Options and the AVF

Attracting qualified personnel, male as well as female, to volunteer for military duty will be increasingly difficult in coming years. In interview after interview with military personnel who are electing to leave the services, low pay scales (when compared to comparable work in the civilian sector, especially in the high-technology areas), and the scaling back on benefits, including college tuition credits and medical services, are cited as determinate variables in making a decision to separate from the U.S. military forces. If the high quality of the personnel of the U.S. Armed Forces is to be maintained, the United States has essentially four options. It can: 1) reinstate the draft or adopt some form of universal service concept, as has been discussed by Senator Nunn; 2) reduce the size of its force structure; 3) lower the entrance qualifications of its personnel: or, 4) utilize more effectively its females. Without exception, none of the alternative options are entirely acceptable from a political standpoint, and all are controversial. While it appears that in the future, barring change in the current budget environment, the United States will be forced to reduce its force structure end-strength, some combination of the other options described above may also be necessary if American interests are to be preserved and protected.

Nevertheless, prospective problems in attracting and retaining qualified male cohorts has encouraged, even among the leadership of the services themselves, fundamental reconsideration of the issue of women and their more effective utilization in the force structures of the Armed Services of the United States. A significant factor in this regard has been the interest of the last two Secretaries of Defense, Caspar Weinberger and Frank Carlucci, in promoting greater opportunities for military women. Both also sought to take the lead in pushing aside traditional notions about the role of women in the military, with Weinberger instrumental in convening a Task Force Study, *Role of Women in the Military*. Chaired by the Principal Deputy Assistant Secretary of Defense for Force Management and Personnel Dr. David Armor, the Task Force found a nexus between combat exclusion and the way in which women were viewed and treated in the services. In many instances women have been viewed as unequal partners whose collective contribution to the force posture of the United States is diminished by the perception that "they" do not carry their full load (of the mission responsibilities) and as a result cannot be counted on in times of crisis or mobilization. These findings, which were substantiated by a separate Navy study, *Progress of Women in the Navy*, suggested that a widespread misconception was prevalent in the services: namely, that women service personnel would not mobilize for deployment overseas in times of crisis and that those women who are stationed in forward areas like Europe and the Republic of Korea would be evacuated "when the balloon goes up." In August 1988, during a trip of the Executive Committee of the Defense Advisory Committee on Women in the Services (DACOWITS), evidence that this view was widely held by both male and female service members was frequently found. Subsequently, Secretary Carlucci, in responding to the issue was raised in the DACO-WITS "after-action report," distributed a memorandum under his signature to the Service Secretaries stating that women would be deployed in crisis contingencies and that their participation in the U.S. Armed forces was instrumental to the successful completion of the mission objectives of each of the services. Carlucci stated:

> To maintain and protect readiness levels, decisions that military women may be assigned to certain missions and units under existing combat exclusion statutes and policies must be made with the understanding that they will be so assigned to duties which they could fulfill in the event of mobilization or other national emergency since there will be no plans or instructions to remove or evacuate them."[13]

It is precisely against the parameters of assessment of the future needs of U.S. force posture that the issue of women in the military must be resolved, and not on the basis of equal opportunity or as part of a "liberation" movement designed to make women exactly like men—if that were possible in the first place. Quite clearly the primary function of the Armed Forces of the United States is to protect our vital national interests and not to redress the perceived or real injustices of our society. To the extent that some view the issue of women in the military in precisely those terms, they do more harm than good to legitimate arguments in support of expanding the roles and opportunities of female service members. In my view it is time to reassess Public Law 80-625, if only to lift the barriers and artificial restrictions that exist and hamper the flexibility of a Commander to assign the best people to perform his (or her) unit's mission objectives. This is not to suggest that all women are appropriate for service in the military forces. Just as all males are not suitable for a military career, it would be a mistake for us to assume that all women understand the obligations and responsibilities that are intrinsic to military service. To ensure a high level of qualified individuals our recruiting practices must be refined and the illusions that some personnel have about their obligations must be dispelled. More importantly, however, if we are serious about maintaining the All-Volunteer Force concept, and, at the same time, continuing to attract women in the services in large numbers, we must be willing to cope with the difficult problems of pregnancy and, even more disturbing, dependent care upon mobilization.

Personnel Policy Issues Relating to Women

There is much disinformation surrounding the issue of pregnancy in the Armed Services. In peacetime, the problem revolves around job absenteeism and the necessity of "covering" in the work force for a colleague who is pregnant and cannot fulfill her mission assignments and/or is on postpartum leave. In wartime, pregnancy could profoundly affect force structure replacement requirements as well as the capacity of a unit to meet successfully its mission objectives. Quite clearly, the issue of pregnancy is of such great concern to the Armed Services that collectively in OSD and individually, as in the case of the Navy, the services are engaged in detailed studies to find out the extent to which the problem negatively affects job performance and unit cohesiveness. At this point the data are incomplete, but initial findings in recent service-sponsored studies indicate that the problems created by pregnancy in the services are not of any greater magnitude than those created by drug or alcohol abuse. This is not to suggest that pregnancy is not a significant issue for the services, which have to find qualified manpower replacements for personnel who are taken off duty status due to pregnancy but that the problems created by pregnancy may not be so great as to pose an insoluble dilemma.

For officers and career-oriented enlisted personnel, pregnancy in general poses no more of a problem than it does for the civilian community— women who are interested in pursuing a career in the military and/or those who are imbued with a sense of professionalism will meet their obligations without compromising their mission responsibilities or their infants' health. Alternatively, in the case of women who view the military as merely a job, or in the instance of a large majority of female single women becoming pregnant while on active duty, especially during first duty tours, the problem is more difficult. In many instances these women have no alternative but to stay in their service because of the financial demands and responsibilities that they now find thrust upon them. In many cases these women become embittered at the vicious cycle in which they find themselves; and, as a result, fail to maintain the performance standards of their jobs. Such women probably should not have been admitted to the services in the first place. Once pregnant, they should be encouraged to separate from the service.[14] Those who elect for whatever reason to stay in the service are then faced with the problem of providing for dependent children, an issue that poses a fundamentally profound challenge to the mobilization contingency planning of the current U.S. force structure.

The issue of dependent children and the potential mobilization crisis that it raises is by no means a women's issue, although traditionally it is framed in that context. It is significant that in our current force structure there are a larger number of single parent males (who have custodial care of their dependents) than there are women. This statistic should not be surprising in light of the larger numbers of males in the services. Nevertheless, the dependent child issue, with all of its attendant aspects, including pressures for larger day care facilities and more home care providers, has just as profound implications for wartime mobilization and the deployment of military personnel as it does for the nature of the peacetime force structure upon which we rely in emergency situations. In the constrained budget environment in which we are likely to continue to find ourselves in the 1990s, the burden for child care for service dependents should not be the responsibility of the military force structure. Yet, the reality is that in the All-Volunteer Force environment, such "perks" are considered to be personnel inducements and are cited as a major reason why some service members elect to re-enlist. Below the surface, there is a very real concern: if mobilization is required, will service members deploy with their units or will the parents among them elect to remain in place to ensure that their dependent children are cared for? There is no easy or clear answer to this very difficult question. What is apparent, however, is that the answer cannot be framed along sexual lines. During a recent visit to military installations in Western Europe, members of the Executive Committee of the DACOWITS heard males as well as females state that they would concern themselves first with their dependents and later with their assigned wartime deployment in a conflict contingency in Europe. If this perspective represents a broad spectrum of the U.S. military, then its implications for the ability of the services to move to their assigned wartime positions will be compromised, with obvious implications for their capacity to meet their mission objectives.

Another issue that has surfaced in the current debate on women in the military relates to allegations that the integration of women into combat formations will degrade the combat performance of military units. The Army, in an attempt to increase readiness, designed exercises (MAX-WAC and REFWAC) to make a case for sustaining a ceiling on the number of women in the force structure. However, the results of both exercises revealed that a unit's performance was influenced less by the integration of women than by the quality of leadership.[15] In this context, the results of a recent Danish experiment in which women were integrated into combat units in Denmark provided evidence that so-called "mixed units" of males and females performed better and had a higher morale than single-sex units, whether male or female. Similarly, in Canada, the initial results of an experiment entitled CREW (Combat-Related Employment of Women) indicates a similar finding even in the case of deployments aboard Canadian submarines. Discussions with U.S. male service members reveals the view that the integration of women in their units provides a "normalization" that makes service life more enjoyable and the inevitable hardships more tolerable. Views such as these raise questions about the old "male bonding" arguments of the 1970s, when the issue of women in the military was often equated with the women's liberation movement. Without commenting on the feminist perspective, I think that it is safe to say that the American debate on women in the military has moved away from these early stereotypes and is now seen in its proper perspective of what is best for the future force posture of the United States.

How we think about the issue of women in the military as we design an adequate force structure for the 1990s cannot be divorced from analytical assessments of the wartime requirements of U.S. forces and the likely conflict contingencies into which U.S. forces may be introduced. Force readiness must be the basis upon which consideration of all force personnel needs are defined. As policymakers grapple with issues raised by the integration of large numbers of women in the military they will be faced with the need to reconcile an institutional bias against further expansion with the requirements to sustain an end-strength large enough and qualified enough to meet any one of a number of global contingencies. The issue of women in the military is complex, raising a host of social policy questions in addition to military factors. Yet, as we stand on the threshold of the twenty-first century and project the types of conflict contingencies into which U.S. forces may be deployed, the question of how, and to what extent, women will perform is less clearly assessed than it needs to be. In the final analysis, the question will be resolved by Congress, which may find it necessary to repeal the combat restrictions embodied in Title 10 and Public Law 80-625, especially if it continues to cut back on military personnel appropriations. In the decade of the 1990s and beyond, the United States will be forced to do more with less as regards its military force structure. For this reason and in light of the march of technology that will contribute to a more lethal battlefield environment, the U.S. Armed Forces will be forced to utilize its female personnel more efficiently than in the past. This will require a new approach to personnel planning, especially assignment policies and recruitment. In the long run, however, it can be expected to pay off in providing greater flexibility (of mission assignment) for the unit commander.

Notes

1. Statement of Lieutenant General John I. Hudson, Deputy Chief of Staff for Manpower, USMC, before House Armed Services Committee, Subcommittee on Personnel and Compensation, February 4, 1988.

2. See Martin Binkin and Shirley J. Bach, *Women and the Military* (Washington, DC: The Brookings Institution, 1977).

3. The successful deployment of female nurses overseas and on board the Hospital ship *Relief* during the Spanish-American War led Congress to establish in 1901 the Nurse Corps as an auxiliary of the Army. In 1908 a Navy nurse auxiliary was established; but it was not until 1944 that nurses were officially recognized as a permanent part of the Army and Navy structures.

4. As characterized by Major General Jeanne Holm in *Women in the Military: An Unfinished Revolution*, 3rd edition (Novato, CA: Presidio Press, 1986), pp. 21–27.

5. Documentation exists to support the contention that Defense Department officials and prominent military leaders at the time supported this legislation as a means of mobilizing women in the event of general war. However, Congressional opposition, particularly from the strong Chairman of the House Armed Services Committee, Carl Vinson, would not agree to passage unless specific restrictions on women in the military were incorporated into the law. See Holm, *Women in the Military*.

6. This law also restricted female officer strength to a figure of 10 percent of the total female enlisted strength.

7. The U.S. Army is not directly restricted by a specific section of Title 10 U.S.C. in its assignment of women. However, section 3012, which sets forth the general policy guidance on women in the military, provides the basis of Army policy for the assignment of women. According to its interpretation of Title 10, section 3012, the Army subsequently developed, as part of its *Women in the Army Policy Review Group*, established in 1981, a methodology by which to assign, or restrict assignment of, women to MOS categories in the Army. This methodology, called District Combat Probability Coding, or DCPC, is based on a Military Entrance Physical Strength Capacity Test, or MEPSCAT, and includes as part of its criteria "location on the battlefield." This aspect of DCPC is currently under review by the Army since it conflicts, in certain cases, with the "Risk Rule" established and adopted by the Office of the Secretary of Defense in 1988 as a result of its Task Force Study on Women in the Military.

8. United States General Accounting Office, *Women in the Military, More Military Jobs Can Be Opened Under Current Statutes*, Report to Senators William Proxmire, William S. Cohen, and Dennis DeConcini, issued on September 1988, p. 11.

9. Laurie Goodman, "Women, War, and Equality: An Examination of Sex Discrimination in the Military," quoted in Karla R. Kelly, "The Exclusion of Women from Combat, Withstanding the Challenge" *The JAG Journal*, 1, (Summer 1984): 84.

10. Carolyn Becraft, "Women in the Military: Organizational Stress and Politics," unpublished paper, 1988.

11. From J. Davis, J. Lauby, and P.B. Sheatsley, *Americans View the Military: Public Opinion in 1982* (University of Chicago: National Opinion Research Center, 1982) in Becraft, "Women in the Military."

12. Linda J. Waite and Sue E. Berryman, *Women in Nontraditional Occupations* (Santa Monica, CA: Rand Corporation, 1985).

13. "Women in the Military," Secretary of Defense Memo, issued September 27, 1988.

14. This would obviously require changing existing service policies, such as the Army's, for example, which requires a woman to serve out her contract obligation even if she becomes pregnant.

15. Holm, *Women in the Military*, pp. 257–58.

21
Resource Implications of Emerging Technology

Stephen J. Flanagan

Overview: Is Emerging Technology an Affordable Force Multiplier?

A variety of technological developments that promise to greatly enhance the effectiveness of non-nuclear weapons systems have been touted as affordable force multipliers for the United States and its NATO allies in this era of dwindling budgets and personnel. Referred to under the general rubric of "emerging technologies," or "ET," what is envisaged is the integration of disparate advances in munitions, precision guidance, sensor, data processing, and communications technologies into complex weapons systems. This chapter outlines the status of various emerging conventional military technologies and considers how their exploitation might affect U.S. and Allied fiscal and personnel requirements in the coming decade. It concludes that fiscal and demographic trends will force the U.S. and its allies to confront difficult problems including choosing between the acquisition of new systems and maintaining force structure; selecting the appropriate mix of high- and low-technology weapons in their inventories; and maintaining the resources to recruit and retain forces qualified to operate and maintain whatever mix of systems is chosen.

Particular attention is given to the proposition that ET may permit Allied military planners to substitute technology for troops. In fact, it seems likely that integration of ET systems will create new demands for both highly trained technicians and unskilled combat service and combat service support personnel that could offset possible decreases in the personnel needs of frontline combat units. High development and procurement costs are likely to limit procurement of ET systems in militarily

The views expressed herein are solely those of the author and do not necessarily reflect the views of the Department of Defense or of any other agency of the United States government.

significant numbers in the near term, given that little or no growth is projected in the defense budgets of most NATO countries.

While a number of these new weapons technologies have been tested and a few are operational, the bulk are still in the developmental stage or have not been integrated into weapons systems. Test data have raised doubts about the operational performance and reliability of many of these complex systems. U.S. predominance in the development of most of the relevant technologies raises additional problems. While West Europeans fear that pursuit of a high-technology defense means concomitant absorption and dependence on U.S. technology, the United States worries that provision of certain advanced technologies to its European partners carries the risk of leakage or unauthorized transfer to the Warsaw Pact. There is also concern in NATO that relatively inexpensive Eastern military countermeasures could erode the effectiveness of these new weapons capabilities.

Because of these hurdles, ET's impact on Western capabilities and resources vis-à-vis the Warsaw Pact will likely be evolutionary rather than revolutionary. ET may have much a more dramatic impact on military requirements in less intense combat environments and against less sophisticated adversaries, as the Israelis demonstrated in the Bekaa Valley campaign. However, even in these situations, technology may not always be decisive. The Argentines inflicted significant damage on the British fleet in the Falklands War with both sophisticated (Super Etendards with Exocets) and relatively archaic (A-4s with one thousand pound iron bombs) weapons systems.[1] Moreover, technology and equipment cannot be considered in isolation. The evolving military environment will be shaped not just by technology but also by such factors as strategy, doctrine, readiness, training, and morale. Despite the better equipment and firepower of Argentine ground forces in the Falklands, the superior training and operational planning of the British forces resulted in their rapid victory.

What Are These New Technologies?

In essence, ET may allow for rapid direction and redirection of more lethal conventional firepower and more capable general-purpose forces to areas of the battlefield where they can be most effective. Emerging and accelerating developments in microelectronics, sensor technology, and munitions could alter considerably the nature of non-nuclear conflict during the coming decade. Moreover, a number of these new systems may be capable of accomplishing some missions presently assigned to tactical nuclear weapons.

The driving force behind this change is the incorporation of advanced data-processing systems and a variety of optical, radar, infrared, and laser sensors into weapons and reconnaissance platforms that enable extraordinarily accurate target acquisition in all types of climatic conditions over a broad area. Critical support to such systems would be provided by rapidly evolving capabilities for all-weather, near-real-time surveillance, and for target acquisition at close range and up to 500 kilometers behind the forward line of own troops (FLOT).

Some of these new technologies are already having an impact on the capabilities of NATO forces against a broad range of military threats. New assets currently being procured may enhance NATO's warning of and ability to counter an initial Warsaw Pact attack, as well as its capabilities to diminish and defend against associated air power, to disrupt Pact C³I—while maintaining the integrity of its own system—and to interdict Warsaw Pact reinforcement efforts.

Under Congressional direction in the 1987 authorization bill, DOD's Balanced Technology Initiative (BTI) has targeted resources on development of new technologies for conventional forces that have the potential to bolster U.S. strengths vis-à-vis Soviet forces.[2] Work is proceeding under the aegis of the BTI on smart and brilliant weapons, armor and anti-armor technology, C³/battle management, high-powered microwaves, and other areas.

DOD's Competitive Strategies Initiative (CSI) has also concluded that a number of advanced technologies offer considerable promise. CSI is a planning concept that seeks to maximize U.S. defense investments in areas that offer the highest operational leverage and that might force stabilizing changes in Soviet force structure and military strategy. The first set of "candidate competitive strategies," which emerged from a 1987–88 review of options for Europe, identified exploitation of emerging missile and target acquisition systems to counter Soviet air operations and deal with penetrations of forward defenses as particularly lucrative military options.[3]

While emerging technologies are certain to have an impact on close combat, the most dramatic innovations could come if capabilities to detect, track, and acquire with precision stationary and mobile targets at very long distances are perfected. In the European context, these "deep-strike" systems have attracted the greatest attention. Some analysts, such as the European Security Study Group (ESECS), have argued that if combined with adjustments in doctrine and tactics, such strikes could enable NATO to prevent a Warsaw Pact breakthrough of its forward defense without resort to nuclear weapons.[4] This ability to acquire targets accurately at great depths could be coupled with advances in munitions and standoff weapons to accomplish some of the counterair, reinforcement interdiction, and counter-C³I tasks presently assigned to nuclear systems.

The extent to which conventional weapons can substitute for tactical nuclear weapons is debatable on several grounds.[5] However, the Soviet military appears to be worried that some of NATO's non-nuclear weapons, particularly precision-guided missile systems, will have similar decisive effects in the early stages of any future war,[6] although it should be noted that these concerns were first raised publicly about the time the Soviets began deploying new self-propelled artillery and the highly accurate SS-21 short-range ballistic missile (SRBM) with new families of improved conventional munitions.[7]

The "Brains" of the Operations

Microcomputers with digital and signal processing capabilities unimagined only a few years ago, and which are likely to expand exponentially in the very near term, are the nerve centers of an increasing number of conventional military systems. As the British government's 1988 Defense White Paper put it, NATO force planners are now ordering "chips with everything."[8] Microcomputers can be found in the guidance systems of most new ballistic and cruise missiles, in the fire control systems of new artillery, rocket launchers, and tanks, and throughout the C³I infrastructure.

The U.S. Department of Defense has spent more than $500 million between 1983 and 1988 on the Strategic Computing Initiative, which has yielded important advances in large-scale parallel computing and on applied use of artificial intelligence, including such projects as the autonomous land vehicle, an aircraft control system, and on a system to plan and control large naval operations.[9] Advances in large-scale and very large-scale integrated circuits (LSI, VLSI) that can process data at rates previously performed only by mainframe computers are already providing tactical surveillance systems with the capacity to track a large number of targets in near real time and pass relevant targeting data onto battlefield commanders. Work is continuing on six new families of smaller, less costly, and more reliable computer chips, developed under the DOD's Very High Speed Integrated Circuit (VHSIC) program. Insertion of VHSIC technology into operational weapons systems began in 1985. Second-generation VHSIC chips promise to yield hundred-fold improvements in processing power and performance reliability at reduced costs in the whole range of military equipment that has microelectronic components.[10]

Developments in surveillance and sensor technology are transforming all aspects of conventional military capabilities. A variety of new sensors on tactical intelligence platforms are already providing NATO commanders with more precise all-weather day and night coverage of stationary and mobile forces at increasing distances. This tactical intelligence data is complemented by improved access to information from U.S. national reconnaissance programs and various space assets. Input of all these data into the terminal guidance systems of a number of "fire-and-forget" and long-range standoff weapons would provide them with near-perfect accuracy.[11]

These new sensors include infrared devices that can detect vehicles at night or under camouflage, synthetic aperture radars that can produce photo-like images through cloud cover and detect movement of aircraft and troop convoys, and electronic intelligence sensors for precision location of hostile air defense radars. These collection systems are becoming more interactive as they are linked together by computers at tactical information fusion centers. Thus, information from one system can be used to alert or tailor the collection activities of another more efficiently.

Development work is under way in the United States on a new long-range radar surveillance system that would be the critical support element for non-nuclear interdiction of second-echelon Warsaw Pact forces. The U.S. Army/Air Force Joint Surveillance and Target Attack Radar System (JSTARS) program, formed in 1982, is designed to provide both services with capabilities, which they presently lack, for real-time monitoring and identification of both stationary and moving ground force targets at long ranges and over a wide field of view. This airborne system would transmit data it collected to a remote truck-mounted ground station for distribution to various weapons systems. JSTARS may also be able to autonomously direct weapons strikes against identified targets. JSTARS, now in full-scale development, is expected to improve management of battlefield interdiction efforts and standoff interdiction attacks. The system is scheduled to begin prototype testing during the late 1980s, with deployment of ten aircraft envisioned in the 1990s. The European allies are developing similar systems.

Developments in Munitions

Many of the emerging weapons capabilities trace their genesis to advances in technologies other than the fabrication of silicon chips. There have been dramatic developments in conventional munitions and in rocket and missile guidance technologies, some of which have already proved their effectiveness in combat as well as on the test range. These weapons have applications in close combat and deep strikes. A number of European as well as U.S. firms are in various stages of developing mid-flight and terminal-guidance packages for a multitude of delivery systems.

Advances in small explosives technology have led to the design of area impact and precision-guided submunitions that multiply and disperse the effects of a single weapons payload delivered to a target. For example, the warhead fitted on a single rocket of the Multiple Launch Rocket System

(MLRS), which is now entering service in several NATO armies, can disperse 844 M-77 submunitions each with an explosive force equivalent to that of a hand grenade.

Two prototypes of "smart" antitank submunitions were tested, with disappointing results, during the U.S. Defense Advanced Research Project Agency's (DARPA) *Assault Breaker* program.[12] New development programs in this area are underway in the United States and Western Europe. It is unclear how effective these smart munitions will be against moving targets or under adverse conditions. In any event, the *Assault Breaker* program illustrated a weakness common to a number of these new high-technology weapons: overall system performance can be critically degraded by the malfunctioning of any of its several components.

New Counterair Capabilities

A number of weapons programs incorporate precision guidance or novel munitions technologies that have the potential to improve Western counter-air capabilities. Four basic types of munitions are required for conventional air attack against airbases: cratering munitions to disrupt runways and taxiways; area effects fragmentation munitions to destroy unsheltered aircraft and equipment; area denial mines to restrict movement of personnel equipment and aircraft; and weapons to destroy protected aircraft. A number of these types of systems have been successfully tested and some are being deployed.

Because of the density and increasing sophistication of Warsaw Pact air defenses, there has been considerable interest in developing guided standoff munitions dispensers for NATO aircraft and utilizing surface-to-surface missiles to deliver airfield attack munitions packages. Several ballistic and cruise missile systems equipped with submunitions are being considered by the U.S. Air Force for standoff counterair missions.

Air Defenses

The other critical element in the counterair equation is the ability to defend one's own airfields. To be able to generate sorties for sustained air combat and ground support, the NATO allies must be able to protect airfields for the recovery of aircraft. The 18 E-3A Airborne Warning and Control System (AWACS) aircraft now deployed with multinational NATO crews in Europe can provide unique early warning and unprecedented air battle management capabilities. E-3As provide high- and low-altitude surveillance of aircraft operations, spotting ground-hugging aircraft, which cannot be detected by land-based radars, shortly after take-off. AWACS controllers can utilize this tracking data to manage several aspects of the air battle.

Systems for the Close-In Battle

The United States and its NATO partners plan to deploy a wide range of weapons systems to meet such challenges of forward defense as stopping the advance of armored units and suppressing Pact artillery and rocket fire. The first units of the Multiple Launch Rocket System (MLRS) have entered service with the U.S. Army in Europe and are being built and fielded by five other members of the Alliance. MLRS offers a significant increase in firepower and important gains in range over existing artillery. Guided artillery is another area where there have been considerable technological advances. Over the past decade, the U.S. Army has developed a laser-guided artillery shell known as *Copperhead*, whose entry into service has been cancelled. For all its technological sophistication, *Copperhead* is still dependent on two forward observers who use a laser target designator and must radio target coordinates to the firing battery. Not only is the laser device cumbersome for soldiers to deploy, but the laser must be held on the target while *Copperhead* is in flight. Soviet tanks equipped with laser detection devices would be able to ascertain that they were being illuminated and could engage the forward observers. It is this vulnerability that has led the Army to develop a number of remotely-piloted vehicles (RPVs) to locate and designate targets for laser-guided weapons.

The United States and NATO are developing and deploying a wide array of anti-armor precision-guided munitions (PGMs) that can be fired from helicopters, vehicles, and artillery and by individual soldiers. Many of these PGMs incorporate laser target designators and guidance systems as well as advanced shaped charges and other armor-penetrating devices that increase their lethality. Most current antitank guided missiles (ATGMs), such as the long-range TOW and HOT and short-range Dragon and Milan, utilize command line-of-sight guidance, necessitating tracking to impact. However, the third-generation fire-and-forget PGMs under development in the West appear likely to overcome several of the significant drawbacks of earlier versions, such as operator vulnerability and weather limitations.[13] They will also be able to distinguish between vehicles of different sizes, thereby permitting selective targeting.

The debate as to whether PGMs favor defense over the offense or can wholly compensate for the quantitative inferiority of NATO's armored forces in the Central Region is unlikely ever to be resolved.[14] It appears that the third generation of these weapons will be more lethal and reliable than their predecessors. However, developments such as Soviet deployment of reactive armor, which diminishes somewhat the effectiveness of infantry-fired ATGMs, is a classic example of the dynamic nature of such competition and of how simple countermeasures can often counter sophisticated technology.[15]

ET's Uncertain Future

Given all these technological and military uncertainties, there is no "magic bullet." Most of the new technologies that promise to correct various problems or enhance certain capabilities are unlikely to be deployed in significant numbers until the end of the 1990s, if only because they will be very expensive. For example, the ESECS study estimated that acquisition of a force of 1,000 short-range MLRS systems to deal with first-echelon forces, 5,000 standoff cruise missiles with smart submunitions to attack follow-on forces, and 900 conventionally armed ballistic missiles for counterair operations could be procured at a cost of $22.5 to 30 billion over a decade. The Office of Technology Assessment has projected that the procurement costs of a "shallow-FOFA" package comprised of JSTARS, MLRS/ATACMS would be more than $15 billion.[16] Some have estimated that a complete shallow-FOFA capability would cost about $25 billion to acquire, about the cost of a NATO corps. Other estimates for these systems vary widely, and at this point it is premature to advance specific cost figures with much confidence.[17] Nonetheless, these costs are non-trivial.

Thus, it may be a misnomer to speak of a technological revolution on the battlefield. U.S. and NATO conventional forces are likely to realize these significant increases in capability in an incremental fashion. Moreover, the impact of technology cannot be considered in isolation. There are many other factors—such as strategy, doctrine, training, readiness, and morale—that must also be considered in any appraisal of the evolving military situation. Some of these factors will now receive closer examination.

The Resource Environment of the 1990s

Trends in Personnel

A shortfall is expected in U.S. and NATO manpower during the 1990s. Demographic trends in all NATO countries will result in a dwindling manpower pool for military service, most acutely in West Germany, Italy, and Denmark. As of 1983, the Western countries had a fertility rate of 1.78, which is 15 percent below the replacement level. Most NATO countries have had fertility rates below the replacement levels for over a decade.[18] Thus, the number of men in the age group best suited for combat roles (17 to 30 years) is declining rapidly. By the year 2000, the European countries that contribute to defense of NATO's Central Region will experience a 20 percent decline in the number of men between the ages of 18 and 22.[19] In addition, West Germany has seen a marked increase in the numbers of men choosing to pursue alternative service, despite the longer term of service.

The impact of the declining birthrate in the United States on military requirements is less severe. In order to satisfy its 1901 personnel needs, the U.S. needed to enlist 5.4 percent of the service-eligible male population. The U.S. service age cohort will reach its nadir in 1998, at which time DOD estimates it will require about 5.1 percent of that group to enlist.[20]

At the same time, manpower pools are aging, with more men in the age group better suited for combat support roles (33 to 40). Solutions to these demographic problems abound, but few are attractive politically. Recent British, French, and West German defense reorganization plans have featured concepts of replacing somewhat diminished active manpower with firepower or reservists. However, dwindling budgets will limit the rate of procurement of new equipment, and it is likely that many of these new weapons with complicated C³ requirements will require additional support personnel.

There is little doubt that the current cadres of enlisted personnel in the U.S. armed forces are among the most capable and best trained in history.[21] Trend lines suggest that this is likely to continue, although it cannot be taken as a given, particularly if military compensation were to fall further behind the civilian sector, as it did by 9.4 percent between 1982 and 1987. The pay raises Congress mandated of 4 and 4.3 percent in 1988 and 1989 are simply designed to prevent any further erosion. Moreover, it is more difficult to predict the availability of *qualified* personnel in the out years to meet the demands of high-tech armed forces. If entry standards must be raised in the 1990s to meet the challenge of new technologies, this could make the recruitment problem much tougher, particularly if compensation erodes.

ET's Growing Demand for Support Personnel

Given the important role that air- and ground-based early-warning and battle management systems would play in NATO defenses, they would obviously be prime targets of Warsaw Pact attacks and electronic warfare measures. Indeed, the Achilles heel of the high-technology conventional battlefield is the C³I system that would be employed in its management.

Development of a C³I system with sufficient protective measures or redundancies to survive in what would be an extraordinarily intense combat environment will be a major challenge for NATO. The Soviet Union has a well-developed radio-electronic combat doctrine, which emphasizes systematic disruption of the opponent's C³I system by employing appropriate lethal and non-lethal means as the situation warrants.[22] Mobility and redundancy are two approaches to limiting system disruption, and NATO is planning to procure land-mobile command posts as well as early-warning and battle-management aircraft. Additional support personnel will be required to operate these redundant systems. The search for ways to cope with these vulnerabilities has also included an examination of the utility of expendable, unmanned aerial surveillance and targeting platforms and the feasibility of greater exploitation of space-based assets, both with direct communications links to battlefield commanders.

There is no doubt that a reduced volume of fire inherent in these more lethal weapons would result in the need for fewer aircraft sorties or artillery rounds and ultimately fewer aircraft and artillery pieces and pilots and gunners. New standoff weapons may also reduce attrition of aircraft and ground forces. However, some of these new systems will also be quite manpower intensive. Some of these additional combat support and service support roles could be filled by women.

Human Engineering Considerations of ET

This growing cornucopia of tactical information has already created new problems for data handling and analysis. Exploitation of radar imagery and other signals is creating new demands for personnel trained in the art of processing, interpreting, and reporting this information in a format that can be used effectively by operational commanders. NATO fusion centers are already suffering from information overload, slowing down processing. In a crisis this situation would be compounded, precluding timely transmission of target acquisition data to users. One way to mitigate this problem is to tailor reconnaissance efforts to target acquisition requirements and develop ways, including use of artificial intelligence packages, to filter out the most critical information.[23] It is also important to recall that the exploitation of new technology involves more than R&D and hardware costs.

The potential of new technology to complicate military operations and exacerbate battlefield stress and confusion should not be overlooked. The circumstances surrounding the downing of Iran Air Flight 855 by the USS *Vincennes* and the Iraqi Exocet attack on the USS *Stark* during 1988 offer tragic illustrations of this pressure. While technology can accelerate the operational performance of weapons systems, it does not necessarily ease the burden on human commanders, who must increasingly make split-second command decisions. This new technology has led to an imbalance between capabilities to attack targets at long ranges and human ability to assess the threat posed by these targets, which are nothing more than disembodied images on a video display. Yet both the Iraqi pilot and the captain of the *Vincennes* would have risked their own demise had they sought further discrimination of their targets. The impact of this imbalance is most poignant in peacetime and low-intensity conflicts. However, it may also result in increased vulnerability to friendly fire in high-intensity combat environments.

The capabilities and difficulties in developing high-technology tactical reconnaissance and surveillance platform are reflected in the TR-1 high-altitude, long-endurance aircraft. The TR-1 was procured to support the Tactical Reconnaissance System (TRS), a combination of active radars and passive surveillance sensors, as well as the Advanced Synthetic Aperture Radar Systems (ASARS) and the Precision Location Strike System (PLSS). ASARS can provide radar images of ground targets such as tanks and parked aircraft at ranges in excess of 150 kilometers. PLSS was designed to yield extremely accurate real-time targeting data on enemy signal emitters (radars, jammers, and communication systems), and can direct aircraft and missile strikes against them. However, during the PLSS prototype tests it was found that processing and analyzing the vast numbers of signals collected during fast-paced combat operations is far more difficult than expected, and the program was cancelled. In addition, the TRS prototype tests revealed several problems that will require modification, resulting in several years' delay in this TR-1 sensor package.[24]

This action on TR-1 reflects the impact of several Defense Department initiatives underway to strengthen its ability to assess the total manpower, personnel, training, and safety (MPTS) implications of future weapons systems.[25] Military and contractor requirements are being carefully reviewed in light of MPTS factors at various acquisition milestones to ensure that maximum operational capability is provided at acceptable cost.

However, predicting personnel and training requirements has been problematic in the past. A study of seven major weapons procured during the 1970s revealed that estimates of manpower needs developed during the acquisition process were generally too low.[26] These underestimates were found to be a consequence of changing operation and support concepts and great uncertainty concerning the manpower needed to maintain the systems. In addition, the study concluded that estimates of new manpower requirements often reflected program goals rather than an unbiased assessment of needs, and that these assessments generally considered only the aggregate manning of the using unit, neglecting the critical issues of overall manpower and skill level requirements.

The Army's experience with development of the TACFIRE field artillery fire-direction system in the 1970s illustrates potential problems in this regard. TACFIRE nearly achieved its initial program goal of having no net impact on manpower requirements in artillery units. However, manning of direct support maintenance battalions to sustain the system had to be expanded because of technological limitations. The program had been designed to allow the system operator to correct 90 percent of system failures. Instead, it was found that operators could only fix 70 percent of system failures, which led to the expanded maintenance requirements.[27]

Skill level requirements can often be as critical as manpower projections in assessing the costs of putting military significant numbers of new systems into the field and then maintaining them. All of the U.S. armed services foresee growing demands for highly trained personnel. As a major 1982 Air Force study concluded:

> ... the expanded operational environment of the future will create an increased demand for people in command, control and communications, in electronic warfare, in computer-assisted design/manufacturing, and in space operations. Although automation and "black box" technology will continue to offset some task complexity, an intensified need for more technically trained workers to operate and maintain complex systems is inevitable.[28]

Despite this general assessment, the services' detailed projections of changes in skill requirements in the early 1990s reveal near continuity with the present force mix—that is, fairly fixed percentages of the total force will require technical or highly technical training.[29]

Policy Options

In pursuing its military technology options in the lean years ahead, the United States and its allies must make several basic choices about an effective high/low technology mix and about means to ensure that qualified personnel join and are retained in the armed services. Emphasis must be placed on developing military systems that are more reliable and easily serviced.

The West should not and clearly cannot forego development of ET systems and attempt to match the Warsaw Pact on a weapons for weapons basis. Firstly, it is mistaken to argue that the Soviets do not push the state of the art in many of their new weapons systems. In fact, Soviet technology in a number of areas may be outpacing similar efforts in the West. Technology has been an important Western strength, and a source of considerable leverage.

Some advocates of pursuit of a high-technology defense have suggested that the new systems will be more complex but more reliable, with easily replaceable "black box" components. Given the record of a number of programs that were similarly touted in the 1980s, like *Copperhead* and the *Sergeant York* DIVADS, a healthy dose of skepticism is warranted. However, DOD has also been seeking ways of enhancing operational simplicity. In the last few years, the Army Research Institute has begun to examine the aptitude and training of operating and maintenance personnel in the development of new weapons. With fewer people there will be fewer skills available. There is a growing need to ensure that the equipment fits the personnel. Such measures will be essential if, as appears likely, U.S. armed forces will have fewer personnel with the requisite skills to maintain and operate sophisticated systems.

Notes

1. Max Hastings and Simon Jenkins, *The Battle for the Falklands* (New York: Norton, 1983), pp. 225–29, 318–25.

2. See U.S. Department of Defense, Secretary of Defense Frank C. Carlucci, *Annual Report to the Congress, Fiscal Year 1989*, February 11, 1988, pp. 272, 115–18.

3. U.S. Department of Defense, Secretary of Defense Frank C. Carlucci, *Annual Report to the Congress, Fiscal Year 1990* January 17, 1989, pp. 46–48.

4. See the reports of the European Security Study (ESECS), *Strengthening Conventional Deterrence in Europe: Proposals for the 1980s*, (New York: St. Martin's Press, 1983); and ESECS II, *Strengthening Conventional Deterrence in Europe: A Program for the 1980s* (Boulder, CO: Westview Press, 1985).

5. On the substitution issue, see Victor Utgoff, "Reshaping NATO's Battlefield Nuclear Weapons Posture," in Stephen Biddle and Peter Feaver, eds., *The Battlefield Nuclear Weapons Debate*, Occasional Paper (Cambridge, MA: Center for Science and International Affairs, forthcoming).

6. See statement of Marshal Kulikov, "For the Sake of Peace on the Earth," *Izvestia*, May 8, 1984, pp. 1–2, in *Current Digest of the Soviet Press, 38* (May 31, 1984): 11–12. See also Mary C. FitzGerald, "Marshal Ogarkov on the Modern Theater of Operation," *Naval War College Review*, 39 (Autumn 1988): 8–22.

7. U.S. Department of Defense, *Soviet Military Power, 1988: Assessing the Threat* (Washington, DC: USGPO, 1988), pp. 75–85.

8. United Kingdom, Ministry of Defence, *Statement on the Defence Estimates, 1988*, Command Paper 334-I (London: HMSO, 1988), p. 39.

9. See Warren E. Leary, "The Battle to Mechanize the Military Mind," *New York Times*, May 15, 1988, p. E-7.

10. U.S. Department of Defense, Secretary of Defense, *Annual Reports to the Congress, Fiscal Year 1988*, February 4, 1985, p. 285, and *Fiscal Year 1989*, pp. 271–73.

11. Edgar Ulsamer, "A Roadmap to Tomorrow's Tactical Airpower," *Air Force Magazine*, December 1983, p. 45.

12. See U.S. Congress, Office of Technology Assessment, *New Technologies for NATO: Implementing Follow-On Forces Attack* (Washington: USGPO, 1988), p. 178, and Michael Gordon, "Highly Touted Assault Breaker Weapon Caught Up in Internal Pentagon Debate," *National Journal*, October 22, 1983, pp. 2152–58.

13. See William J. Perry and Cynthia Roberts, "Winning Through Sophistication: How to Meet the Soviet Challenge," *Technology Review* (July 1982): 27–35.

14. See John Mearsheimer, "Precision-Guided Munitions and Conventional Defence," *Survival* (March/April 1979): 88–78, and Daniel Goure and Gordon McCormick, "PGM No Panacea," *Survival* (March/April 1980).

15. See DOD, *Annual Report, FY 1989*, p. 275.

16. See ESECS II, *Strengthening Conventional Deterrence*, pp. 125–38, and OTA, *New Technologies for NATO*.

17. For estimates of FOFA systems costs, see U.S. Congress, Office of Technology Assessment, *New Technology for NATO: Implementing Follow-On Forces Attack*, (Washington: USGPO, 1987), pp. 32–33.

18. Ben J. Wattenberg and Karl Zimmeister, "The Birth Dearth: The Geopolitical Consequences," *Public Opinion* (December/January 1988): 8–11.

19. See Susan L. Clark, "Who Will Staff NATO?" ORBIS 32, (Fall 1988): 522–23.

20. See the testimony of Chapman B. Cox, Assistant Secretary of Defense for Force Management and Personnel, in U.S. Senate, Committee on Armed Services, l00th Cong., lst. sess., Senate Hearing 100-242, Pt. 3, *DOD Authorization for Appropriations for Fiscal Years 1988 and 1989* March 3, 1988, p. 739.

21. Cox testimony, pp. 727–28.

22. U.S. Department of Defense, *Soviet Military Power: An Assessment of the Threat, 1988* (Washington, DC: USGPO, 1988), p. 88.

23. See John E. Rothrock and Timothy E. Kline, "RAAP: Lethal Focus for the Information Technology Explosion," *Military Technology*, 8 (1987): 159–85.

24. U.S. Department of Defense, Secretary of Defense Caspar W. Weinberger, *Annual Report to the Congress, Fiscal Year 1988*, January 12, 1987, pp. 200–1.

25. DOD, *Annual Report, FY 1989*, pp. 151–52.

26. Norman E. Betaque, et al., *Manpower Planning for New Weapons Systems*, Report to the Department of Defense By the Logistics Management Institute, Washington, DC, December 1978, pp. 39–50.

27. Ibid., pp. 43–44.

28. U.S. Department of the Air Force, *Air Force 2000: Air Power Entering the 21st Century* USGPO (1982), p. 253.

29. See Martin Binkin, *Military Technology and Defense Manpower*, Brookings Institution Studies in Defense Policy, (Washington, DC: Brookings Institution, 1988), pp. 37–43.

22

On Theory and Reality: The Need for Consensus and Reconciliation of Contractions in Arms Control and Defense Policy

Benson D. Adams

There are contradictions between arms control theory and deterrence theory that require reconciliation if we are to: 1) have a coherent and consistent national security policy; 2) provide better and clearer guidance to our military planners and the acquisition community; 3) obtain more security for our money in a period of scarce resources; 4) have more realistic arms control expectations and agreements; and 5) deny the Soviet Union the opportunity of exploiting these contradictions. In my opinion, there are three areas around which consensus must form in the 1990s: the need for a more relevant arms control theory, strategic defense, and compliance.

If we continue with current arms control theory we are more than likely to not only get bad and irrelevant arms control, but to weaken our security as well. If we don't recognize and admit that strategic defenses make very real contributions to deterrence and arms control, we are going to lose the ability to constrain the offense, increase instability in the U.S.-Soviet nuclear balance, and alter qualitatively that balance. Without a compliance policy, the credibility of our foreign policy, diplomacy, and commitments could adversely be affected by a perception that we lack the will to address violations.

I am going to discuss each of these issues by making use of three rules that I have discovered as a result of my eighteen years of government service.

The Lysenko Rule

This rule is named after Trofim Lysenko, the infamous Soviet biologist who set Soviet genetics back at least fifty years by his nonsense about

The views expressed herein are solely those of the author and do not necessarily reflect the views of the Department of Defense or of any other agency of the United States government.

organisms passing acquired characteristics onto succeeding generations. This rule states that if you cannot change reality to conform to theory, then keep trying to change reality.

One might logically ask, why is it necessary to develop a new theory of arms control? Isn't the present one good? Hasn't it successfully guided our efforts to date? Indeed, modern arms control, as we know it, has been in various forms and guises a part of every administration's foreign and/or defense policy since 1945, and a mainstay and central feature of every administration's national security policies since 1969. But has it been meaningful and successful? Has it enhanced our security? Has it achieved the goals set for it nearly thirty years ago?

Arms control was originally conceived of as an interim step on the road to disarmament—an historic Western dream—and was to serve three purposes:

> reduce the likelihood of war,
>
> reduce damage from war, and
>
> save money.[1]

In fact, none of these objectives has been achieved.[2] Why? First, because weapons do not cause wars. Men and the states they govern decide whether there is to be war. The reasons are few and simple: 1) they think they can win; 2) the alternatives are worse; or 3) a combination of both. In fact, Michael Howard's brilliant work, *War and the Liberal Conscience*,[3] demonstrates convincingly that every time a presumed cause of war is removed by treaty, agreement, or technological change, wars continue to occur. Second, if there were a nuclear war between the superpowers, the very theory of arms control that led to those agreements and the force structures they permitted would guarantee greater damage than if there were no agreements. Third, arms control has not saved money because the money presumably not spent has gone into verification or other pressing defense needs.

On the other hand, the reason that arms control has become a central feature of U.S. foreign and domestic policy is that the issue has become political and emotional, based on the following fears and beliefs:

1. The people's fear of nuclear war, as though reducing or controlling nuclear arms will remove the cause of or reduce the occurrence or likelihood of war.

2. The belief that the so-called nuclear arms race must be halted because too much is being spent on "overkill," and sooner or later these weapons, since they exist, will be used.

3. The naive belief that limitation, reduction, and control of nuclear armaments will lead eventually to the disarmament Garden of Eden and thus to a peaceful and tranquil nuclear-free world.

4. The belief that arms control is a cheaper way of containing the threat, since we cannot or will not build the military establishment needed to safeguard our interests and commitments. It does not seem to have occurred to anyone that we could reduce our security risks by either buying and deploying what is needed or reducing our interests and commitments to bring them into conformity with the means of our military establishment.

5. The belief that arms control will result in reduced expenditures for defense, and those resources otherwise spent on defense could be used for domestic purposes.

6. The bottom line: How can anyone be against arms control and disarmament?

None of the previous arms control agreements we have entered into or the outcome of the current START or Defense and Space negotiations is likely to fulfill the classic goals of arms control theory or the six reasons noted.

Like any endeavor of statecraft, the "raison d'être" for the current nuclear arms talks is more complex than any of these reasons. It is rooted in power and strategy. For the United States it may be an attempt to reduce or contain a threat that it allowed to get out of hand by its unwillingness to maintain nuclear superiority. Superiority conflicted with the theory of mutual deterrence/arms control, which postulated the need for the Soviet Union to catch up with us in nuclear arms so they would not feel threatened and thus a basis for strategic stability would be created. Not only does this logic sound absurd, because it resulted in the absolute and relative growth of Soviet power at our voluntary expense, but it goes against all human experience involving competition.[4] This does not mean cooperative measures are eschewed when one has superiority, but it does mean you do not give up your competitive advantage unless you have some other way to maintain it. We did not. The Soviets, on the other hand, could view these negotiations (among other economic and strategic reasons) as an opportunity to constrain, reduce, and control U.S. (Western) arms spending and programs, especially SDI. There are some in the West who see it this way too. To illustrate this point of theory versus reality somewhat differently, consider: Arms control is about strategy and not just numbers. There are some who believe the numbers of warheads permitted in a future START agreement are so high as to be meaningless, even if the agreement represents a significant treaty involving reductions.

There are others, however, who worry that the remaining number of delivery vehicles is getting so small that one side's undetected cheating could seriously threaten strategic stability. Unmentioned is the fact that at deep levels of reductions the relative strength of other nuclear powers increases.

None of this, then, has to do with altruism, saving money, disarmament, or seeking a peaceful world. It is about strategy. It has to do with power, interests, and advantage, the hallmark of human existence from the time man first organized into communities. It certainly does not represent the shared value and assumptions of arms control theory as expounded in the late 1950s and early 1960s. This leads me to conclude that there is something wrong with the theory of arms control as propounded in the late 1950s and its application in the 1990s. In the late 1950s and early 1960s, the United States had nuclear superiority; missile defenses were in their primitive development stage; no one but the United States and the Soviet Union had ICBMs, SLBMs, or even intermediate-range rockets; the U.S. was a creditor nation whose technological and industrial prowess and creativity were unsurpassed; Vietnam, Watergate, SALT I and II, the ABM Treaty, the INF Treaty, Iran, and the War Powers Act had not yet happened; and the social, political, and sexual revolutions were years off. How, then, can one continue a theory propounded in the 1950s and 1960s in the face of this reality?

The theory is bankrupt and irrelevent. It has to change to conform to the strategic, political, economic, and technological reality of the 1990s. There must be a consensus about the need for a new theory and its contents. This brings me to my second rule—The "Real" Rule, which illustrates why both arms control and deterrence theory must change.

The "Real" Rule

The "Real" Rule states, except for the case of the victor imposing on the vanquished limits, controls, reductions, and prohibitions on weapons, the real reasons nations enter into arms control/disarmament agreements are that: 1) political, economic, strategic, and technological expediency, interests, and objectives make it attractive and in some cases necessary (to buy time); 2) technology has rendered the weapons being considered for control or limitation obsolete; 3) new systems, technology, and weapons are available to replace obsolete weapons; and 4) the value of certain weapons is not considered militarily significant or useful (the converse is that certain technologies or weapons may have tremendous potential so you do not close the door on them by controlling them). This is not to say that there cannot be a coincidence of "realpolitik" and the objectives of stability, reduced tensions, arms reductions, or disarmament. But it does say that there may not be a mutual and long-term shared commitment and consent among nations to arms control. Rather, arms control may be used as a temporary expedient to buy time to assimilate new weapons technology, to change doctrine and organization, or to restructure an organization or force in order to ready it for the kind of future foreseen by military planners. This being the case, I would contend, therefore, that the continued adherence to an outmoded theory of arms control is like clinging to the Ptolemaic view of the universe in the face of the evidence of the Copernican revolution. Technology and politics have outstripped and bankrupted it, and continued adherence to the theory is not only out of step with reality but is a threat to our national security.

One area where this should be self-evident, and which exemplifies what I am talking about, is the issue of strategic defense. Arms control theory must no longer continue to oppose strategic defenses, while deterrence theory must admit their value and integrate them into its framework.

The theory of mutual deterrence was postulated in the late 1950s, but not publicly discussed until the mid-1960s. Proponents of the theory argued that to deter nuclear war and to achieve greater stability in the U.S.-Soviet strategic balance, it would be desirable if both sides were mutually vulnerable to each other's secure second-strike capability. Mutual deterrence depends on some undefinable combination of finite military capability and political will to be credible, and to influence Soviet perceptions in order to deter them from taking any action inimical to our interests that might lead to nuclear war. This theory presumed the Soviets had a common interest in subscribing to mutual deterrence and in being satisfied with nuclear parity based on an offensive capability. The theory never assumed, and its proponents could not accept, a Soviet view of defense that included a warfighting and war-winning component, in addition to strategic defenses. The Soviet preoccupation with strategic defense was dismissed as an aberration or as an inability to escape from their historical experience, even though the Soviets have always favored a balance between offensive and defensive nuclear forces.

Throughout most of the nuclear era, U.S. and Soviet views of nuclear war, the forces both sides acquired to support those views, and their respective strategies have been radically divergent, a fact only conceded at official levels of our government in the late 1970s. The U.S. forces which were procured well before the latest generation of Soviet forces have always been justified on the basis of a deterrent strategy. The U.S. view of deterrence remained remarkably consistent, although our rationalization of our forces and their capabilities changed at different times as the Soviet nuclear buildup continued. Similarly, our views on the nature of nuclear war remained unambiguous and consistent until 1974, when a series of changes in our employment policy began to occur, shifting our views from the simple, spasmodic holocaustic view of a nuclear exchange we had held since the late 1950s to a complex, protracted view of nuclear war.

In contrast, the Soviets have held that war is a continuation of policy and that nuclear weapons, while more powerful than conventional explosives, are still weapons that may be used. The Soviets believe nuclear war is wageable and winnable, which is not to say they desire one or want to start one. The Soviets, like ourselves, recognized early that nuclear weapons brought about a qualitative change in the nature of warfare—that the opening phase of a conflict might be the only phase before war termination. This conclusion led the Soviets to place a great emphasis on preemption as well as defenses to limit damage, because the existence of nuclear weapons creates the possibility of their use. This is a view the United States subconsciously understands but wants to deny. Thus, the United States has consciously sought to prevent this understanding from becoming a reality by maintaining a high nuclear threshhold to ensure nuclear weapons are not used early, complemented by a deterrent strategy that threatens unacceptable damage to an aggressor. The Soviets, on the other hand, reject as irrational the threat of nuclear war if it leads to suicide.

Mutual deterrence was also viewed as consistent with an arms control regime based on a finite, offensive, dominant deterrent force. It was thought that if the technological development of the offense could be kept ahead of the defense, and if the defense were restrained or not permitted, then the offense would continue to deter and dominate without a new round of offensive improvements or a race in defensive systems. Defenses were identified as provocative and destabilizing because their deployment would upset the offensive retaliation/mutual vulnerability/hostage relationship which was central to mutual deterrence. Any advantage that protected people or increased the residual number of offensive weapons left after an attack was anathema to the advocates of mutual deterrence. This thinking coincided with the arms control theory that advocated preventing the deployment of strategic defenses, ballistic missile defense (BMD) in particular, in order to preclude a new dimension in the U.S.-Soviet arms competition. The mutual deterrence and arms control theories combined to denigrate the value of strategic defenses, whose value is not based on theory but on military fact. These arguments, combined with the offense-dominant doctrine dating to the earliest days of air power and the strategic bombing experiences of World War II, mutually reinforced one another to prevent the serious deployment of strategic defenses.

The United States unilaterally withheld deployment of BMD from 1965 to late 1967 in the hopes of persuading the Soviets to accept mutual deterrence and not to deploy a BMD for reasons of arms control. Even though the United States decided to deploy a BMD in 1967 (*Sentinel*), and later altered its mission in 1969 to ICBM defense (*Safeguard*), it was never seriously prepared to deploy missile defenses, since it was prepared to give them up in SALT. The arguments marshaled against developing or deploying BMD were also used against deploying civil defense programs, and are also being used today against the development of SDI for defense, even before the feasibility of such weapons has been evaluated. The objective, opponents of BMD argue, is to preserve mutual deterrence through mutual vulnerability, not to find a defense against ICBMs.[5]

There are several advantages that accrue from robust defenses, and these should be borne in mind during the current debate over SDI. First, penetrating defenses can be very costly in terms of resources and forces so as to make the effort either not worthwhile or very expensive. The multibillion-dollar penetration aid and multiple independently targetable reentry vehicle (MIRV) programs for ICBM and sea-launched ballistic missiles to penetrate Soviet missile defenses is an excellent example. Such programs are not cheap, nor were the technical solutions easy. Second, defenses cause great uncertainty for the conservative offense planner about the ability of his resources to accomplish their objectives. This also strengthens deterrence. Third, defenses exert virtual attrition on the payloads of the offense by forcing either defensive armaments and/or penetration aids to be carried at the expense of payload or range. Fourth, strategic defense provides a military option, and preserves the offense for future use. Finally, there are some who view defenses as a way out of the moral and religious dilemma posed by an offense-dominated nuclear deterrent doctrine.

Defenses are intended to make any attack extremely costly, repel an attack, and preserve or protect a target in order to allow its essential functions to continue even when damaged or under attack. The value, vulnerability, and priority of targets in terms of their worth to the defender and his strategy must be carefully assessed, and only those targets essential to the success of the defender's strategy or that can defeat the attacker's strategy should be defended. If the offense in the nuclear age cannot be sure of success or absolute decisiveness in its initial attacks in the presence of defenses, then the defense may well have contributed to deterrence in a manner uniquely different from an offense-dominant or offense-only deterrent. An offensive dominant deterrent can only be credible if the attacker believes it will and can be used. If the attacker has a way to neutralize the deterrent, the deterrent no longer deters. In the presence of defenses, the attacker must assume there will be no hesitancy to use it, which complicate his decision of whether to attack in the first place. In a deterrent strategy in which defenses are present, they are there to be used if deterrence fails. Whereas, in an offense-dominant deterrent strategy, in which it is almost impossible to consider that deterrence could fail, the offense is there so it will not have to be used. This makes no military or strategic sense. It leads to offensive arms races and efforts to upset stability, and makes a mockery of arms control, since the latter must preserve the offense at any price. The presence of strategic defenses allows a reconciliation between reality and the U.S. version of nuclear war on a strategic rather than an emotional plane, without having to adopt the Soviet view of nuclear war. Strategic defenses not only contribute to deterrence by making the outcome of an attack more uncertain, but defense can repulse an attack, shield the homeland, protect the offense, and dampen an offensive arms race.

For these reasons there must be a national consensus that defenses are not only *good*, but *necessary*, because they contribute to deterrence. Moreover, arms control and deterrence theorists have to rethink their earlier opposition to defenses and find a place for it in their respective theories.

The "Sorry" Rule

The third rule I want to discuss is the "Sorry" Rule. This rule states that the Western powers have a sorry history of enforcing compliance with arms control/disarmament agreements and treaties.

Since the 1921 Washington Naval Treaties, the West has acquiesced to treaty noncompliance and violations by the Germans (Versailles Treaty, Naval Treaty), Japanese (Naval Treaties), Italians (Naval Treaties), and Russians (SALT I and II, ABM Treaty) by ignoring them, making diplomatic protests, allowing the violation to stand without trying to reverse it, denigrating the military significance of the violation, concluding that nothing that can be done about it, or debating whether the evidence or facts constitute a violation. Historically, what has been even more remarkable is the unwillingness of the Western powers to build up to the the military levels permitted by these treaties to offset regional superiority or advantage by other powers. This willingness to accept any kind of violation, cheating and/or noncompliance is insidious. It results in the violator's perceiving a lack of will on the part of the aggrieved party to stand up and challenge him, thus encouraging further testing of will and possible cheating. This has been the case with Soviet violations of SALT I and II and the ABM treaty. Contributing greatly to our current problems is that we lack a compliance policy to deal with violations from the outset of a treaty regime. Without such a policy, there appears to be very little a party can do to compel another party to comply with a treaty if the latter is not inclined to do so. Sanctions, protests, force, diplomatic means, and so forth, are usually unable to reverse a noncompliant action. A compliance policy accompanied by a plausible set of actions designed to make the cost of cheating and noncompliance so high it is no longer worthwhile is likely to deter noncompliance. That policy, to be credible and offer a real potential to deter noncompliance, must exist before a treaty is ratified. It will put teeth into any arms control treaty, because certain things will happen automatically in the event of a determination of a violation.

The following questions are invariably raised during treaty negotiations and later during the ratification process: How do we know they will not cheat? How can we trust them? How will we know if they cheat? Can we detect the cheating? Can we monitor the agreement? Can we verify an agreement? What will we do if they have cheated and we catch them? Fred Iklé, in his classic article, "After Detection, What?" asked these very questions, and they have yet to be answered satisfactorily.[6] Invariably, the further the ratification process recedes into the past, the greater has been the West's moral and political reluctance, inability, or unwillingness to confront a violator with their violations. The reasons are many, but they essentially boil down to:

> The unwillingness of authorities to believe information that has awkward political implications. The tendency of . . .[those] who have taken part in negotiations to become advocates of the integrity of the persons with whom they secured agreement, and to lose the scepticism which is a part of vigilance. . . . Technicians may not be the best judges of enemy intentions and achievement. They find it hard sometimes to believe that what they cannot do or have not thought of doing has been done by the other side."[7]

While it is not necessary to discuss the types of compliance issues or controversies that may arise, it should be noted that compliance issues are not just violations, but include ambiguous activities and actions, some of which may be as innocent as those resulting from different interpretations of an agreement or treaty provision. It is critically important not only for arms control but for the credibility of our diplomacy and foreign policy that we have a consensus on the need for a clearly stated arms control compliance policy so allies and parties to the agreement understand that forces and processes will be set in motion automatically to offset violations and that we will not sign agreements to watch them be broken and violated.

The purpose of a compliance policy is to enforce the agreement, to deter violations, cheating, and noncompliance by providing a means to determine if such activities took place, and if they did, to provide an appropriate response to such activities. Such a policy might have the following elements:

316 • U.S. Defense Policy

1. A declaratory statement setting forth what our compliance policy is and what will happen if a violation is detected.

2. A reasonable period for resolution, after which any questionable activities, behavior, ambiguities, and outright violations are made public so that the problem (and thus the violator) is not shielded by prolonged and ineffective diplomatic efforts at resolution.

3. A planning and analysis capability to anticipate cheating scenarios and possible violations that might occur in order to prepare candidate responses. The responses must be militarily and politically significant in that if invoked, they have a reasonable chance of offsetting the violation, and reversible if their execution results in restoring the compliance regime.

4. An annual report on the status of all arms control agreements to include compliance regardless of whether there are violations.

5. A Compliance Advocate to serve as the institutional advocate and conscience for arms control treaty compliance, who would be the focal point for all arms control treaty compliance issues.

6. A formal process to analyze the verification, technical, and political aspects of all compliance issues.

7. A process which results, when appropriate, in a presidential declaration of a violation and the forwarding to Congress by the president of such a declaration accompanied by an appropriate response and a request for funds to offset the violation, which must be voted up or down by the Congress in a reasonable amount of time.

8. A sunset provision that allows a compliance issue to be escalated to other diplomatic levels after a significant amount of time has passed to resolve the issue in the appropriate compliance forum.

9. Introduction of legislation for an arms control compliance act to take the politics out of the compliance process and make it easier to address and deal with noncompliance when it occurs. This would make compliance less a bureaucratic and partisan political issue and more a national security issue.

Conclusion

I have tried in this chapter to draw together three aspects of our national security policy which require a consensus in the 1990s if that policy is to be consistent, logical, realistic, credible, and strong. The first is the need for a new theory of arms control for the 1990s to replace the obsolete one of the 1950s and 1960s. The second is the need to accept the value and

role of strategic defense in deterrence and arms control theory. The third
is that in order to put teeth into present and future arms control agreements and make the agreements support our defense and foreign policy,
we need an arms control compliance policy so violators know they cannot
violate agreements with the United States and U.S. allies believe we will
enforce agreements and not condone violations.

Notes

1. Donald G. Brennan, ed. *Arms Control Disarmament and National Security*
(New York: Braziller, 1961). This book is based on the Fall 1960 special issue of
Daedalus.
2. See for example, Bruce D. Berkowitz, *Calculated Risks: A Century of
Arms Control, Why It Has Failed and How It Can Be Made to Work* (New York:
Simon and Schuster, 1987); Malcolm Wallop and Angelo Codevilla, *The Arms
Control Delusion: How Twenty-Five Years of Arms Control Has Made the World
Less Safe* (San Francisco: IUCS Press, 1987); Colin Gray, "Nuclear Delusions: Six
Arms Control Fallicies," *Policy Review* (Summer 1986), pp. 48–53; Joseph Kru-
zel, "What's Wrong with the Traditional Approach?" *Washington Quarterly*
(Spring 1985), pp. 121–132; Joseph Kruzel, "Arms Control and American De-
fense Policy: New Alternatives and Old Realities," *Daedalus* (Winter 1981), pp.
137–153; John Steinbrunner, "Arms Control: Crisis or Compromise," *Foreign
Affairs* (Summer 1985), pp. 1036–1049; Edward Luttwak, "Why Arms Control
Has Failed," *Commentary* (January 1978), pp. 19–28; Wayland Young (Lord
Kennet), "Disarmament: Thirty Years of Failure," *International Security* (Winter
1978), pp. 33–51; Seymour Weiss, "The Case Against Arms Control" *Commentary* (November 1984), pp. 19–23; Christoph Bertram, "Rethinking Arms Control," *Foreign Affairs* (Winter 1980/81), pp. 352–365; William R. Hawkins,
"Arms Control: Three Centuries of Failure," *National Review*, August 9, 1985,
pp. 26–32; Thomas C. Schelling, "What Went Wrong with Arms Control," *Foreign Affairs* (Winter 1985/86), pp. 219–233.
3. Michael Howard, *War And The Liberal Conscience*. (London: Temple
Smith, 1978).
4. This theory is a prize-winning, cannot-miss candidate for the *Journal of
Irreproducible Results.*
5. See my: *Ballistic Missile Defense* (New York: Elsevier, 1971); "In Defense
of the Homeland," *US Naval Institute Proceedings*, June 1983; "Strategy and the
First Strategic Defense Iimitative," *Naval War College Review* (November/
December 1985); Statement before the SDI Panel, *House Armed Services Committee*, 100th Cong., 2nd sess., September 29, 1988. See also B. Bruce-Briggs, *The
Shield of Faith*, (New York: Simon and Schuster, 1988).
6. Fred Iklé, "After Detection—What?" *Foreign Affairs*" (January 1961), pp.
208–220.
7. The three points made here are attributed to Rear Admiral John Godfrey,
Director of British Naval Intelligence from 1939 to 1942, who made them in the

context of the internal Admiralty debate about the size and displacement of the battleship *Bismarck* and whether it complied with the Anglo-German Naval Treaty of 1936. Indeed, this case study illustrates two other points: 1) the danger of "wishful thinking," that ever lurking temptation for politicians dealing with military affairs—and for serving officers involved in politics" (p. 135) and 2) how deceit, lying, deception, and trusting one's negotiating partner can lead to being fooled (p. 139). See Donald McLachlan, *Room 39: Wherein Took Place The Exciting Story of British Naval Intelligence During World War II* (New York: Antheneum, 1968). The three points as quoted are on p. 142.

23
Managing National Security

Carnes Lord

I n the public consciousness, questions relating to the management of
national security affairs in the United States generally assume the guise
of personality disputes between powerful members of a president's
cabinet. The classic case in point is of course the quarrels between the
Secretary of State and the National Security Adviser that have marked
virtually every administration since that of Richard Nixon. This is unfortunate. Individuals and personalities *are* important in our political system.
More often than not, however, their impact is grossly exaggerated, and
the role of the powerful organizations that make up the nation's permanent government is overlooked.[1]

Many of those who regard presidential control of the national security
bureaucracy as a non-trivial problem tend to make a similar error. "People," so it is said, are more important than "organization." Though probably true at some level of analysis, this proposition is not very helpful.
Examples abound of bad organization that wastes the talents of good
people—or worse yet, puts those talents to work in a bad cause. Part of
the reason the proposition is inadequate has to do with the overly narrow
conception many have of organizational questions. What is at issue here
are not simply organizational charts. Anyone familiar with the federal
bureaucracy knows that such charts do not tell the whole story about the
locus of power in an agency or how it is exercised. More important are
aspects of bureaucratic life that do not show up at all on organizational
charts—standard operating procedures, personnel management practices,
and perhaps most important of all, an agency's institutional interests,
spirit, and culture.

Whatever may be true of the federal government as a whole, in the
national security area the challenge of managing the bureaucracy has been
for some time, and remains today, an acute one. The U.S. military, diplomatic, and intelligence bureaucracies all have unusually powerful and dis-

The views expressed herein are solely those of the author and do not necessarily reflect the
views of the Department of Defense or of any other agency of the United States government.

tinct institutional interests and cultures, and have demonstrated considerable aptitude over the years in resisting, deflecting, or coopting the policy preferences of the president and the Congress. What is at stake here is much more than the efficient management of a sprawling bureaucratic empire or the rooting out of waste, fraud, and corruption, necessary as all this may be. Rather, it is the fundamental question of the reality of democratic—and most especially, of presidential—control of those agencies of government that are the immediate guardians of the nation's most vital interests.

This is by no means to argue that the primary problem is the protection of the nation's liberties (or for that matter, its moral sensitivities or its purse) from potential threats posed by a rogue intelligence or military establishment. The primary problem is not so much negative as it is positive control—the ability of the nation's elected leaders to use the bureaucracy to develop and implement policies of their own. The lack of responsiveness of the national security bureaucracy as a whole to (especially) presidential leadership is a function of a set of bureaucratic pathologies that have altered little over the years, and that account for much of the general incoherence as well as many of the specific failings of recent U.S. national security policy.

Many examples of bureaucratic pathologies that have directly and significantly influenced national security policymaking under the Reagan administration could be cited, but several areas stand out particularly. In the critical area of arms control, bureaucratic warfare has gone on almost uninterruptedly since the beginning of the administration.[2] The State Department and the Office of the Secretary of Defense (OSD) have been the primary antagonists; but State has often had to contend with internal differences as well, while the Joint Chiefs of Staff (JCS), the Arms Control and Disarmament Agency (ACDA), and the National Security Council (NSC) staff have all frequently played independent roles. The result has been a lack of overall strategic direction, bureaucratic confusion and delay, and a policy framework in which political and military requirements are very imperfectly integrated, to say the least. After the Reykjavik summit meeting between Resident Reagan and Soviet General Secretary Gorbachev, which nearly produced an agreement in principle to eliminate nuclear-armed ballistic missiles, it became clear that the position presented there by the United States had been developed without benefit of serious analysis by the JCS. The virtual coup engineered at Reykjavik by the State Department is a particularly striking case, but hardly atypical given the relentless promotion of arms control by an agency institutionally obsessed with improving relations with the Soviet Union, as well as the growing unwillingness of the JCS to buy political trouble for itself by appearing to oppose progress in arms control.[3]

   In the low-intensity conflict area, in spite of the success of administration actions in Afghanistan, Grenada, and elsewhere, the overall picture has been nearly as bleak. As has become apparent in the wake of the Iran-Contra revelations, the administration's halfhearted attempt to run a Kissinger-style NSC operation in the areas of counterterrorism and insurgency/counterinsurgency warfare reflected frustration not only with the Congress but with the relevant executive branch agencies as well. As regards Central America in particular, a convincing case has recently been made that the seeds of NSC policy entrepreneurship in these areas were sown by the State Department in its repeated efforts, beginning in the early 1980s, to circumvent or preempt presidential policy on Nicaragua.[4] But one also has to look at the performance of the Pentagon and the intelligence community on the ground in Central America. A recent study of the history of the U.S. military advisory effort in El Salvador by four U.S. Army officers suggests that the U.S. military as an institution has yet to come to grips fully with the requirements of counterinsurgency warfare in the Third World.[5] Similar questions can be raised about the strategic and operational competence of the CIA in managing the Nicaraguan Contras.[6] On top of all this is the seemingly intractable problem of interagency coordination in supporting U.S. involvement in conflicts such as those in Central America. The absence of an appropriate mechanism at the national level remains a key problem in spite of recent legislation designed to address it. Less noted but equally important is the tangle of problems relating to command and control of U.S. low-intensity activities in the field.[7]

   What, if anything, can be done about this state of affairs? There are a number of steps that could be considered to address the general pathologies of the national security bureaucracy. These will be presented and discussed first in summary form. I will then move to a discussion of specific remedies that might be applied in the areas of arms control and low-intensity conflict.

   Of general remedies, the most obvious, as well as the most important, is a stronger role for the National Security Adviser and the NSC staff. Contrary to a very general misconception, the alternatives here are not an NSC essentially limited to the administrative coordination of agency positions on the one hand, and a Kissinger-style operational NSC on the other. Although NSC has important functions of an operational nature, it cannot and should not attempt to do the business of the State Department—or any other national security organization. Indeed, an excellent argument can be made that the NSC should ideally spend less time on foreign policy than has usually been the case in the past, and more time on other aspects of national security policy, especially in contentious areas (such as arms control, low-intensity conflict, counterintelligence, and strategic economics) where there is large overlap in agency responsibilities and a history of poor policy performance. But the key point is that NSC should be empowered not merely to craft bureaucratic compromises between contending agencies but to create a coherent framework for national security policy as a whole.

What the NSC needs to be truly effective in such a role, in the first instance, is a clear grant of authority from the president to act as his surrogate, and more generally to represent in an impartial and comprehensive fashion the "national level" of national security policy. This authority should enable the NSC to act as arbiter and manager of the national security policy process, with a mandate to develop, in cooperation with the relevant agencies and with the Congress, coherent national strategies reflecting the president's policy views, and to oversee and enforce the implementation of those strategies by the bureaucracy. This is not very far from the way many assume the NSC actually works, and it approximates the way the NSC has worked in certain areas at certain periods in the past. Yet it is far from the norm of NSC performance. This is especially the case under the Reagan administration, which entered office determined to downgrade the position of NSC Adviser in order to avoid the open conflicts between State and NSC that had marked the Nixon and Carter administrations.[8] The fact of the matter is that such conflicts can never be avoided entirely precisely because of the institutional imperatives that shape the behavior of both organizations—imperatives that are quite independent of the motivations of the individuals at their helm. A better approach is to recognize this reality, and take deliberate steps to adjust the State-NSC relationship so as to achieve a more stable balance between conflicting organizational requirements and clearer expectations concerning their primary spheres of responsibility.

A second and closely related remedy is a greater emphasis on strategy, planning and doctrine. This should be a prime concern both within the White House and throughout the national security agencies.

Within the White House, to begin with, new mechanisms are needed to couple the NSC and the NSC interagency structure more firmly to White House offices with responsibilities for the budget, legal issues, congressional relations, and public affairs. All too often, established policy channels in the executive branch are undermined or circumvented by pressures generated by or through these White House offices, sometimes acting in collaboration with their counterparts in the agencies. There needs to be greater recognition of the strategic character and significance of budgetary, legal, congressional and public affairs issues, and the necessity of integrating them fully in executive branch policymaking. Developments during the Reagan administration have underlined the need to regularize and institutionalize relations between the National Security Adviser and his staff and other officials and staffs within the White House complex. In important respects, the traditional State-NSC rivalry has been superceded in recent years by rivalry or tension between the National Security Adviser and the White House Chief of Staff. While personal relationships have clearly been an important factor here, they reflect a deeper institutional problem that has not yet received the attention it deserves.

Within the NSC staff itself, major organizational innovation is needed to encourage integrated strategic approaches and a more serious effort at strategic planning. Two key elements of such a reorganization are a separate and coequal NSC planning component, and procedures designed to break down the compartmentalization of the staff—something that contributed importantly to the Iran-Contra fiasco and that continues to vitiate the NSC's effectiveness more generally. NSC planning should encompass a variety of distinct though related functions: long-range planning, crisis and short-range planning, budget and resource planning, strategic intelligence and net assessment, and speechwriting. Within the agencies, planning staffs (where they exist) need to be strengthened and given greater authority, as well as greater latitude in working together with similar staffs in other agencies and at the NSC.

One of the first objectives of these changes should be to develop a body of national-level doctrine concerning policy, organizations, and procedures in bureaucratically contentious areas such as low-intensity conflict and arms control. In the absence of such an agreed framework, the most well-intentioned effort at strategic planning is likely to founder on persisting and fundamental differences in agency outlook. The very notion of developing national security "doctrine" is apt to be repugnant to many within as well as outside the government, and regarded as an unnecessary limitation on the flexibility of the agencies in responding to international developments and adjusting U.S. strategy and tactics accordingly. But if doctrine is seen to be essential to the effective functioning of the nation's military establishment, it is difficult to see why it would not also be beneficial in the equally complex world of national-level policy. This is especially the case given the severe problems the government as a whole faces in the area of personnel continuity and institutional memory.

The third remedy is enhancement of political or civilian control of the national security agencies. No serious effort to reform the national security bureaucracy will be possible without a deliberate effort by the president to assert and extend his authority through the process of appointment to office. Perhaps the most unremarked development in national security affairs under the Reagan administration has been the ability of the various career services to coopt senior presidential advisers and to limit the number and authority of political appointees at lower levels. Nor is the problem limited to the bureaucracy. For a number of reasons, neither the National Security Adviser himself nor his deputy should be a serving military officer, contrary to what has become the practice under the Reagan administration; and the senior echelon of the NSC staff should consist of persons who, at a minimum, are retired from government service, and who ideally should lack close identification with agency interests and perspectives while sharing the president's general policy orientation. Some presence of the career bureaucracy at the NSC is possible and indeed desirable, but it is inappropriate for such persons to occupy positions where they are inevitably called upon for policy advice and expected to place loyalty to the president over attachment to their parent agency.

In the second place, the number of political appointees in the State Department needs to be sharply increased, especially at top management levels (under and assistant secretary). The Foreign Service has been notoriously resistant to efforts to do this; but especially given State's history of recalcitrance to White House policy direction, it is unclear why the president should not insist on a degree of personnel control there that is taken for granted in most federal agencies. Gaining working control of the State Department's seventh floor is infinitely more important for a president than disposing of more ambassadorial appointments, the more conspicuous arena of State–White House personnel disputes.

Finally, the possibility should at least be explored of filling positions with non–career appointees at CIA and elsewhere in the intelligence community. In spite of the predictable resistance to such a step from the career service as well as from the Congress, it would arguably improve both the quality of CIA personnel in key policy-relevant jobs and the coordination and integration of the agency's activities with the rest of the national security bureaucracy. The venerable notion that CIA is merely a technical organization whose integrity is threatened by too much intimacy with the White House or the policy agencies generally is one that stands up poorly to scrutiny. A thorough reexamination of its relationship to the White House and to the intelligence requirements of the presidential office is long overdue.[9]

The fourth remedy is a greater emphasis on the implementation of policy, both at the national level and throughout the agencies. Many observers have grossly underestimated the problems involved in translating national-level policy into agency operational planning and its tactical implementation. Some of these problems are procedural and administrative, but others reflect deliberate agency efforts to reinterpret or even subvert White House directives. NSC planning and presidential decision documents should pay more detailed attention to implementation than is now the case. NSC follow-up on presidential decisions and monitoring of agency operations should be made systematic and routine, and NSC should be given the authority necessary to do it effectively. Political appointees in the agencies should have special responsibilities for monitoring and enforcing implementation of national policies, and the NSC adviser should have a watching brief on the performance of these political executives, including cabinet-level officials. All of this presupposes, of course, a president who is able and willing to involve himself in potentially unpleasant personnel matters and take decisions that may prove controversial. It is unrealistic to expect the president to fire a senior official over every policy disagreement or failure of implementation, nor is it necessary that he do so. At a certain point, however, the visible prospering of officials who are disloyal or incompetent or both begins to be seen as a sign of administration weakness and lack of seriousness.

A fifth remedy is enhancement of personnel continuity and institutional memory throughout the national security agencies. Two bureaucratic pathologies with crippling effects on the implementation of policy are a lack of historical knowledge and perspective and career management practices that favor short duty tours and a generalist approach to professional advancement.[10] Obviously, these pathologies are related and aggravate one another, and they cannot be compensated for entirely by a greater reliance on written doctrine, as important as that may be in its own right.

One element of such an effort would be the strengthening and integration of computerized information systems throughout the various agencies and at the national level. Considerable progress has been made over the last five years in this area, particularly within the White House.[11] However, much remains to be done in this very complex area. Databases on policy-relevant intelligence and on national policy need to be maintained and refined, and procedures and formats devised for the processing of information suited to the needs of senior policymakers throughout the national security bureaucracy.

The area of personnel policy poses some of the most daunting challenges to anyone interested in improving the management of the government for national security. The pathologies created by irrational personnel management practices are frequently both pervasive and elusive, and, for a variety of reasons, very resistant to change. A strong case can be made that the time has come for a high-level review of personnel practices throughout the national security bureaucracy within a framework of overall national objectives and strategy. Such a review, perhaps conducted by a blue-ribbon presidential panel, should look comprehensively at the military, diplomatic, and intelligence establishments. It should make recommendations especially concerning ways to enhance career stability in key policy and operational areas, to create greater incentives for career specialization in strategy and planning, and to increase cross-agency training and assignment.

A sixth remedy is to give greater scope to centrally managed programs in select areas. Government by committee, reflecting as it does the management style and political culture of the country as a whole, is the norm throughout the national security bureaucracy, and probably increasingly so. Dissatisfaction with this approach periodically leads to calls in Congress and elsewhere for the creation of "czars" in the executive branch to administer programs cutting across agency boundaries. Unfortunately, precisely because they run against the grain of normal bureaucratic practice, czars are easy to create but difficult to sustain and make effective. More systematic attention ought to be given to the czar question and recent experience with it—for example, the use of the vice president to spearhead government-wide efforts in areas such as drugs, or the role of the Strategic Defense Initiative Organization (SDIO) in the Pentagon. Of particular interest is the possibility of czars at the national level with directive and funding authority over operational programs. Such authority is arguably the key to real effectiveness in any area, and is likely to be essential to the success of any high-level interagency committee, perhaps even one chaired by the vice president.

Also worth considering, though, is the possibility of greater devolution of policy development and implementation tasks in certain areas from interagency committees to specific agencies, or even specific offices within agencies. This would have the great merit of assigning clear responsibility for performance, as well as dispensing with much bureaucratic red tape. Of course, it could only be expected to work effectively if coupled with aggressive monitoring and disciplining of the process by political executives in the agencies and the White House.

Finally, there are the organizational remedies proper—reforms in the internal organization and the relationships of the various national security agencies. This is a large subject. A good case can be made, to begin with, that significant if not sweeping changes are needed within State and OSD, particularly as regards the areas of responsibility and the authority of the under secretaries. Clarifying and enhancing the authority of these senior officials would seem highly desirable, if not essential, in any attempt to strengthen strategic and operational planning at State and the Pentagon. One change particularly worth exploring is the creation of new under secretaries for political-military affairs in both buildings to deal with the complex of troublesome issues that tend to fall between these agencies' stools—notably, low-intensity conflict.

Equally important, and certainly long overdue, is a critical examination of the role of the smaller national security agencies as well as the international or security-related components of the domestic agencies. In the public diplomacy area, for example, an excellent case can be made for dismantling the U.S. Information Agency and/or returning key functions to the State Department, perhaps under another newly created under secretary.[12] An argument might be made for rethinking the role of the Arms Control and Disarmament Agency (ACDA), possibly including its merger with the On-Site Inspection Agency newly established within the Department of Defense to monitor the provisions of the U.S.-Soviet treaty on intermediate-range nuclear forces (INF) signed in 1987. Finally, thought should be given to improving the organization of the government for international economic policy. In addition to new (and much needed) coordinating arrangements at the national level, this might include the creation of a new superagency for international trade and development.

Let us return at this point to the question of specific remedies for the problems in the two neuralgic areas of arms control and low-intensity conflict. The bureaucratic problem in the arms control arena is a complex one, and the institutional interests of the various players less obvious than is frequently assumed. Although many imagine that the Defense Department as a whole is institutionally hostile to arms control, this is far from the case, especially among the uniformed military, who have increasingly tended to take the position that arms control is an essentially political matter that is not within their area of competence. In actuality, the overriding institutional concern of the Pentagon in arms control matters is to ensure that prospective agreements do not foreclose important weapons options. This view is entirely compatible with the idea that arms limitation treaties genuinely contribute to U.S. security. The problem with the Pentagon is rather that it tends to take a myopic view of arms control issues and is uninterested in developing a coherent overall approach to arms control or to particular treaty areas. The same problem is evident in the State Department's institutional attitudes toward arms control, though its basis is different. For State, arms control is seen primarily as a tool or adjunct of U.S. diplomacy toward the Soviet Union (as well as our NATO allies), not as an area requiring strategic coherence and policy consistency over time. To the extent that this latter approach has an institutional embodiment within the government, it is the Arms Control and Disarmament Agency. The problem with ADCA, however, is its institutional mandate to promote arms control agreements, which hurts its credibility and reduces further its already very limited bureaucratic clout.

The Pentagon's role in arms control is further complicated by the existence of two separate and essentially coequal representatives of that building, the JCS and the Office of the Secretary of Defense (OSD). In recent years, OSD has taken a leading role within the administration in attempting to define an overall posture or strategy toward arms control, though it has often done so without the full support of the JCS. In addition, the NSC staff has from time to time chosen or been forced to play a similar role, though without enjoying real authority to do so. The result of this bureaucratic fragmentation has too often been confusion, delay, and ad hoc and spasmodic decisionmaking at the top. Particularly since the advent of the Gorbachev era in the Soviet Union, with its fast-paced arms control diplomacy, the U.S. has increasingly found itself out-maneuvered by the Soviets in the public relations aspects of arms control, if not in actual negotiations.

The case for relatively drastic reform of the arms control policy process is almost self-evident. This is an arena of very high policy stakes, high political salience both at home and abroad, and one in which the Soviets hold an innate advantage by virtue of the greater centralization and se-crecy of their decisionmaking processes. It is more difficult to make rec-ommendations for changes here. A special requirement in the arms control area is an effective mechanism at the national level for the consideration and resolution of arms control issues by senior policymakers, given the demanding technical character of these issues and the detail usually neces-sary for addressing them adequately. Though the public record is not clear on this score, it would appear that some progress has been made over the last several years in bringing technical arms control expertise directly to bear at senior policy levels. Nevertheless, there would still seem to be room for improvement—particularly in the highly technical yet politically volatile area of verification and compliance.

However this may be, the core problem in arms control remains the cumbersomeness and fragmentation of authority of the interagency arms control process at lower levels. There are a number of ways this could be remedied. One would be to exclude the JCS and ACDA from interagency arms control committees and give the NSC broad authority to adjudicate State-OSD disagreements. (Under this option, ACDA's role would be re-duced to a more strictly operational one.) A second option would be to give primary responsibility for arms control policy to OSD, with State explicitly limited to dealing with the broad political and diplomatic di-mension of arms control as opposed to substantive detail. A third option would be to give primary responsibility for arms control policy to a greatly strengthened and expanded ACDA. Fourthly, ACDA might be merged wholly or in major part with the State Department, and primary policy responsibility for arms control given to a new Under Secretary of State. Finally, ACDA might be divided between State and OSD, and re-sponsibility for different arms control areas split between these two agen-cies, with OSD receiving U.S.-Soviet nuclear-related arms control matters and State receiving multilateral arms control matters.

It has to be acknowledged that any effort to eliminate ACDA or even significantly reduce its charter is virtually certain to face stiff opposition in

the Congress, and may not be worth the investment of political capital it
would require. But some change in the agency's role might be feasible. A
very useful reform might even involve enhancing ACDA's policy and operational responsibilities—notably, in the area of verification and compliance assessment. Rationalizing the arms control policy process would seem
to merit serious consideration in any event quite apart from this issue.

Turning finally to low-intensity conflict, a few points may be made
about specific organizational or institutional fixes. Several years ago—
ironically, shortly before the breaking of the Iran-Contra scandal—
Congress took some major steps to enhance U.S. capabilities for
low-intensity conflict. The ongoing controversy surrounding the new Special Operations Command and the new position of Assistant Secretary of
Defense for Special Operations and Low-Intensity Conflict are well
known. Less well known is the congressionally mandated Low-Intensity
Conflict Board, supposedly headed by a deputy to the National Security
Adviser. The model for this body seems to have been the Special Group
(Counterinsurgency) of the Kennedy era, which was intended to provide
high-level coordination of U.S. involvement in revolutionary warfare in
Southeast Asia and elsewhere.[13] What is missing, unfortunately, both in
the conception and the implementation of the recent reforms, is precisely
the key insight that led to the creation of that committee—recognition of
the essentially political nature of low-intensity conflict and the need for
full integration of the civilian agencies in the overall U.S. government
effort. The unfortunate identification of low-intensity conflict with special
operations in the recent legislation (and much public discussion of the
subject) has reinforced the notion that insurgency/counterinsurgency warfare is essentially a military problem. As long as this misconception pre-
vails, the NSC Low-Intensity Conflict Board will be stillborn.

The question of the nature of revolutionary warfare of course goes
beyond organization to strategy; but it also highlights the fundamental
organizational problem. An adequate discussion of this question is not
possible here. Suffice it to say that if—as the recent history of the new
U.S. Special Operations Command (USSOCOM) and related changes
strongly suggests—the U.S. military is unwilling or unable to organize
itself to undertake the revolutionary warfare mission, then one of two
things is necessary: either a LIC Board at the national level with a dedicated staff under a czar-like manager with directive and budgetary authority, or a new civilian agency with policy and operational responsibilities
for the full range of U.S. insurgency/counterinsurgency involvements short
of the command of U.S. forces in combat. Either solution would be a
radical one. But the record of U.S. performance in this area makes serious
consideration of solutions of this type long overdue.

As the two cases just discussed clearly demonstrate, the very different histories, policy characteristics, and organizational pathologies of any given national security policy area preclude the possibility of a single administrative remedy to the organizational and management difficulties that continue to face U.S. government officials. Indeed, in some areas fundamental improvement through such methods may not be possible at all—only new policies or people will help. Nevertheless, it would seem that the administrative resources are available to cure real problems, if they are applied with appropriate creativity and determination.

Notes

1. This argument is developed at greater length in my *The Presidency and the Management of National Security* (New York: The Free Press, 1988).

2. See, for example, Strobe Talbott, *Deadly Gambits: The Reagan Administration and the Stalemate in Nuclear Arms Control* (New York: Alfred A. Knopf, 1984).

3. The circumstances surrounding the Reykjavik meeting are authoritatively discussed in *The Reykjavik Process: Preparation for and Conduct of the Iceland Summit and Its Implications for Arms Control Policy*, Report of the Defense Policy Panel, U.S. House of Representatives, Committee on Armed Services, December 15, 1986.

4. Constantine Menges, *Inside the National Security Council* (New York: Simon and Schuster, 1988).

5. A. J. Bacevich, James D. Hallums, Richard H. White, and Thomas F. Young, *American Military Policy in Small Wars: The Case of El Salvador* (Cambridge, MA: Institute for Foreign Policy Analysis, 1988).

6. Consider, for example, the remarks of Gen. Paul F. Gorman, former Commander-in-Chief of the U.S. Southern Command, in *National Security Strategy*, Hearings before the Committee on Armed Services, U.S. Senate, 100th Cong., 1st sess. (Washington, DC: USGPO, 1987), pp. 783–88.

7. On this subject see especially Paul F. Gorman, "Command, Control, Communications and Intelligence: USCINCSO'S Perspective, 1983–85," paper delivered at a conference at the National Defense University, June 25, 1986; and Wallace Nutting, "Organizing for Low-Intensity Warfare," *Global Affairs* (Summer 1987): 92–105.

8. See, for example, Alexander M. Haig, *Caveat: Realism, Reagan, and Foreign Policy* (New York: Macmillan, 1984), pp. 12–13, 58.

9. Highly relevant in this connection is Kenneth deGraffenreid, "Intelligence in the Oval Office," in Roy Godson, ed., *Intelligence Requirements for the 1980's: Intelligence and Policy* (Lexington, MA: Lexington Books, 1986), pp. 9–31.

10. Pertinent observations on this issue may be found, for example, in Edward N. Luttwak, *The Pentagon and the Art of War* (New York: Simon and Schuster, 1984), pp. 157–203.

11. See Ronald H. Hinckley, "National Security in the Information Age," *The Washington Quarterly*, (Spring 1986): 125–39.

12. See Gifford D. Malone, *Political Advocacy and Cultural Communication: Organizing the Nation's Public Diplomacy*, (Lanham, MD: University Press of America, 1988).

13. See, for example, Douglas S. Blaufarb, *The Counterinsurgency Era*, (New York: The Free Fress, 1977), p. 88.

24
Reforming the Procurement Process: Lessons from Recent Experience

Robert T. Marsh

I have adopted the title for this chapter because "reform" is the current buzzword of popular choice when speaking of the Department of Defense's (DOD's) weapon system acquisition process. In my opinion, it has a pejorative connotation. It implies that the DOD acquisition system is ineffective and in need of major overhaul. I do not agree.

The purpose of the acquisition system is to equip our military forces with cost-effective weapon systems and equipment to deter war, and failing that, to defeat the enemy. I believe it has fulfilled this purpose admirably ever since World War II. It has produced, and is producing, the world's finest weapon systems. They are the envy of the world's military forces and are actively sought by all our friends and allies. This nation's deterrent posture has been so effective since World War II that our systems have seldom been challenged in conflict. But those few times that we or our friends have had to use them in battle leave no doubt of their superior capability. I also note that this highly effective deterrent and warfighting capability has been maintained utilizing a declining share of both our gross national product and federal budget since shortly after World War II.

This is not to say that all is right with the acquisition system and that there is no room or need for improvement. This immense enterprise, which dwarfs in size and complexity the largest businesses in the world, has been evolving since World War II—and is still evolving. As the postwar DOD organization took shape, countless acquisition problems were encountered and solved, and lessons were learned. Every administration and Congress since has instituted changes to improve the organization and process. As one might expect, these changes did not always bring about the improvement desired, and in fact sometimes created new problems, more serious than the ones for which cures were intended. A brief review of this evolution is instructive as we look at the system today, to assess recent changes and determine what further improvements are needed.

The acquisition system immediately after World War II and extending through the 1950s was managed independently by the services in a decentralized fashion much as it had been in World War II. Following the DOD Reorganization Act of 1947, broad oversight was instituted by the newly formed Office of the Secretary of Defense (OSD), but the services still advocated their programs to Congress, managed their acquisition efforts independently, and were solely accountable for the results. Thus, common procurement practices and policies among the services, even between the fledgling Air Force and its former parent, the U.S. Army, were rare. Emphasis on unexploited technology resulting from the war efforts posed special difficulties. These technologies offered opportunities for dramatic new capabilities. The services, impressed with the role that technology had played in World War II, and increasingly worried about the growing Soviet threat, pursued these new capabilities aggressively. In a number of cases, more than one service pursued the same or similar capability. Many weapon system "new starts" were undertaken—far more than the services could afford to procure for the inventory.

Additionally, the ability to estimate costs was very poor. Optimism in the services and industry concerning program costs was unconstrained. And, cost growth was almost assured by the widespread use of letter contracts with long-delayed definitization, a practice that can be characterized as "blank check" procurement. This combination of factors resulted in a few real "lemons," a number of high-visibility program cancellations, and substantial cost growth in most programs.

Concern mounted in the Congress and the public over the cancellations, cost growth, and the apparent duplication of many of the service's programs. The response by both the Congress and the administration in the late 1950s and early 1960s was to exert much more management and control over the entire process. Experienced business executives, industrialists, and technocrats were appointed to many of the key posts in the upper levels of the DOD and charged with organizing the Department's acquisition efforts in a more business-like fashion. Congress strengthened its oversight by expanding the number of committees overseeing the DOD's activities, increasing the depth of staff surveillance, and scrutinizing the DOD's budget requests in greater detail.

If the word "reform" is applicable to any period in the evolution of the acquisition process, it is this period from the late 1950s to the late 1960s. It was, though, reform mainly of the organizations and activities above the execution level of the process, that is, above the services' acquisition management organizations and their program offices. For throughout the 1950s, the services had been steadily reshaping their system development and acquisition organizations and refining their system procurement and management techniques. In fact, the highly successful ballistic missile programs and a number of other weapon system programs of the late 1950s and early 1960s are testimony of the fairly advanced state of systems acquisition management at the time.

The changes put into place in OSD represented a profound change in the upper-level management of the acquisition business. A formalized system of OSD weapon system program reviews and milestone approval was instituted. A systems analysis and evaluation capability was formed to address system utility, force structure, and weapon system trade-offs. A formalized and highly structured planning, programming, and budgeting system (PPBS) was established to produce a balanced, DOD-wide, five-year defense program. Collectively these changes represented a major centralization and consolidation of control of acquisition efforts in OSD. And, of course, the services responded by strengthening their top-level civilian and military acquisition management staffs accordingly. Unquestionably, these changes produced substantial improvement in a number of weak areas as mentioned, however, they also gave rise to some significant new problems.

The implementation of the program review and milestone approval system created a new bureaucracy and detailed procedures which slowed the acquisition process and lengthened the weapon system acquisition cycle considerably. Also, it created a fertile environment for micromanagement of the acquisition programs by people far removed from the program execution level and all levels in between. The systems analysis and evaluation organization became highly influential in weapon system definition and selection and, at times, granted more weight to cost-effectiveness than military judgment. And the PPBS system produced a fine-grain composition of the DOD budget, which was seized upon by the Congressional staffs as a ready-made spreadsheet for Congressional microattention and micromanipulation.

At the same time, the acquisition agencies of the services were vigorously pursuing improvements of their system management practices. To cope with cost growth, increased attention was placed on risk assessment in the early phases of programs. Risk reduction was made an essential feature of program planning and structuring. Concurrency of the acquisition phases was analyzed and guidelines for program structuring were developed. Prototyping was stressed as a preferred approach to risk reduction. Major efforts were made to improve cost estimating, including development of databases and models, special training programs, and independent peer reviews. The use of letter contracts was drastically curtailed, and early definitization was mandated. Cost-reimbursement contracts were restricted to high-risk undertakings. Incentive-type contracts rewarding lower costs and increased quality and performance were structured. Scheduling tools were developed. Configuration management methods were refined and formalized. Contractor data submittal requirements were defined and tailoring methods developed. Procedures were developed to track contractor cost and performance to provide early warning of developing problems. In summary, by the end of the 1960s, formalized, advanced methods and procedures had been developed in all of the disciplines of acquisition management required at the execution level.

Unfortunately, most changes, no matter how beneficial, also carry costs, and there were several unexpected consequences of these improvements of the 1960s. The formalized management practices and tools developed for use of the program offices were picked up by higher levels, expanded and made more detailed, and imposed as required practices for all acquisition activities. Congress even incorporated some of these practices in statutes. This followed from the mistaken belief that a standard management scheme was optimum for all programs regardless of their different characteristics. Reporting requirements were established to permit higher staff levels to track program progress. Many of the newly established contractor reports and data submittals were requested by higher level staffs, thereby giving them the same management information available to the program manager. This facilitated detailed scrutiny, meddling, and micromanagement by all levels, further eroded the authority and responsibility of the program manager, and generated new opportunities for cost growth and schedule slippages. Also, the application of these many management and reporting requirements was viewed by industry as an unwarranted encroachment by the government into its internal management, and as creating a large, costly, and unproductive paperwork burden.

As we entered the 1970s, the new OSD leaders recognized that centralization and the concomitant micromanagement by all levels had proceeded too far. Mr. David Packard, then the Deputy Secretary of Defense, moved out in a highly visible manner to reverse it. A fundamental of his approach was to give program managers the authority commensurate with their responsibility for system acquisition. His stated philosophy was to give program managers much freer rein—then reward successful managers and deal firmly with unsuccessful ones. He attempted to overcome micromanagement by streamlining direction and reporting channels, and he insisted that program managers be given flexibility to tailor their contracting approach, management approach, and management systems to the unique demands of their programs. Additionally, he initiated important improvements in professional training and qualification of the acquisition work force. In short, he made a major, albeit temporary, move to decentralization. The movement lost momemtum—and in fact reversed—after Mr. Packard's departure.

Cost growth was still headline news well into the 1970s, even though some of the more celebrated cases were programs initiated years earlier. Several of these, including the C-5 and F-111 aircraft programs, might be called management experiments directed by the upper-level acquisition management staffs. Additionally, much of the cost growth was caused by program instability and stretchouts resulting from the fiscal demands of the Vietnam War and later in the decade, by the declining defense budget and double-digit inflation.

Nevertheless, OSD fixed on unrealistically low initial cost estimates as a prime cause of cost growth. An independent cost analysis group was formed to review program managers' cost estimates and the services' independent cost analyses of those estimates. This new organization had the authority to revise program estimates if deemed necessary. There is no doubt that the change forced increased attention to program cost estimates; whether it improved their quality is a matter of conjecture.

Congress joined the effort and made independent cost analyses a matter of law, even specifying their frequency—and imposed a comprehensive cost and performance reporting system on the DOD. The cost and performance estimates for all major systems had to be reported quarterly—from the first development estimates through production. Additionally, Congress legislated strict measures for dealing with variances from those estimates.

The press also seized on a number of performance deficiencies in new generation systems entering the inventory in the late 1960s and early 1970s. They echoed critics' contentions that more rigorous testing should have uncovered these problems earlier. Special attention was focused on reliability and maintainability problems. In response, OSD and the services formed new independent test agencies—independent, that is, from the acquisition agency and the program manager. The OSD was given the authority to review and approve program test plans. This new thrust did result in more thorough and realistic testing, and it garnered needed support for improved testing facilities and capabilities. On the other hand, it further eroded the program manager's authority, stretched the weapon system acquisition cycle even more, and highlighted complex testing issues and test results for scrutiny and debate by a public generally ill-equipped to understand the issues. Congress followed this development closely and made the organization, conduct, and reporting of weapon system testing matters of law.

Finally, to appreciate the status of the acquisition process of the 1970s, we must address personnel. The badly lagging government pay scales in the mid-to-late 1970s, the trend back to centralized management, increasing micromanagement, and the unfavorable publicity targeted at the acquisition community caused an exodus of experienced mid- and senior-level managers. Consequently, program offices were left with mostly junior people who lacked experience in the complex and demanding business of acquisition management.

And so as we entered the 1980s, the weapon system acquisition process in place to support the aggressive modernization efforts of the Reagan administration was mature and capable. It was, however, still managed in a highly centralized manner, and subject to ever increasing scrutiny, regulation, and control by the Congress. It was characterized by micromanagement at all levels, and was manned by fewer experienced acquisition professionals than required. Cost growth had been exacerbated by the budget-induced program stretchouts and double-digit inflation of the late 1970s, and was still a high visibility topic. Past budget pressures had resulted in inadequate funding to support the weapon systems in the field; consequently, operational readiness and sustainability were suffering badly. I should add that this lack of readiness was misinterpreted and exploited by some as indicative of unduly complex and overly sophisticated weapon systems incapable of being adequately operated and maintained by our service personnel. The real problem was the lack of adequately funded logistic support.

As the new administration advocated its major modernization program, it recognized that it needed to "tune up" the acquisition system as much as possible as it embarked on the buildup. A thorough bottom-up assessment of the system was undertaken, and thirty-two initiatives for improvement were identified. These became known as the Carlucci Initiatives. They represented a consensus of the most knowledgeable people in the acquisition community at the time. They covered the gamut from competition, multiyear procurement, baselining, estimating, budgeting, and contracting to centralizing policy and decentralizing execution to logistics support and personnel training and selection. In the main, they were not newly identified weaknesses, but areas where further improvement appeared practical, and which promised high payoff. In my opinion, only two of these initiatives highlighted newly identified weaknesses—program instability and the poor state of the industrial base. Several analyses had been completed shortly before that showed in quantitative terms the staggering costs of program stretchout and production at less than economical rates. Likewise, recent studies of the industrial base had highlighted the very long lead times required to surge defense production, the increasing dependency of our weapon systems on foreign materials and components, the lagging manufacturing productivity in the defense industry, and the limited capability of the lower tier supplier base. Program instability was increasingly recognized as a major inhibitor of contractor capital investment. Further, it directly degraded the health of the supplier base. Program stability was thus elevated to the top of the initiatives list. And multi-year procurement, which can produce important savings, but also promote program stability was stressed. Special emphasis was placed on these two initiatives. I believe that good progress was made with most of the thirty-two initiatives, however, the initial progress with program stability was short-lived, and very few gains were made in the health of the industrial base.

Concurrently, but separate from the Carlucci Initiatives, the new administration launched a major government-wide campaign targeted at "fraud, waste, and abuse." New organizations and councils were set up and charged with the program's execution and oversight. "Hot lines" were established, and the program was given wide publicity. There is no doubt that more malpractices were uncovered than there would have been without this initiative. However, the publicity given resulting revelations was detrimental to careful improvement of the system. Although intended to portray a government carefully guarding the taxpayer's dollar, this publicity produced just the opposite effect.

In cases involving DOD acquisition, the findings were given front-page press coverage, but that coverage failed to communicate that these problems were uncovered by the DOD and were being dealt with by the DOD. This led to highly publicized hearings by Congress and much to-be-expected "remedial" legislation. Among other matters, the legislation strengthened the role and responsibility of the DOD Inspector General, shifted the authority for determining allowability of contractor costs from the contracting officer to the auditors, delineated specific unallowable contractor costs, and mandated contractor certification with regard to such costs. More importantly, though, the publicity weakened the public's confidence in the DOD acquisition process and in the ethics and efficiency of the defense industry. Ultimately, it undermined public support for continuation of the defense buildup. The resulting downward budget adjustments created a new wave of program instability—the root cause of so many problems in the past.

Soon thereafter another bombshell burst—the spare parts scandal involving such items as high-priced toilet seats and coffee pots. In retrospect, we should keep in mind that these incidents were uncovered by the DOD, that many cases were the result of cost allocation practices and were not actual overchargings, that many of the cases were the direct result of very small buys after a hiatus of production, and that the DOD obtained restoration in most cases of actual, and even perceived, over-pricing.

True, there were cases of actual price gouging, but they were few in number. As I noted, the DOD uncovered the problems and set out aggressively to fix them. The services thoroughly investigated each incident and the spare parts procurement process in general, and instituted a wide range of corrective measures. Despite its best efforts, though, the DOD could not retain control and put the matter to rest. The media would not relent and Congressional committees moved out aggressively with extensive hearings. Congress settled on open competition as the panacea, and followed with numerous pieces of legislation to effect that solution.

At this point I would stress that the scandal involved spare parts procurement, a specialized activity quite different from weapon system acquisition. An initial supply of spares is usually acquired as part of the weapon system acquisition, but the procurement responsibility for follow-on supplies is then shifted to those responsible for supporting the weapon system in the field. In the case of the Air Force—the principal target of the scandal—the logistics centers, or depots, perform this role. As the media and Congress addressed the problem, though, the focus of remedial action shifted subtly from spare parts procurement to the subject of procurement in general, and finally to weapon system acquisition. This, then, explains the ensuing legislation directing two competing sources for major weapon systems, directing establishment of Competition Advocates for all acquisition, and the coverage of the Competition in Contracting Act for all acquisitions.

As a footnote, and as one might guess, the increased competitive procurement of spare parts is not without its drawbacks. It is obviously manpower-intensive, complicates warranty matters, and because it takes longer, can adversely affect readiness. Further, there are already several celebrated cases of defective spare parts provided by low-cost but low-quality suppliers.

The spare parts scandal had whipped the reform movement into a frenzy, and the administration came to the conclusion that it could not be quieted. The administration had to seize the initiative. The response was the Packard Commission. It is ironic that the critical event leading to the creation of the Packard Commission was the spare parts scandal, a problem of procurement execution, but that the Commission charter, as it finally evolved, dealt with such macro issues as the organization of the Joint Chiefs of Staff (JCS), military command and control, development of national strategy, the role of the commanders-in-chief of the combatant commands in the requirements process, the Congressional budgetary process, and industry ethics. This broad focus can be attributed to the administration's desire to fold into the Commission charter the major ongoing public and Congressional concerns arising from the Iranian rescue attempt; the Grenada operation; the fraud, waste, and abuse revelations; and the debate on the role of the Chairman of the JCS. As a result, the Commission devoted most of its attention to these broader issues and spent little time on the execution aspects of the acquisition process.

There were, of course, important recommendations aimed at improving the higher level management of the acquisition process. The Commission recommended consolidating the many diverse activities of the OSD staff into a newly created position of Under Secretary of Defense for Acquisition (USD/A), creating in effect a "czar" for DOD acquisition. It also recommended the creation of a Vice-Chairman of the Joint Chiefs of Staff to provide a stronger JCS voice in weapon system requirements, especially joint service requirements, and represent the views of the commanders-in-chief of the combatant commands on weapon system requirements, priorities, and resource allocation. It echoed earlier recommendations for adoption of a two-year DOD budget, and Congressional authorization of weapon system acquisition only at the two key milestones of full-scale development and high rate production. It emphasized program stability, baselining, and increased use of commercial products.

A more controversial recommendation, which was not as well supported, was the streamlining of the reporting hierarchy above the program manager within the services. The Commission was fixated on a maximum of two reporting officials, or layers, between the program manager and the to-be-created USD/A. The logic or origin of the specific two-layer reporting recommendation is not clear. It may have been to pressure the Army and Air Force to emulate the recently restructured Navy system since the elimination of the Naval Material Command, or it may have followed from observations of some successful industrial operations. However, while this made for good press, in my many years of working with industry, I have not observed this minimal reporting structure very often, nor seen a strong correlation between it and program success.

However, this was an obvious attempt to reduce layering and the attendant micromanagement, and hence had merit in that regard. But it required the Air Force and the Army to alter their organizational and reporting arrangements considerably to accommodate the change in ways that, in my opinion, are inconsistent with good management principles. Specifically, it presented those two services with the choice of altering their development and acquisition organizational structure or creating a new program management reporting chain separate from the acquisition organization's command and control. They reluctantly chose the latter.

At the time of this writing, it has been over two and a half years since issuance of the executive order implementing the Commission's recommendations, and passage of the complementary Goldwater-Nichols legislation. The new organizations and management procedures are still evolving. I believe that most experts will agree that the creation of the new USD/A has to this date resulted in little perceptible improvement in top level OSD management of the acquisition process. A highly structured committee and board structure bureaucracy has been created to support the new office. The total staff has not been substantially reduced, no fewer briefings are required, the time to obtain milestone decisions has not been reduced, and program managers see little reduction in micromanagement. A two-year DOD budget is no nearer realization, Congressional manipulation and micromanagement have not slackened, and program stability has not been enhanced. And, despite increased study and discussion, the industrial base is no stronger.

This brings us to the present. I have no priviledged information on the emerging new scandal involving consultants and certain present and former acquisition officials. I can only urge that it be kept in perspective, although I am not optimistic that this is possible. It appears that this is another instance of the DOD uncovering some suspected wrongdoing and aggressively pursuing the matter. If government officials are found to have accepted bribes or favors for government information, or to have been improperly influenced in their official capacities, or if others have attempted to influence government officials improperly, then they have committed criminal acts and should be dealt with accordingly. But it is premature to conclude that some weakness in the acquisition process encourages criminal conduct—anymore than banking procedures encourage embezzlement.

However, I feel that, after all the facts are known, a review of the process is appropriate to determine if any areas require strengthening. For example, there is speculation that the "Best and Final Offer" process promotes industrial espionage and invites improper auctioneering on the part of government personnel bent on forcing costs down. It might even be determined that the elimination of a layer in the Navy's acquisition hierarchy reduced certain checks and balances below a desired minimum. If confirmed, these are easy matters to correct. But this is speculation, and there should be no knee-jerk reaction until the investigation has run its course. One matter of serious concern, though, is that the increased involvement of Congress in detailed acquisition decisions obviously invites industry and others to attempt to influence such decisions. I see no remedy for this other than withdrawal of the Congress from such decisions.

What, then, can we conclude about the state of the acquisition process today? I believe that the DOD acquisition process is basically sound, and still produces the best military capabilities in the world. The "horror stories" regarding spare parts, overhead charges, and isolated fraudulent incidents are blown far out of proportion and are not indicative of fundamental weaknesses in the process. The continuing stream of "reform" legislation and regulation is not only misdirected and unnecessary, but will serve to further complicate—perhaps even suffocate—an already badly overregulated and overmanaged process.

I can think of no single change that would have more beneficial effect on the acquisition process than a longer-term Congressional and administration commitment, and accompanying funding support, to a given defense program. Only such long-term stability will bring out the best of U.S. industry in terms of keen competition, labor-saving capital investment, acquisition and retention of top talent, and quantum advances in efficiency and productivity. A cooperative initiative between Congress and the administration for such change would have a dramatic effect on the acquisition process, both in industry and government.

Basic to the success of any complex human endeavor is the principle of delegation of responsibility with commensurate authority. The DOD and service directives stress the importance of this principle to the acquisition process, but day-to-day practice does not reflect it. Programs are still subject to too many formal and informal reviews by all echelons, including the Congress, which produce innumerable changes and redirections, many of which have significant impact on costs and schedules, but lack acknowledged accountability. There is a compelling need to insulate program managers from outside meddling and micromanagement and to institutionalize the delegation of necessary authority and responsibility. Such change can and should be implemented by both the administration and the Congress—and should be effected without the usual resort to reorganization.

The health of the industrial base is a profoundly complex matter. At the risk of overgeneralization, the defense industry suffers from insufficient capital investment resulting in excessive tough labor, and hence, less than desired quality and productivity. This, in turn, leads to unduly high costs for our weapon systems, as well as reduced international competitiveness. These weaknesses exist throughout the prime and lower tiers of the industry.

Ironically, there is generally an overcapacity in a number of areas at the prime supplier level but a shortage of qualified suppliers for many critical materials and components in the lower tiers. The industry is increasingly reaching out to foreign countries to obtain needed materials and components—with the primary objective of cutting costs. The specifics of this practice throughout the various tiers of the industry are not known, but it is widespread and sure to be creating an ever increasing dependency on such foreign sources.

These weaknesses raise two principal concerns. Will an industry characterized by such lagging capital investment be able to develop and produce affordable, yet ever more technologically advanced, weapon systems needed in the future? And can this industry, especially considering its lower-tier limitations and dependency upon foreign sources, fulfill the nation's potential surge and mobilization requirements? These concerns are currently being studied by Congress, the USD/A, and by such independent organizations as the Air Force Association. It is clear that changes in acquisition practices alone will not constitute a panacea. A cooperative, broad-based, sustained effort of the Congress, the administration, and industry is required. We must get it under way.

Finally, the proper attention to personnel in support of the acquisition process is critical. Major difficulties still exist in attracting and retaining quality personnel to carry out this vital mission. The changes discussed above will contribute to increasing the attractiveness of this career area for both military officers and civilians. But much more needs to be done. Pay comparability with civilian counterparts must be achieved and maintained. The image of the civil servant must be elevated to match his and her real worth to government and society. Civilian system procurement positions must be professionalized. Career paths in acquisition management must be developed for civilians. Opportunities for high-grade civilian positions in system acquisition management must be increased. Military careers in system acquisition must be accorded equal status and promotion opportunity with other career areas. Revolving-door restrictions must be narrowly focused to prohibit only true conflict-of-interest situations. They should then be rigidly enforced. Special efforts must be made to recruit highly qualified personnel with business and industrial experience for political appointment to the senior management positions in the DOD acquisition hierarchy. The well-known barriers to this goal must be mitigated. Since this activity of such vital importance to our national security and is of such interest to the public and the Congress, it surely deserves to be manned with the highest quality force possible. A perfect process will not yield good results without good people.

In summary, the overall acquisition process is profoundly complex, but it works and produces good results. There is obviously room and need for improvement to yield even better results. The administration, working with the Congress, must strive for a well-conceived, stable, longer-term defense program. Increased emphasis is required on implementing the principle of centralized policy formulation and decentralized execution, both in the Congress and the administration. Special attention must be given to attracting and retaining top quality personnel at all levels, but especially at the execution level. Finally, based upon this historical review of the evolution of the acquisition process to date, all are well advised to thoroughly evaluate each proposed improvement to assure that it addresses a true deficiency rather than a symptom, and that it is likely to produce the desired improvement without undesireable side effects.

25
Toward a Long-term Integrated National Security Strategy for the United States

Michael A. Freney

L ast summer, fifty years after Hitler began terrifying the world, I sat comfortably in a club in a stylish European capital with the head of one of the leading strategic research institutes there. After amenities, my host began conversation. "Talking with an American about strategy," he said, "is like having a conversation about sex with a seminarian." I replied with a question. "George Marshall?" After choking on his fine Cuban cigar, swallowing hard, and ordering another drink, my companion launched again. Interestingly, he turned the conversation not to 1939, 1941, or 1945, but toward 1992 and beyond.

As we talked, it became apparent that we agreed on three simple propositions, none of them new, all of them prevalent in Marshall's thinking, as essential qualities of a useful long-term strategy in today's world. First, strategy must combine military and economic considerations with dynamic appreciation of political will in democracies. Second, successful strategy must be based more on cooperation than competition among allied nations (to say nothing of individual military services). Third, strategy must explicitly include attention not just to military preparedness but especially to improvement in the quality of human life.

Those struggling to think about and build strategy today may quickly observe that these three agreed conclusions are typical products of discussion over brandy and cigars rather than significant observations on the difficulties our policymakers face. I would counter that it is necessary, although hardly sufficient, to reflect upon those three qualities of mean-

The views expressed here are those of the author and do not necessarily reflect the views of the Department of Defense or of any other agency of the United States government. Whatever merit exists in the ideas that follow proceeds in substantial measure from deliberations in 1988 and 1987 with Dr. Robert Hunter, Director of European Studies, Center for Strategic and International Studies; Dr. Geoffrey Kemp, Senior Associate, Carnegie Endowment for International Peace; and General W. Y. Smith, U.S.A.F. (Ret.), President, Institute for Defense Analysis. The four proposals, along with any absurdities, inconsistencies, and inadequacies are my own.

ingful strategy before proceeding to the more difficult work of trying to build a long-term integrated national security strategy for the United States.

Indeed, it is useful to establish early whether or not those toiling toward such a strategy are building on a common base. Put another way, it is useful to parse the problem presented in the title of this chapter. The discussion that follows is intended to be suggestive rather than definitive. In the worst tradition of the U.S. defense establishment, it is written substantially "to specification." The designated objective of the piece is to provide grounds for discussion of the desirability, practicability, and sustainability of a long-term integrated national security strategy for the United States. Hopefully some of the points raised will lead to a clarification of assumptions underlying strategic discussion. With that objective in mind, and with great risk of appearing or being pedantic, attention to concepts is in order.

Key Concepts

Strategy

In the context of present discussion, the most important observation about the nature of strategy is that it is a process, not an event. The heart of the process consists in reconciling objectives and capabilities. Statements of strategy should not be confused with strategy as a process. The President's annual report, *National Security Strategy of the United States*, the recent Iklé/Wohlstetter document *Discriminate Deterrence*, the Lehman-touted maritime strategy, and so forth, are snapshots reflecting the point of view of the photographers. In reality, though, strategy is a moving picture.

That is not to say that such statements are unimportant. On the contrary, they are critical events, essential ingredients in the process of focusing attention on objectives and capabilities, building public support for programs and policies, and reconciling the gaps which will continue to exist between our conception of national security and the resources and determination we apply in pursuit of that goal.

National Security Strategy

Those who define national security, a critical objective, as the capacity to prevent or defeat military aggression focus upon factors too narrow and too few to guarantee achievement of broad national objectives. If we regard international politics as who gets what in terms of trouble and treasure in our highly interdependent international environment, we see that national security involves not only the capacity to resist military pressures but also the determination to consistently improve the quality of human life.

The capacity to balance threat against opportunity in a forward-looking way is the essence of Marshall's genius before World War II, throughout its course, and in its wake. It is the basis upon which the present security and prosperity of the free world rests.

Integrated National Security Strategy

In the 1980s, national security concepts require integration along at least three dimensions. Robert Schumann and Jean Monnet foresaw and indeed demonstrated that integration of economic interests among nations can lead not only toward reduction of tensions among traditional adversaries but toward sustained improvement in the quality of life in populations previously plagued by war. The processes they set in motion have not eliminated competition, but the potential for outright conflict on the basis of national disagreements has been substantially reduced. Cooperation within NATO, broad enough to envelop France's roguish behavior, is a quality that we should celebrate and that potential adversaries should treat with respect, if not necessarily apprehension.

Within nation-states, integration of the political, economic, and military elements in national policy becomes increasingly important. One can separate political capabilities, economic capabilities, and military capabilities only in the abstract. They are inevitably and irrevocably interwoven. It is a challenge to the policymaker to be able to understand the interrelationships among those factors and to be able to explain those interrelationships in a way in which political support for defense programs can be mobilized.

The third dimension along which strategic thinking must be integrated is more purely political. A vital, realistic, and productive strategic process depends upon input not only from leaders of governments, but from bureaucratic institutions, from universities, from industry, from the professions, and from the latent wisdom in our citizenry that democratic theory explicitly acknowledges.

But strategy cannot exist in the world of ideas alone. It must proceed from a marriage of ideas with the capacity to build and implement policies. Institutions and individuals like those who were instrumental in commissioning this work and contributing to its content are in a unique position to augment national capabilities to integrate on all three and among all three of the dimensions identified.

Long-Term Integrated National Security Strategy

Nowhere in strategy is the tension between the practical and the theoretical more evident than in trying to determine the meaning of "long term." Economists and technologists, to say nothing of politicians, have proved themselves gloriously inept at establishing the periodicity of change. It is useful, by default perhaps, to fall back on human biology and concentrate on two generations forward as a realistic planning window. In asking ourselves where we want to be in terms of trouble and treasure forty years from now, we will surely have provided enough of a challenge to stimulate thought. Simultaneously, given the pace of technological change, including improvements in information systems, a forty-year threshhold is not totally unrealistic. It conveniently captures two design-to-production cycles for complicated systems like aircraft. It allows fairly reliable demographic forecasting, barring major catastrophe. It even corresponds to the U.S. election cycle. In any case, if there is no philosophical virtue in such a choice, at least it is a blatant statement of assumption from which one might proceed.

Dilemmas

The inherent difficulty in trying to look forward forty years, much less determine a desired state of affairs, is complicated even further in the United States by a variety of factors. Some of those are outlined briefly below.

Confidence and Uncertainty

Sustained U.S. involvement in the great sweep of world affairs is recent. Popular confidence in our ability as a nation to develop and pursue realistic objectives is transitory at best. Uncertainty is viewed as the single constant in world affairs. Our inability to confidently predict the future accentuates a serious tendency among many Americans to shrink from what Geoffrey Kemp has described as "an angry, ungrateful world."

Threat and Opportunity

The difficulty for the United States in anticipating future threats becomes glaringly clear if one reflects upon the wide divergence in popular and expert perceptions of recent developments. Gorbachev's intentions and future prospects, the meaning of the continuing Soviet buildup in conventional forces, or the likely future course of the Communist Nicaraguan regime are topics that can start an argument in even the most civilized and informed circles.

On the opportunity side, there is no agreement on the desirability of better economic relations with the Soviet Union and its satellites. Indeed, how we attempt to mend trade rifts with Japan or deal with the advent of inter-European cooperation in 1992 are issues that create difficulties not only within our decisionmaking bodies but within business, academia, and the populace at large.

Strengths and Weaknesses

Whether we in the United States label circumstances in the international environment as threats or opportunities depends in substantial measure on how we perceive our own strengths and weaknesses. Most Americans concerned with national security agree that one of our major strengths is the commonality of values that we enjoy with our principal allies. We also continue to enjoy major leverage in the realm of defense policy, military capability, and economic affairs.

In the economic dimension, however, Americans in general and decisionmakers in particular are viewing with increasing alarm the decline in relative economic influence of the United States on a global basis. Indeed, there are those who argue that by carping on our decreased ability to dominate in world economic affairs we are establishing a self-fulfilling prophecy that will deprive the United States of the kind of influence it requires to pursue a better quality of life for our own people.

Still others argue that we have weakened ourselves by consumer spending, failure to save, failure to invest in long-term research and development, and other economic choices to the point where our former friends will quickly move to take advantage of us. Some see military capability and the capacity to expand economically as opposed to one another in a zero-sum fashion. These wide divergences of opinion about our basic political, economic, and military postures contribute to disagreement over the nature of threat, the existence of opportunity, and the ability to confidently set and pursue goals in today's and tomorrow's world environment.

Strategic Coherence and Political Pluralism

A process to reconcile objectives with capabilities is, of course, much more efficient when there can be clear goal setting by a relatively centralized authority. In the United States, constitutionally, the responsibility for setting goals is not clearly defined. Most importantly, the responsibility for developing capabilities is, at best, shared, and at its most inefficient, divided between the executive and legislative branches of the government. Further, neither of those branches can ignore the competing pulls of foreign affairs against requirements for domestic policies and programs. Institutionally, then, the United States labors under burdens not altogether so constraining to parliamentary democracies when they attempt to develop and sustain a long-term integrated national security strategy.

Consistency and Pragmatism

Ideally, a long-term strategy should allow for reorientation as goals and capabilities change. Simultaneously, it should be broad enough to make such reorientations necessary only infrequently. The history of the United States in world affairs, however, has been one in which shifts in direction sometimes have been quite rapid and in which the capacity to mobilize capabilities has been ignored until crisis is imminent.

There is widespread recognition in the United States, both in the policy community and among the population at large, that we will no longer be able to maintain our position in world affairs if we fail to maintain a credible defense posture. There is, nevertheless, a national tendency, evident in the arts, business, education, and most evidently in politics and policy, to pay the most attention to the most immediate problems. Whatever the cultural roots of that prediliction, Americans are not inclined to plan far ahead. Longer term diplomatic, defense, and economic policies are therefore endemically more difficult to formulate, sustain, and execute.

In spite of all these difficulties, few Americans dispute the desirability of trying to plan ahead. Most Americans will support well articulated positions and programs developed by their leaders. Americans appreciate fast results. They are also violently intolerant of long-term disappointments. Nonetheless, they are usually optimistic.

National Values and the International Environment

Commerce and telecommunications are bringing home to an increasing number of Americans the interconnectedness among their own personal standards of living, the health and welfare of the nation collectively, and the general state of affairs in the international environment. This is not to say that intense effort to educate Americans about our nation's place in the world is not increasingly essential. Indeed, our appalling ignorance of geography is a most telling symptom of the need for education in world affairs.

More important, however, there exists at this juncture an opportunity for leaders in the United States to define our national interests in broad political, economic, and military terms that average Americans can understand. How should our leaders proceed to attempt this?

The values that dominate our pursuit of national security should be consistent with the values we pursue in our domestic environment. Politically, economically, and militarily, we must seek safety, security, well-being, and an improved quality of life not only for our own people but, to the degree that it is possible, for the people who pursue values common to ours.

In short, when we choose friends and adversaries, our choices should reflect our views on the importance of individual rights, democratic philosophy, free market economics, and the territorial integrity and legal equalities of states. We should throw our support to international organizations and nation-states that share those preferences. We should be prepared to oppose, if necessary with force of arms, those who would attack such values. We should reward pursuit of and adherence to the values we favor, and make clear our displeasure with those who do not actively pursue them.

Priorities

We should make clear on a continuing basis the priorities among our own values. Clearly, the physical safety and survival of the United States is the primary value. We must maintain strategic and conventional capabilities that deter potential adversaries. Simultaneously, we should seek every opportunity to reduce the risk of war, and not just war involving ourselves and our friends. Peaceful resolution of conflict is not only in the interest of our own national security in its broadest sense, but it is also consistent with our fundamental values, as outlined above.

Along with reducing the risk of war, we should attempt wherever possible to reduce the cost of defense. By so doing, we allow ourselves to increase the possibility of greater benefit from open economic and financial transactions in a free international environment.

Broad and repeated statements of our values and priorities serve a variety of useful functions, the most important of which is to build and sustain a consensus behind our leaders with respect to foreign policy and to illustrate the connection between sound foreign policy and the quality of life at home. Reiteration of these basics, while boring to some specialists, is a necessary tonic for our people against demagoguery and harebrained schemes to manipulate in the international arena. It is also a means of reassuring our allies and keeping our potential opponents on notice. We need not be so explicit as to invite challenge. We can be forthright and positive short of that.

Problems

While fundamental values should change very slowly and while objectives and priorities will shift somewhat more quickly, a variety of problems will constantly change their content and portent. A long-term strategy will hopefully place great emphasis on those problems that are most persistent. An example would be the ideological competition between the Soviet Union and the United States, along with its diplomatic, economic, and military manifestations. Another problem would be the serious strains along all three of those dimensions that exist in so-called North-South relations. A third problem would be the tensions that always exist between economic competition on the one hand and cooperation on the other. Specific problems which change more rapidly should be dealt with in a variety of policymaking fora, but in a fashion consistent with the values, priorities, and problems identified in a long-term strategy.

Opportunities

Similarly, the capacity of the United States, alone or with its allies and friends, to shape the international environment should focus on long-term trends that we can affect to the betterment of all. A long-term strategy would seek to identify how we might spread the benefit of industrial advancement, technological know-how, medical knowledge and practice, and forms of political organization in ways designed to make the world a less threatening place. This is not an argument for social engineering on a global scale. It is an argument for testing policy decisions and programmatic behaviors. They should be tested for consistency among themselves but, more importantly, for consistency with goals and priorities identified in long-term strategy.

In line with the notion that strategy is a process, testing for consistency must be an ongoing practice in the policy arena. Here are some suggestions on how to build a long-term integrated national security strategy that lends itself to constant review and that can guide policies and programs.

A Four-Part Proposal

The dilemmas faced by the United States in our attempt to develop and sustain a long-term strategy will never be completely overcome. There is, however, an opportunity to come to grips with some of the difficulties in the process of developing and prioritizing goals and applying resources against them.

Presidential Council on Strategy

First, the Executive Branch could be well served by emulating the example set by the President's Foreign Intelligence Advisory Board. That diverse group of talented people, all of them removed from the daily pressures of policymaking and resource allocation, but all experienced in different ways in affairs of state and in some cases the details of intelligence, provide a kind of sounding board against which policy decisions can be tested.

It is possible for the President of the United States to take a lead by establishing a Presidential Council on Strategy as a standing body. Unlike the short-lived Kissinger Commission or the Scowcroft Commission, such a body, composed of a dozen individuals not presently in government but with extensive experience, appointed for three-year terms, and combining expertise in foreign and domestic affairs, intelligence, science, and public communication, and supported by a small staff, could focus upon the considerations outlined above at the expense of attention to all except the most expensive and longest range policy and program decisions. The aim of such a group would be to articulate long-term national security objectives and provide the president with guidance quietly, outside the existing policymaking channels.

By rotating membership so that four counselors are appointed each year, continuity could be established to avoid severe problems faced by changes of administration. Similarly, because two-thirds of the group will have served together for at least two years during each annual series of meetings, there will be a continuity in thinking that is essential in long-term strategy. Simultaneously, there will be an infusion of new blood each year. Obviously, the group will have to be bipartisan, especially to assure transition across changes of administration when succeeding presidents are from different parties. Similarly, private reporting to the president is essential if the group is not to deteriorate into just another debating society in which party positions are aired. Lastly, some of the members of the group should be old. A person trying to plan forty years ahead who has less than twenty years of work behind him is unlikely to be as effective, in most instances, as an individual whose career has spanned several decades.

Joint Congressional Committee on Strategy

Again, in the interest of continuity and bipartisanship, it should be possible to build a Joint Congressional Committee on Strategy, which would draw senior members of Congress expert on political, economic, and military matters. If the membership of that committee were limited once again to about twelve people, four from the Senate and eight from the

House, and if there could be some bipartisan flexibility (which current long-term incumbency in the House would favor), a three-year term could be applied to the Congressional group as well.

By concentrating upon questions and considerations with substantial half-life, rather than upon details of appropriation and authorization, such a group might contribute significantly to the quality of normally fractious Congressional debate on a variety of policies and programs that, taken together, presently represent "strategic resource allocation." An annual report by such a committee, in which no minority or dissenting opinions would be permitted, might also provide extraordinarily useful guidance to those in the Executive Branch trying to develop and execute policies and programs.

Council on Global Concerns

The chairman of the President's Council and the ranking Republican and Democratic members of the Joint Committee could appoint a third body, which would have an extraordinarily challenging but very important task. The Council on Global Concerns would bring to bear, in an institutional way, empathy for our allies and friends and appreciation of the positions of our potential adversaries on a variety of long-term strategic issues. A dozen distinguished individuals chosen from among business leaders, academics, former members of the diplomatic and military services, the media, and even from the arts, could apply their extensive experience in dealing with principal allies or with adversaries to inform strategic debate. They would be rotated in the same fashion as previously described. They would be bipartisan to the degree that they are partisan at all.

These twelve individuals would produce annual recommendations which would be submitted to the president, to the Chairman of the President's Commission, and to the leaders of the Joint Congressional Committee. In the interest of continuity, the departure point for the Council on Global Concerns each year would be the reports of the President's Council and of the Joint Congressional Committee from the preceding year. Once again, focus would be upon a threshhold roughly twenty years in the future and beyond.

Annual Report of the President on Global Affairs

Finally, the time has come to ask the President of the United States to deliver a second annual address to a joint session of the Congress. That speech would focus specifically upon long-term integrated national security strategy. Such an address, delivered in the fall at the beginning of that Congressional session, could benefit from the deliberations of the three bodies previously described. It could be used as an occasion to identify and provide appreciation to the counselors composing those three groups. It also might be amplified in a brief question and answer session not dissimilar to those which take place in a number of parliamentary systems.

The danger of having partisan attacks distract from the quality of such an event is far outweighed by the opportunity to demonstrate concensus on vital long-term issues. Preparation for such an event could provide an opportunity for key policymakers at the highest levels to focus on long-term considerations rather than on the consuming details of their daily responsibilities. Finally, such an address would provide an opportunity both for U.S. citizens and for our friends and potential adversaries abroad to understand in general terms the directions in which our administration and our Congress intend to proceed.

Summary

Inherent in the preceding very general proposal is the potential for legions of lawyers to argue over questions such as appointment processes, funding, and the like. The proposal, nonetheless, attempts to take into account the great difficulties that we in the United States face when we attempt to come to grips with long-term strategic questions.

When we require our political system simultaneously to account for and to distinguish among the most threatening circumstances we face and the most likely threats; when we ask our defense establishment to be simultaneously ready for conflict now while building capabilities for twenty years out and beyond; when we ask our diplomats and others to struggle between leading our friends and allies on the one hand and, on the other, dragging them along; we should quickly see how essential it is to have an integrated long-term perspective on national security. Failing to develop such a perspective will lead at best to confusion and at worst to paralysis.

When we attempt to set up machinery for pursuing long-term national security strategy, we should remind ourselves that nowhere more than in the arcane world of strategy are conceptual confusion and imperfect communication more likely or more insidious. Simultaneously, we must consider the audience for a long-term integrated national security strategy. We must seek to build a basis for agreement among the various interested parties in the Executive Branch. We must recognize the key role played by the Congress as well as others "inside the Beltway." We must try to design strategic concepts and statements of strategy that will sell in Peoria, in Europe and Japan, and in Moscow and Beijing.

356 • U.S. Defense Policy

To give such a task a short fuse is to render it impossible. As George Marshall demonstrated so admirably, ranging from the days of unpreparedness in 1938 through the days of victory in 1945 and into the days of recovery in Europe in the mid-1950s, strategy is iterative. It must contain not only military but also economic and political dimensions. Most important, it must be legitimized. There must be common ground between our leaders and our people in the United States if we are to pursue a long-term integrated national security strategy. By focusing on basic concepts and seeking innovative structures through which we might identify and pursue our goals, we improve our chances for safety and security, and for the continuing improvement in the quality of our lives, the lives of our allies and friends, and perhaps even the lives of our potential adversaries.

26
A New National Strategy

Bradley C. Hosmer

S ince the end of World War II, the Soviet Union, and therefore the United States, has focused on the diplomatic and military aspects of the U.S.-USSR confrontation. Although that competition continues, significant changes have taken place both in the nature of the relationship between the two superpowers and in other global factors. It is time to consider choosing a different approach to our national strategy.

Criticisms of Traditional National Strategy

The U.S. strategy with the longest tradition is isolationism. As a deliberate policy, the United States initiated very few actions outside our boundaries once our nation spanned the continent. Typically, we acted only to counteract events that threatened us directly and immediately: a defensive strategy. Following World War I, President Wilson tried to bring the United States into the League of Nations, but even this degree of involvement in foreign affairs was not supported by the Congress. We maintained a stubbornly defensive attitude virtually until December 7, 1941.

Following World War II, with an imminent Soviet threat to Western Europe, the United States adopted the national strategy of containment. This countered the Soviet threat, broke our habit of peacetime isolationism, and led to a constant military presence and to diplomatic activities beyond our borders. Still, as containment evolved, it was on the whole defensive: Once our perimeters were set up, we considered ourselves secure unless those perimeters were disrupted.

This traditional U.S. national security policy has been criticized by some as reactive, inconsistent, and unrealistic; and with some justification. Yet, despite the carping, our traditional national strategy has worked. Much has changed in the two generations since World War II, and the

The views expressed herein are solely those of the author and do not necessarily reflect the views of the Department of Defense or of any other agency of the United States government.

world has now evolved to a point where weaknesses behind those criticisms can no longer be ignored.

In this chapter I will detail two major changes to our current peacetime national strategy that could make it more active, more consistent, and more realistic—if we choose to go that route. I believe we cannot achieve these changes unless we do make such a choice, and, furthermore, make it consciously, publicly, and as a nation. These possible changes are:

> Broaden the formal participants in national security policymaking beyond just the Department of State and the Department of Defense.
>
> Discard our tradition of a national strategy based on defensive actions.

The reason we need to focus on process and tradition is that these two elements place strong limits on how effective a national strategy we can achieve and sustain.

Background

Today's power centers are more complex and more numerous than they were immediately following World War II. The result is many new sources of risk for the United States. But this fact should not distract us from the present concrete Soviet military threat. The Soviets are very strong militarily—at least at parity with the United States. General Secretary Gorbachev's promise at the United Nations that he would reduce the strength of the Soviet Armed Forces by 500,000 troops and withdraw some 50,000 troops and 5,000 tanks from East Germany, Czechoslovakia, and Hungary, seems to be a constructive gesture, but I see it as one that still has to be evaluated. For example, Soviet production of military equipment continues to expand without apparent restraint. Another consideration is that public support for NATO's military capability may be waning, both in the United States and in Europe. Finally, even if the present Soviet leadership is benevolent, the Soviet Union is still an autocracy—it can change key individuals or policies overnight. Let's be candid about the threat: The Soviets (and only the Soviets) have the capability to destroy us.

The Soviet threat is very serious, and I focus on it as a military officer. But there are other risks to U.S. security as well, and in this chapter I will discuss how we might better handle *all* of the risks.

Indirect Threats

It is obvious to me that the Soviets are now on the diplomatic and political offensive. They are very good at political warfare. By putting their own actions under *glasnost* and *perestroika* in the most favorable light possible, they are making the West seem reactive and uncertain. This political warfare affects each country differently and could even lead to the decoupling and splitting of NATO—a longstanding Soviet objective.

Secretary General Gorbachev has set up a strategic dilemma for us. I see four possible outcomes for the Soviet Union as a result of his initiatives.

They work, leading to eventual renewal of Soviet power with no basic changes in Soviet attitudes.

They work, leading to a renewal of the Soviet economy, but with a fundamental change in Soviet culture to the point that the Soviets live peacefully with the West.

They barely work or fizzle gradually, leading to no significant change in the present situation. This outcome probably would produce a gradual deterioration of Soviet military strength over time.

They don't work, and in fact fail catastrophically, leading to chaos or perhaps a reversion to Stalinism. This outcome is potentially disastrous.

The two middle outcomes are acceptable to the United States, while the first and fourth are fraught with danger. So the dilemma is clear: How to take advantage of the openings and opportunities to encourage the good outcomes, while preserving the military capability to deal with the bad outcomes in case one of them comes to pass. Meanwhile, any actions we take to encourage an acceptable outcome could either backfire and encourage the wrong result or reinforce a growing public sense that the military threat is going away. An eventual cost may be the loss of our ability to deter war if the actual outcome is a dangerous one.

I believe that we are at a point today where the United States would be prudent to have a strategy based on specific security goals for the future, thus providing a countervailing agenda and the initiatives to push it.

Multipolar Complications

The growth of regionalism, or "multipolarity," is a topic with related strategic issues. Our allies and other countries have developed to become nations of consequence with their own interests and ideas—just as we had hoped. Of course, that development creates both opportunities and problems. And many of these nations, some of them our allies, now have an impact on our security.

But issues other than security issues also exist between us. Some examples: trade policies, technology transfer, and access to natural resources. Thus, security interests will occasionally trade off against other interests or against each other. And the United States and other nations often fail to agree on the appropriate course of action. Therefore, I feel it is necessary to have a view of national security that includes *all* of the major activities that affect it. For example, wouldn't it be important to know all the major impacts of U.S. actions on country X, and country X's on the United States, before deciding what position we should take on base negotiations? On technology transfer? On microchip dumping? On opposing their support for terrorism?

It is my opinion that to guide such judgments, and therefore to help shape our national strategy, we must have specific and achievable long-term goals in all areas that affect the well-being of this nation; for example, for key capabilities in our industrial base.

Issues Without Citizenship

There exists another group of risks to our security, which we might call "transnational," meaning that the risks are largely outside the control of individual nations as we do things today. Examples of these risks are uncontrolled pollution, uncontrolled disease, drug cartels, some drastic ecology changes, and changing global patterns of industrial production as a result of multinational business decisions. No nation by itself can fix these risks or avoid their consequences. And yet they have a big impact on the distribution of political and economic power and on the well-being of populations—more so, in fact, than many government decisions have.

Classical political/military security relations are zero-sum, but transnational issues can result in a net plus or minus for the globe, depending on how nations collectively deal with these issues. One can even speculate that transnational issues could eventually take us beyond the balance-of-power approach to security by offering compelling reasons for nations to work together solving problems that can only be solved by cooperation.

Again, specific long-range goals seem the best basis for initiatives that could represent global leadership by the United States on issues of this type.

Recapitulation

To summarize, our past approach to national strategy has been successful. We have countered the Soviets. When they used a political/military approach, with the emphasis on military power, they were most effective. We responded in kind. But in the past the United States was really *the* globally dominant power. For example, about 45 percent of the world's production in the early 1950s was made in the United States. We didn't need to use all of the dimensions of our national strength, and typically we didn't.

The one telling exception to a string of successes came in Vietnam. I read Vietnam as a competition between our defensive political/military national strategy against a North Vietnamese active (not defensive) national strategy. Moreover, their active strategy had a political/psychological angle with a long-term payoff. The Vietnamese stuck with their broader, longer-term national strategy—despite terrible short-term costs—and were successful.

Taking into account the altered world situation, we may want to consider two major changes in how we approach national security strategy:

The factors that are normally brought into play in our national strategy—diplomacy and military power—may not be enough. Perhaps we should formally include all the factors that are sources of national strength and impact national strategy.

And we may need to consider altering our long-held defensive approach to national strategy in peacetime and shift to an active national strategy.

I do not mean to throw away what we do now—I mean to build on it.

Broadening the National Security Community

Earlier, I said that one way to improve our current peacetime national strategy is to broaden the formal participants in U.S. policymaking. I refer, for example, to other departments of the Executive Branch being formally included in the National Security Council (NSC).

Consider, for instance, the appropriate government participants on the issue of technology transfer. This issue has an unmistakable bearing on national security. In this case the departments involved could include State, Defense, Commerce, Justice, Treasury, and possibly others. An NSC expanded with these other departments would be better able to formulate true national policy. The resulting policy would likely be different from that proposed by any single department. Developing that policy would involve building on each, and should include the key aspects of each. When departmental disagreements cannot be reconciled, the final policy would reflect choices made according to national priorities. With such a process, an NSC-created proposal would be a truly unified proposal, defensible and supportable by all Cabinet participants.

Reconsidering Defensive National Strategy

Just adding more people at the table during strategy formulation is not enough. My second thought is that we may want to consider altering our traditional defensive (reactive) approach to national strategy. Our defensive strategy of containment has worked up until now, but in coming years we may prefer not to wait for potential difficulties to become problems before we act.

Allow me to elaborate. It seems to me that any national strategy will be more powerful if it is based on specific choices about how the future should be shaped—that is, on fairly specific national goals. I believe the time scale of national strategy must be long enough to allow a nation to seek and deliberately achieve such long-term goals—like the nearly ten years it took the North Vietnamese to erode United States political support for the Vietnam War.

Mine is not a universal view. Some people hold that strategy is a matter of understanding how all factors affect a current situation and then making a decision accordingly. And that by itself can be a truly formidable challenge. Yet, in my opinion, that approach is more nearly appropriate to a strictly military strategy either in war or in the close approach to war. It overlooks a powerful tool essential for strategy at the national level: creating a view of the future—through specific long-term national goals that are consistent with our other long-term goals—and shaping events to gradually achieve changes that are too fundamental to be achieved quickly.

I see four distinct advantages to this approach:

Decisions on current issues can sometimes nudge events toward long-term objectives—once we have decided our specific long-term objectives.

Knowing where we want to go provides a basis for designing and putting forward initiatives to get there. Without specific strategic goals, initiatives are likely to be meager or aimless.

Making the deliberate choices of long-term goals should expose the priority trade-offs needed to reach consistent goals. Strategy based on specific and consistent goals becomes more realistic.

When followed persistently through time, objectives become attainable that would otherwise be beyond reach. And, our attention remains on the results of actions, not on the surface cosmetic reaction to the actions.

The result would be an *active* national strategy, as opposed to the current, and in my view primarily defensive, national strategy.

Choosing an active strategy would be a substantial change in approach for the United States. Big changes in our national attitude would have to occur as well. To make such a change, I believe we have to put the issue on the national agenda and talk explicitly about the advantages and costs of an active national strategy. Without such discussion and widespread understanding, specific strategic decisions will not stick—they are likely to be altered because national security issues have become fuel in our political bonfires. National understanding of the reasons to embark on an active national strategy is, in my view, the only effective answer to the frequently heard complaints that our national strategy is reactive, inconsistent, and unrealistic.

If we do adopt an active strategy, we will have to make serious choices about the future. Some decisions will involve choosing between security now and security later. Others will involve choosing between consumption now and productive capacity later. And yet other decisions will involve choosing between security now and consumption now.

We will also have to stop reshaping our national security every year, or every four years. Fundamental strategic decisions cannot be changed annually. That is not changing national strategy—that is destroying it. So, clearly, such decisions as we would take for the future would have to be taken carefully because they would represent long-term commitments. Of course refinements and adjustments would be needed as events unfold.

Congress and the Public Have a Role

The adoption of an active national strategy goes beyond the Executive Branch. Congress has a role, too. The congressional leadership must be involved in national strategic decisions, because Congress must make and stand by the long-term commitments or any resulting strategy will be ineffective. A bipartisan security policy will probably be necessary to keep elections from reopening and making uncertain basic strategic decisions and commitments.

Finally, the public has a key role. It can help advise on key choices through such devices as commissions and blue-ribbon panels. This is appropriate because the public should help determine whether the nation should embark on an active strategy, and should share in the making of hard priority choices. Also, public participation in national strategy would also have an important educational role for the nation.

Conclusion

Today the United States may need a national strategy that is a major departure from the past defensive approach. Making the transition to an effective long-term active strategy would not be easy, but making a deliberate transition is necessary if we expect to gain more benefit from our national strategy than we enjoy now. Ultimately, the reward will be worth the effort.

27
Thinking Strategy Through

Steven P. Adragna

A mid the crush of the day-to-day responsibilities confronting U.S. policymakers, thinking about national strategy and its implementation is often abandoned to an unfortunate degree. The various contributors to this volume have endeavored to refocus our collective attention on the critical parameters, goals, and elements of an effective and long-term national strategy. The bulk of their effort has been directed toward defining the requirements for U.S. defense policy in an era of constrained resources, while later chapters offer some recommendations on how best to shape our future national strategy in light of the aforementioned requirements. The purpose of this chapter is to tie together some of the disparate conceptual threads woven throughout this book in order to cast them in an appropriate strategic context. Obviously, just as no single book can serve as an exhaustive treatment of sound national strategy (the present volume, for example, being primarily concerned with the subcomponent of national security policy), no individual chapter can embrace all aspects of what ought to comprise that strategy. The objectives of this chapter, therefore, are rather more modest. They are: to address briefly the question of what national strategy is; to outline what ought to comprise the content of that strategy; to distill a set of national security policy recommendations from the analyses contained in this volume; and, to offer some concluding thoughts on incorporating these recommendations into a broader national strategy.

What Is National Strategy?

The Report of the President's Commission on Integrated Long-Term Strategy, *Discriminate Deterrence*, has defined the post–World War II strategy of the United States as "forward deployment of American forces, assigned to oppose invading armies and backed by strong reserves and a capability to use nuclear weapons if necessary. Resting on alliances with other democratic countries, the strategy aims to draw a line that no aggressor will dare to cross."[1] In a similar fashion, a 1979 Joint Chiefs of Staff (JCS) publication defined national strategy as: "The art and science of developing and using the political, economic, and psychological powers of a nation, together with its armed forces, during peace and war, to secure national objectives."[2]

These definitions are simply too narrow, and they fail to take account of several factors which will condition the formulation of effective strategy into the twenty-first century. Compounding this problem is the degree to which we tend to use the terms "national strategy," "military strategy," "national security policy," "defense policy," and "global strategy" interchangeably. Although much time is frequently spent over academic hairsplitting with respect to terminology, it is important that we begin our discussion from a common point of departure. First and foremost, we must address the question of what it means to *think strategically*. True strategic thought implicitly requires the ability to link the present to the future, to relate near-term policies to clearly defined long-term objectives. Strategy (and strategic thought) embraces an ability to discern objectives that lie beyond the (foreseeable) short term, to establish goals to be achieved, to develop conceptual approaches for achieving those goals, to establish a logical relationship between shorter and longer time frames, and to outline the necessary capabilities (as well as the means of developing those capabilities).

National strategy (or grand strategy) fuses all of a state's powers, during peace and war, for the purpose of attaining national interests and objectives.[3] Contributing to this national strategy there may be, theoretically, a political strategy, a military strategy, an international economic strategy, and so on, which flow from the goals of the national strategy. It is unlikely, however, that such a detailed and well-structured set of strategies could be devised. More likely, a state will have political, economic, military, and other *policies* which may or may not conform to a sound national *strategy*.[4] Ideally, these several policies should work in concert to support an effective national security policy (which, in turn, should constitute the primary vehicle for implementing national strategy). In other words, national strategy serves as a plan or roadmap for achieving national objectives, while national security policy (through its several components) serves as the means by which those objectives are attained.

How does this theoretical construct apply to the United States? As a global power with global interests, the United States must have a global strategy. Thus, U.S. national strategy is synonymous with global strategy. Almost by definition, therefore, such a strategy must integrate all of the state's policy tools—foreign policy and diplomacy, military power, economic and industrial resources, science and technology, statesmanship and national will, bluff, psychological pressure, and moral suasion—in a consistent and coherent fashion. Inherent in a global strategic view is an understanding of the relationship between geostrategic/geopolitical considerations and the other elements of national security policy (military, political, economic, psychological, and so on).[5] Moreover, like any other national strategy, a global strategy must be developed by planners able to view specific issues from a number of perspectives, and to meld these multidimensional analyses of seemingly discrete and/or isolated events into a clear picture of the threat to one's global interests and the steps needed to counter that threat.

National security policy (and its subcomponents), because it serves as the means of realizing strategic goals, must be attuned to the stated national strategy. As Robert Pfaltzgraff correctly observed:

> All grand strategies, however elegant in their simplicity, depend for their realization upon the development of specific plans, priorities, and tactics. On a day-to-day basis the tactics in support of strategy call for planning related to the posited long-term strategic objectives adapted to take advantage of opportunities that become available and to overcome the obstacles of the moment.[6]

Obviously, the farther out into the future a strategy projects, the more general and broadly gauged will be its principal components. As the time frame for realizing certain strategic objectives becomes shorter, national security policy must become more concrete, and plans must become more detailed. The challenge inherent in harmonizing policy and strategy is compounded by the political pressures generated in any pluralistic society as well as by the bureaucratized nature of the U.S. decisionmaking apparatus.[7]

Nevertheless, proceeding from this view of the nature of strategy, we can construct a model of what the strategy-making and national security policymaking processes ought to look like; an ideal which, while perhaps unattainable in reality, at least provides a goal toward which national leaders should direct their efforts. Based upon our definition of national (global) strategy, we can depict the strategic planning process schematically as shown in figure 27–1.

According to this model, the goals and objectives of national strategy become increasingly general as the time frame expands, but they are nevertheless oriented in specific directions (physical security for the United States and allies, support for democracy around the world, free market economies and international free trade, and so on). Extending through the near term and into the mid-term, national security policy serves as the principal mechanism for implementing strategy. Acting within the broad

368

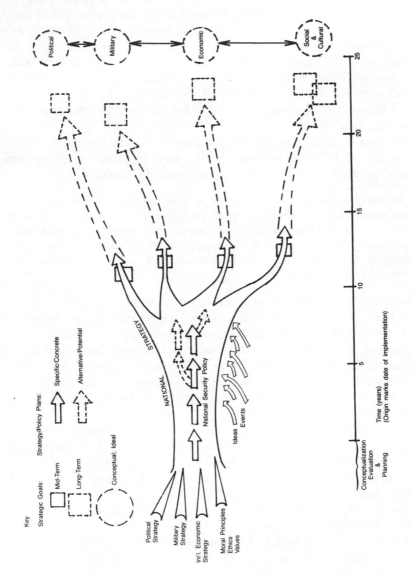

Figure 27–1. A Conceptual Schema for National Strategy

parameters of the national strategy, national security policy should still be flexible enough to allow for "mid-course corrections" at various points in time, and it must be responsive to unanticipated opportunities and challenges if it is to keep the broader national strategy more or less "on course." Bound up as it is with future goals and a host of intangibles (national will, moral-psychological factors, and statesmanship, to name but a few), strategy-making is a dynamic and continuous process (vice the more discrete and systematic approach associated with short-term policy planning). Even so, it is useful—to borrow Michael Freney's analogy—to take a "snapshot" of the moving strategic picture at selected points in time in order to ascertain whether course corrections in national security policy are in order and, periodically, to readjust and sharpen the focus of the goals and objectives of national strategy itself.

National security policy, too, is composed of a number of distinct but overlapping elements. A sound national security policy can be represented schematically as shown in figure 27–2.

As should be readily apparent, an ideal national security policy should embrace all other aspects of national policy: defense policy, foreign policy, international economic policy, and science and technology, all of which mutually influence and reinforce one another as well as contribute to the national security policy. It should also be noted that, according to this model, arms control policy does not exist as a co-equal with national security policy, but instead serves as one of several policy tools that may be used in support of national security policy. Moreover, arms control policy cannot be developed in a vacuum, but must be formulated in light of defense and foreign policy.

Likewise, our public diplomacy and psychological activities should not be merely a reflection of declaratory foreign policy, but should be informed by defense, economic, scientific-technical, and other factors as well. Moreover, we should take steps to imbue our public diplomacy efforts with the moral and social values in which we believe. As the student demonstrations in Beijing and the emigrations from totalitarian regimes and to the United States during the 1970s and 1980s have demonstrated, words do matter—especially if they are backed up by a firm moral commitment to basic values.

Proceeding from these conceptual frameworks, we can cut through much of the semantic debate over strategy: A true U.S. national strategy is by definition global, long term, and integrated. Conversely, if it is not characterized by these features, then it is not a true national strategy. While these conceptual models are useful for illustrating *how* to think about strategy, they do little to show *what* we should think. The goals and content of strategy, as well as the policies employed in support of strategy, are and ought to be topics for reflection and discussion. It is to

370

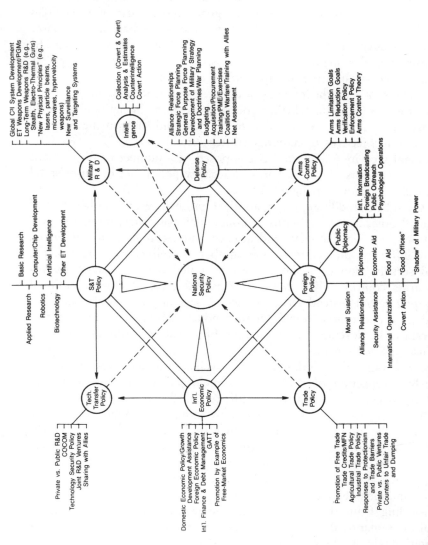

Figure 27-2. Elements of National Security Policy

Note: Obviously, other elements of national security policy can be identified. These schema merely represent the major policy elements and their complex interrelationships.

the problem of developing a sound national strategy for the United States, therefore, that we now turn our attention.

Shaping a National Strategy for the United States

Generally, there is broad agreement on the goals of U.S. national strategy. To be more precise, one can identify (as the Reagan administration did) five key national interests, as well as a number of broad and specific objectives to be pursued in support of those interests. While neither exhaustive nor set in stone, the following list of major U.S. interests should enjoy broad popular support and therefore should serve as a suitable base from which to begin the process of strategy-making. These key national interests include:

1. The survival of the United States as a free and independent nation, with its fundamental values and institutions intact.
2. A healthy and growing U.S. economy.
3. The growth of freedom, democratic institutions, and free market economies throughout the world, linked by a fair and open international trading system.
4. A stable and secure world, free of major threats to U.S. interests.
5. The health and vigor of U.S. alliance relationships.[8]

The same report that identified these national interests went on to outline a number of objectives which support those interests, and which can be summarized as follows:

> "To maintain the security of our nation and our allies" by deterring aggression or, if deterrence fails, by being able to defeat an attack and end the conflict on favorable terms. This includes securing access to the oceans and space, and preventing Soviet domination of the Eurasian landmass.

> "To respond to the challenges of the global economy" in an economically interdependent world. This includes addressing the problems of Third World debt and protectionism, while at the same time promoting U.S. competitiveness, ensuring access to foreign markets and energy resources, and maintaining a stable international economic environment.

> "To defend and advance the cause of democracy, freedom, and human rights throughout the world." This objective embraces the pro-

motion of national independence, economic development, and pluralistic sociopolitical orders in the Third World.

"To resolve peacefully disputes which affect U.S. interests in troubled regions of the world," and to dampen the likelihood of their escalation to wider conflict. This includes addressing the root causes of regional instabilities, maintaining stable global and regional military balances with respect to Soviet-aligned states, assisting states threatened by Soviet-sponsored insurgencies, and attempting to "neutralize the efforts" of the Soviet Union to increase its global influence.

"To build effective and favorable relationships with all nations with whom there is a basis of shared concern." This means supporting the establishment of pro-U.S. associations of states, reducing tensions with hostile states, and strengthening U.S. alliance relations and U.S. influence throughout the world.[9]

While it is not the purpose or intent of this analysis to delve into the merits of the Reagan administration's view of strategic interests and objectives, the two lists above do highlight a few important points about current strategy which should be borne in mind when attempting to formulate strategy for the future. Specifically, current U.S. strategic interests and objectives are:

1. *Multidimensional.* Foreign, defense, economic, and scientific-technical policies each condition particular aspects of our national interests, and each has a role to play in implementing national strategy.

2. *Interrelated.* Internal and external policies mutually affect one another and are inextricably bound. For instance, domestic objectives (such as a healthy U.S. economy) are affected by external policies and events (U.S. trade policy, other nations' trade policies, and so on). Likewise, foreign policy goals (healthy alliance relationships and international stability, for example) are affected by internal policies and events (such as budget cuts, political discord, and protectionism).

3. *Global in scope, continental in emphasis.* Clearly, our national interests are worldwide and must therefore be analyzed and addressed from a global strategic perspective. At the same time, those same national interests are most directly affected by territorial considerations: threats to friendly governments; access to energy resources and strategic minerals; the presence of hostile powers on territory from which that access could be interdicted; and the promotion of democratic movements in various parts of the world. Our national strategy must embrace both perspectives if it is to satisfy the requirements of each.

4. *Essentially "reactive."* While it is perfectly acceptable to posit protection of our own interests and of our allies' security as national objectives, the fact remains that most statements of current U.S. strategy are characterized principally by such phrases as "to maintain," "to respond", and "to defend." The question of whether our national strategy should place more emphasis on "achieving," "initiating," and "promoting" is still an open one. Bradley Hosmer has presented one perspective on this question in his contribution to this volume, and more will be said on the subject later in this chapter as well.

Even if the goals of U.S. strategy are generally agreed upon, the means and nature of that strategy remain a source of debate. There are (and have been), of course, a number of schools of strategic thought, each emphasizing a particular dimension of strategy or a particular approach to realizing strategic objectives.[10] Basically, however, the theories of these various schools of thought fall into one of two discernible strategic views: peripheral (or maritime), and continental.

In general terms, the peripheral strategy emphasizes power projection capabilities (to include not only naval forces, but also air power and strategic nuclear forces) and greater burden sharing on the part of allies. Proponents of this school of thought contend that, since resource limitations will constrain the ability of the United States to project power in several vital theaters at the same time, other states must absorb a greater share of the burden in defending their respective regions (Western Europe and Japan immediately come to mind) so that U.S. forces will be better able to deal with contingencies in other regions (such as Southwest Asia, Central America, and Southeast Asia). In countering the Soviet threat, moreover, this school of thought holds that instead of vainly attempting to match Soviet land power, the United States should take greater advantage of its status as a maritime power (by strengthening its strategic nuclear power and enlarging its navy), while simultaneously encouraging the modernization and strengthening of West European and Japanese (ground) forces for regional self-defense.[11]

In contrast, the continental strategy argues for a balanced force posture and the maintenance of forward-deployed U.S. ground forces in Western Europe and Northeast Asia, both as a counter to Soviet forces and as an escalatory link to the U.S. strategic nuclear deterrent. While proponents of this view may enthusiastically support greater allied burden sharing, they argue that the withdrawal of forward-deployed U.S. forces might prompt a severe erosion of political will and overall defense capability on the part of our allies (especially in Europe). Moreover, continental strategists argue, the withdrawal of U.S. ground forces would probably create a defense "gap" which would not be filled by allies. More likely, they say, is the prospect of an increasingly neutral Western Europe (highly susceptible to Soviet influence operations), which would in turn allow the Soviet Union to reallocate resources to other vital military theaters. Being in greater geographic proximity to most regions of importance to U.S. interests, the Soviet Union would then be in a position to negate any potential benefits that might otherwise accrue from improved U.S. power projection capabilities, thereby defeating the very logic of the peripheral strategy.[12]

In general, peripheral strategists maintain that the continental strategy is too preoccupied with large forces-in-place, positional warfare and static defense, and time-worn balance-of-power logic. According to this view, the continental strategy locks the United States into a fool's game of trying to compete against the Soviet Union in the area in which we are at an automatic disadvantage—land power—instead of accentuating our strength as a maritime power by emphasizing power projection capabilities and strengthened nuclear forces. Continental strategists, on the other hand, contend that the peripheral strategy would, in effect, concede our core area of interest—Western Europe—and subsequently produce a series of possibly insurmountable challenges in distant but vital regions of the globe.

Although the singular merits of each of these strategies are debated and defended with great fervor in academic and policy circles, it should be fairly obvious that a sound U.S. national strategy should include elements of both schools. As noted earlier, our strategy should be global in scope and continental in emphasis. A primary objective of our strategy must be to deny Soviet (or other hostile powers') control and/or influence over the Western European and Southwest Asian "rimlands," and naval and air forces for power projection alone are insufficient to ensure reliably our ability to meet this objective. Moreover, the nature of the global security environment and the reality of resource constraints mean that our strategy will continue to rely necessarily upon the alliance structure. This will require continued effort both to maintain alliance cohesion and to avoid using legitimate but modest burden-sharing arguments as cudgels with which to batter the alliance system in order to serve domestic political ends.[13]

At the same time, however, the fact remains that the United States will continue to have global interests and commitments, and it must therefore have the ability to counter threats to those interests outside the core area of Europe. In some instances, it may be possible to forge a common allied response to an "out-of-area" issue: the multinational naval escort operations in the Persian Gulf provide a recent example. Nevertheless, political consensus may be impossible to achieve in some cases, and the United States will therefore have little choice but to undertake unilateral action in these situations. Clearly, designing and maintaining the necessary power projection capabilities for undertaking unilateral action throughout the maritime periphery must also be a component of our national security policy.[14] In short, our national strategy must be conditioned by both perspectives: we should endeavor to work with allies to the greatest possible extent, while retaining a capability to act unilaterally in those situations where consensus cannot be reached and U.S. national interests are directly at stake.

This appreciation for the character of U.S. national strategy—while important and necessary—serves only to highlight strategy's modus operandi, its geostrategic world view. As noted earlier, it is equally important that we bear in mind the other requisite components of a sound national strategy, elements which contribute to strategy's strength and durability. The most important of these have been discussed in earlier chapters, but they merit restating in the present context.

1. *Strategy must be based on consensus.* A strategy that is not supported by political will cannot be sustained over time (as Bradley Hosmer has argued with respect to our involvement in Vietnam). In order for that political will to be present and enduring, bipartisan support is essential, and it must come not only from the several agencies of the Executive but from Congress as well. Moreover, public debate and discussion must also be encouraged, because the electorate will almost certainly refuse to support a strategy that it does not understand or the goals of which are unclear (even in broad terms). In a pluralistic system such as ours, however, with its highly bureaucratized but decentralized decision-making apparatus, forging and maintaining a consensus of opinion will be exceedingly difficult.[15]

2. *Strategy must be integrated, in its content and in its formulation.* We have already discussed the necessity of melding the several components of strategy—political, military, economic, scientific-technical, moral-psychological, and so on—into a coherent and consistent whole. By the same token, strategy stands the greatest chance of being integrated if its formulation process is equally integrated. As several contributors to this volume have argued, all the relevant federal agencies should be charged with the task of addressing specific strategic concerns that fall within their respective areas of expertise, and the subsequent conclusions and proposals of these agencies should be considered, streamlined, integrated, and implemented in accordance with declared strategic objectives. The National Security Council (NSC) would appear to be the most appropriate institution for performing this function, but this will require an NSC staff that is both sufficiently large to grapple with the probable work load and relatively free from allegiance to any particular department or agency.

3. *Strategy should take a long-term view.* As we have already noted, a key component of strategic thinking is the ability to link the present to the future. Establishing long-term goals can help to clarify and direct near-term decisionmaking, which in turn makes it easier to achieve those long-term objectives. The four distinct advantages of a long-term approach identified by Hosmer need no further elaboration here. As the old adage puts it, if you don't know where you want to go, any road will take you there. A coherent national strategy with specific long-term objectives provides a needed roadmap for national security policy formation.

4. *Strategy should be active.* It should set specific goals, anticipate potential difficulties, and outline alternative approaches. Here again, it is not necessary to repeat arguments made earlier. What should be emphasized here is the fact that "active" does not mean "aggressive." On the contrary, as Michael Freney has argued, American national strategy should be directed toward improving the quality of human life, promoting the development of democratic institutions, and securing such other positive goals as are within our capability. At the same time, "offensive" policy tools (such as support for anti-Marxist insurgencies, psychological operations, and "proactive" public diplomacy campaigns) can and should play a role in support of a positive, active national strategy. At the most fundamental level, the transition from a reactive strategy to an active strategy begins with the recognition of the subtle but important distinction between saying that "there are goals to be achieved" and merely saying that "there are conditions to be guaranteed." Once that conceptual change is made, all else follows.

In short, our strategic thinking must be innovative, active, and dynamic, and it should be conditioned by the moral and political precepts upon which our society and system of government are based. A greater emphasis on improving the quality of our strategy should not come at the expense of our attention to national security policy, however. On the contrary, a strategy that rests upon weak and ill-considered policies is a strategy devoid of effective tools with which to achieve its objectives, and is therefore likely to fail. Thus, it is to the matter of shaping near-term national security policy that we now turn.

Policy Recommendations

The contributors to this volume have presented a variety of policy recommendations with respect to the various dimensions of national security. Although these tend to focus primarily upon defense policy, in concert they raise important points and ideas for consideration by policymakers. It will perhaps be useful, therefore, to encapsulate here some of the principal conceptual recommendations sown throughout this volume.

With respect to the process of formulating policies that contribute to strategy, our efforts must be directed toward producing a national strategy that is: integrated, drawing upon the inputs from a variety of institutional actors; coherent and consistent; global and long-term in scope; the product of an informed national debate and bipartisan consensus; and, a dynamic, active, "living" concept. Equally important, this strategy formulation process must address and take account of inevitable constraints on resources.

The security environment for which our national security policy must be designed will be characterized by a growing number of power centers, as well as potentially hostile states that will be more technologically advanced and more militarily capable. Our national security policy must also take account of the growing strategic importance of the Pacific Rim, and it should explore the possibility of creating a true regional security framework. Low-intensity conflict (LIC) will be a persistent hallmark of international relations, and U.S. national security policy must address the "LIC phenomenon" soberly and honestly. We must have the capability to wage successful LIC campaigns, and we should also work to redress the root causes of insurgency. In spite of this proliferation of threats, the Soviet Union will remain at the center of our national security concerns at all levels. Change is indeed taking place in the Soviet Union, but this change is not necessarily in our long-term interest. The long-term Soviet view with respect to the contradictory nature of the two social systems and the necessity of combatting "imperialism" remains largely unchanged, and planning our security in accordance with the notion that this is not the case would be dangerous and naive.

U.S. defense policy should be directed toward maintaining an effective and survivable strategic nuclear deterrent (to include a mix of offense and defense); ensuring the readiness and combat capability of our foreward-deployed and CONUS-based forces for all levels of conflict; and modernizing our weaponry and training our troops within constrained budgetary parameters. Greater attention should be given to the role of space in military affairs, and a detailed program for space policy should be worked out. Moreover, a firm rationale should be promulgated for the Strategic Defense Initiative (SDI) if the United States is serious about deploying it (which means that the program ought to be debated openly on its merits), and various spinoffs from SDI research should be aggressively pursued.

Our foreign policy should continue to be directed toward the promotion of democratic values. The content of foreign policy embraces far more than simple inter-state discourse. All the available tools of foreign policy should therefore be brought into play: alliance relationships; political example and moral suasion; security assistance; diplomatic mediation; the "political shadow" cast by military power; political/diplomatic support for foreign democratic movements and insurgencies; skillful diplomacy; public information; and others. Many of these, of course, overlap defense and economic policy in some area; what is important is that they are all policy tools that can be used to influence the behavior of other states and to promote the spread of democratic ideals and institutions.

In a similar fashion, our international economic policy should not focus on the narrow objective of providing economic assistance in support of our foreign policy. Instead, it should strive to promote and support market-oriented economic policies and economic development throughout the world (while simultaneously providing grant-in-aid assistance to the needy). By encouraging free trade, market-oriented economies, and private enterprise, our international economic policy helps move us toward the goals of improving the quality of human life, maximizing opportunity, and reinforcing democratic values by promoting individual welfare.

Science and technology policy can, in one sense, be viewed as a subcomponent of foreign policy, in that granting or denying access to U.S. scientific-technical resources can be a powerful policy tool. The robustness of our scientific-technical potential is extremely important in its own right, however, and not only for its domestic implications. Historically, the ability to innovate technologically has proved to be a weapon like any other, and as powerful as any other weapon. With the advent of an era in which high-technology weapons are increasingly likely to find their way into the hands of potentially hostile regional powers, the ability to maintain a technological edge will become even more important. In addition, a scientific-technical policy designed both to anticipate patterns of technological development and to innovate in unanticipated ways contributes materially to a sound national strategy.

Arms control policy must not be placed on a co-equal basis with defense policy or foreign policy. Arms control is but one of many policy tools to be employed in support of national security policy and national strategy. It can have a very useful role in heading off wasteful proliferation of certain types of arms; enhancing deterrence; reducing certain elements of risk; and denying unilateral advantage to an adversary. It should not, however, be regarded as an end in itself. Reliable verification measures and a bipartisan policy on treaty compliance and enforcement are necessary adjuncts of a sound and effective arms control policy.

These and other components of national security policy must be examined individually for soundness and realism, and then must be harmonized so as to support and reinforce one another mutually. National security policy, in turn, should then be applied in support of near-, mid-, and long-term strategic goals, and should be modified and adjusted over time as circumstances dictate. It should be readily apparent that, in our increasingly complex world, coordinating all of these efforts successfully will not be an easy task. Therein lies the challenge for the 1990s.

Into the 1990s

In order for the United States to have a sound, integrated long-term strategy, we must develop a better understanding of strategy as a whole: what it is, how it is formed, what its perspective ought to be, and how to develop and implement it over time. A true national strategy is coherent and cohesive, integrated, global in perspective, and goal-oriented. National strategy must necessarily be long-term, and it must therefore transcend near-term debates over specific initiatives, policies, or programs. In other words—to use an already overused metaphor—we must not become so caught up in debating the policy "trees" that we lose our perspective on the strategic "forest."

This does not mean that policy issues should be allowed to lapse, regardless of how clear our strategy is. Without movement on policy and programmatic initiatives, strategy stagnates and becomes rigid (and therefore out of touch with developments in the real world). To give but one example, our national strategic goal of maintaining a secure nuclear deterrent and the operational requirements of our military strategy cannot be satisfied over time if the issue of ICBM vulnerability is not addressed and a consensus on how to proceed with the modernization of our strategic forces is not achieved. This particular problem serves to highlight the fact that one of the basic responsibilities incumbent upon decision-makers is that they do, in fact, *make decisions* and have the resolve and fortitude to carry them out.

It is easy to say that formulating a sound national strategy and appropriate policies will not be easy; the real challenge lies in actually finding the solutions and securing the necessary support for them. The importance of statesmanship and vision cannot be overstated, and the ability to inform and influence the national debate over strategic issues and to develop policies that are visionary and workable will become increasingly important. Essentially, the business of shaping national strategy hinges on the nature of our values and goals, and the depth of our commitment to seeing these translated into reality. Thus, visionary leaders are needed in order to see that those values are clearly articulated, skillfully embodied in policy, and implemented faithfully but in innovative and creative ways.

Above all, time is not a commodity we can afford to waste: We must make a concerted effort now if we are to forge a national strategy that can guide our policy decisions into the next century. Simply thinking about strategy—as largely an academic exercise—is not enough, since no strategy can ever hope to succeed in the future if it is not actually implemented at the time it is conceived. Of course, in all probability, the United States could continue to "muddle through" in world affairs without a true national strategy. The questions we must ask ourselves, however, are whether we can (or should) be content to do so and, more importantly, whether—in the emerging security environment of the 1990s and beyond—"muddling through" will be good enough.

Notes

1. *Discriminate Deterrence*, Report of The Commission on Integrated Long-Term Strategy (Washington: U.S. Government Printing Office, January 1988), p. 5.

2. JCS Publication 1, Dictionary of Military and Associated Terms (Washington: U.S. Department of Defense, June 1, 1979), p. 228.

3. See John M. Collins, *Grand Strategy: Principles and Practices* (Annapolis, MD: U.S. Naval Institute Press, 1973), pp. 14–21.

4. Conversely, skeptics might argue that the United States may have a military strategy, an international political strategy, and a foreign economic strategy, but no effective national strategy.

5. For an interesting (though slightly dated) treatment of the relationship between geopolitics, national security, and strategy-making, see Ray S. Cline, *World Power Trends and U.S. Foreign Policy for the 1980s* (Boulder, CO: Westview Press, 1980). See also Colin S. Gray, *The Geopolitics of the Nuclear Era: Heartland, Rimlands and the Technological Revolution* (New York: Crane, Russak, 1977).

6. Robert L. Pfaltzgraff, Jr., "U.S. Strategy for National Security," in Terry L. Heyns (ed.), *Understanding U.S. Strategy* (Washington: National Defense University Press, 1983), p. 222.

7. See Pfaltzgraff, "U.S. Strategy for National Security," pp. 222–223.

8. These "national interests" are taken directly from *National Security Strategy of the United States* (Washington: U.S. Government Printing Office, January 1987), p. 4.

9. Adapted from *National Security Strategy of the United States*, pp. 4–5. It

is interesting that this document (actually a White House report) fails to generate much discussion in policy-making and legislative circles. Although lacking in terms of concrete proposals for near-term challenges, it is nevertheless commendable for the scope of its perspective and its analysis of the interaction of the various components of national security policy. This lack of general interest in the report, however, bespeaks a general lack of interest in addressing long-term goals and objectives.

10. Space constraints preclude a review of each of the major schools of strategic thought. The major schools and their respective theories are ably summarized in Collins, *Grand Strategy: Principles and Practices.* For primary source writings on strategy, the best-known anthologies are Peter Paret (ed.), *Makers of Modern Strategy: From Machiavelli to the Nuclear Age* (Princeton, NJ: Princeton University Press, 1986); and the earlier edition of the same volume, Edward Mead Earle (ed.), *Makers of Modern Strategy: Military Thought from Machiavelli to Hitler* (Princeton, NJ: Princeton University Press, 1971). The contents of the two latter volumes are not identical, and each merits attention in its own right.

11. For a concise assessment in favor of the peripheral, or "maritime," strategy, see Stansfield Turner and George Thibault, "Preparing for the Unexpected: The Need for a New Military Strategy," *Foreign Affairs, 61,* (Fall 1982), pp. 122–135.

12. For a defense of the continental strategy, see Robert W. Komer, "Maritime Strategy vs. Coalition Defense," *Foreign Affairs, 60,* (Summer 1982), pp. 1124–1144. Komer's concept of coalition defense is one which holds that uniform and stable growth in defense spending among all NATO members, coupled with a skillfully managed defense plan, would allow for a robust non-nuclear defense of Western Europe. It should be noted that there is another variant of the continental strategy that maintains that theater nuclear weapons serve the important and dual purpose of deterring a potential Warsaw Pact attack while simultaneously providing a coupling link with U.S. strategic nuclear forces. For an explication of this view, see Bernard W. Rogers, "The Atlantic Alliance: Prescriptions for a Difficult Decade," *Foreign Affairs, 60,* (Summer 1982), pp. 1145–1156. For another pair of contrasting views on U.S. national strategy, see Jeffrey Record and Robert J. Hanks, *U.S. Strategy at the Crossroads: Two Views* (Cambridge, MA: Institute for Foreign Policy Analysis, 1982).

13. For a thorough discussion of the facts and myths surrounding the burden-sharing debate, see Anthony Cordesman's chapter, "Economics, Strategy, and Burden Sharing," chapter 13 in this volume.

14. The challenges and requirements that will confront the United States with respect to the forward defense of Europe and the maintenance of an effective forward-based power projection capability are addressed in chapters 14, 15, 19, and 20 of this volume.

15. For some interesting suggestions on how to address the problem of achieving consensus and bipartisan support for national strategy, see Michael Freney's chapter, "Toward a Long-Term Integrated Strategy for the United States," chapter 25 in this volume.

About the Contributors

Steven P. Adragna is Research Staff Director, International Security Studies Program, The Fletcher School of Law and Diplomacy. Before joining the staff of ISSP, he served as a policy analyst with High Frontier, Inc. He is the author of *On Guard for Victory: Military Doctrine and Ballistic Missile Defense in the USSR*, as well as several articles on international security affairs.

William F. Burns recently retired as Director of the U.S. Arms Control and Disarmament Agency. He has represented the Joint Chiefs of Staff on the U.S. Delegation to the Intermediate-Range Nuclear Force Negotiations in Geneva, Switzerland. Immediately prior to becoming Director of ACDA, he served as Principal Deputy Assistant Secretary of State in the Bureau of Politico-Military Affairs, Department of State.

Jacquelyn K. Davis is President of National Security Planning Associates, Inc., and Executive Vice President of the Institute for Foreign Policy Analysis, Inc. Her publications include: *The Cruise Missile: Bargaining Chip or Defense Bargain?* and *The Atlantic Alliance and U.S. Global Strategy*.

John E. Endicott most recently served as Director of the Institute for National Strategic Studies at The National Defense University. Previously, he has served in the Plans Directorate of Air Force Headquarters in the Pentagon, and as the Deputy Air Force Representative to the Military Staff Committee of the United Nations.

Stephen J. Flanagan is a member of the Policy Planning Staff, Department of State. Before assuming his current position, he was a Senior Fellow in the Strategic Concepts Development Center and a member of the National War College faculty at the National Defense University. Dr. Flanagan has published widely on European security, arms control, and intelligence issues, and is the author of *NATO's Conventional Defenses: Options for the Central Region.*

Michael A. Freney is currently a Senior Research Fellow at the U.S. Naval War College. He was formerly Senior Fellow and Deputy Chief Operating Officer at the Center for Strategic and International Studies, Washington, D.C.

Paul F. Gorman (General, USA, Ret.) left the Army in 1985 after 40 years of military service. In his final assignment he was Commander-in-Chief, United States Southern Command, responsible for all U.S. military activities in Latin America. He is currently President of Cardinal Point, Inc., a consulting and research firm.

Robert E. Harkavy is Professor of Political Science at The Pennsylvania State University, specializing in national security policy, arms control, and U.S. foreign policy. He is the author of several books, the most recent being: *Bases Abroad: The Great Powers' Foreign Military Presence.*

Robert F. Helms, II (Colonel, USA) is currently Chief of the Joint Strategy and Concepts Office, U.S. Forces Command. He has been Chief of the Concepts, Doctrine and Force Integration Headquarters, and of Long-Range Planning in the Department of the Army.

G. Paul Holman, Jr., is a professor at the National Security Decision-Making Department, U.S. Naval War College. A career intelligence officer, Professor Holman is co-editor of the multivolume series, *Foundations of Force Planning.*

Bradley C. Hosmer (Lieutenant General, USAF) is Inspector General of the Air Force, and previously served as President of the National Defense University. He is a former commander of two Air Force wings and an air division. He has served in numerous positions at Headquarters, Pacific Air Force; Headquarters, United States Air Force; and at the Office of the Joint Chiefs of Staff.

Phillip A. Karber is Vice President and General Manager of National Security Programs at The BDM Corporation. He has written extensively on European security issues and his articles have appeared in various U.S. and European journals, including *Comparative Strategy, Armed Forces Journal International, International Spectator*, and *Politique Etrangere.*

Ilana Kass is Professor of National Security Policy at the Department of

Military Strategy, National War College. She has authored a book on Soviet national security decisionmaking, as well as numerous articles on Soviet military strategy, which have appeared in such journals as *Strategic Review, Comparative Strategy, Air University Review,* and *Signal.*

Carnes Lord is National Security Adviser to the Vice President. Before assuming his current post, he was Director of International Studies at the National Institute for Public Policy, Inc. He is the author of *The Presidency and the Management of National Security.*

Robert T. Marsh (General, USAF, Ret.) is the former Commander of the Electronic Systems Division at Hanscom Air Force Base. He also served in Air Force Systems Command at Hanscom before his retirement. He is currently an aerospace consultant.

Keith B. Payne is currently Executive Vice President of the National Institute for Public Policy, Inc. He has served as a consultant to both the White House Office of Science and Technology Policy and the Arms Control and Disarmament Agency. He is also an Adjunct Professor at Georgetown University and a member of the editorial board of *Comparative Strategy.*

John L. Piotrowski (General, USAF) is Commander-in-Chief of the North American Aerospace Defense Command and the United States Space Command, both headquartered at Peterson Air Force Base in Colorado Springs. Prior to his present assignment, he was the Vice Chief of Staff of the United States Air Force.

Diego A. Ruiz Palmer is Manager of the NATO Studies Center at the BDM Corporation. Since 1979, he has been a member of a high-level task force evaluating the U.S./Soviet and NATO/Warsaw Pact balance of forces in Europe for the U.S. Department of Defense.

Jeffrey Salmon is Senior Speech Writer to the Secretary and the Deputy Secretary of Defense. At the time this book was written, he was on leave from DOD while serving as a Senior Fellow at the Institute for National Strategic Studies of the National Defense University. Prior to assuming his current position, he was Managing Editor of *Comparative Strategy.*

Sam C. Sarkesian is Professor of Political Science at Loyola University of Chicago. He is also the Chairman of the Research Committee of the National Strategy Forum and the author of numerous books, including

America's Forgotten Wars: The Counterrevolution Past and Lessons for the Future, and *The New Battlefield: the United States and Unconventional Conflicts.*

William J. Taylor, Jr., is Vice President for Political-Military Affairs at The Center for Strategic and International Studies in Washington, D.C. and an Adjunct Professor at Georgetown University. Author, co-author, and editor of a number of books, his most recent publications include *The Strategic Dimension of Military Manpower* and *Strategic Requirements for the Army to the Year 2000.*

Horatio W. Turner, IV (Captain, USN) is Deputy Director of Plans for Operational Space Systems, United States Space Command. As such, he directs the development of operational requirements for space systems to support all unified and specified commanders and their forces. His operational experience includes both carrier and surface combatant deployments as an antisubmarine warfare helicopter pilot.

R. James Woolsey, Jr., is a partner in the law firm of Shea & Gardner. He has served as Program Analyst in the Office of the Secretary of Defense and as General Counsel to the Armed Services Committee of the U.S. Senate. He has also been a member of the President's Commission on Strategic Forces and the President's Commission on Defense Management. He is the editor of *Nuclear Arms: Ethics, Strategy, Politics.*

Elizabeth G. Wylie (Captain, USN) is Dean of Academics, U.S. Naval War College. She has served as Commander, Military Sealift Command Atlantic and as Deputy Director of the Navy Staff in Current Plans and Policies.

About the Editors

Robert L. Pfaltzgraff, Jr., is Shelby Cullom Davis Professor of International Security Studies at The Fletcher School of Law and Diplomacy, Tufts University, and President of the Institute for Foreign Policy Analysis, Inc. Dr. Pfaltzgraff has written and lectured widely on Alliance policies and strategy, the interrelationships of political, economic, and security policies, technology transfer, arms control, emerging trends in both global and regional security environments, international relations theories, and U.S. foreign policy. Among his many books, the most recent are: *Guerrilla Warfare and Counterinsurgency: U.S.-Soviet Policy in the Third World* (Lexington Books, 1988); and the third edition of *Contending Theories of International Relations* (Harper & Row, 1990).

Richard H. Shultz, Jr., is Director of the International Security Studies Program and Associate Professor of International Politics at The Fletcher School of Law and Diplomacy, Tufts University. He is the recipient of a Secretary of the Navy Senior Research Fellowship for 1989–90. He has been a Hoover Institute Fellow, and recipient of an Earhart Foundation Research Fellowship, and a U.S. Institute of Peace Research Fellowship. He is a frequent lecturer at U.S. war colleges and military academies as well as at universities and world affairs groups across the United States. His most recent books include: *The Soviet Union and Revolutionary Warfare: Principles, Practices, and Regional Comparisons* (Hoover Institution Press, 1988); and *Guerrilla Warfare and Counterinsurgency: U.S.-Soviet Policy in the Third World* (Lexington Books, 1989).